MINIATURE EMPIRES

MINIATURE EMPIRES

A Historical Dictionary of the Newly Independent States

James Minahan

Greenwood Press
Westport, Connecticut

Library of Congress Cataloging-in-Publication Data

Minahan, James.
    Miniature empires : a historical dictionary of the newly
independent states / by James Minahan.
       p.   cm.
    Includes bibliographical references and index.
    ISBN 0–313–30610–9 (alk. paper)
    1. States, New—Dictionaries. I. Title.
  D860.M55   1998
  940.55'9—dc21   98–13979

British Library Cataloguing in Publication Data is available.

Library of Congress Catalog Card Number: 98–13979
ISBN: 0–313–30610–9

First published in 1998

Greenwood Press, 88 Post Road West, Westport, CT 06881
An imprint of Greenwood Publishing Group, Inc.

Printed in the United States of America

The paper used in this book complies with the
Permanent Paper Standard issued by the National
Information Standards Organization (Z39.48–1984).

10 9 8 7 6 5 4 3 2 1

Contents

Preface

The collapse of totalitarian regimes at the end of the Cold War brought a collection of nearly unknown countries to the world's attention. This volume covers those countries and the nations that dwell within their borders. *Miniature Empires: A Historical Dictionary of the Newly Independent States* follows the development of these countries from the earliest periods of their national histories to the present. This collection of country surveys is an essential guide to the new states that the world ignored or suppressed during the decades of the Cold War, both the twentieth century's most protracted conflict and the longest and most stable peace in the history of the modern world.

The Cold War did give the world a fragile peace, but for many it was at the price of their national freedom. In the name of stability historic nations were held captive and denied the right to self-determination. The suppression that kept these nations in bondage was also extended to the many other national groups inhabiting their national territory. Intergroup and interethnic conflicts, which result mostly from the expression of group rights, were also suppressed in the name of state unity and national integrity.

Each of the newly independent states, sometimes referred to as the NIS, has claimed or reclaimed its independence based on the right of the titular national group to govern itself. The titular or predominant nationalities, the historic national cores, have been the center of the attention focused on these new states. Yet all of the new states are actually miniature empires, inhabited by many different ethnic, religious, and national groups. The ethnic and national conflicts that followed the independence of many of these new nations have their roots in their own multiethnic populations. Until now no reference book has addressed the post–Cold War nationalist resurgence by focusing on the nations within the new nation-states, both the core nationalities and the so-called national minorities.

This dictionary was prepared to fill that void. It contains twenty-five articles highlighting the historical, political, social, and economic evolution of the new nations that are now emerging to claim a role in the post–Cold War world order. Each survey gives a breakdown of the country's population, with information about the size and composition of each of the national groups that inhabit the new state. The worth of the dictionary derives in part from its up-to-date information on the relatively unknown nations that inhabit the countries that have been recognized as independent states since 1989.

The decision to use the term newly independent states as a collective description was made for lack of a better term. None of the terms applied to these newly independent states has proved entirely successful, and only NIS applies to the entire group of countries included in this study. The only factors that the twenty-five states included in this book have in common are their multiethnic populations and the fact that they gained their independence from the rubble of collapsing totalitarian regimes between 1989 and 1998. With each passing year the use of the term newly independent states or the search for a better one will become increasingly unnecessary.

Webster's Unabridged Dictionary defines the word *nation* as "a body of people, associated with a particular territory, that is sufficiently conscious of its unity to seek or possess a government particularly its own." This definition applies to the core nation group or groups of each of the new states, but not to the nation-state itself. Even the few new states with a core national group that accounts for more than 80% of the total population are inhabited by dozens of different national, religious, and ethnic groups.

The newly independent nations included in this volume played little or no role in international politics before the end of the Cold War. Some of the nations will be familiar, either historically or more recently as news items. Some of these nations will be familiar to millions of Americans and Canadians whose families trace their roots to these historic regions.

The states that broke up following the collapse of their totalitarian regimes left behind not only numerous secession states, but also the truncated remains of the former state inhabited by the previously predominant core national groups. The core states of the disappeared countries are also newly independent states with different governments, names, national territories, and populations. These new states, the Russian Federation, the Federal Democratic Republic of Ethiopia, the Federal Republic of Yugoslavia, and the Czech Republic, have all been widely accepted as the direct successors of the disappeared states. The advantages to successor status include control of the former state's assets, including national treasuries, armies, embassies, and other properties. Claims to successor status have also allowed these newly independent states to take over established United Nations seats and memberships in many other national organizations.

One of the states, Namibia, is not usually included as a newly independent state, although it was the first of the group to gain independence. The apartheid White-dominated South African government, which controlled Namibia under an expired UN mandate, was permitted to defy world opinion and hold onto the territory because of its staunchly anti-Communist stance. When communism began to crumble and the Cold War ended, the South African government too came under intense pressure, finally ceding power to a majority government, while Namibia was granted independence under UN auspices.

Each national entry is divided into several parts or headings: the name and alternative names; the capital city; population statistics, incorporating the total population, the largest national groups, the major languages and religions, and the largest cities and urban areas; geography, including size, location, physical geography, administrative divisions, and political status; independence declarations; the national and other pertinent flags; a brief sketch of the national groups living within the country's borders; the nation, including the history and national development to the present.

The emergence of these new nations has brought many changes to the fields of geography and cartography. Place names, previously known in the language of the controlling state, are still in the process of translation to the new national languages, with cartographers and geographers attempting to settle on the definitive forms of the names of nations, national groups, and languages. In this volume, where new names are used, the more familiar form is shown in parentheses.

The population figures are the author's estimates for the year 1998. The figures are designated by the abbreviation (98e) before the appropriate statistics. These figures were gleaned from a vast number of sources, both official and unofficial, representing the latest censuses and official estimates. Official rates of population growth, urban expansion, and other variables were applied to the figures to arrive at the statistics included in the dictionary.

The population statistics are accompanied by the national breakdown of the total population of the national territory. Territorial claims are invariably based on historic association, not modern ethnic demographic patterns or international borders, so that all of these new nations are multiethnic and multireligious. Along with the population of the primary national group or groups, the national and religious divisions within each nation are detailed in percentages. Detailed population information is available in Appendix A. The population figures for the major cities include the population within the official city limits and, where appropriate, the population of the surrounding urban or metropolitan area (shown in parentheses). The two figures are included in an effort to reconcile the vastly different methods of enumerating urban populations used by the various governments and international agencies. A list of the principal statistical sources used is provided at the end of the preface.

The geographic information incorporates the size of the territory, in both square miles (sq.mi.) and square kilometers (sq.km.). Where nationalist claims to additional territory are an issue, both the official territorial extent and the extent of the nationalist claims are included. Additional geographic information includes location of the territory in relation to neighboring states, information on the principal geographic features, the internal administrative divisions, and data on the state's declaration of independence.

A number of the newly independent states have, at some time over the past century, been declared independent states. These dates, along with the dates of declarations since 1990, form part of each national survey. Several of the states have enjoyed years or even decades of independent existence, only to disappear as the result of wars or upheavals.

An overview of the people of each national territory is followed by a brief description of each of the national groups living within its borders. The descriptions highlight the linguistic, religious, cultural, and national influences that have shaped each national group.

Each of the newly independent nations has its own particular history, the events and conflicts that have shaped its national characteristics. The largest part of each national survey is therefore devoted to the historical development of the nation. The historical survey follows the evolution and consolidation of the nation from its earliest history to the present, including information on the numerous conflicts and controversies that emerged following the independence of these new nations.

The two appendices included in this volume will allow the reader to develop a better understanding of the historical evolution of the newly independent nations. Appendix A sets the numerous declarations of independence in a historical and chronological context, explicitly illustrating the earlier attempts of these nations to win permanent independence. Appendix B provides an overview of the geographic and international distribution of the national groups included in this volume.

Few of the newly independent nations developed in isolation; most were shaped by their relations with various governments and neighboring peoples. As an aid to the reader, the names of nations mentioned in the text for which separate national surveys are included here are followed by an asterisk (*). An extensive subject index at the end of the volume provides a convenient way to access desired information. Each entry also includes a short bibliographic list as a guide to sources that pertain to the nation in question.

This dictionary was compiled to provide a guide to the old nations, but new states, that emerged at the end of the Cold War. It is presented as a unique reference source to the newly independent states that are spearheading one of the most powerful and enduring political movements of the twentieth century, the pursuit of democracy's basic tenet, self-determination.

PRINCIPAL STATISTICAL SOURCES

1. National Censuses 1995–1998.
2. World Population Chart 1995 (United Nations).

3. Populations and Vital Statistics 1996 (United Nations).

4. World Tables 1997 (World Bank).

5. World Demographic Estimates and Projections, 1950–2025, 1988 (United Nations).

6. UNESCO Statistical Annual 1997.

7. *World Bank Atlas 1996.*

8. The Economist Intelligence Unit (Country Report series 1997).

9. OMRI Open Media Research Institute 1997.

10. *Europa Yearbook 1997.*

11. United States Department of State publications.

12. *The CIA World Factbook 1996.*

13. *United Nations Statistical Yearbook 1996.*

14. *United Nations Demographic Yearbook 1996.*

15. *The Statesman's Yearbook 1997.*

16. *Encyclopaedia Britannica.*

17. *The Columbia Encyclopedia.*

18. *Webster's New Geographical Dictionary.*

19. National Geographic Society.

20. Royal Geographical Society.

21. *World Almanac and Book of Facts 1997.*

22. *Political Handbook of the World.*

23. The Urban Foundation.

24. The Blue Plan.

25. Eurostat, the European Union Statistical Office.

30. International Monetary Fund (IMF) publications.

Introduction

The twentieth century has witnessed more and faster changes to the map of the world than all the centuries that went before. In 1900 the world was dominated by the empires of Great Britain, France, Germany, Russia, Turkey, Italy, Belgium, the Netherlands, Portugal, Spain, China, Ethiopia (Abyssinia), Austria-Hungary, and Japan. A century later the empires have disappeared and the family of independent states counts more than 185 nations.

The nationalist resurgence that has overshadowed the twentieth century has spawned numerous conflicts, but nationalism is not only a divisive force. Nationalism provides citizens with an identity and a sense of responsibility and belonging. The striving to take their place among the world's recognized states has been one of the century's most powerful impulses. The desire to be recognized as an independent nation-state is the motive that drove and continues to drive the nationalist movements that have proliferated around the globe.

A branch of the eighteenth-century doctrine of popular power, nationalism became a driving force in the nineteenth century, shaped and animated by the principles of the American and French revolutions. The first wave of modern nationalism culminated in the disintegration of Europe's multinational empires after World War I. The second wave began during World War II and continued as the very politicized decolonization process that engulfed the overseas territories of the remaining European empires as part of the Cold War. The end of Cold War factionalism released a third wave of nationalism, which has thus far led to the breakup of Europe's last empire and the collapse of several multinational states.

Nearly all the world's nation-states, with the exception of some tiny island nations, are actually multiethnic political entities, miniature empires most often dominated by the state's titular or core national group or groups. The world's newest nations are not exceptions to this rule, as each of these newly independent nations is inhabited by dozens and up to hundreds of distinct ethnic, religious, and national groups, many already pulling at the fabric of these new states.

Democracy, although widely accepted as the only system that is able to provide the basis of humane political and economic activity, can also be a subversive force. Multiparty democracy often generates chaos and instability as centrifugal forces, an inherent part of a free political system, are set loose. The post–Cold War restoration of political pluralism and democratic process has given rise to a rebirth of ethnicity and politicized national identity, while the collapse of totalitarian regimes in much of the world has shattered the political equilibrium that had prevailed for over four decades.

The Cold War political blocs had mostly succeeded in suppressing or controlling the regional nationalisms in their respective spheres, nationalisms that now have begun to reignite old national desires and ethnic rivalries. Around the globe numerous stateless nations, their identities and aspirations long buried under decades of Cold War tensions, are emerging to claim for themselves the basic principle of democracy, self-determination. Nationalism, with the striving for independence that accompanies it, is set to shape the world's political agenda well into the twenty-first century.

Nationalism has become an ascendant ideology that is increasingly challenging the nineteenth-century definition of the unitary nation-state. The post–Cold War nationalist revival is an amplified echo of the nationalism that swept Europe's numerous stateless nations in the late nineteenth and early twentieth centuries. The idea that political and economic security could only be guaranteed by the existing political order set in place after World War II was one of the first casualties of the revolution brought on by the world's new enthusiasm for democracy and self-determination. States held together by ideology and totalitarian power quickly disintegrated under the influences of democratic procedures.

Politicians and geographers have a tendency to simplify national reality and to identify it with state structures, but this century's last and most powerful resurgence of nationalism is a movement against the existing state structures. The nationalism of the world's stateless nations is rooted in the mismatch of state frontiers relative to the peoples claiming national status. Very few of the world's nation-states are homogeneous, made up of just one nation; most are in fact multiethnic, multinational, and multireligious political entities increasingly threatened by the aspirations of their constituent nations. The new nation-states included in this volume are the forerunners of this latest nationalist resurgence.

The Cold War emphasis on the rights of states, rather than the rights of the individuals and nations within them, has long dictated international attitudes to nationalism and the striving of stateless national groups for international recognition. The use of condemnatory labels—separatist, secessionist, rebel, splittist, and so on—has been a powerful weapon against those who seek a different state structure on behalf of their nations. The collapse of the ideological basis of the totalitarian regimes overturned the idea of state authority. In the multi-ethnic states government authority was quickly replaced by regional nationalist movements.

Two major trends are shaping the post–Cold War world. One is the movement to form continental or regional economic-political groupings that would allow for smaller political units as members. The other is the emergence of smaller and smaller national units as older states are broken up. The two trends are not mutually exclusive. The nation-state, along with its absolute sovereignty, is fading and giving way to new trends, the nation rather than the nation-state, in one direction, and supranational bodies, such as the United Nations, the European Union, and regional trading and political blocs in the other.

The rapidly changing political and economic realities of the world have challenged the old arguments that population size, geographic location, and economic viability are deterrents to national self-determination. The revival of nationalism is converging with the emergence of continental political and economic units theoretically able to accommodate smaller national units within overarching political, economic, and security frameworks.

The post–Cold War spread of national sentiment, affecting even nations long considered viable nation-states, is attracting considerable attention, but the focus of that attention is invariably on its impact on recognized governments and international relations. As the Cold War withered away it was replaced by a confusing number of nationalisms that in turn spawned the breakdown of the existing state systems no longer held together by totalitarian ideology.

The third wave of twentieth-century nationalism, with its emphasis on democratic self-determination, is set to top the international agenda well into the twenty-first century. The nationalist revival, global in scope, has strengthened submerged national, ethnic, and regional identities and has shattered the conviction that assimilation would eventually homogenize the existing nation-states. The newly independent nation-states are already feeling the tug and pull of regional nationalisms, religious conflicts, and irredentist territorial claims.

The political and cultural renaissance spreading through the world's stateless nations is inexorably moving global politics away from the present system of sovereign states, each jealously defending its authority, to a new world order more closely resembling the world's true national and historical geography. A world community dominated by democracy must inevitably recognize the rights of the world's numerous national groups, including the right to choose their own future. A world dominated by political blocs is now in the past; the future looks to be dominated by smaller and smaller national units grouped into overriding political, economic, and military alliances.

The world increasingly espouses democracy, but often continues to deny the democratic rights of stateless nations, including the right to choose their own future. The newly independent states included in this volume are the heralds of the twenty-first century. Their histories and their determination to take their place among the independent states of the world must be studied and understood in the context of their populations. The relationships between the governments of the newly independent states and their various national groups will determine their future as united nation-states or as the targets for further fragmentation along ethnic, religious, and historical fault lines.

ARMENIA

Republic of Armenia; Hayastani
Hanrapetut'yun; Haikakan
Hanrapetoutioun; Hayastan

CAPITAL: Yerevan

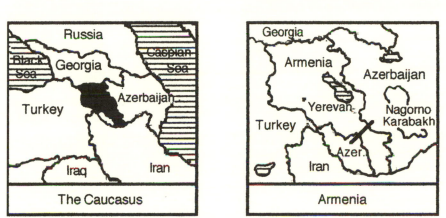

POPULATION: (98e) 3,472,000 : 3,300,000 Armenians in Armenia and large numbers in neighboring states, 421,000 in Georgia,* 553,000 in Russia,* about 90,000 in Turkey, and 175,000 in Artsakh (Karabagh) and Azerbaijan.* The Armenian Diaspora is estimated to number over 7 million. MAJOR NATIONAL GROUPS: REPUBLIC OF ARMENIA: (98e) Armenian 95%, Kurd 1.7%, Russian 1.5%, Azeri (Azerbaijani), Rom (Gypsy), Ukrainian, Assyrian, Greek, Belarussian, other. MAJOR LANGUAGES: Armenian, Russian, Kurdish. MAJOR RELIGIONS: Armenian Orthodox, Russian Orthodox, Roman Catholic, Protestant, Shi'a Islam, Sunni Islam, Yezid. MAJOR CITIES: (98e) REPUBLIC OF ARMENIA: Yerevan (Erivan) 1,345,000 (1,790,000), Gumry (Leninakan) 240,000 (275,000), Karaklis (Kirovakan) 185,000 (230,000), Hoktemberyan (Oktembran) 77,000, Echmiadzin 67,000, Razdan 50,000, Kafan 40,000. ARTSAKH (KARABAKH): Stepanakert (Khankendi) 35,000 (60,000).

GEOGRAPHY: AREA: Republic of Armenia 11,506 sq.mi.-29,808 sq. km. LOCATION: The Republic of Armenia, incorporating less than a quarter of traditional Armenia as defined by militant national groups, lies in the mountainous Transcaucasus region of southeastern Europe, bordering Azerbaijan on the east, Georgia on the north, Turkey and the Nakhichevan region of Azerbaijan on the west, and Iran on the south. PHYSICAL GEOGRAPHY: Much of Armenia is a rugged plateau of ridges, narrow valleys, extinct volcanoes, and small rivers and streams. The republic's major rivers include the Araks River, which flows into the Caspian Sea, and the Hrazdan, which flows from Lake Sevan into the Araks River in a series of majestic waterfalls. The Araks and Hrazdan Rivers provide almost all of Armenia's electric power. Lake Sevan, the largest lake in Armenia, is surrounded by extinct volcanoes. Known as Armenia's Pearl, this lake serves as the main reservoir of Armenia's irrigation system. The Ararat plain in the northwest is now the most densely populated area in Armenia, and, with irrigation, supports crops such as cotton, fruit trees, and vineyards. Armenia was once covered by dense forests. During the industrialization drive of the Soviet era, most of these forests were cut down. Due to the continuing blockade of energy supplies to Armenia from neighboring Azerbaijan, almost all the remaining trees have been cut down to provide desperately needed fuel for heating and cooking. Mount Ararat, the legendary landing place of Noah's Ark, is located in what is now modern Turkey. Situated near the border, the peak is visible from nearly every area of Armenia. Historically, the mountain has been the Armenian people's most treasured landmark. ADMINISTRATIVE DIVISIONS: Thirty-seven regions (shrjanner, singular—shrjan) and twenty-three cities (kaghakner, singular—kaghak). POLITICAL STATUS: The Republic of Armenia was recognized as an independent state in 1991. "Greater Armenia," the territory claimed by some nationalist groups, also includes the enclave of Artsakh or Eastern Armenia (Nagorno-Karabakh) in neighboring Azerbaijan, and Turkish or Western Armenia, part of independent Armenia from 1918 to 1920, but an integral part of the Turkish state since 1921.

INDEPENDENCE DECLARATIONS: ARMENIA: 28 May 1918 (from Russia and Turkey); 23 September 1991 (from the Soviet Union); ARTSAKH (NAGORNO-KARABAKH): 31 December 1991 (from Azerbaijan).

FLAG: The Armenian national flag, the official flag of the Republic of Armenia, is a horizontal tricolor of red, blue, and orange. OTHER FLAGS: The flag of the Artsakh Armenians in Azerbaijan is the traditional red, blue, and orange with the addition of a white step triangle on the fly.

PEOPLE: Armenia is the most homogeneous of the former Soviet republics, with only small non-Armenian national groups living in the state. Since independence in 1991 an estimated 700,000 people have left the republic, including the formerly large Azeri population. Many ethnic Russians, Ukrainians, and Belarussians have also left Armenia, along with many Armenians who have migrated to the United States or Russia seeking economic opportunities. The Republic of Armenia covers only about a quarter of the territory that historically comprised Armenia. The largest part of historic Armenia, Western or Turkish Armenia, was largely depopulated by war and massacres and is now populated by ethnic Turks and Kurds.

Armenian—an estimated 95% of the population, numbering about 3,300,000.

An ancient people first mentioned in the seventh century B.C., the Armenians form a separate branch of the Caucasian peoples. Heirs to an ancient culture, the Armenians feel culturally superior to both their powerful neighbors, the Russians and the Turks. The Armenian nation, often subjugated and their lands frequently devastated, nevertheless survived while most ancient peoples disappeared into history. The Armenian Christians were often persecuted by the conquerors, creating martyrs and keeping alive Armenian nationalism.

The Armenian language is the only surviving example of the Thraco-Phrygian group of the Indo-European languages. The language is written in a separate alphabet called Mesrobian, invented by an Armenian, St. Mesrob, in the fifth century. The alphabet is unique, although it is based on ancient Greek uncials and the Armazi script of the Aramaic language. The language is spoken in two major dialects, Western Armenian and Eastern Armenian.

The majority of the Armenian population is Christian, belonging to an independent Armenian Orthodox Church. A small minority, called Khemsil, adopted the Islamic religion during the centuries of Turkish rule, but remains Armenian in culture and history. Turkish Armenia, populated by over 2 million ethnic Armenians in 1890, is now mostly inhabited by Muslim Turks and Kurds. The Armenian Diaspora, estimated to number over 7 million, includes large populations in the United States and Canada, Russia, Iran, Syria, Lebanon, Romania, Bulgaria, Greece, France, Cyprus, and Egypt, and the neighboring states of Georgia and Azerbaijan. Some sources estimate the Armenian Diaspora to number around 10 million.

The Armenian church has been the unifying force for the Armenian people throughout centuries of foreign invasion, occupation, and dispersal. Christianity remained strong in Armenia despite many efforts to stifle its expression. The Armenian church is an independent entity with the seat of its Katholikos, the supreme spiritual head of the church, in the town of Echmiadzin, about twelve miles from the Turkish border and twelve miles west of Yerevan. The Armenian church, with its unique blend of nationalism and religion, has long been the safeguard of Armenian culture. During the Soviet era, however, many Armenians believed that their nation's membership in the Union of Soviet Socialist Republics provided a measure of protection for their church, language, and way of life against their traditional enemies.

Kurd—an estimated 1.8% of the population, numbering about 64,000.

The majority of the Armenian Kurds are Yezid, the descendants of refugees fleeing persecution in Muslim lands to the south. The majority of the Armenian Kurds speak Kurmanji or Northern Kurdish.

The Armenian Kurds have maintained their culture, religion, and traditions through centuries of persecutions and migrations. In the modern world they are the only ethnic Kurds to have established ethnic institutions such as radio, press, and education in their language. A literary language was established in 1921 on the basis of one of the Kurmanji dialects spoken in Armenia. It was first written in the Armenian script, but in 1929 the Soviet authorities changed the alphabet to Latin, and in 1945 the Latin script was replaced with the Cyrillic alphabet of the Russian language.

Russian—an estimated 1.5% of the population, numbering about 52,000.

The Russian-speaking population in Armenia is mostly concentrated in the urban areas of Yerevan and the other large cities. Most of the Russians settled in the republic during the industrialization of the 1930s and after World War II.

The majority of the Russian population does not speak Armenian, which has made them ineligible for most government employment. A very low birthrate and migration to central Russia or North America have greatly reduced the Russian-speaking portion of the population, a process accelerated by the ongoing conflict with neighboring Azerbaijan.

Azeri—estimated at less than 1% of the population, numbering about 10,000.

Most of the Muslim Azeris, the majority of them adhering to the Shi'a branch of Islam, have left the republic since the conflict between Armenia and Azerbaijan broke out in 1988. They now form only a small minority of about 10,000, concentrated primarily along the border areas of Nakhichevan in the southwest.

During the Soviet era the Azeris formed the largest of the minority national groups in Armenia, an estimated 3% of the total population. Many fled the fighting along the Azeri border or fled Armenian attacks that formed part of the vicious war over the enclave of Nagorno-Karabakh, an Armenian-populated region within Azerbaijan.

Rom (Gypsy)—estimated at less than 1% of the population, numbering about 8,000.

The Rom or Gypsy population of Armenia was formerly nomadic, but now mostly lives in the larger towns and cities. Most of the Rom belong to the Armenian church and have begun to assimilate into Armenian society.

The majority of the Armenian Rom speak Lomavren (Bosha), a Gypsy language that has been grammatically restructured to be like Armenian. The language's phonology and lexicon have also been greatly influenced by the Armenian language.

Ukrainian—estimated at less than 1% of the population, numbering about 8,000.

The Ukrainian population of Armenia mostly settled in the area after World War II. Transported to Armenia to work in the newly industrialized cities in the late 1940s and the 1950s, the majority still reside in Yerevan and the other large northern towns. Since Ukraine and Armenia became independent in 1991, the Ukrainian population of Armenia has been greatly reduced by immigration to Ukraine or southern Russia.

Assyrian—estimated at less than 1% of the population, numbering about 6,000.

The majority of the Assyrians are the descendants of two waves of migration, the first in the nineteenth century and the second after World War II. Most Assyrians belong to the Nestorian and Jacobite Christian religions, although other Christian sects and denominations are also represented. The Assyrians originally migrated to Russian territory to escape persecution by Muslims in the Turkish Ottoman Empire. After World War II remnants of the formerly large Christian populations fled to the Soviet Union to escape persecution by Arab nationalist governments in the Middle East.

The Assyrian language belongs to the Western branch of the Semitic language family. The Urmiye dialect is the most widely spoken in Armenia and other former Soviet republics.

Greek—estimated at less than 1% of the population, numbering about 5,000.

Most of the Armenian Greeks live in the capital, Yerevan, and a few other large cities, where they prospered as merchants or professionals. The Greeks speak an archaic dialect of Greek called Pontian Greek, but the majority also speak Russian or Armenian as their second language.

Descended from the so-called Pontian Greeks, the Greek-speaking population of the Black Sea region, many migrated inland to Armenia during the nineteenth century. Since 1991 many Greeks have accompanied the Armenian exodus from the contested province of Abkhazia in Georgia. The Greek government has subsidized immigration of the Pontian Greeks wishing to resettle in Greece.

Belarussian—estimated at less than 1% of the population, numbering about 3,000.

The Belarussians, the third largest of the Eastern Slav nations, are the smallest of the Slav national groups in Armenia. The Belarussian population mostly migrated to the republic during the postwar industrialization. The majority speak Russian and are nearly indistinguishable from the large Russian population.

THE NATION: According to Armenian tradition, Noah's Ark, after weathering the great flood, landed on Mount Ararat, the sacred symbol of Armenian nationhood, now in Turkish territory. The Armenians claim descent from Noah through Haik, thus the name for their homeland, Haikakan.

The first records of Armenia date back to the ninth century B.C. The nation was established by the union of local tribes known as Urartu (the ancient word for Ararat). This kingdom, sometimes called the Vannic kingdom, was founded by Arame, a legendary national hero. Although the Urartu enjoyed about a century of power, the kingdom eventually fell to invading tribes. The name Armenia comes from a Persian word describing those who conquered and settled the region in the sixth century B.C. The earliest known mention of the "Armenian" people, called the Armenoi, was found in the writings of the Greek historian Hecataeus of Miletus, about 550 B.C. "Armenia" (Armina) was mentioned in the Behistun inscription of Darius I of Persia about 520 B.C.

Historians believe that the Armenians are descendants of various indigenous people who merged with the people of Urartu between the tenth and seventh centuries B.C., although ancient historians and geographers often repeated the tradition that the Armenians migrated to their homeland from Thrace, Phrygia, or Thessaly. The various tribes are thought to have emerged as one linguistic family around 600 B.C.

From 518 B.C. the region formed a satrapy of the Persian Empire until the arrival of the Greeks of Alexander the Great. Following Alexander's death and the disintegration of his empire, Armenia became part of one of the successor states, the Seleucid Empire. After the destruction of the Seleucid Empire, the first Armenian state was founded in 190 B.C. under the Artaxid dynasty. At its zenith under Tigran (Tigranes) the Great, from 95 to 55 B.C., Armenia extended its rule over the area of what is now eastern Turkey and, with Pontus, formed a short-lived Armenian-Hellenistic empire that stretched from the Caucasus to Lebanon and from Mesopotamia to the Black Sea coast.

For a time, Armenia was the strongest state east of the Roman Empire. The empire was destroyed by the Romans, who were gradually expanding into the Caucasus and the Middle East. Western Armenia thus fell under Roman hegemony in 30 B.C., while the eastern territories came to be dominated by the Parthians.

The Armenian nation was the first to adopt Christianity as the national religion. Trdat (Tiridates) III accepted Christianity for the Armenian people, traditionally in A.D. 301, but possibly as late as 314. Their distinct national church was established in 491 when the Armenian church separated from the Greek rite prevalent in the eastern half of Christendom. Armenian tradition maintains that Christianity was introduced by Sts. Bartholomew and Thaddeus, while St. Gregory (Grigor) the Illuminator is credited with the conversion of King Tiridates in 301. It is also known that small Jewish colonies, dating back probably to the period of the Babylonian Captivity, existed in Armenia and probably served as nuclei for the spreading of the gospel.

Following the conversion of the Armenians, church services were held in Greek or Aramaic, depending on the district. The liturgy was read in Armenian churches in one or the other of these languages, with an immediate translation into Armenian made by a special order of clerics called Translators. The lack of a native writing system was seen by the ecclesiastical and political leaders as inimical to both the nurturing of Christianity and national cohesion. To remedy this national lack, the Katholikos Isaac and King Vramshapuh appointed a learned monk, Mesrob Mashtots, to devise an alphabet, which was introduced around 404. The introduction of the alphabet began a great flowering of Armenian culture.

The collapse of Roman power left the small Christian nation vulnerable to neighboring states and peoples. However, in spite of the threat, the golden age of Armenian culture continued, reaching its zenith around 600. Original works were also composed during the golden age, including works on history, philosophy, hagiography, homilies, hymns, and apologetics. Later, works on the sciences were written. The Armenian church became the repository of the cultural works, providing the Armenian people with a strong national culture just at the time that the Armenian state was losing its national independence. The golden age continued until the Byzantine Empire, the successor to Rome in the East, ceded Armenia to the expanding Arabs in 653.

In 806 the Arabs installed the Bagratid family to govern Armenia as a vassal state. The revival that began under the Bagratids led to a second golden age from 862 to 977, coinciding with Armenian independence from Arab rule in 885 under the Bagratid dynasty. Armenia was again conquered in 1046 by the Byzantine Greeks. As a part of the Byzantine conquest of the Armenian states, many nobles lost their estates in Armenia and were resettled in Cilicia, in southern Asia Minor.

The defeat of the Byzantines by the Seljuk Turks at the Battle of Manzikert in Armenia in 1071 brought all Armenia under Seljuk rule. Many Armenians, fleeing the Turkish Seljuk invasion of Anatolia after 1073, and then the Mongol invasions of the thirteenth century, also fled to Cilicia. A new, prosperous Armenian state was established in Cilicia or Little Armenia by the Rubenid dynasty in 1080 while Armenia proper was rapidly declining. In 1293 the Katholikos moved his seat to Sis, the capital of Cilicia. Little Armenia survived until destroyed by the Egyptian Mamelukes in 1373–75. The Armenians of Cilicia were close allies of the Crusaders who came to the Middle East to free the Holy Land.

The devastating Mongol invasion began in 1220 and ended with the complete occupation of Armenia in 1236. Unlike the Russians, the Armenian elite eventually prospered under the Mongols, serving as agents and being able to engage in international trade via the newly secured routes through Central Asia to India and China. As the Mongols declined in power, the Armenian territories were devastated by raiding bands of nomadic tribes.

Tamerlane (Timur), one of the successors to the Mongols' far-flung empire, invaded Armenia in the late fourteenth century. His forces massacred a majority of the Christian population between 1386 and 1394. The surviving Armenians came under the rule of the advancing Ottoman Turks in the fifteenth century, although Turkish control, particularly of the eastern districts, was disputed by the Persians. Even though subject to cruel restrictions and special taxes as Christians under Muslim rule, the industrious Armenians acquired a vital economic role in the workings of the Ottoman Empire, some even rising to high office.

The Persian conquest of eastern Armenia in 1639 effectively partitioned the nation. Suffering persecution and discrimination under Muslim rule, the Armenians welcomed the advance of the Christian Russians in the Transcaucasus in the late eighteenth and early nineteenth centuries. In 1828 the Russians took control of eastern Armenia from Persia, setting off a wave of pro-Russian sentiment among the harshly treated Armenian population living under Ottoman Turkish rule.

Russian interest in the region triggered a period of repression and persecution of the Ottoman Christians that worsened in the latter half of the nineteenth century. The focal points of Armenian life, due to the repression, lay outside the nation's heartland, in the great centers of Armenian culture, Constantinople, Tiflis (Tbilisi), and Van. The major European nations, uncomfortable with the persecution of Christians, demanded reforms in the Ottoman Empire in 1878 and again in 1883, but the demands only increased Turkish distrust of their Christian subjects.

A small number of educated Armenians founded the Armenian national movement in the relatively more liberal Russian Armenia in 1840. National sentiment, fueling a cultural revival in the mid-nineteenth century, rapidly spread through the Armenian populations in Russia, Turkey, and Persia.

Determined to crush the perceived Christian threat to the Ottoman Empire, the Turkish authorities, beginning in 1890, officially encouraged attacks on defenseless Armenian towns and villages, leading to horrible massacres by rampaging Turks and Kurds. In 1895 over 300,000 died in attacks and massacres. An 1896 attack by Armenian nationalists on the Ottoman Bank cost the Armenians over 50,000 lives in official reprisals. Nationalists, in the late 1890s, formed the Armenian Revolutionary Federation, the Dashnaktsutium, which soon had cells in most towns and villages in both Russian and Turkish Armenia. The nationalists, led by the Dashnaks, openly opposed Turkish oppression and the Russian policy of assimilation.

The official policy of the Russification of the Armenian population in Russian Armenia increased in parallel with the growth of Armenian national sentiment. Attempts to forcibly convert the Armenians to Russian Orthodoxy greatly increased tensions in the region. The threat to their religion, an integral part of Armenian culture, spurred the growth of Armenian nationalism. In 1903 all the holdings of the Armenian Church in Russia were confiscated and turned over to the Russian Orthodox Church. The outraged Armenians joined in the revolutionary activities that swept the Russian Empire in 1905. As part of the concessions promised by the government to end the revolution, all church property was returned to the Armenian Church and the 1903 decree retracted.

Divided Armenia became a battleground when war broke out in 1914. The Christian Armenians, led by the Dashnaks, generally supported Christian Russia against the hated Turks. Ottoman Turkey, allied to the Central Powers, Germany and Austria-Hungary, continued to view its Christian minorities with suspicion.

The Armenian majority in the town of Van, in Turkish Armenia, rebelled on 13 April 1915. The rebels quickly captured the important fort and held off the Ottoman military until relieved by Russian troops on 19 May. In June the Ottoman government, controlled by the pan-Turk clique known as the Young Turks, claiming that the over 2 million Armenians in the empire were aiding the Russian enemy, ordered non-Muslim populations removed from all points of military concentrations and lines of communication.

The orders, carried out with incredible cruelty, were interpreted as sanctioning the virtual annihilation of the Armenian minority in the empire. Hundreds of thousands of Armenian civilians were driven into the Syrian Desert to perish from hunger, thirst, and violence. Armenian men were systematically murdered; the women were raped and, with the surviving children, sold into slavery. The deserted Armenian towns and villages were eradicated, with particular attention devoted to the destruction of churches. Over half a million scattered survivors fled to sanctuary in Russian Armenia or escaped abroad. Estimates of the number murdered in the century's first genocide, 1915–16, range from 1 to 1.5 million.

The Russian Provisional Government, coming to power following the revolution in Petrograd in February 1917, gave vague promises of unification of all the Armenian lands, giving the Dashnak nationalists reason to support the new government. The Bolshevik coup, in October of the same year, alienated the new Armenian government, which sought protection by joining with neighboring Georgia and Azerbaijan in an independent Transcaucasian Federation. Tensions between the federation partners, particularly between Christian Armenia and Muslim Azerbaijan, ended the attempt to form a strong federation even as new threats appeared to menace the fragile independence of the Transcaucasian republics.

The Armenian authorities, with the collapse of the Transcaucasian Federation, declared Armenia a separate independent state on 28 May 1918. The new state laid claim to the traditional Armenian lands, including the Armenian populated parts of newly independent Azerbaijan and the largely depopulated provinces of Turkish Armenia, where only a few thousand Armenians remained alive, mostly in Allied-controlled refugee camps.

Armenian troops moved west into the Ottoman provinces, hailed as liberators by the surviving Armenians and the numerous Greek Christians living along the Black Sea coast. Looting of Muslim properties, as well as massacres in retaliation for the earlier Turkish massacres, became widespread before the government in Yerevan could restore order. In May 1919, taking advantage of Ottoman Turkey's defeat by the Allied powers, Armenia formally annexed Turkish Armenia even though much of the region remained outside Armenian control. The Armenian republic, claiming an area of over 68,000 square miles, had a population of over 2 million in 1919, 65% Christian and 33% Muslim.

Cilicia, in southeastern Turkey, with a large Armenian population, was taken by Allied forces in 1918. In 1919 the French took control of the Cilicia region. Due to the non-Turkish majority, the region was separated from Turkey and was given as a mandate to France by the new League of Nations in 1920. The beleaguered Armenian government in Yerevan also sought British and French protection, but without success.

The delegates sent by the Armenian government to the Paris Peace Conference, in 1919, put forward territorial claims to former Russian Armenia, plus the former Turkish Armenian provinces of Van, Bitlis, Diyarbakir, Kharput, Sivas, Erzurum, Trebizond, and Cilicia in the south. The Turks rejected the Armenian claims to former Ottoman territory completely. On 23 July 1919 the Turks held the first Turkish National Congress in Erzurum, in Armenian claimed territory. The Allies, over Turkish objections, made provision for recognizing an independent ''Greater Armenia'' in the 1920 Treaty of Sevres, which formally ended hostilities with Turkey. The Allies refused to accede to all of the Armenians' territorial demands, which were thought excessive, but recognized Armenian claims to parts of former Ottoman Armenia. The new state's western border, as defined by the treaty, was delimited personally by U.S. president Woodrow Wilson, a staunch advocate of Armenian independence.

The new republic, threatened by the advancing Red Army and a resurgent, nationalist Turkey, appealed to the Allies for protection. In April 1920, at the San Remo Conference of Allied Powers, the Allies urged the United States to accept Armenia as a mandate under the new League of Nations. The U.S. Senate, having kept the United States out of the League of Nations, voted 52 to 23 against the mandate proposal. The vote sealed the fate of the beleaguered Armenian republic.

The Soviet government, emerging victorious from the Russian Civil War, and Turkey, under its new nationalist leader, Kemal Ataturk, by tacit agreement planned the demise of the bothersome Armenian republic. The Red Army, in the east, and the Turks, in the west, launched a simultaneous attack on the republic in September 1920. In November Turkish troops, led by General Osman Karabekir, abetted by the Soviets, overran the poorly defended former Ottoman provinces in western Armenia. The Turkish conquest of the Armenian territory in eastern Anatolia ended with near obliteration of the Armenian presence in the region. The renewed massacres of the remaining Armenian population sent the survivors fleeing to the meager protection of the eastern districts of the besieged republic. In December 1920 the Red Army finally defeated the starving, ill-equipped, and seriously overcrowded remnant of the Republic of Armenia.

The defeated Armenians rebelled against their new Communist masters in February 1921 while the Red Army was occupied with the conquest of neighboring Georgia. In March the Soviets defeated the rebels, and a purge of the Armenian leadership began.

In the south the victorious Turkish troops expelled the French forces from the Cilicia Mandate in 1921. The Turkish conquest of Cilicia forced thousands of Armenians to flee across the border into French territory in Syria, the last large refugee Armenian population to be driven from their homelands.

The fallen republic, partitioned between the Turkish and Soviet states, ceased to exist. In the Turkish zone the new nationalist government sponsored Muslim settlement in the depopulated region. In the east the Soviets proclaimed, on 2 April 1921, the independent Soviet Republic of Armenia, which was joined to Soviet Georgia and Azerbaijan in a new Transcaucasian Federation. The federation joined the new Union of Soviet Socialist Republics on 30 December 1922.

The Soviet government, distrustful of minorities—particularly the Armenians, with their ties to the Armenian Diaspora—purged potential leaders, writers, intellectuals, and professionals during the 1920s and 1930s. The federation of the Transcaucasian states was finally abolished, and Armenia became a separate republic within the Union in 1936.

In 1953, on behalf of the Armenian people, the Soviet government formally renounced all claims to Turkish Armenia. After World War II the Soviet government, despite decades of purges that had eliminated the Armenian political and cultural leadership, urged Diaspora Armenians to return to the world's only Armenian state. Over 200,000 Armenians returned from exile, preferring to live among their own people, even under Soviet rule.

Armenian nationalism, sustained by the large Armenian Diaspora, reemerged in the 1970s, led by the pro-Western Dashnaks. Militant groups demanded that Turkey admit to the crime of genocide and as partial compensation cede Turkish Armenia to a reconstituted Armenian state. Armenian terrorist groups struck at Turkish targets around the world, particularly Turkish diplomatic missions in

Europe and the Middle East. More moderate nationalist groups lobbied Western support from offices in Europe, the United States, and the Middle East. The French government, in 1983, announced its support for an independent Armenian state.

Nationalism in Soviet Armenia grew rapidly in the more relaxed atmosphere begun by the Soviet leader Mikhail Gorbachev in 1987. The introduction of the *glasnost* and *perestroika* reforms allowed the expression of ideas and sentiments unthinkable just a few years before. Renewed Armenian territorial claims to Nagorno-Karabakh, an Armenian majority enclave controlled by neighboring Azerbaijan since 1923, became a rallying point. Nationalists formed the Karabakh Committee, demanding that Nagorno-Karabakh, called Artsakh in Armenian, be returned to Armenian administration. Crowds estimated to number over 1 million people demonstrated in Yerevan when the Soviet government refused to alter borders within the Soviet Union. Nationalist sentiment grew rapidly as the Soviet government loosened its grip on the union republics.

The Karabakh Committee, like the popular front groups in the Baltic republics, demanded greater economic, political, and cultural freedom. The nationalists insisted on a veto on all development projects in the republic, freedom to fly the Armenian national flag, the right to open consulates in countries with large Armenian populations, and the creation of a separate Armenian detachment to the Red Army so that young Armenians could perform their military service on home soil. The most politically charged nationalist demand, the unification of the Armenian populated areas of the Soviet Union, starting with Nagorno-Karabakh, immediately led to open disputes with neighboring Azerbaijan.

In February 1988, the Armenian population of Nagorno-Karabakh voted to secede from Azerbaijan and to unite with Armenia. The Armenian nationalist demands sparked a parallel nationalist upsurge among the Muslim Azeris, leading to attacks on the Armenian districts of Azerbaijan's largest cities. Azeri mobs tore into the Armenian quarter in the industrial city of Sumgait, killing over thirty Armenians and injuring hundreds. In an effort to quell the growing ethnic violence, the Red Army sent troops to occupy both Armenia and Azerbaijan, but the mob violence and confrontations continued. Over 200,000 Armenian refugees fleeing the growing violence in Azerbaijan poured across the Armenian border, only to be engulfed in a new disaster, the most destructive earthquake to hit the region in over a thousand years.

On 7 December 1988 the massive quake that struck northern Armenia leveled whole cities and left 55,000 dead, thousands wounded, and over half a million homeless. Leaders of the Karabakh Committee, critical of the Soviet rescue effort, and blaming poor planning and construction techniques for the massive death toll, were arrested at the height of the disaster and charged with spreading false information and slandering the Soviet state. New Armenian protests erupted, leading to clashes between demonstrators and the army and police. Army units, withdrawn from Azerbaijan to aid the earthquake rescue effort, freed the Azeri mobs to renew their attacks. Even after the enormously destructive earthquake, trains full of terrified Armenian refugees continued to arrive in Yerevan.

Battered by an Azeri rail blockade that crippled the economy and brought earthquake reconstruction to a halt, the Armenians quickly lost faith in the ability of Gorbachev's reform government to protect them from their Muslim neighbors. Shortages of food and other essential goods further inflamed Armenian nationalist sentiment as the advantages of Soviet citizenship rapidly withered away.

On 26 March 1989 the citizens of the Soviet Union, for the first time in over seven decades, voted in free, multicandidate elections for a new Chamber of Deputies. The Armenians, defying the occupation troops of the Red Army and an official ban on demonstrations, took to the streets to protest the elections being held while their proposed candidates, members of the Karabakh Committee, were in prison in Moscow. A mass boycott negated the results of the vote in Armenia, where most refused to vote while their entire nationalist leadership remained in jail or in hiding. Mass demonstrations in Yerevan finally achieved the freedom of the imprisoned Armenian nationalist leaders.

The Armenians of Nagorno-Karabakh, feeling unable to count on the Red Army to protect them from attacks by their Muslim neighbors, formed self-defense groups. In an attempt to stop the growing violence and confrontations between Armenia and Azerbaijan, in early 1989 the Soviet government placed Nagorno-Karabakh under direct rule from Moscow. Both the Armenian nationalists and the Azeri government refused to accept the solution as final. The sporadic fighting turned into full-scale war in Nagorno-Karabakh and neighboring areas in January 1990.

In May 1990 the Armenian parliament suspended the spring draft of military conscripts following massive antidraft demonstrations in Yerevan. Only 7% of the Armenian draftees bothered to answer their induction notices. In late May renewed violence broke out after Interior Ministry troops fired on demonstrators in Yerevan, killing at least twenty-two people.

The Armenian National Movement, a coalition of several separate nationalist organizations, grew out of the Karabakh Committee and rapidly gained support in the republic, even among longtime Armenian Communists. Nationalists quickly moved into local governments and soon controlled the major organs of the republic. On 23 August 1990 the Armenian parliament declared the sovereignty of the renamed Republic of Armenia and announced that the declaration was the beginning of a process of establishing independent statehood. The clauses of the declaration asserted Armenian control of its own army, along with the republic's natural resources, banks, economic system, and foreign policy, and extended Armenian control to the disputed enclave of Nagorno-Karabakh.

On 30 April 1991, for the first time in the dispute, Soviet troops openly sided with the still Communist-controlled Azerbaijan against the nationalist-controlled Armenia. In May, following a two-week campaign by Azeri and Soviet troops along the Azeri-Armenian border, thousands of Armenians were forced to flee, further eroding support for the maintenance of the tottering Soviet Union.

In the wake of the failed military coup in Moscow in August 1991, the Armenian government organized a referendum on independence on 21 September. The vote was 94.05% in favor of immediate independence. On 23 September 1991 the Armenian president, Levon Ter-Petrossian, formally declared the republic's independence as the Republic of Armenia, Haikakan Hanrapetoutioun. In December 1991 the United States and other world governments extended formal diplomatic recognition to the new Armenian state.

The new republic, strongly supported by the Armenian Diaspora, faced massive economic and political problems, as the change from communism to capitalism was further complicated by an economic blockade begun by neighboring Azerbaijan in November 1991. The dispute over Nagorno-Karabakh fueled a continuing war involving the local Armenian military in the besieged enclave, which was supplied by Armenian helicopters. On 31 December 1991 the Armenian-controlled government of Nagorno-Karabakh declared independence from Azerbaijan, further escalating the war between the two newly independent states.

On 4 January 1992, Armenia began radical free-market economic reforms. With its economy crippled by the ongoing Azeri blockade, the change from a command to a free-market economy caused massive suffering and hardships, alleviated only by the support of the Armenian Diaspora and aid from friendly world governments.

Azeri forces besieged Nagorno-Karabakh in November 1992, forcing the residents of the enclave's capital to live in underground shelters. The enclave's only lifeline was a dangerous helicopter route to Armenia. The Armenian forces of Nagorno-Karabakh, backed by troops of the Republic of Armenia, went on the offensive to break the siege, finally opening a secure land corridor between the enclave and the republic in late 1992. By April 1993 the Armenian forces had occupied up to a tenth of the national territory of Azerbaijan, mostly the districts lying to the west and south of Nagorno-Karabakh that connect the enclave to Armenia.

Armenia, surrounded on three sides by Muslim states, sees itself as the standard-bearer of Western civilization in the region. The new republic's ties to the large diaspora reinforce the Armenians' view of themselves as an outpost of Western culture. Armenia continues to have the active support of the rich and vigorous diaspora, especially in America, earning it the sobriquet "Israel of the Caucasus." In spite of the Azeri blockade and a partial blockade by neighboring Turkey, Armenia has proved a model of economic self-discipline. And despite severe energy shortages, industrial production is rising rapidly.

Karabakh Armenians, supported by the Republic of Armenia, in 1997 continued to hold about one-fifth of Azerbaijan and have refused to withdraw from occupied territory until an agreement on the status of Nagorno-Karabakh is reached. Armenia and Azerbaijan continue to observe the cease-fire that has been in effect since May 1994, and in late 1995 both also agreed to allow European field representatives, based in Tbilisi, Georgia, to help facilitate the peace process.

President Levon Ter-Petrosian, though untainted by a Communist past, is secretive and nervous. His government won parliamentary elections in July 1995, and he was reelected president of the republic on 22 September 1996. Despite the democratic nature of the elections, opposition political parties continue to denounce the undemocratic practices and the corruption of the Ter-Petrosian government.

In 1997 the republic signed a new economic and military treaty with the Russian Federation as part of the Armenian government's attempts to break out of the diplomatic isolation of the Nagorno-Karabakh conflict. In August 1997 the government announced that a border crossing would soon be opened between Armenia and Turkey, which had formerly refused diplomatic ties and border crossings due to the Nagorno-Karabakh conflict.

President Levon Ter-Petrosian, having dared to suggest that Armenia should be more flexible over Artsakh (Karabakh), in the autumn of 1997 endorsed a step-by-step peace plan put forward by the Organisation for Security and Co-operation in Europe (OSCE). His conciliatory moves outraged many Armenian leaders, who finally forced him from office in early February 1998. The ouster of Ter-Petrosian, who has dominated Armenia since independence in 1991, diminishes the chances of a peaceful solution to the long-running dispute with neighboring Azerbaijan.

SELECTED BIBLIOGRAPHY:

Chorbajian, Levon, ed. *The Caucasian Knot: The History and Geopolitics of Nagorno-Karabagh.* 1994.

Libaridian, Gerald J., ed. *Armenia at the Crossroads.* 1991.

Malkasian, Mark. *'Gha-Ra-Bagh': The Emergence of the National Democratic Movement in Armenia.* 1996.

Sunny, Ronald Grigor. *Looking Toward Ararat: Armenia in Modern History.* 1993.

Walker, Christopher, ed. *Armenia and Karabagh: The Struggle for Unity.* 1991.

AZERBAIJAN

**Republic of Azerbaijan;
Azerbaidzhan; Azerbaijchan
Respublikasy; Azarbaycan
Respublikasi**

CAPITAL: Baku

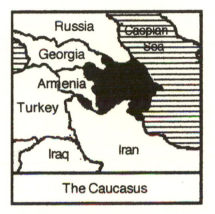

The Caucasus

Azerbaijan

POPULATION: (98e) 7,721,000 : 6,663,000 Azeris in Azerbaijan and large numbers in neighboring states, 315,000 in Georgia,* 342,000 in Russia,* and 10,000 in Armenia.* An estimated 15 to 20 million Azeris inhabit the region called Iranian Azerbaijan, just across the southern border of the republic. MAJOR NATIONAL GROUPS: REPUBLIC OF AZERBAIJAN (98e): Azeri 86.3%, Dagestani 3.2%, Russian 2.4%, Armenian 2.3%, Talysh 1.8%, Kurd 1.4%, Georgian 1.2%, Ukrainian, Jew, Tatar. MAJOR LANGUAGES: Azeri, Russian, Armenian, Kurdish. MAJOR RELIGIONS: Shi'a Islam, Sunni Islam, Russian Orthodox, Armenian Orthodox, Georgian Orthodox. MAJOR CITIES: (98e): AZERBAIJAN: Baku 1,835,000 (2,220,000), Gyandzha (Gandja, Kirovabad) 291,000 (330,000), Sumqayit (Sumgait) 270,000, Mingechaur 88,000 (103,000), Nukha (Sheki) 76,000, Lenkoran 55,000, Ali-Bayramly 50,000, Nakhichevan 47,000, Khankendi (Stepanakert—under Armenian control) 35,000 (60,000). IRANIAN AZERBAIJAN: Tabriz 1,175,000 (1,400,000), Orumiyeh 375,000, Ardabil 345,000, Khvoy 180,000, Marangeh 145,000, Marand 110,000, Mianeh 105,000, Ahar 90,000, Miandowab 85,000, Namin 82,000, Benab 73,000, Ahar 68,000, Mahabad 67,000, Sarab 52,000.

GEOGRAPHY: AREA: 33,436 sq.mi.—86,621 sq.km. "Greater Azerbaijan" 74,581 sq.mi.—193,215 sq.km. LOCATION: Azerbaijan lies in the Transcaucasus region of southeastern Europe, a mountainous region sloping down to the Caspian Sea on the east, and bordering Georgia and the Dagestan Republic of Russia on the north, Armenia on the west, and the Aras (Araks) River on the south, the river forming the international border between the Republic of Azerbaijan and Iranian Azerbaijan. A small region, Nakhichevan, is separated from Azerbaijan proper by Armenian territory and forms an enclave lying between the western border of the Republic of Armenia and the northwestern frontier of Iran. PHYSICAL GEOGRAPHY: In the north of the country lie the Greater Caucasus Mountains, which descend rapidly to form a band of low, arid hills. The Lesser Caucasus Mountains, in the south, which consist of the Shakhdag, Qarabag (Karabakh), and Murordag ranges, also contain a vast lava plateau as well as extinct volcanoes. The Kura Depression, a low, fertile, almost treeless plateau, also called the Kur-Araz Lowlands, which lies between the Greater and Lesser Caucasus and part of which is below sea level, is the heartland of the country. Baku lies on the Abseron (Apsheron) Peninsula, which juts into the Caspian Sea in the east of the country. ADMINISTRATIVE DIVISIONS: Fifty-nine counties or rayons (rayonlar; singular—rayon), eleven cities (saharlar; singular—sahar), one autonomous republic (muxtar respublika). POLITICAL STATUS: The Republic of Azerbaijan was recognized as an independent state in 1991. Iranian Azerbaijan, claimed as part of ''Greater Azerbaijan'' by some nationalist groups, forms the Iranian provinces of East and West Azerbaijan.

INDEPENDENCE DECLARATIONS: 28 May 1918 (from Russia); 8 September 1945 (from Iran); 30 August 1991 (from the Soviet Union).

FLAG: The Azeri national flag, the official flag of the Republic of Azerbaijan, is a horizontal tricolor of pale blue, red, and green, bearing a white crescent moon and eight-pointed star centered on the red stripe.

PEOPLE: Azerbaijan has a mixed population, with about seventy national groups represented in the republic. Since 1988 the majority of the formerly large Armenian population, with the exception of the Armenian population of the breakaway region of Nagorno-Karabakh, has left Azerbaijan. Many ethnic Russians, Ukrainians, and Belarussians have also left Azerbaijan. Most of the Armenians fled to Armenia following the outbreak of violence in 1988, while the Slavs mostly migrated to Russia or the United States seeking better economic opportunities. Up to 1 million Azeris are displaced within the country due to the fighting in Nagorno-Karabakh and adjoining regions.

Azeri (Azerbaijani)—an estimated 86.3% of the population, numbering about 6,663,000.

The Azeris are a Turkic people, the descendants of early Caucasian peoples, with later Persian and Turkic admixtures. In the past, the clan-type family structure was common among the Azeri. The clan, or hoj, was usually named after a common ancestor. Clan members shared pasture land and were bound to provide mutual aid to each other. They frequently acted as a unified entity in business dealings. It was also common for up to forty members of an extended family to live together in large dwellings called gazma. Landless peasants, the *tavyrga*, made up the lowest social class.

The Azeris speak a Turkic language belonging to the Southwestern or Orguz branch of the Turkic language family. There are two main subgroups of Azeri: Azerbaijani North, spoken mostly in Azerbaijan, and Azerbaijani South, spoken in Iran. The main differences are in the sounds and basic grammatical structure of the dialects. Azeri has a written tradition that dates back to the fourteenth century. Arabic or Persian script is used in Iran, and the Cyrillic alphabet is used in Azerbaijan. Azeri serves as the somewhat hybrid, yet common, language of eastern Transcaucasus, southern Dagestan, and northwestern Iran.

Officially, about 70% of the Azeris adhere to the Shi'a branch of Islam, the predominant sect in neighboring Iran, while some 20% practice the Hanafite rite of Sunni Islam, primarily in the northern districts of the republic. However, the number of practicing adherents is considerably lower than the official figures. Among the Azeri Muslims, religious practices are less restrictive of women's activities than in most of the other Muslim countries. The majority of Azeri women have jobs outside the home, and a few have attained leadership positions. However, some evidence of the traditional, restrictive female role remains.

The Azeri population of the former Soviet Union and Iran, although separated by political borders for nearly two centuries, retains strong cultural and linguistic ties. Some Azeri nationalists continue to work for the union of the two Azerbaijans in one sovereign Azerbaijani republic. Considered the most sophisticated of the Muslim peoples of the former Soviet Union, the Azeris have reestablished their old ties to Turkey, particularly after Turkey supported Azerbaijan in its conflict with Armenia.

Dagestani—an estimated 3.2% of the population, numbering about 248,000.

The Dagestanis are North Caucasian peoples living mostly in the Dagestan Republic of the Russian Federation just north of Azerbaijan. The Dagestanis speak various Caucasian and Turkic languages. However, most of the Dagestani peoples living in Azerbaijan speak Northern Caucasian languages.

The largest of the Dagestani peoples in Azerbaijan are the Lezgi or Lezgins, numbering about 173,000, a figure much lower than that quoted by Lezgin nationalist groups. The majority of the Lezgins live in the northeastern districts near the border with Russian Dagestan and on the southern slopes of the main spur of the Caucasus Mountains. Most of the Lezgins are Shi'a Muslims, with a Sunni Muslim minority. Within Azerbaijan, the Lezgins have faced mounting pressure to assimilate. Their literary language was banned in 1939, and virtually all Lezgin are bilingual, speaking Lezgin and Azeri. A growing national movement aims to unite the 1.2 million Lezgins in Azerbaijan and the Russian Dagestan Republic.

The Avars, numbering about 53,000, mainly inhabit districts of the Zaqatala and Balakan regions along Azerbaijan's northwestern border with Russia. The Avars are mostly Sunni Muslims. The Avars include various peoples who were once considered distinct ethnic groups. Each distinct language is now considered a dialect of Bolmat's, the Avar language.

The third largest group of Dagestanis are the Tsakhur, numbering about 16,000. The Tsakhurs live among the Avars and Azeris inhabiting the districts along the northwestern border with Russia. Like the Avars, the Tsakhurs are mostly Sunni Muslims.

The other Dagestani peoples in Azerbaijan are small in number, and most speak languages related to the Lezgian language. The majority of these small groups use their own language as a spoken language, but use Azerbaijani as their literary language.

Russian—an estimated 2.4% of the population, numbering about 185,000.

The dwindling Russian population in Azerbaijan is concentrated mainly in the urban areas of Baku and the other large cities. Most moved to Azerbaijan in government-assisted immigration after World War II, although a substantial Russian minority has lived in Baku since the oil boom of the early twentieth century.

Armenian—an estimated 2.3% of the population, numbering about 175,000.

The Armenian population of Azerbaijan is mostly concentrated in the breakaway Nagorno-Karabakh region near the western border with Armenia. The formerly large Armenian populations of Baku and the other large cities in eastern Azerbaijan mostly fled to Armenia to escape the anti-Armenian violence that accompanied the outbreak of the Nagorno-Karabakh conflict in 1988.

Talysh (Talish)—an estimated 1.8% of the population, numbering about 141,000.

The Talysh are an Iranian people living along the Caspian Sea between the Viliazh-Chai River and the Iranian border. An estimated 120,000 Talysh live in adjoining areas of Iran. The Talysh speak their own Indo-Iranian language, while the majority are bilingual in Azerbaijani. The Talysh are mostly Shi'a Muslims, as are their Azeri and Iranian neighbors. Descendants of the old Iranian groups of present-day Azerbaijan and northern Iran, most have been assimilated by Azeri Turks who migrated into these areas. Except among the elderly, the main spoken and literary language of the Talysh is Azeri.

Since the independence of Azerbaijan in 1991, many younger Talysh have rejected the assimilation promoted by the Azeri government. New interest in their language and culture has spurred the formation of an autonomy movement, with a small but growing separatist movement in the Talish homeland in the south. Government figures estimate the Talysh population of Azerbaijan at less than 2% of the total population, but nationalists claim a much higher proportion, estimating that 11% of the total population of Azerbaijan is ethnic Talysh. The different figures would seem to be based on language rather than ethnic origins. Nationalists claim that the combined Talysh population of Azerbaijan and Iran numbers over 2 million.

Kurd—an estimated 1.4% of the population, numbering about 108,000.

The Kurds, other than a small minority living in Baku, live along the southern border with Iran and in the Nakhichevan region, an autonomous republic divided from Azerbaijan proper by part of Armenia. Many of the Kurds are Yezids, practicing a form of Islam for which they were formerly persecuted. The ancestors of the present Kurdish population fled to Russian territory in the nineteenth century and after World War I to escape persecution in the Muslim lands to the south. The Kurds speak an Indo-Iranian language, and many support the aims of the Kurdish nationalists working for an independent Kurdistan in present Turkey, Iraq, Iran, and Syria.

Georgian—an estimated 1.2% of the population, numbering about 92,000.

The ethnic Georgians in Azerbaijan mostly inhabit the frontier districts along the northwestern border with the Republic of Georgia. The majority are Georgian Christians, with a minority that adhere to the Sunni branch of Islam. Culturally and politically, they are oriented more toward Tbilisi than Baku.

Ukrainian—estimated at less than 1% of the population, numbering about 32,000.

The Ukrainians, like the Russians, mostly settled in the republic during and after World War II. Most live in Baku and the other large urban areas in the east of the country. The second largest of the East Slav nations, the Ukrainians of Azerbaijan form part of the large Ukrainian nation in Ukraine.* However, most speak Russian as their first language. The majority are Orthodox, with smaller numbers of Uniate Catholics.

Tatar—estimated at less than 1% of the population, numbering about 32,000.

The Muslim Tatars, from the upper Volga region, were conquered by the Russians in the sixteenth century. Their language, a West Turkic language, is related to Azeri, although the languages are not mutually intelligible.

Many Tatars became administrators and government officials in the newly conquered Muslim lands in the nineteenth century, making the Tatars the most widely dispersed of the peoples of the old Russian Empire and the later Soviet Union. The majority live in Baku and the large cities of the eastern region of the country.

Turk—estimated at less than 1% of the population, numbering about 19,000.

The Turks are the remnant of a larger Turkish population that has mostly assimilated into Azeri culture since the seventeenth century, aided by the similarity between the Turkish and Azeri languages and cultures. Many of the Turks came to the region when Azerbaijan formed part of the Turkish Ottoman Empire. Unlike the majority of the Azeris, the Turks are mostly Sunni Muslim.

Jew—estimated at less than 1% of the population, numbering about 6,000.

The Jews of Azerbaijan are mostly descendants of early Jewish populations that lived in the Caucasus Mountains. Their native language, called Tat or Judeo Tat, is an Iranian language. Other Jews, mostly Russian-speaking, settled in the region during the Soviet era. The majority of both groups have now immigrated to Israel or the United States.

Belarussian—estimated at less than 1% of the population, numbering about 5,000.

The majority of the Belarussian population arrived in Azerbaijan after World War II, mostly from the devastated western provinces of Belarus, then called Byelorussia. They were resettled in government programs and given work in newly industrialized Baku and other eastern cities. The Belarussians of Azerbaijan are mostly Russian-speaking and belong to the Russian Orthodox Church.

THE NATION: An ancient Caucasian region inhabited by early Caucasian tribes, Azerbaijan is thought to have been settled by the ancient Medes in the eighth century B.C. The region formed part of successive Persian empires and is traditionally the birthplace of Zoroaster, the founder of Persia's pre-Islamic religion. A Persian governor, Atropates, appointed by Alexander the Great, established an independent Mede kingdom in the region in 328 B.C. Known as Atropatene or Media Atropatene, the region, lying on the major invasion route between Asia and Europe, was often conquered by migrating armies. Under Roman rule the region was called Albania.

The area was claimed by the Parthians, and later by Persia, although continuous Persian control was not firmly established until the third century B.C., when Azerbaijan became a province or satrapy of the Persian Empire. Except for a brief period of Byzantine control in the early seventh century, the area remained Persian until the Arab conquest of the region.

Muslim Arabs conquered the area in the seventh century, forcibly converting the inhabitants to Islam. The region was ruled by the Muslim empire, the Caliphate, until the eleventh century, when it fell to migrating Seljuk Turks. The conquerors adopted the Islamic region of the inhabitants. Turkish language and culture replaced the earlier Persian.

For centuries a frontier district at the confluence of the competing Turkish and Persian empires, the region often changed rulers. The Safavid dynasty, established in 1499, from its beginnings in Iranian Azerbaijan, restored internal order in the Persian Empire. Under Safavid rule the Shiite sect was established as the state religion.

Wars between Safavid Persia and the Turkish Ottoman Empire marked the next centuries. Between 1578 and 1603 the Azeri homeland again fell to Turkish rule. In the seventeenth century Azerbaijan was once again under firm Persian control. As Safavid power waned, Russia and the Ottoman vied for power in the region.

The Russian Empire, expanding south into the Caucasus Mountains region, annexed northern Azerbaijan piecemeal from a weakened Persia between 1805 and 1813. Baku came under Russian control in 1806. The territories taken by the Russians were formally ceded by Persia in the treaties of Gulistan in 1813, which divided Azerbaijan into Russian and Persian spheres, and the Treaty of Turkamanchan in 1828, in which Persia ceded the Nakhichevan. Southern Azerbaijan remained under Persian rule as a separate satrapy with its capital at Tabriz. Russian attempts at further expansion to the south were unsuccessful.

Following the discovery of oil, Baku, a small and dusty Muslim town in newly annexed Russian Azerbaijan, became the first, and at the time, the greatest petroleum producing center in the world. Azerbaijan's oil industry, then the largest in Europe, was established in 1872. Baku's oil fields, tremendously important to the industrializing Russian Empire, brought an influx of Slavic oil and industrial workers. By 1900 the Baku fields were producing half the world's oil.

The wealth generated by oil brought an unprecedented rate of growth and development, and made millionaires of the first investors, including the Nobel brothers, later known for the prizes awarded to world leaders in various fields. These new millionaires financed a massive array of public institutions, schools, and buildings in Baku. In 1907 Baku boasted not only the first opera house in the Muslim world, but also the first Muslim opera, Uzeir Ghajibekov's *Leila and Majnun.*

The sudden economic importance of the area exposed the Azeris to urbanization, Western education, and technology, with the accompanying growth of national consciousness. Resentment of Slavic privileges sparked an Azeri cultural and religious revival in the late nineteenth century, the revival fanned by government programs aimed at the Christianization and assimilation of the Azeri population.

Although less developed than their northern kin, the Azeri population in Persia, affected by the nationalism spreading across the border from Russian Azerbaijan, also began to espouse nationalism as a reaction against the corrupt and feudal rule of the Iranian state. The Russian government often cooperated with the Persian authorities to combat the growing nationalism in the region.

Serious nationalist-religious rioting rocked Russian Azerbaijan in 1901 and 1904, escalating into a popular revolt during the revolution that swept all of Russia in 1905. During the revolution the Azeri nationalists controlled Baku and the surrounding areas until routed by tsarist troops.

The national movement led to the formation of specifically Azeri political parties. The most important, Hemmat (Endeavor), the Muslim Marxist party, formed in Russian Azerbaijan in 1904 and participated in the 1906 revolution in Persian Azerbaijan. Severe anti-Russian rioting swept Russian Azerbaijan in 1907. During the repression that followed, Hemmat and the other political parties were forced underground, while the rioters were put down by Cossack troops. The nationalist political party, Mussavat (Equality), was founded in 1911 with supporters in both Russian and Persian Azerbaijan.

Nationalist unrest spread to Persian Azerbaijan during the same period, inciting serious Azeri revolts against Persian rule during the 1906 revolution and again in 1909. The second revolution in Persia in 1909 gave the Russian government the opportunity to occupy Persian Azerbaijan, but the troops were later withdrawn under the terms of economic and political agreements with the Persian government. Nationalist sentiment, based on the idea of a united Azeri homeland and promoted by the newly formed political parties, spread rapidly on both sides of the international border.

The nationalist Mussavat Party became the largest political organization in Russian Azerbaijan, winning popular support with its demands for Azeri autonomy within the Russian Empire and religious freedom for the Muslims. Russian and Persian government policies restricted contacts between the two halves of the Azeri nation, but clandestine contacts continued, particularly between Mussavat activists and nationalists in Persian Azerbaijan.

The Azeris' sympathies were overwhelmingly with Ottoman Turkey when World War I broke out in 1914. Turkish overtures to the Turkic peoples living in the Russian Empire sparked ethnic and religious conflicts in Baku and other cities in Russian Azerbaijan.

Effectively freed from Russian rule by the Russian Revolution in early 1917, the Azeris, fearing Turkish and Persian designs on the region, and destabilized by Russian soldiers returning from the Turkish front, agreed to join neighboring Georgia and Armenia to form a Transcaucasian federation. The federation cut all ties to the collapsing Russian Empire following the Bolshevik coup that overthrew the democratic Russian Provisional Government in October 1917.

The federation, weakened by severe ethnic and religious differences, particularly between the Muslim Azeris and the Christian Armenians, was further threatened by fighting between nationalists and Russian soldiers, many supporting the radical Bolsheviks, returning from the Turkish front. The returning soldiers, taking advantage of the collapse of civil government, occupied Baku. The tensions and fighting between the Azeris and the Armenians in the federation culminated in the massacre of some 12,000 Azeris in Baku by radical Armenians and Bolshevik troops in March 1918.

The federation was finally dissolved, and the three states were proclaimed separate republics. The Republic of Azerbaijan, led by nationalists of the Mussavat Party, proclaimed its independence on 28 May 1918. The capital of the new country was established at Ganja, as Baku, the Azeri metropolis, remained under the control of Bolshevik forces. In June 1918 Azerbaijan signed a treaty with Turkey and won recognition by Great Britain and other nations. In the summer of 1918 Muslim rioters killed an estimated 4,000 Armenians; the killings stopped only when British troops occupied the port and oil facilities in Baku in July.

Turkish troops supported the Azeris in their reconquest of Baku on 15 September 1918, and two days later the government was transferred to the city from Ganja. Over 8,500 Armenian residents of the city were killed in retaliation for the March massacre of Azeris. British troops occupied Baku to protect the important oil fields. The British occupying forces in Baku gave the Azeri government some stability.

The nationalist revolution in Russian Azerbaijan sent ripples of unrest across the border into Persian Azerbaijan. In 1917 nationalists in Tabriz, formed the Democratic Party of Azerbaijan (Firqeh-i Demokrat-i Azerbayjan), which established close ties to the nationalist Mussavat Party in the former Russian zone.

The republic, caught up in the vicious Russian Civil War, frantically sought Allied assistance as the Bolshevik threat neared. In November 1918, following the Turkish military withdrawal from the republic, the Azeri government appealed directly to President Woodrow Wilson of the United States for help from the Allies, particularly the British, whose troops occupied Baku and the oil fields. Pressured by the Allies, the Azeris formed an alliance with the anti-Bolshevik White Russian forces. The alliance, for the most part, was unsuccessful, as the Whites were unsympathetic to non-Russian national aspirations and vehemently opposed the secession of any part of the Russian Empire. In August 1919 the British, trusting that Azeri independence was assured by the recent Soviet declaration concerning the rights of national minorities, withdrew their troops from Baku, leaving the Azeris at the mercy of the advancing Red Army.

An agreement between the new National Republic of Turkey and the Soviet Union to end the uncomfortable independence of the Transcaucasus republics gave the Turks and Soviet military forces virtually a free hand in the region. The Western Allies, exhausted from the war, refused to intervene more forcibly to protect the nascent democracies, relying instead on their anti-Communist White allies. The Azeri delegation to the Paris Peace Conference in 1919 pleaded for continued British protection, but the pleas were mostly ignored.

The Soviet defeat of the anti-Bolshevik Whites brought the Red Army to Azerbaijan's northern border in early 1920. Betrayed by its former allies, the Turks, the new state was caught in a two-front war. The Soviet authorities, ignoring their earlier assurances to the Azeri government, massed troops on the Azeri border. The Red Army overran the northern districts of the republic while the Turks occupied the south in April 1920. The small Azeri army fought bravely, while the republic's leaders issued frantic appeals for assistance that went unanswered. On 20 April 1920 the Red Army occupied Baku and the Azeri national government collapsed, its leaders imprisoned, shot, or fled abroad. The Soviet victors set their soldiers loose on the city of Baku for twenty-four hours, looting, raping, and murdering. The Red troops were allowed to "amuse" themselves with the city's large number of class enemies—the middle and upper class inhabitants, whether Azeri, Armenian, or Russian. Hundreds died in the orgy of violence.

The victorious Bolsheviks declared Azerbaijan a Soviet republic on 1 May 1920, and oil from Azerbaijan's rich fields began to flow to Soviet Russia. The republic, along with Armenia and Georgia, also under Soviet control, again became part of a Transcaucasian federation, which joined the Union of Soviet Socialist Republics as a constituent republic on 30 December 1922. In 1936 the federation was disbanded and the three republics were made separate constituent republics within the Union.

Azeri nationalism, during the purges and oppression of the 1920s and 1930s, shifted to Iranian Azerbaijan, where many Mussavat leaders had taken refuge. In concert with the nationalists in Tabriz, the exiled Azeri leadership continued to work for a free, united Azeri nation. In 1938 Iranian Azerbaijan was reorganized into two separate provinces in an attempt to dilute growing Azeri nationalist sentiment.

Neutral Iran, when war broke out between the Soviet Union and Nazi Germany in June 1941, refused transit rights to the Soviets and their British allies. To ensure the vital southern supply route during World War II, Soviet troops, in concert with their British counterparts, occupied Iran on 25 August 1941, the Soviets in the northern provinces, the British in the south. A tripartite agreement, signed on 29 January 1942, stipulated that the occupying troops would leave within six months of the end of the war. In 1945, as the end of the war seemed certain, Azeri Communists of the Tudeh Party formed an alliance with the Azeri nationalists of the Democratic Party of Azerbaijan. The alliance, with Soviet support, declared the independence of Iranian Azerbaijan as the Azerbaijan Democratic Republic on 8 September 1945. The Soviets, in spite of the January 1941 agreement and the end of the war, refused to withdraw their troops.

The rebellion in Iranian Azerbaijan, supported by the Soviet occupation troops, led to a serious immediate postwar crisis. One of the main ingredients in the crisis was the Iranian refusal to grant the Soviets an important oil concession. Under growing international pressure, including a U.S. offer to help the Iranians expel the Soviet troops, the Soviets finally withdrew the occupation troops, having first extracted a generous oil concession from the Iranian government. With the Soviet withdrawal, Iranian troops invaded the breakaway Azeri state. The Azeri government collapsed, and the rebellion was brought to a bloody end.

The forced Russification of local government, education, and publishing during the Stalinist era, including changing the alphabet used for the Azeri language from the traditional Arabic alphabet to the Russian Cyrillic alphabet, placed the Slav minority in Azerbaijan in a privileged position. Slav immigrants, encouraged by the government to resettle in the republic, took many of the prestigious government positions in local administrations and education. After World War II, the Stalinist government also staged repeated purges in Soviet Azerbaijan. The elimination of Azeri Communist leaders for alleged "bourgeois nationalism" was a common occurrence in the late 1940s and early 1950s. Following Stalin's death in 1953 and the gradual relaxation of Stalinist vigilance, the republic slowly recovered from the purges and persecution. The growing Azeri resentment of Slav privilege, more acute following Stalin's death, fueled a modest cultural and national revival in the late 1950s and the 1960s.

Improved medicine and food production fostered rapid population growth beginning in the 1930s. The demographic explosion undermined Stalin's plan to colonize and assimilate the republic into a Soviet nationality. The population of the republic grew a startling 26% between 1939 and 1959, giving the Muslim Azeris an overwhelming majority. The demographic explosion worried the authorities in Moscow, as it paralleled a drop in the Slavic birthrate in the region. Soviet government attempts to introduce family planning, seen by the Azeris as yet another attack on their persecuted religion, led to new confrontations in the 1960s and 1970s. The confidence of the post-Stalin era manifested itself in a renewed interest in their culture, language, and Muslim religion. On 21 August 1956 the Supreme Soviet of Azerbaijan decreed that henceforth Azeri would be the only official language of the republic. Periodic purges between 1966 and 1969, and again in 1975, saw top Azeri leaders removed for nationalist tendencies.

The prohibition on contacts between Soviet Azerbaijan and Iranian Azerbaijan became increasingly hard to enforce as the use of radios became widespread, allowing the Azeris in the Soviet Union to lend some covert aid to their kin suffering under the oppressive rule of the Iranian government. The Azeris formed the middle class in Iran's stratified society, dominating the bazaars and providing two-thirds of the army officers as well as many of Iran's intellectuals, writers, and teachers. Despite the repression of the Shah's government, the Iranian Azeris prospered.

The prelude to revolution in Iran spurred a renewed interest in the Iranian Azeris' ties to their northern kin and in their unique culture and language. With the fall of the Shah of Iran's government in 1979, Azeri nationalism reemerged in opposition to the excesses of the revolutionary clique. Azeri opposition to the Islamic Revolution fueled nationalist rioting in Tabriz and other large cities. The Azeri spiritual leader, Ayatollah Shariamadari, was placed under house arrest in Tabriz after his followers clashed with Revolutionary Guards during nationalist rioting in the city. In 1983 the Democratic Party of Azerbaijan and the leftist Tudeh Party were officially dissolved by Iran's Islamic government. In a massive crackdown hundreds of party members and suspected Azeri nationalists, including many women, were imprisoned.

In the years after the revolution in Iran, Azerbaijani radio broadcasts from the Soviet Union were jammed, while broadcasts in Azeri from the Islamic Republic of Iran attempted to stir up Islamic fundamentalist zeal in Soviet Azerbaijan. The Soviet Azeris, after decades of official atheism, were less stirred by religious fundamentalism than by the demands of the increasingly open economy and the perceived Armenian threat. The vast majority of the republic's urbanized population found little attraction in the radical, restrictive doctrines of the Islamic Republic. Azeris wishing to visit relatives across the border were subjected to lengthy paperwork and scrutiny.

The liberation of Soviet society, the result of the introduction of *glasnost* and *perestroika* by Mikhail Gorbachev in 1987, loosed long-simmering ethnic and nationalist tensions in the region. Economic stagnation, mostly due to the region's petroleum fields being neglected in favor of the Siberian oil fields, became a serious problem for the Azeri republican government. Production dropped from 21.5 tons in 1965 to just 3.7 tons in 1988.

A resurgent Azeri nationalism, spurred by Armenian nationalist claims to Nagorno-Karabakh, an Armenian-populated enclave added to Soviet Azerbaijan by Stalin in 1923, sparked mass demonstrations, strikes, and protests. The Azeris claim that Nagorno-Karabakh, an autonomous region with a population 80% Armenian, was historically Azeri territory. The claim is vehemently disputed by the Armenian inhabitants of the small region.

Azeri nationalist sentiment grew rapidly as the conflict with Soviet Armenia escalated into violent confrontations in February 1988. Tensions between the Christian Armenians, often viewed as Russian surrogates, and the Muslim Azeris increased dramatically, often focusing on the large Armenian minorities in Baku and other Azeri cities.

In February 1988 rioting erupted in the important industrial city of Sumgait, north of Baku. Azeri mobs attacked the Armenian quarters of the city, killing between thirty-two and seventy-eight (the official and Armenian estimates) and leaving hundreds injured. Over 10,000 Armenians fled the city. The Armenians charged that Azeri nationalist groups from outside the city were brought in to participate in the anti-Christian crusade. In spite of official denials after the riots, the city's mayor, the police chief, and the local party leader were dismissed and expelled from the Communist Party.

On 12 July 1988 the local legislature of the autonomous region of Nagorno-Karabakh voted to secede from Azerbaijan over Azeri government protests that there were no political, economic, or legal grounds for changing the borders of the enclave. The Soviet government rejected the move, but in September, following renewed ethnic violence, Nagorno-Karabakh was placed under curfew and Soviet troops moved into the region. In an effort to control the publicity surrounding the Soviet Union's worst outbreak of ethnic violence since the civil war period, the Soviet authorities closed Azerbaijan to foreign journalists.

In November 1988 the ethnic clashes began again, particularly in Baku and the large industrial cities in the east of the republic. As the violence spread, thousands of Armenians fled west to Armenia, bringing stories of atrocities and horrors that further widened the growing rift between the two Soviet republics. Soviet troops occupied Baku, Kirovabad, Nakhichevan, and Stepanakert to prevent wholesale massacres of Armenians, many of whom sent their women and children on evacuation convoys to Armenia and stayed to form self-defense committees. The ethnic confrontations added to the nationalist fervor, with mass Azeri demonstrations against Armenian aggression against Azeri sovereignty.

In December 1988 most of the Soviet government troops were withdrawn from Azerbaijan to aid with the rescue effort following a massive earthquake in neighboring Armenia. The newly formed Azeri Popular Front (APF) called for new demonstrations and the establishment of an independent Azeri republic.

The Azeri Popular Front, openly nationalist, threatened war if Nagorno-Karabakh was turned over to Armenia, and in August 1989 called a general strike that effectively blockaded Armenia, which received 87% of its goods and fuel through Azerbaijan. By the end of September the Azeri Popular Front virtually controlled the republic, having moved more quickly from obscurity to power than any similar organization in the Soviet Union. Under nationalist pressure the republic's Supreme Soviet passed new laws on citizenship, the right of the republic to secede from the Soviet Union, and laws that gave the republic control of its abundant natural resources.

In November 1989 a more radical faction, National Salvation, won control of the APF. The faction, openly separatist, demanded the unification of the Azeri nation. Protest rallies in the Nakhichevan region on the Iranian border, organized by the APF, demanded an open frontier with Iranian Azerbaijan. In mid-December leaders of the movement issued an ultimatum to dismantle the border crossings by 31 December 1989. The government's response—the easing of tourist restrictions—was found unacceptable, and demonstrations broke out, quickly spreading to the Azeri heartland on the Caspian Sea.

In early January 1990 violent confrontations were erupting across the republic, fueled by the fighting in Nagorno-Karabakh. Nationalist mobs resumed their attacks on the republic's Armenian minority, and mass demonstrations led to clashes in Baku and other large cities. Azeri demonstrators on the Iranian border tore down the border posts and the frontier fence that divided the two halves of the Azeri homeland, while leaders called for independence for a reunited "Greater Azerbaijan." In spite of Soviet government threats, mass demonstrations continued to sweep the Azeri cities amid calls for a referendum on secession from the Soviet Union. In mid-January 1990 nationalists erected barricades around Baku and demanded immediate independence. The nationalist control of the Azeri capital and the threat of secession provoked a strong government response.

Seventy years of communism had turned Soviet Azerbaijan into a secular society, with Muslim fundamentalism holding little attraction. The Iranian government, no longer trying to export its Islamic revolution to the republic, and increasingly aware of the effect of the independence movement in Soviet Azerbaijan on its own Azeri population, cracked down on antigovernment activities in Tabriz. Envoys to Moscow demanded a curb on the Azeri drive for independence in Baku. Pressured by the Iranian government, which had contended with rising Azeri nationalism in Iran since the 1979 revolution that installed an Islamic state, the Soviet authorities finally sent troops to Baku.

On 19 January 1990 Soviet troops smashed through the barricades and occupied the city. Officially, 83 people died in the occupation, but nationalists claimed that the number of martyrs exceeded 500. The use of violence ended the de facto power of the APF but united most of the diverse Azeri factions—the nationalists, the republican government, and even the Azeri Communist Party. Anti-Armenian sentiment quickly became anti-Russian and anti-Soviet as even the most virulently anti-Armenian groups began to see the Soviet government, not Armenia, as the real enemy of the Azeri nation. The Soviet authorities installed a new government, led by Ayaz Mutalibov, but in order to cling to power he quickly began to outdo the nationalists in supporting Azeri nationalist causes.

The Azeri Popular Front, with its military wing, the National Defense Council, negotiated a cease-fire along the Armenian border and demanded negotiations with the Soviet government on the peaceful secession of Azerbaijan from the Soviet Union. The Communist Party, all but discredited in the republic, lost much of its membership to the nationalists, who represented the only force able to speak for the majority of the Azeri nation. Despite continued occupation by the Red Army, over a million Azeris turned out to publicly mourn, on 2 May 1990, the martyrs killed when the Soviet troops attacked Baku. In a further act of defiance thousands took to the streets to commemorate the seventy-seventh anniversary of Azeri independence on 28 May 1918.

A coup attempt, on 19 August 1990, supported by the Communists, aimed to return the republic to firm Communist control. Tanks in the streets restored calm but further alienated the growing nationalist forces. The Communist-controlled government increasingly supported a more nationalist platform in order to remain in power, including erecting a full state border on the frontier with Armenia, replete with customs posts, passport controls, and the other trappings of an international frontier. On 23 September the government declared Azerbaijan a sovereign state within the Soviet Union. The republic's first multiparty elections were held on 30 September 1990. Led by Ayaz Mutalibov, who ran uncontested, the Communists and their allies won over the nationalists, whose leaders were in prison or had fled. In February 1991 the government voted to drop ''Soviet Socialist'' from the republic's name.

The failed Soviet coup of August 1991 against the continuing reforms of Mikhail Gorbachev shook the republican government. The Communist Party chief and president, Ayaz Mutalibov, supported the coup against Gorbachev. The subsequent breakup of the Soviet state pushed the Communist Azeri government to embrace popular nationalism in order to retain power. On 30 August 1991 the government declared Azerbaijan independent of the collapsing Soviet empire. In October the government nationalized all military equipment and recalled 140,000 Azeri conscripts serving with the Soviet forces.

The continuing territorial conflict with Armenia over the autonomous republic of Nagorno-Karabakh presented the new state with its most pressing problem, bringing Azerbaijan and newly independent Armenia close to war. When negotiations, held soon after Azerbaijan and Armenia gained independence, failed, the Soviet troops in Nagorno-Karabakh withdrew and violence again escalated. Nagorno-Karabakh's autonomy was abolished by the Azerbaijani Supreme Soviet on 26 November 1991. In response the local legislature of Nagorno-Karabakh voted for independence from Azerbaijan, and on 31 December 1991 declared the independence of the Republic of Artsakh.

Heidar Aliyev, named head of the Azerbaijani Communist Party in 1969, became a full member of the Soviet Politburo in 1982 and replaced Mutalibov as head of Azerbaijan's independent government in 1991. Antigovernment feeling continued to mount as Armenian victories pushed Azeri troops back from the western border.

The Azeri government, in January 1992, opted for Latin, used in Turkey, to replace the Russian Cyrillic alphabet. The two regional powers, Turkey and Iran, both vying for influence in the oil-rich republic, have extended economic and political support. But after decades of ''revolution'' Azerbaijan has little interest in Iran's Islamic Revolution, which threatens the large Azeri population of Iran, with whom Azerbaijan wishes to eventually unite.

Nationalist groups, led by the Azeri Popular Front, openly opposed Aliyev's neo-Communist government and continued to press for a stronger response to the Armenian threat and for the reunification of ''Greater Azerbaijan.'' In May 1992 a brief uprising in Baku overthrew the ex-Communists turned nationalists. Following new elections in June, an APF government, led by Abulfaz Elchibey, took power in Baku.

The new nationalist government, unable to stem the military defeats inflicted by the advancing Armenians, saw the Armenians occupy up to 10% of the republic's territory and displace up to a million Azeris by April 1993. The APF government, under extreme pressure, lasted only until June 1993, when Abulfaz Elchibey was overthrown by local rebels, reportedly supported by Russia. The former Communist leader, Heidar Aliyev, returned from exile as head of the Nakhichevan region to lead the new government.

In November 1995, the Aliyev government was reelected by voters longing for stability. Under new government policies oil wealth again began to flow, but for ordinary Azeris the benefits have barely started to arrive. The Aliyev government has brought inflation under control and has begun a tentative privatization, but democratic institutions have suffered.

The Azeri government has become less eager to appease Russia and refuses Russian demands for military bases or for a say in the terms of the exploitation of the rich Caspian Sea oil fields. Closer ties to the United States, the European Union, and even Israel are being actively pursued.

The most pressing of Azerbaijan's problems remains the status of the break-away enclave of Nagorno-Karabakh. The Karabakh Armenians, with the aid and support of the Republic of Armenia, continue to hold about 20% of the country's territory while up to a million Azeri refugees languish in camps in the east of the country. Both sides have generally observed a Russian-mediated cease-fire in place since May 1994. Nevertheless, Baku and Stepanakert, called Khankendi by the Azeris, remain far apart on most substantive issues, from the placement and composition of a peacekeeping force to the enclave's ultimate political status. The prospects for a negotiated settlement remain dim.

Heidar Aliyev's Soviet-style personality cult is reinforced by a heavy-handed intimidation and the self-censorship of the tame national press. On 28 May 1997, on the anniversary of the proclamation of the Azeri republic in 1918, President Aliyev announced the end of all student deferments to military service and stated that the defense of the country and the restoration of its territorial integrity are more important than education. On 2 July 1997 the president announced a new official state holiday to be celebrated on 15 June. Called National Salvation Day, the holiday is to commemorate his taking power in Azerbaijan in 1993.

Azerbaijan's gross domestic product has contracted about 60% since 1991, and the downward trend only began to reverse in 1997 due to expanding oil production. Foreign oil companies are vying for part of Azerbaijan's massive oil reserves. Western governments, mostly ignoring the abuses and dictatorial aspects of the Aliyev government, continue to court the Azeri government.

Israeli Prime Minister Benjamin Netanyahu, shopping for oil on his way home from the Far East, held talks with Azerbaijan's President Heidar Aliyev during a brief stopover in Baku in August 1997. The visit, strongly denounced by neighboring Iran, characterizes the differences between the world's only two primarily Shi'a Muslim countries. Azerbaijan, unlike Iran, has embarked on a secular, pro-Western model of development, reinforced by seven decades of officially atheist Soviet rule.

In November 1997, in a ceremony attended by both American and Russian officials, the Azeris officially started oil production in the Caspian Sea. The offshore oil reserves, thought to rival those of the Middle East, have become a divisive issue for Iran and the new states that border the Caspian Sea, particularly the conflicting claims to the Caspian oil fields by Azerbaijan and Turkmenistan.*

SELECTED BIBLIOGRAPHY:

Altstadt, Audrey L. *The Azerbaijani Turks: Power and Identity under Russian Rule.* 1992.

Atatbaki, Touraj. *Azerbaijan: Ethnicity and Autonomy in Iran after the Second World War.* 1995.

Roberts, Elizabeth. *Georgia, Armenia, and Azerbaijan (Former Soviet States).* 1992.

Swietochowski, Thadeusz. *Russia and Azerbaijan.* 1995.

————. *Russian Azerbaidzhan 1905–1920: The Shaping of National Identity in a Muslim Community.* 1985.

BELARUS

Respublika Byelarus'; Byelorussia; Belorussia; Bietarrussiya

CAPITAL: Miensk (Minsk)

Northeastern Europe

Belarus

POPULATION: (98e) 10,421,000 : 8,170,000 Belarussians in Belarus and another 3,450,000 in adjacent areas of Russia,* Ukraine,* Poland, Lithuania,* and Latvia.* MAJOR ETHNIC GROUPS: Belarussian (Belarusy) 78.4%, Russian 10.6%, Polish 4.4%, Ukrainian 3.1%, Rom (Gypsy) 1.1%, Jew 1%, Tatar, Lithuanian. MAJOR LANGUAGES: Belarussian, Russian, Polish. MAJOR RELIGIONS: (98e) Russian Orthodox 60%, Roman Catholic 18%, Jewish 2%, Sunni Muslim. MAJOR CITIES: (98e) Miensk (Minsk) 1,711,000 (1,893,000), Homyel (Gomel) 572,000, Mahilyow (Mogilev) 408,000, Vitsyebsk (Vitebsk) 382,000, Hrodna (Grodno) 311,000, Brest 274,000, Babruysk (Bobruysk) 263,000, Baranavichy (Baranovichi) 237,00, Barysaw (Borisov) 162,000, Piensk (Pinsk) 133,000, Vorsha (Orsha) 127,000 (165,000), Mazyr (Mozyr) 118,000 (180,000), Soligorsk 108,000, Maladzyechna (Molodechno) 105,000, Lida 94,000, Polatsk (Polotsk) 88,000 (213,000), Svyetlahorsk (Svetlogorsk) 85,000.

GEOGRAPHY: AREA: 80,134 sq.mi.—207,601 sq.km. LOCATION: Belarus occupies the western extremities of the East European Plain in eastern Europe, bordering Russia on the east and northeast, Latvia and Lithuania on the northwest, Poland on the west, and Ukraine on the south. Small, militant nationalist groups also claim parts of Smolensk, Pskov, and Bryansk oblasts of Russia, the Chernikov region of Ukraine, the Dvinsk (Daugavpils) region of Latvia, and the Bialystok region of Poland. PHYSICAL GEOGRAPHY: Most of the territory of Belarus is hilly lowland drained by several large rivers. Forests cover about 30% of the country, and lumbering is important to the economy. The flat plains of Belarus are crossed by several large rivers such as the Dnieper, the Neman, and the Zapadnaia (Western) Dvina. Belarus has Europe's largest tract of swamp, the Pripat Marshes, in the south. The southern provinces are still affected by the Chernobyl nuclear disaster of 1986, which spread nuclear radiation over a wide area of southern Belarus. ADMINISTRATIVE DIVISIONS: Six voblastsi (singular—voblasts') and one independent municipality, Minsk (harady, singular—horad). POLITICAL STATUS: Belarus was recognized as an independent state in 1991.

INDEPENDENCE DECLARATIONS: 25 March 1918 (from Russia); 25 August 1991 (from the Soviet Union).

FLAG: The Belarussian state flag is a horizontal bicolor of red over green, the green half the width of the red, bearing a white vertical stripe at the hoist charged with the traditional Belarussian design in red. OTHER FLAG: The Belarussian national flag—the flag adopted by the independent state in 1918, the first official flag of the republic in 1991, and still the flag of the Belarussian nationalists—has three equal horizontal stripes of white, red, and white.

PEOPLE: The flat plains of Belarus have been overrun and conquered numerous times in the history of the region. Each group of conquerors left behind a portion of their people. To this mixture of national groups the Soviets added others, forcibly or voluntarily, so that today 123 distinct nationalities call Belarus their homeland. The majority of the population is ethnic Slav, mostly belonging to the East Slav group that includes Belarussians, Russians, and Ukrainians, but this group remains divided along linguistic, regional, and religious lines.

Belarussian (Belarusian)—an estimated 78.4% of the population, numbering about 8,170,000.

The Belarussians, calling themselves Belarusy, are a Slavic people, the smallest of the three main divisions of the Eastern Slavs. The Belarussians emerged as a separate nation in the thirteenth century and were called *byelo* (white) for the color of their traditional costumes. Considered the purest of the Slav nations, the blond Belarussians more closely resemble the Baltic and Scandinavian peoples than their Russian neighbors.

The Belarussians speak an East Slavic language of the Slavic group of Indo-European languages that utilizes many borrowings from Russian and Polish. The language, standardized only after the Russian Revolution, was developed from several dialects spoken in the region. The use of the language has been increasing since the Revolution; only 71.9% considered it their mother language in 1926, but by 1959 84.2% considered it their first language, and in 1992 an estimated 89% considered Belarussian their mother tongue. The Belarussian language is spoken in three major dialects, Northeast Belarussian, Southwest Belarussian, and Central Belarussian. The language is written in the Cyrillic alphabet. Linguistically, Belarussian lies between Russian and Ukrainian and has transitional dialects to both.

The majority of the Belarussians are Orthodox Christians, with a large Roman Catholic minority in the western provinces bordering Poland and western

Ukraine. Official figures often represent nominal membership in a religious group rather than the actual figure of practicing adherents. Seven decades of official atheism have greatly reduced religious belief in Belarus.

Russian—an estimated 10.8% of the population, numbering about 1,135,000.

The Russian population of Belarus lives mostly in the eastern provinces along the border with the Russian Federation and in the center, around the capital, Minsk. The largest of the East Slav peoples, the Russians have dominated Belarus for centuries, and many ethnic Russians settled in the region during the imperial and Soviet eras. The Russian language is very close to spoken Belarussian.

Pole—an estimated 4.1% of the population, numbering about 427,000.

The Poles, concentrated in the western provinces that formed part of Poland between the wars, are the remnant of a larger Polish population that formerly inhabited the western region of Belarus. Many ethnic Poles left for Poland after World War II; others have migrated since 1991, looking for economic and political stability.

The language of the Poles, a West Slav language, is spoken as a second language throughout a large part of western Belarus, particularly by the older generation. The inhabitants of the western provinces, Poles and Belarussians, are mostly Roman Catholic.

Ukrainian—an estimated 2.9% of the population, numbering about 302,000.

The Ukrainian population is concentrated in the southern provinces adjoining Ukraine. The second largest of the East Slav peoples, the Ukrainians have lived in the region for centuries, although a large number settled in the area after World War II in government-sponsored migrations.

The Ukrainians of Belarus are mostly Russian-speaking, although in recent years a new interest in the Ukrainian and Belarussian languages has become evident. The Ukrainians, like the Belarussians, are divided religiously between the Orthodox and Catholic churches.

Rom (Gypsy)—an estimated 1.1% of the population, numbering about 115,000.

The Rom or Gypsy population is scattered through the republic and is divided into several linguistic and cultural groups. Although the Rom have had a strong influence on the Slav culture of Belarus, they have traditionally been relegated to the margins of society. Rom groups in the country claim an ethnic Rom population of between 300,000 and 500,000. The majority of the Rom are Orthodox, with Roman Catholic and Muslim minorities.

Jew—an estimated 1% of the population, numbering about 112,000.

The Jewish population of Belarus is the remnant of a much larger number, most of whom were massacred by the Fascist forces, including some Belarussians, during World War II. The majority of the Jews living in the republic speak Russian as their first language, while Yiddish is still spoken among the older people.

Discrimination and persecution, while not as severe as in other parts of the former Soviet Union, continue to threaten the Jews of Belarus. In recent years Jewish emigration from Belarus has grown rapidly, mostly to Israel and the United States.

Tatar—estimated less than 1% of the population, numbering about 72,000.

The Tatars, the descendants of the Golden Horde, settled in the region in the fourteenth and fifteenth centuries. Some were brought to Belarus as prisoners of war; others settled in the area voluntarily to escape persecution in other regions.

The Tatar language, a West Turkic language, is spoken by about 12,000 of the Tatars. Most of the remainder speak Russian as their first language, while in recent years many have learned Belarussian. They form the largest Muslim group in the country.

Lithuanian—estimated less than 1% of the population, numbering about 11,000.

The Lithuanians, living mostly in the northwestern region adjacent to Lithuania, are a Baltic people not related to the Slavs ethnically or religiously. Lithuanians have lived in the region since the Middle Ages, when Belarus formed part of the Lithuanian state. After World War I, and again after World War II, many ethnic Lithuanians left for Lithuania. The Lithuanians are mostly Roman Catholics.

Latvian—estimated at less than 1% of the population, numbering about 5,000.

The Latvians, a Baltic people related to the Lithuanians, live in the northwestern provinces. The majority of the Latvians speak Russian as their first language, although Latvian is spoken in the home. Most of the Latvians in Belarus are Roman Catholic Latgalians from the southeastern region of Latvia.

THE NATION: Originally inhabited by Finnic peoples, the region was populated by Slavs during the great Slav migrations of the fifth and eighth centuries. The migrating Slav tribes displaced the region's original Finnic peoples and divided the area into tribal territories. The largest of the tribes, the Kryvichy, occupied the northern districts. In the center the Dreulane became the predominant tribe, in the south the Drehavichy, and in the east the Radzimichy. The northwestern part of the territory was occupied by a Baltic tribe, the Yatviags. These tribes, the historical ancestors of the Belarussian people, had become distinct political entities by the sixth century A.D. All these tribes had much in common in their languages, customs, and beliefs.

The Kryvichy in the north founded the principalities of Polotsk and Smolensk and the Pskov republic. The Dreulane united into the principality of Turau. The principalities of Polotsk and Turau became the first states on the territory of modern Belarus. They are first mentioned in the chronicles of the ninth century, and are also the oldest centers of Belarussian culture. Some Scandinavian songs mention Polatsk as already being a strong and powerful town in the sixth century.

The area formed the northern part of the first great Slav state, Kievan Rus, in the ninth century. After the people of Kiev were baptized in 988, the Belarussian principalities adopted Christianity together with the other Slavic states. However, some historians believe that Christianity came to Belarus much earlier from Scandinavia. Allied to Kiev, or at times fighting it for control of the region, the Polotsk principality reached its greatest territorial extent, wealth, and power in the eleventh century.

Called the White Rus (Belarusy) for the white clothing worn by both men and women, the Slavs of the northwest began to separate culturally and linguistically from the other East Slavs in the tenth century, about the same time that Christianity spread north from the Slav capital, Kiev. The newly Christian Belarusy remained split into several petty principalities, tributary states to Kievan Rus or dependencies of the powerful Novogorod republic, to the northwest, after it broke away from Kievan rule in 1136.

The separation from the main body of the East Slavs was completed when all the East Slavs except the White Rus came under the rule of the Mongol Golden Horde in the thirteenth century. Coming from the northwest, the Catholic Lithuanians, under their prince, Ryngold, began to take control of the petty Belarussian principalities. His successors extended their growing federation to control Potolsk, Vitebsk, Smolensk, and Turau in the fourteenth century, often by marrying their children into the Belarussian princely families.

The federation of principalities called Great Lithuania defeated the invading Tatars in 1249. Prince Gediminas, who took the Lithuanian throne in 1316, limited the power of the members of the federation, making the principality of Great Lithuania a true monarchy. Gediminas, taking advantage of the Tatar invasion of the Slav lands, extended Lithuanian control to the principalities of Kiev, Chernigov, and Volyn. Protected by the vast swamps in the south of the country, the Belarussian territories remained free of Tatar incursions.

The region, called Byelorussia or Belorussia (White Russia), prospered as part of the medieval Lithuanian empire while the other East Slavs languished under Mongol rule. The Belarussians' Slav language became the dominant language of the multiethnic Lithuanian empire. The mid-fifteenth century saw a great flowering of Belarussian arts and culture, the apex of a golden age that flourished to the end of the sixteenth century. Large Jewish populations, fleeing persecution in the west, settled in the region in the sixteenth century, forming an urban middle class of bankers, merchants, and traders.

Rivalries between the empire's Catholic and Orthodox aristocracies and near constant wars with the expanding power of Moscow weakened the empire in the early sixteenth century. The Belarussians lost importance in the empire after the merger of Lithuania and Catholic Poland in 1569. Many people in the upper classes adopted the predominant Polish language and culture of the expanded empire, relegating Belarussian to the position of the language of serfs and peasants. In 1697, following a series of revolts, the Poles forbade the use of the Belarussian language in the courts and local administrations, and in 1699 they forbade the election of Orthodox citizens to local governments.

Lacking natural barriers, the flat plains of Belarus were repeatedly overrun during the wars fought in the region between the sixteenth and eighteenth centuries. The region ultimately came under Russian rule during the Polish partitions of 1772, 1793, and 1795. The official policy of assimilation to Russian culture eventually achieved the conversion of the majority, particularly in the eastern provinces, from Catholicism to Orthodox Christianity, but was less successful culturally. To further its aim of assimilation, the Russian government banned the Belarussian Uniate Church, which had become a bastion of Belarussian culture and traditions, in 1839.

The formerly prosperous region declined under Russian rule. Widespread poverty, especially among the Jews, fueled the massive immigration in the early nineteenth century, mostly to North America. The Russian government finally banned the Belarussian language and forbade the use of the name Belarusy or White Russian in the 1840s. Called the Northwestern Region by the tsarist government, the area eventually was divided into several Russian provinces.

Serfdom, widespread in Byelorussia (Belarus), was officially abolished in the empire in 1861, the former serfs being promised lands of their own. In 1863 the former serfs of Byelorussia, still without the promised lands, led a rebellion that quickly attracted support among the upper classes and the free peasant farmers. The revolt, suppressed by tsarist troops, virtually ended all economic activity in the Belarussian provinces. Dependent on subsistence farming, the region became a cheap labor pool for the tsarist authorities. The grinding poverty and the harsh conditions sent a new wave of immigrants, including many Jews, to the New World between the 1880s and the turn of the century.

Russian suppression of the Belarussian culture and language nearly achieved the desired assimilation. By the late nineteenth century most of the Belarussians had no clear identity, considering themselves ethnic Russians or Poles, the distinction determined by religion, the Orthodox being closer to the Russians, and the Catholic minority thinking of themselves as Poles.

In 1888 an estimated 82% of the population was illiterate, retarding the ethnic revival that swept most of Europe in the latter half of the nineteenth century. Only in the 1890s did a national revival take hold, much later than the cultural revival of neighboring nations. The revival, more modest than in most of Europe, was retarded by the backward condition of the majority of the population in one of Europe's least developed areas.

The spread of revolutionary ideas after the turn of the century added to the growth of the Belarussian national movement. Nationalists formed the Byelorussian Revolutionary Hramada in 1902. A year later the organization was renamed the Byelorussian Socialist Hramada. The nationalists participated in the abortive 1905 revolution in Russia, most supporting calls for reforms and limited autonomy for Byelorussia. The revolution was brought to an end following concessions by the tsarist government, including some freedoms of language and publishing previously forbidden the Belarussians.

The nascent Belarussian national movement, active particularly among the Catholic minority, was overtaken by the outbreak of World War I in 1914. Over the next three years thousands of Belarussians perished, mostly from hunger and disease. Poorly equipped Belarussian military units suffered massive losses. The massacre of nearly an entire generation of young men added to the growing discontent with the war and with the tsarist autocracy. The Germans overran western Belarus, while the Russians retained control of Minsk and the eastern provinces.

The Belarussians of the eastern provinces enthusiastically joined the revolution that overthrew the hated Russian autocracy in February 1917. A new government formed by the nationalists gained importance with the onset of the revolution, quickly organizing to fill the vacuum left by the collapsing Russian civil administration. In March 1917 the Hramada-dominated Byelorussian National Committee demanded autonomy within a newly proclaimed democratic Russia. A Belarussian parliament, the Rada, was convened in July-August to debate the region's future relations with the Russian government. The debate was made more urgent by the German and Polish occupation of the western Belarussian provinces and the occupation, in the east, of some territory by soldiers of the Russian Provisional Government. The military occupation of territories in the west and east added to the growing confusion and chaos in the region.

The Bolshevik coup, the overthrow of Russia's fledgling democracy in October 1917, set off a power struggle between the Belarussian nationalists, led by the Hramada, and the local Bolshevik forces. On 14 November the numerous Bolsheviks took control of Minsk and other major cities in the eastern provinces. The nationalists, driven from the capital, convened the All-Byelorussian National Congress in December. The delegates to the congress, on 17 December 1917, declared Byelorussia an autonomous state and later voted by a majority for immediate independence. Before they could consolidate their power, German troops invaded the infant state in February 1918, quickly driving the Bolsheviks from Minsk and the other important centers.

The new Bolshevik government of Russia, desperate for peace in the west while threatened by the White forces in the growing Russian Civil War, signed a treaty with Germany that left most of the former western provinces of the Russian Empire to German and Austrian control. The Treaty of Brest-Litovsk, signed in western Byelorussia by the Central Powers and the new Soviet government in March, left much of Byelorussia under German authority.

The nationalist leaders of the Hramada emerged from hiding and, with German protection and support, reconvened the Rada. The delegates again voted overwhelmingly for independence from Russia. The Rada declared Byelorussia independent on 25 March 1918 as the Byelorussian National Republic. The new republic quickly severed all remaining ties to Russia and was recognized by many national governments.

The new republic laid claim to the regions historically inhabited by the Belarussian peoples, including the disputed regions claimed by Soviet Russia in the east, the western Russian oblasts of Smolensk, Bryansk, and Kalinin, and the southern districts of Pskov Oblast, the Dvinsk (Daugavpils) region claimed by Latvia, and the Bialystok region, also claimed by Poland. In the west the Poles occupied the Bialystok region and on 28 November 1918 held a plebiscite for incorporating the region into the Polish state despite the protests of the Belarussian national government to the Allies at the Paris Peace Conference. With no effective fighting force to oppose the Poles, as the Germans had prohibited armed groups in the region, the Belarussians could not militarily oppose the Polish annexation of the western districts.

The German withdrawal in December 1918, following the armistice that ended World War I in November, left the new Belarussian republic virtually defenseless as the Russian Civil War spread to the west. In January 1919 the Red Army occupied the eastern districts, creating a Byelorussian Soviet Republic at Smolensk as a rival to the nationalist government at Minsk.

Newly independent Poland, in April 1919, declared war on Soviet Russia. Polish troops stopped the advancing Bolsheviks and occupied the western Belarussian provinces. The Poles refused to recognize Belarussian independence. The Poles offered the Belarussians major autonomy in a "Greater Poland" and gained the support of many nationalists by driving the Soviets from the eastern provinces. The Soviets, embroiled in a massive civil war, were unable to hold the region against the Poles and their Belarussian allies, but with their victory over the Whites in 1920 troops were freed for the Polish front.

In July 1920 the Bolsheviks went on the offensive. The Belarussian nationalists, caught between the Poles in the west and the Soviets in the east, lost all remaining political power in the region. The Soviet promises of independence within a federation of Soviet states, which had some support in the region, were set aside following the brutal suppression of a Belarussian nationalist uprising against Communist rule in Slutsk province in 1920.

The Treaty of Riga, signed on 18 March 1921 by Poland and the Soviet Union, partitioned Byelorussia between the Polish and Soviet states. The Polish government annexed the mostly Roman Catholic western districts, which had a population of 4 million. In 1922 the eastern provinces under Bolshevik control were organized as a separate Soviet republic that joined the new Soviet Union as a constituent state. The consolidation of Soviet power in the eastern provinces ended all manifestations of Belarussian nationalism. Between 3% and 5% of the population died of starvation following the forced collectivization of agriculture.

The purges of the Stalinist era, especially severe in Byelorussia in 1929–30 and 1933–34, destroyed all remaining national and cultural leadership. The Soviet government, in 1933, charged that nationalists had formed a Byelorussian National Center, its aim the secession of the republic from the Soviet Union—a right guaranteed in the Soviet constitution but never allowed. The entire Belarussian republican government, including the president of the Soviet Central Committee, was purged for advocating a united Belarussian republic, to include both the Soviet and Polish zones, in 1937. The victims of the Stalinist purges, numbering in the thousands, were buried in mass graves; later, the Soviet government claimed that the remains were those of victims of Nazi atrocities.

The Belarussians under Polish rule, although free of the fear and panic of the Stalinist purges, were also deprived of their rights and language. Belarussian schools were closed, and the Belarussian language was forbidden in Catholic churches. In 1927 the Polish government cracked down on all specifically Belarussian organizations and arrested a number of national leaders. A program of assimilating the Belarussian population into Polish culture became the official government policy.

The Ribbentrop-Molotov Pact between Nazi Germany and the Soviet Union divided the small countries that lay between the two powers into spheres of influence on 23 August 1939. In September 1939 the Soviet Union and Nazi Germany signed the pact that effectively divided the smaller nations between the two powers. The pact allowed the Soviets to occupy eastern Poland and to unite all of the Belarussians in an expanded Byelorussian Soviet Socialist Republic. With ruthless efficiency, anti-Soviet Belarussians were eliminated in the newly annexed western provinces. Thousands, including many Roman Catholic priests and nuns, were deported or quickly executed.

Many Belarussians, their nation decimated by planned famine, forced collectivization, and periodic purges, welcomed the German invasion of the Soviet Union in June 1941. The Germans and their allies were hailed as liberators from Soviet rule. Despite the harsh Nazi occupation, Belarussian nationalists were encouraged to collaborate in an anti-Communist crusade. Those nationalists working with the occupation administration convened the Byelorussian Central Council and the Second All-Byelorussian National Congress at Minsk in 1944. A Byelorussian National Guard, created as a national army, helped to massacre the republic's large Jewish population. Many of the traditionally anti-Semitic Belarussians served as guards at the notorious Minsk concentration camp.

A Belarussian national uprising began with the Nazi defeat in 1944. Poorly armed partisan units fought the victorious return of the Red Army to Belarus. Guerrilla units continued to operate in the republic, especially in the Pripat swamps, well into the 1950s.

A battleground during the war, Belarus suffered the worst devastation in all of Europe. An estimated quarter of the prewar population died in the war, the postwar uprising, and the deportations of the "ideologically contaminated" survivors that accompanied the reimposition of Soviet rule.

The Soviet leader, Joseph Stalin, intent on the assimilation of the Belarussians, instituted a policy of intense Russification, the Belarussian language once again banned and the culture suppressed. In an effort to placate the surviving Belarussian nationalist sentiment, the Soviet constitution was amended to allow Byelorussia and Ukraine to maintain separate armed forces and diplomatic representation. But these provisions were only implemented one time, to secure United Nations seats for the two Soviet republics in 1945.

A national revival, a reaction to Stalin's excesses, began at his death in 1953 and gradually gained momentum, particularly in the Roman Catholic west, until it was stifled by renewed suppression in the 1970s and early 1980s. The introduction of reforms in Soviet life, *glasnost* and *perestroika*, in 1987 by Soviet leader Mikhail Gorbachev, allowed the expression of ideas and sentiments unthinkable under former Soviet leaders. Unofficial political groups began to form, but the changes that occurred in rapid succession in the neighboring Baltic republics were resisted by the old-line Communists who continued to control the republican government.

The national movement gained support due to the poor government response to the 1986 Chernobyl nuclear disaster, which affected thousands of Belarussians living near the path of the radioactive contamination. The nuclear disaster, the worst in modern history, released radiation into the air, contaminating areas in Ukraine and Byelorussia, which received 70% of the radiation.

Soviet newspapers, as part of a massive official cover-up, claimed that only 238 people had been affected by the nuclear accident and published radiation levels that were 1% or less of the true levels. While local officials advised pregnant women in the contaminated areas to have abortions, the government continued to deny that the Chernobyl accident had any links with the sudden outbreak of thyroid problems, cancers, and freak animal births. In late 1989 the Soviet government finally published a map of the contaminated area, but only in early 1990 did it publish the results of the investigations of the incident: 20% of Byelorussia's farmland was contaminated, and over 2 million Belarussians had received dangerous doses of radioactive pollution. A subsequent report confirmed an 18% rise in birth defects in the republic.

In May 1988 news of the discovery of mass graves at Kurpaty, on the outskirts of Minsk, further galvanized the growing anti-Communist feeling in the republic. The graves held the remains of between 100,000 and 300,000 Belarussians systematically murdered by the NKVD, the predecessor of the KGB, between 1937 and 1941. The discovery that the Soviets had committed these murders, formerly attributed to the Nazis, added fuel to the antigovernment movement taking hold in the most obedient of Soviet republics.

The Belarussian Popular Front, called Adradzhen'ne (Rebirth or Renewal), modeled on the Baltic movements, was formed in 1989 despite official opposition and harassment by the secret police, the KGB. Official opposition to perestroika in the republic forced the Popular Front to hold its first congress in Vilnius, the capital of neighboring Lithuania. Partly in resentment for the failure of Belarussian officials to endorse the changes that were rapidly reshaping the Baltics, the Popular Front adopted an openly nationalist platform, demanding a separate budget for the republic, control of the local economy, cultural and economic autonomy, the right to fly the long-banned national flag, and an open accounting of Stalinist era crimes against the Belarussian people.

The Soviet Union's first "multicandidate elections" since 1917 were held on 26 March 1989. Many Communist officials in Byelorussia, through devious means, ran unopposed. Where there was a choice, local candidates viewed as pro-change easily won, while even some officials running unopposed failed to receive the 50% of the vote needed to retain their positions, including the Communist Party chief of the republic. The elections galvanized the nationalist opposition, and by February 1990 Adradzhen'ne had over 100,000 members, a tenth of the republic's population. On 17 July 1990 the Belarus government, pressed by the growing national movement, issued a declaration of state sovereignty.

The republic's conservative Communist leaders, under increasing nationalist pressure, declared the Byelorussian Soviet Socialist Republic a sovereign state on 27 July 1990. The declaration proclaimed Byelorussia a nuclear-free zone and designated the entire republic a nuclear disaster area.

The Belarussians voted by an overwhelming 83% to retain the Soviet Union in a referendum organized in early 1991. In the wake of the aborted coup against Gorbachev in August 1991, the Belarussian leaders reluctantly declared the republic's independence from the Soviet Union on 25 August 1991. The republic, a separate member of the United Nations since 1945, was recognized as an independent state by the United States and most of Western Europe in late 1991.

Nationalist organizations that were increasingly winning support at the expense of the republic's neo-Communist leadership were mostly driven underground in the mid-1990s. Intent on creating the first truly independent Belarussian state, the nationalists must first wrest political control from the old Communist hierarchy, which continues to govern the republic under the guise of a national government.

Belarus, once one of the more advanced regions of the Soviet Union, in the first seven years of independence slipped to the levels of the poorest regions of Europe. Among the causes of this decline were poor management, clinging to the old Soviet forms, and looking to Russia before making any decisions. The severe economic decline has accelerated the republic's economic and military integration with Russia. The Belarussian government subordinated its military policy to that of Russia in December 1993, and in January 1994 subordinated its economic policies to those of Russia.

On 23 June 1994 Belarussians voted to follow the rest of the former Soviet republics in establishing an office of president. Six candidates, including the prime minister, ran for office. On 11 July 1994 Alexander Lukashenko, formerly a collective farm director, received 80.1% of the vote and became the first elected president. Lukashenko's favorite themes, anticorruption and closer ties to Russia, appealed to the weary voters of the republic. Buffeted by a continuing economic crisis and mounting crime, the voters turned to the man who promised to restore their former prosperity. Since his election, President Lukashenko has severely undermined democracy in the republic. In parliamentary elections, held in November 1995, many of the candidates voted into office opposed a return to a Soviet-style economy and growing Russian domination. The parliamentary elections set the stage for serious conflicts between the president and parliament.

The historic white-red-white national flag, which was adopted as the official state flag upon the declaration of Belarus' independence in 1991, was replaced as the result of a 1995 referendum whose legitimacy is still questioned. The new state flag, almost identical to the Soviet era flag, is not accepted by the nationalist groups or the democratic opposition.

At the time it declared independence in late 1991, Belarus was one of the most developed of the former Soviet states, inheriting a modern—by Soviet standards—machine building sector and a robust agricultural sector. However, the breakup of the Soviet Union and its traditional trade ties, as well as the government's failure to embrace market reforms, has resulted in a sharp economic decline. Privatization is virtually nonexistent, and the system of state orders and distribution persists. Despite the economic disaster in the country, the Belarus government startled the world by claiming a growth rate of 9% in the first quarter of 1997. The state still owns 85% of industry.

The majority of the Belarussian people, long accustomed to seeing themselves as part of the Russian sphere of influence, support Lukashenko's aims of closer relations with Russia. A new constitution and a revamped parliament aid Lukashenko's dictatorial government. The oppression of democratic forces in the country brought protests from within and from outside the country. Since the spring of 1996 a number of rallies and demonstrations against the president's policies have served to unite the fragmented democratic groups.

The country, strategically placed in the middle of eastern Europe, is the least democratic of the former Communist states. The republic's chief problem is its autocratic, erratic president, Alexander Lukashenko. Although he was democratically elected, he quickly destroyed the country's fragile democracy and established one-man rule. In March 1997 the government moved to severely curb human rights in the country, instituting bans on the political opposition and groups with foreign affiliations. The freedoms of the Belarus people have deteriorated severely under the regime of President Lukashenko. Three opposition newspapers, banned in Belarus, are printed in neighboring Lithuania.

In May 1997 Belarus and Russia signed a union charter drawing the two countries closer to full integration. Nationalists in Belarus, increasingly run as a Stalinist dictatorship, demonstrated against the agreement. In spite of growing opposition, the Belarus government has clung to a Soviet-style economy and has rapidly slipped back into the totalitarian ways of the past.

SELECTED BIBLIOGRAPHY:

Applebaum, Anne. *Ukraine, Moldova, Belarus: Between East and West.* 1995.
Keep, John. *Last of the Empires: A History of the Soviet Union, 1945–1991.* 1995.
Marples, David R. *Belarus: From Soviet Rule to Nuclear Catastrophe.* 1996.
Zaprudnik, Jan. *Belarus at a Crossroads of History.* 1993.
———. *Historical Dictionary of Belarus.* 1998.

BOSNIA AND HERZEGOVINA

Bosna; Republika Bosna i
Hercegovina; Republic of Bosnia
and Herzegovina

CAPITAL: Sarajevo

Southeastern Europe

Bosnia and Herzegovina

POPULATION: All population figures are subject to considerable error due to the dislocations of war and ethnic cleansing. In 1991 Bosnia and Herzegovina had a population of 4,365,000. (98e) 3,116,000 (including about 600,000 refugees within the country, but not the estimated 1.5 million refugees outside the country). Muslim region 1,671,000; Serb region 1,104,000; Croat region 341,000, MAJOR NATIONAL GROUPS: (98e) Bosniak (Bosnian, Bosnian Muslim) 36%, Serb 34%, Croat 21%, Rom (Gypsy) 5%, Montenegrin 1%, Albanian, Jew. MAJOR LANGUAGE: Serbo-Croatian. MAJOR RELIGIONS: (98e) Orthodox 39%, Sunni Muslim 36%, Roman Catholic 17%, Protestant 4%, Uniate, Jewish. MAJOR CITIES: (98e) (Muslim-controlled region) Sarajevo 404,000 (511,000), Tuzla 78,000 (123,000), Zenica 71,000 (100,000), Travnik 40,000 (55,000), Bihac 35,000 (50,000), Goradze 30,000 (65,000); (Serb-controlled region) Banja Luka 185,000 (254,000), Bjeljina 34,000, Prijedor 33,000, Doboj 28,000, Zvornik 27,000. (Croat-controlled region) Mostar 53,000 (90,000). (Disputed) Brcko 33,000.

GEOGRAPHY: AREA: 19,741 sq.mi.—51,142 sq.km. LOCATION: Bosnia and Herzegovina lies in the central Balkan Peninsula, bordering Croatia* on the north and west, and Yugoslavia* to the east and south. The republic has a narrow outlet to the Adriatic Sea, but lacks port facilities. PHYSICAL GEOGRAPHY: Most of the republic is a hilly region of high valleys rising to the high mountains of the Dinaric Alps in the west, which run parallel to the Adriatic coast. About half the republic is forested, with about a fourth cultivated. The Sava River separates the republic from Croatia on the north, and the Drina River forms the border with the Yugoslav Republic of Serbia in the east. The Sava and its tributaries are the main rivers. ADMINISTRATIVE DIVISIONS: One hundred nine districts or opstinas (singular—opstina). POLITICAL STATUS: Bosnia and Herzegovina was recognized as an independent state in 1992–93; however, the Serb portion of the population rejected independence and wishes to unite with neighboring Serbia.

INDEPENDENCE DECLARATION: 3 March 1992 (from Yugoslavia).

FLAG: The Bosnian state flag is a white field bearing a centered blue shield charged with a diagonal white stripe and six gold fleur-de-lis. OTHER FLAG(S): The Bosnian Muslim national flag is a white field with narrow green stripes top and bottom charged with a centered white crescent moon outlined in green. The flag of the Bosnian Croats is a horizontal tricolor of red, white, and blue bearing a centered shield charged with twenty-five red and white squares. The flag of the Bosnian Serbs is a horizontal tricolor of red, blue, and white bearing a centered white eagle or the traditional Serbian Orthodox cross. The proposed flag of the new federation is a horizontal tricolor of red, white, and green bearing a centered shield divided horizontally with a circle of ten yellow stars on blue representing the ten counties of the federation and two shields above, a yellow fleur-de-lis on a blue background representing the Bosniaks, and a red and white check shield representing the Bosnian Croats.

PEOPLE: The most ethnically mixed of the former Yugoslav republics, the major national groups in the region had a very high incidence of intermarriage; 16% of the population were the product of mixed marriages, and the various national groups mixed freely until war began in the republic in April 1992. Hundreds of thousands of refugees, representing every national group in the republic, have been displaced, both internally and externally, with large refugee populations living outside the republic.

Bosniak (Bosnian Muslim)—an estimated 36% of the population, numbering about 1,122,000.

The Bosnian Muslims, now popularly called simply Bosniaks or simply Bosnians, are a South Slav people. Ethnically related to the neighboring Croats and Serbs, the Bosnians are distinguished by their Muslim religion, their unique background, and recent history. Until the post–World War II era, the Muslims of Bosnia-Herzegovina usually identified themselves as Serbs or Croats, depending on their geographic location.

The Bosniaks speak a dialect of Serbo-Croatian that they have begun to call Bosnian or Serbo-Bosnian. The language, which can be written in either the Latin or the Cyrillic alphabet, uses many Turkish forms and words absent from the dialects spoken by the Croats and Serbs of Bosnia. Many in the country have begun to call their dialect the Bosnian language.

Highly secularized and well educated, the Bosniak population has traditionally formed an urban middle class in Sarajevo and the other large urban areas. Since the ethnic cleansing that accompanied the war, the majority of the rural Bosniaks have also sought refuge in Sarajevo, Tuzla, Zenica, and other large towns under Bosnian government control.

In the 1991 census the Muslims accounted for 44% of the population. Since the war began in 1992 hundreds of thousands have been forcibly expelled from areas overrun by the Serbs or Croats. Many sought refuge abroad and now live in 127 countries worldwide.

Serb (Bosnian Serb)—an estimated 34% of the population, numbering about 1,060,000.

The Bosnian Serb population, mostly concentrated in the north and east of the country, is part of the greater Serb nation that predominated in neighboring Yugoslavia. Most Bosnian Serbs lived in rural areas until the outbreak of war in 1992. Since the war the cities and towns that formerly had large Muslim and Croat populations are now almost entirely Serbian in population.

According to the 1991 census the Serbs accounted for 31% of Bosnia's population. The mainly rural Serbs have since extended their hold to around 70% of the country. Many refugees from other areas of former Yugoslavia, particularly Croatia, have settled in the region.

The Serbs are overwhelmingly Serbian Orthodox. Their religion is yet another tie to the Serbian heartland in Yugoslavia. The Serbs speak a dialect of Serbo-Croatian that is written in the Cyrillic alphabet and is now called Serbian.

Croat (Bosnian Croat)—an estimated 21% of the population, numbering about 655,000.

The Croat population of Bosnia and Herzegovina, which numbered 17% of the population in 1991, is concentrated in the southwest and west of the country bordering the Dalmatian coast of Croatia. The Croat region, centered on the historic Herzegovina region, is the Catholic heartland of Bosnia-Herzegovina. Until the early years of the twentieth century, all the inhabitants of Bosnia called themselves Bosnians. Only since World War I have the Roman Catholic Bosnians been called Croats based on their religion.

The Croats speak the same language as the Bosniaks and Serbs, Serbo-Croatian, although since the wars in the Balkan region, the dialects have been adopted as national languages. The Croat dialect, called Croatian, is written in the Latin alphabet.

Rom (Gypsy)—an estimated 2% of the population, numbering about 65,000.

The Rom population of Bosnia and Herzegovina is made up of several different groups, including Muslims, Roman Catholics, and Orthodox Christians. Many Rom habitually registered as ethnic Muslims, Croats, or Serbs according to their religion.

The Rom dialects most commonly spoken in Bosnia are Machwaya and Machvano. Most Rom are bilingual in Serbo-Croatian. Traditionally, the Rom have suffered persecution and discrimination in the region.

Turk (Rumelian Turk)—estimated at less than 1% of the population, numbering about 50,000.

The Turks of Bosnia are a distinct people, the descendants of Anatolian Turks settled in the region during the Ottoman era. Unlike the Slav Bosniaks, the Turks are a large non-Slav population. Their language, a Turkic dialect, is spoken as a second language, while the Bosnian dialect of Serbo-Croatian is the first language. The majority of the Turks are Sunni Muslims, but tend to be highly secular.

Montenegrin—an estimated 1% of the population, numbering about 32,000.

Closely related to the Serbs, the Montenegrins are concentrated mostly in the southwestern part of the country close to the border with Montenegro, which forms part of the Yugoslav Federation. Historically, the Montenegrins were ethnic Serbs, but are divided from the Serbs by a thousand years of separate history.

The Montenegrins are Orthodox Christians mostly belonging to the independent Montenegrin Orthodox Church. Their language, a dialect of Serbo-Croatian, is, like Serbian, written in the Cyrillic alphabet.

Arab—estimated at less than 1% of the population, numbering about 30,000.

The Arab population of Bosnia-Herzegovina was settled in the region under Ottoman rule. Brought from the Middle East in an attempt to strengthen the Muslim population of the region, the majority later returned to their homelands, with only a remnant remaining in Bosnia, mostly in the capital, Sarajevo. The Arabs speak standard Arabic along with Bosnian and are Sunni Muslims.

Albanian—estimated at less than 1% of the population, numbering about 25,000.

The majority of the Albanians are concentrated in Sarajevo and the other major cities. They left poor, backward Kosovo in Serbia during Tito's long dictatorship to find work in the factories and munition works in Bosnia and Herzegovina. Most of the Albanians are Sunni Muslim, like the Bosniaks, and have also suffered from forced expulsion from Serb- and Croat-held areas.

Jew—estimated at less than 1% of the population, numbering about 17,000.

Most of the Jews of Bosnia are concentrated in Sarajevo, where a Jewish population has existed since medieval times. The latter include Jews, who found a haven in the tolerant city of Sarajevo in 1492 following their expulsion from Spain. Unlike many of the Jewish populations in Western Europe, the Jews of Bosnia were never forced to live in a ghetto.

The Jews of Sarajevo played an important commercial and intellectual role in the life of the city until the outbreak of hostilities. Since the war began in 1992 many Bosnian Jews have left the country for Israel or the United States.

THE NATION: Originally inhabited by Illyrian peoples, Bosnia was part of the Roman Empire during the first centuries of the Christian era. After the fall of Rome, the Balkan territories were contested between Byzantium and Rome's successors in the West.

Slavic tribes, migrating from the north, settled the mountain valleys of the Dinaric Alps in the sixth and seventh centuries. Coming under nominal Byzantine rule, the majority gradually adopted much of the Byzantine culture and converted to Orthodox Christianity. The Slavs formed a number of small counties and duchies too weak to oppose the powerful Byzantines.

Two neighboring kingdoms, Serbia and Croatia, were established in the ninth century. They rose to prominence among the small Slav states in the region. The two kingdoms were often at war over the division of authority and territory in the region.

In the tenth century many of the Christian Slavs of the high mountain valleys of the Dinaric Alps converted to a dualistic creed attributed to Bogomil, a Bulgarian priest. The creed, intensely nationalistic and political as well as religious, opposed Slavic serfdom, church authority, and Byzantine cultural influences. The Slav believers in the creed, known as Bogomils, suffered severe and violent persecution as religious heretics.

Ruled by Croatian kings from 958, a separate Bosnian state formed in the twelfth century as a vassal of the Kingdom of Hungary. In 1180 a local ruler, Kulin, declared himself the *ban* (governor) under nominal Hungarian rule, and established the Bosnian state in the center and north of the present Bosnia and Herzegovina. In the same year Kulin openly declared his adherence to the Bogomil sect.

The population of medieval Bosnia, although professing Christianity, adhered to not one but three different beliefs, Roman Catholicism, Eastern Orthodoxy, and the local schismatic Bogomil sect. All three belief systems were organizationally weak, and religious leaders were largely uneducated. None of the three could count on steady and exclusive state patronage. The weakness of the religious systems contributed to the later conversion of many Bosnians to Islam.

Herzegovina, an independent principality dominated by the Huns from the tenth century, came under Serbian rule in the fourteenth century. The region, influenced by the Venetian territories along the coast, remained a separate duchy until the thirteenth century, when it came under the rule of the *bans* of Bosnia.

The region, after a period of Serbian rule, became a strong Christian lordship with territory extending to the Adriatic Sea under the leadership of Ban Stephen Kotromanic (1322–53). The *ban* Stephen Tvrtko took the title of King of Bosnia and Serbia in 1376. The Bosnian kingdom joined an alliance of Balkan Christian nations in a vain attempt to block the northward advance of the Muslim Ottoman Turks. In 1389, at Kosovo Polje, the Field of Blackbirds, the Slavs were defeated in one of medieval Europe's largest battles. Legends tell of blackbirds feasting on the corpses of thousands of dead for weeks after the battle.

The kingdom, weakened by war and religious strife among the Bogomils, Roman Catholics, and Orthodox Christians, split into several small, weak states in the fifteenth century, including Herzegovina, which became an independent duchy. In 1463 Bosnia fell to the expanding Turkish Ottoman Empire, as did Herzegovina in 1482. The Ottoman authorities, while allowing the Christian churches to continue under Muslim rule, stopped the periodic religious persecutions of the Bogomil sect.

The Bogomils, hated and persecuted by their Christian neighbors, largely converted to the Turks' Islamic religion. As Muslims under Ottoman rule they formed a favored minority, the Bosnian Muslim nobility. Augmented by a Turkish military aristocracy who confiscated the lands of annihilated Christian nobles, the Muslims controlled large estates worked by mostly Christian serfs, the *rayas*, who were treated little better than slaves. Although the serfs were forbidden weapons, insurrections against harsh Muslim rule were frequent.

Sporadic peasant rebellions during the nineteenth century culminated in a widespread Slavic uprising against weakening Turkish rule in 1875, a major factor in the Russo-Turkish War of 1877–78. The Congress of Berlin, convened to revise the treaty forced on the defeated Ottoman Turks by Russia, assigned the Turkish territories south of Croatia and west of newly independent Serbia to the Austro-Hungarian Empire. The Slav rebellion was finally crushed by the Austrian military occupation of Bosnia, Herzegovina, and Sanjak (Sandzak) in 1878. Bosnia and Herzegovina were annexed outright by the Austro-Hungarian Empire in 1908. The Sanjak, the province of Novibazar, was returned to Turkish rule as partial compensation for the annexation of Bosnia and Herzegovina.

The nationalist dream of a great South Slav state united under the leadership of Orthodox Serbia was supported and promoted from Serbia and financed by Russia, the self-appointed guardian of the Eastern Orthodox peoples. The Muslim Slavs saw no place for themselves in this proposed new Orthodox order, and many embraced the Austro-Hungarian authorities as protectors. Some Bosnian Muslims immigrated to Turkey and other parts of the Ottoman Empire, fleeing Austrian military conscription and a politically uncertain future, but the majority stayed, taking advantage of the educational and economic opportunities brought in by the new rulers. Under Austrian rule the Bosnian Muslim and Roman Catholic Croat communities grew more modern and prosperous than their Orthodox rival.

Serbian nationalists in Bosnia, meanwhile, were plotting to overthrow Austro-Hungarian rule not only in Bosnia, but also in the neighboring South Slavic lands of Croatia and Slovenia.* The Austro-Hungarian government's decision to annex the region formally only added to the Serbian sense of urgency. The annexation of Bosnia and Herzegovina aroused Serbian nationalists who dreamed of the resurrection of the medieval Serbian empire.

On 28 June 1914 a Bosnian Serb, Gavrilo Princip, an ardent Serbian nationalist, assassinated Archduke Francis Ferdinand, the heir to the Austro-Hungarian throne, in Sarajevo. Francis Ferdinand was an advocate of a triple monarchy to include a Slav state alongside Austria and Hungary. The proposal to add a third crown to the dual empire had won the enmity of the powerful pan-Serbian nationalists, who viewed a Slav state in the empire as an impediment to the Serb dream of dominating the South Slav nations of the Balkan Peninsula. The Austrian reaction led to war with neighboring Serbia, and the conflict spread rapidly to engulf Europe and eventually most of the world.

Bosnia, the object of competing Croatian and Serbian claims during World

War I, was one of the more difficult points for the delegates of the Croats, Slovenes, Serbs, and Montenegrins to settle at the meeting of South Slav leaders on the island of Corfu in 1917. The leaders, determined to forge a South Slav state out of the Balkan Peninsula, finally declared a union of all South Slav peoples and agreed to the principle of unity once the Central Powers had been defeated.

The South Slav territories of defeated Austria and Hungary, Slovenia, Croatia, and Bosnia and Herzegovina were joined to the independent states of Serbia and Montenegro to form a separate South Slav kingdom in 1918. The Bosnians suffered persecution and discrimination in the years after the end of World War I. On 26 October 1918 Bosnia and Herzegovina were annexed by Serbia, and remained part of Serbia within the new Kingdom of the Serbs, Croats, and Slovenes, called Yugoslavia from 1929. As the original name indicates, no special provision was to be made for people who considered themselves neither Serbs nor Croats, and in the interwar years Bosnia's Muslim Slavs were pressured to register themselves as one or the other. Insofar as the Muslims counted on the political scene, it was as a weak population of despised non-Christians caught between Serb and Croat nationalist ambitions.

The Bosnian Muslims, generally opposed to inclusion in the Serb-dominated kingdom, became increasingly anti-Serb following the abolition of serfdom, which brought economic ruin, and the increasing domination of their traditional territories by the Serbs, the most powerful segment of the Yugoslav state. The violent ethnic and religious conflicts, particularly acute in Bosnia, worsened with the rise of Fascist ideology and an oppressive Serb-dominated dictatorship of the Yugoslav kingdom in the interwar period.

Invaded by the Fascist German and Italian armies in 1941, the Yugoslav state was quickly overrun and divided by the victors. A German-sponsored Croat republic, including Bosnia and Herzegovina, declared its independence of Yugoslavia. Bosnia-Herzegovina, in 1941, had a population 40% Muslim, 37% Serb, and 21% Croat.

The Bosnians, called Muslim Croats by the Fascist Croat government, generally supported the Croats against the hated Serbs. Ideological and religious violence, especially severe in ethnically mixed Bosnia, led to widespread atrocities and massacres perpetrated by all sides. Following the German withdrawal in 1944, several thousand Bosnians were murdered in savage Serbian reprisals.

Josip Broz Tito, a local Communist leader, organized a partisan army in Bosnia in 1942. The Communists were opposed by the Fascist Croats and Muslims and the Serb nationalists and royalists, led by Draja Mikhailovich. A civil war raged in Bosnia in parallel to the wider World War II. Mikhailovich's group, mostly ethnic Serbs, often clashed with Tito's Communist resistance, which increasingly won the support and material aid of the Allied governments.

Postwar Yugoslavia, under a Communist government led by wartime partisan leader Tito, was reconstructed as a federation of socialist states under a new 1946 Communist constitution. The constitution, promulgated on 31 January

1946 and modeled on that of the Soviet Union, replaced the Yugoslav monarchy with a federation of six republics and two autonomous provinces within the Serbian republic. Bosnia-Herzegovina was the only constituent republic of the new federation not created within discernible ethnic borders; it included large Muslim, Serb, and Croat populations, plus minorities of Albanians, Jews, and Montenegrins. In spite of the federation form of the constitution, real authority remained at the center, in Belgrade, and was exercised by the Communist Party.

The republic prospered under the national communism practiced in Tito's Yugoslavia. Many of the Yugoslav state's important industries, including munitions, were situated in the republic. The three largest national groups, the Muslims, Serbs, and Croats, mostly put aside historic grievances and lived peaceably in the multiethnic republic.

The 1948 census listed the population of the republic as Serb, Croat, and undetermined Muslim, while the census of 1953 listed the Bosnian Muslims as undetermined Yugoslavs. Not recognized as a separate nationality until 1969, the Bosniaks were only counted as a separate Yugoslav people, called Muslims, in the 1981 Yugoslav census. The Bosniaks, having identified themselves only by their religion, or as Serbian or Croatian Muslims, up to World War II, in the decades after the war slowly developed a distinct national identity around their traditional Muslim beliefs and their secular, urbanized culture.

Tito, an ethnic Croat, held the disparate nations together in the Yugoslav federation by allowing cultural autonomy and more rights and freedoms than was usual for the postwar Communist dictatorships of the Cold War period. In 1974 a new constitution allowed for greater republican autonomy and recognized the Muslims as a nationality. Ethnic relations in Bosnia remained fairly peaceful, with intermarriage among Muslims, Catholics, and Orthodox very common. Despite the fairly good relations between the national groups, some 600,000 ethnic Serbs left the republic for Serbia between 1945 and 1986.

In May 1980 Tito died, fatally weakening the federal institutions. Tito's position as the leader of the Yugoslav state was turned over to a rotating presidency of the leaders of the republics and autonomous provinces. Without Tito's strong hand the various nationalities began to move in separate directions, straining the fabric of the multiethnic federation. The one strong federal institution that remained, the military, came increasingly under the domination of the Orthodox Serbs.

The collapse of communism across Eastern Europe in 1989 aroused the old nationalisms buried under decades of Communist suppression. Political parties quickly formed in the region, mostly along ethnic lines. The Muslim Party of Democratic Action (SDA) represented the majority Muslim population, the Serbian Democratic Party the large Serb population, and the Croatian Democratic Union the Croats living mostly in Herzegovina and western Bosnia. On 15 October 1990 the parliament of Bosnia-Herzegovina declared the republic's sovereignty.

On 18 November 1990 free elections in Bosnia resulted in a governing coalition of the three ethnically based parties generally corresponding to the three major ethnic groups. Muslims and Croats in the governing coalition favored independence for Bosnia-Herzegovina, while most Bosnian Serbs rejected independence amid calls for union with neighboring Serbia. On 20 November, fearing violence, the Bosnian government requested the deployment of United Nations troops in the republic, but the appeal went unanswered.

Lying between the increasingly combative Croat and Serb states, the Bosnian coalition government carefully maintained a neutral stance. But the Croatian war fatally damaged the fragile balance of nationalities in Bosnia. In early May 1991 violence spilled over into the republic from Croatia, raising tensions in the republic. The secession of neighboring Croatia from Yugoslavia in June 1991 provoked Serb claims, backed by the Yugoslav government in Belgrade, to much of the territory of Bosnia-Herzegovina.

In August 1991, as the war in neighboring Croatia wound down, the Serbs stepped up pressure on Bosnia-Herzegovina. The Bosnian Serbs, led by the Serbian Democratic Party and supported by the Yugoslav government in Belgrade, gained control of most of northern Bosnia in August 1991. In September the Serbs declared three large, mainly Serb-populated areas autonomous regions and prepared for unification with Serbia. Armed clashes erupted between Serbs and Bosnian Muslims in several areas.

Serbian territorial claims to Bosnian territory pushed the Bosnian government, supported by the Muslims and Croats, to hold a referendum on independence in October 1991. The referendum, boycotted by the ethnic Serbs, favored independence for Bosnia-Herzegovina.

On 24 December 1991 the governments of four Yugoslav republics, Bosnia-Herzegovina, Croatia, Macedonia,* and Slovenia, requested recognition as sovereign states from the European Community. However, on 9 January 1992 European Community leaders announced that the risk of ethnic conflict was too great for Bosnia-Herzegovina to qualify for recognition. The United States and the major European states pressed for the continuation of a looser Yugoslav confederation. The assembly representing the Bosnian Serb population declared an autonomous republic and announced that Bosnia-Herzegovina's government no longer represented the Serb portion of the population in international forums. Sporadic fighting broke out between Muslims and Serb irregulars, units of the Yugoslav army, and Croat irregulars.

Following international recognition of Croatian and Slovene independence in January 1992, and news that Macedonia's secession was imminent, the elected Bosnian government found itself faced with an impossible choice. The prospect of remaining part of a rump Yugoslavia dominated by advocates of ''Greater Serbia'' was clearly unacceptable to the majority of Bosnia's population, while Bosnian independence was anathema to Serb nationalists both within Bosnia and in Serbia.

On 29 February 1992, with 63% of eligible voters taking part, including many ethnic Serbs, 99.4% opted for full independence. The referendum, one of the conditions demanded by the international community before Bosnia's independence would be recognized, was boycotted by the majority of the Bosnian Serb community. On 3 March 1992 the government formally declared the independence of the Republic of Bosnia and Herzegovina. The Bosnian Serbs, rejecting the independence referendum, moved their parliamentary representatives from the Bosnian capital to the ski resort of Pale, outside Sarajevo. The new Bosnian Serb parliament at Pale declared the autonomy of the areas under Serb control.

On 18 March leaders of the three major ethnic groups signed an agreement, under European Union threats of withholding recognition, which provided for the division of the republic into three autonomous units. The agreement was signed even though all agreed that it would be extremely difficult, if not impossible, to implement because very few areas of the republic were exclusively Muslim, Croat, or Serb. The Bosnian Serbs declared the independence of their region on 27 March. On 6 April ministers representing the European Union recognized the independence of the republic. Fighting between the different national groups intensified week by week.

On 5 April 1992 there was a mass demonstration by citizens of Sarajevo's three major communities, including moderate Serbs who favored Bosnian independence. Yugoslav National Army (JNA) snipers and Serb nationalist militants hidden on surrounding rooftops opened fire on the crowd, killing and wounding scores of unarmed citizens. The following day, Yugoslav army units began to shell Sarajevo from prepared positions on the hillsides overlooking the city, and columns of troops and tanks crossed the Drina River from Serbia into eastern Bosnia. Initially armed only with police sidearms and hunting rifles, later with captured and smuggled weapons, the Bosnian forces, including Muslims, Croats, and Serbs, tried to defend their newly independent country against the onslaught of radical nationalism.

On 22 May 1992, Bosnia-Herzegovina, already recognized by many states, was admitted as a full member of the United Nations. An arms embargo, imposed on all of the former Yugoslavia by the UN in 1991, in effect barred the internationally recognized Bosnian government from acquiring the means to exercise its right to self-defense as guaranteed under the UN Charter. The Serb forces, armed and supported by the Yugoslav National Army, were well armed and quickly overran many districts.

Islamic volunteers entered Bosnia. Called mujahideen, the volunteers formed the Muwafag and the Muwafaqah brigades. The presence of foreign volunteers fed the propaganda put out by the Serbian and Croatian press that the Bosniaks were intent on turning the country into an Islamic state modeled on Iran.

Crippled by an arms embargo imposed by the West, the Bosniaks fell back under concerted attacks. The Bosnian Serbs and the Yugoslav army quickly defeated the poorly armed republican forces and overran much of Bosnia's national territory. Employing a new and brutal weapon called ethnic cleansing—the murder, rape, and expulsion of entire populations—the triumphant Serbian forces surrounded Sarajevo and several other enclaves held by the forces of the Bosnian government.

The fragile Bosnian-Croat alliance collapsed in March 1993. Severe fighting between Muslims and Croats spread across the south and west, devastating ancient monuments and cities, including the traditionally Muslim and Croat city of Mostar, the capital of Herzegovina. The Croats declared the autonomy of their statelet in the southwest, called Herzeg-Bosne.

The Bosnian War, a three-sided conflict among the Bosnian Muslims, the Bosnian Croats, and the Bosnian Serbs, aided by the truncated Yugoslavia (Serbia and Montenegro), quickly escalated into the most brutal conflict to take place in Europe since World War II. The international community, reluctant to get involved in the conflict, failed to react strongly to the ethnic cleansing, reports of mass rape, concentration camps, and massacres. Refusing direct involvement, many governments called on the United Nations to act.

Representing the United Nations and the European Union, Cyrus Vance and Lord David Owen presented a peace proposal for Bosnia-Herzegovina on 2 January 1993. The proposal included the reorganization of the republic into ten provinces, the establishment of safe corridors for the movement of civilians and humanitarian aid, a large measure of autonomy for the provinces under a decentralized state, and cease-fire and demilitarization arrangements.

In late April the Bosnian Serb Assembly rejected the proposed territorial arrangements in the Vance-Owen peace plan for Bosnia, which had been endorsed by Bosnian Croats and Muslims. Many interpreted the Bosnian Serb decision as a calculated gamble that the West's response to the crisis would remain tentative and that there would be no direct international military intervention. However, under strong pressure from Serbia, the Bosnian Serbs signed the Vance-Owen plan in May, but then the Serbian parliament in Pale refused to endorse the agreement and submitted the final decision to a referendum. The Bosnian Serbs rejected the plan and with a 96% majority voted for the independence of the Bosnian Serb–held areas.

After a year of war, in April 1993, the Bosnians and Croats accepted a UN peace plan that would divide the country into two areas, a Muslim-Croat federation and a Serbian republic. The plan, formalized in March 1994, reduced the warring factions from three to two and created a projected federation of Bosnia and Herzegovina. The plan, rejected by the Bosnian Serbs, remained as the principal bargaining position taken up by the Western powers. Several subsequent peace plans foundered on the inability of the combatants to agree on an equitable division of territory between the three national groups.

The Bosnian state, devastated by continuing war that left some 200,000 dead, was overwhelmed by 2 million refugees, most "ethnically cleansed" from their villages in areas held by the Bosnian Serbs. The UN, supported by troops from many member nations, attempted to secure a fragile peace, but failing that took over the job of trying to keep transportation routes open and the flow of desperately needed food and medicine moving.

Bosnian Serb troops, disregarding the UN and NATO, overran the UN-protected enclaves of Srebernica and Zepa in eastern Bosnia in July 1995. Reported massacres of Bosniaks and continued attacks on the other so-called protected zones, particularly a brutal attack on a market in Sarajevo, finally provoked a massive NATO air attack on the Bosnian Serbs on 30 August. Pressed militarily by the NATO attacks, the Serbs began to lose territory in western Bosnia to renewed attacks by the Bosnian government forces and their Croat allies.

The August 1995 NATO attacks on Bosnian Serb military targets set the stage for a United States–brokered peace plan. On 21 November 1995, in Dayton, Ohio, the former Yugoslavia's three warring parties signed a peace agreement that brought to a halt over three years of interethnic civil strife in Bosnia and Herzegovina. The Dayton Agreement divides Bosnia and Herzegovina roughly equally between the Muslim and Croat Federation (51%) and the Bosnian Serb Republic of Srpska (49%) while maintaining Bosnia's currently recognized borders.

An international peacekeeping force (IFOR) of 60,000 troops began to enter Bosnia in late 1995 to implement and monitor the military aspects of the agreement and was scheduled to depart the country within one year. Under the new constitution initialed in Dayton, the name of the country will be changed from Republic of Bosnia and Herzegovina to simply Bosnia and Herzegovina and will be made up of the Muslim and Croat Federation and the Bosnian Serb entity now called Republika Srpska. In March 1996 the Serb suburbs of Sarajevo were turned over to the control of the mostly Muslim Bosnian government. The majority of the Serb population evacuated before the handover, leaving behind them only charred ruins.

Despite the general compliance with the military aspects of the peace agreement, little progress was made toward implementing those aspects relating to human rights, such as freedom of movement and the right of displaced people and refugees to return to their homes. About 1.5 million Bosnians driven from their homes remain refugees.

In 1997 a serious split among the leadership of the Republic of Srpska threatened to divide the Bosnian Serbs into warring camps. The split is between supporters of the hard-line leaders, most now accused of wartime atrocities, and a more moderate group, including the republic's president, who want the Serbs to renew their ties to the world beyond the republic. With the economy in freefall, corruption rampant, and the Serbs vilified as aggressive and brutal, the moderate Bosnian Serb leadership has looked to the West for support.

The country, with the first relative peace since 1992, began the task of reconstruction. By mid-1997 some 300,000 of the 2.1 million displaced persons had returned to their homes, but fewer than 30,000 had returned to territory controlled by a different ethnic group. The country, experts estimate, will need around $20 billion to resettle the refugees and displaced and to reconstruct the major war damage.

According to Bosnian leaders, survival of the Bosniak nation is now just as important as the survival of the internationally recognized state of Bosnia-Herzegovina. Should fighting again break out in the republic, Bosnian leaders fear that the survival of the nation, not just the country, will be at stake.

In August 1997 US envoy Richard Holbrooke returned to Bosnia to try to restore the fractured peace accord he put together at Dayton, Ohio, in 1995. He settled a dispute over the appointment of ambassadors, giving the Serbs the right to name the ambassador to Washington. Muslims will name the UN representative, and the Croats the envoy to Tokyo. A more serious threat to the peace accord is the refusal of the Bosnian Serbs to allow Bosniak and Croat refugees to return to areas controlled by them. Attempts by Bosniaks and Croats to return to their homes in Serb-held areas have been blocked by hard-liners loyal to Radovan Karadzic, the wartime leader.

SELECTED BIBLIOGRAPHY:

Donia, Robert J., and John V.A. Fine, Jr. *Bosnia and Hercegovina: A Tradition Betrayed.* 1994.

Friedman, Francine. *The Bosnian Muslims: Denial of a Nation.* 1996.

Greenberg, Keith Elliott, and John Isaac. *Bosnia: Civil War in Europe.* 1996.

Malcolm, Noel. *Bosnia: A Short History.* 1994.

Manuel, David. *Bosnia: Hope in the Ashes.* 1997.

CROATIA

Hrvatska; Republike Hrvatske

CAPITAL: Zagreb

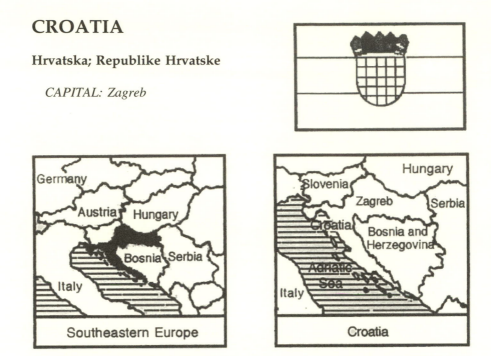

POPULATION: (98e) 4,621,000 : 3,678,000 Croats in Croatia and another 750,000 in adjacent parts of Bosnia.* MAJOR NATIONAL GROUPS: (98e) Croat 79.6%, Serb 10.4%, Hungarian 3.7%, Italian 2.6%, Muslim 1.1%, Bosnian 1%, Slovene, Czech. MAJOR LANGUAGES: Croatian (Hrvatski), Serbian, Hungarian, German. MAJOR RELIGIONS: Roman Catholic, Serbian Orthodox, Muslim, Uniate, Jewish. MAJOR CITIES: (98e) Zagreb 961,000 (1,190,000), Split 238,000 (311,000), Rijeka 193,000 (235,000), Osijek 131,000 (167,000), Zadar 61,000, Sisak 54,000, Karlovac 53,000 (82,000), Slavonski Brod 53,000 (71,000), Vukovar (91e) 49,000, Pula 48,000 (61,000), Sisak 48,000, Varazdin 43,000, Dubrovnik 39,000 (60,000), Sibenik 38,000.

GEOGRAPHY: AREA: 21,824 sq.mi.—56,538 sq.km. LOCATION: Croatia lies in the northern Balkan Peninsula in south-central Europe bordering Slovenia* and Hungary on the north, Bosnia on the south and east, and the Serbian Republic of Yugoslavia on the east. PHYSICAL GEOGRAPHY: Topographically, the country can be divided into three regions. The barren, rocky mountains of Dalmatia are part of the Dinaric Alps and extend through the center of Croatia. The rolling hills of the Zagorje region, located north of Zagreb, and the Pannonian Plain, a flat area bordered by the Drava River in the north and the Danube and Sava Rivers to the east and south, are the most productive regions of the country. Croatia includes a string of islands lying in the Adriatic Sea along the subtropical Dalmatian coast. A small sliver of Croatian territory, in the far south, is separated from the rest of the country by a small stretch of territory belonging to Bosnia and Herzegovina. The country's principal rivers are the Drava and Sava. ADMINISTRATIVE DIVISIONS: Twenty-one counties or zupanijas (singular—zupanija). POLITICAL STATUS: Croatia was recognized as an independent state in 1991–92.

INDEPENDENCE DECLARATIONS: 10 April 1941 (from Yugoslavia); 25 June 1991(from Yugoslavia).

FLAG: The Croatian national flag, the official flag of the Republic of Croatia, is a horizontal tricolor of red, white, and blue bearing a centered shield of twenty-five red and white squares surmounted by a crown of five crests representing the regions of Croatia, Slavonia, Dalmatia, Dubrovnik, and Istria.

PEOPLE: In the Republic of Croatia over forty national groups are represented. Other than the major national groups, Macedonians, Germans, Roms (Gypsies), Ruthenians, Slovaks, Ukrainians, and many others are also present in the republic. The Croats and most of the minority national groups in the republic are generally Roman Catholic, with a small Protestant minority. The only sizable religious minority is the Orthodox Christians, mostly ethnic Serbs.

Croat—estimated 79.6% of the population, numbering about 3,678,000.

The Croats are a South Slav people whose name comes from an old Slavic word meaning mountaineer. They are ethnically related to the neighboring South Slav peoples, and their claim to national identity is based on their separate history and their Roman Catholic faith.

Traditionally oriented to western Europe since the breakup of the Roman Empire in the fourth century, Croats continue to see themselves as the frontier of the Western world. According to Croat tradition, the Orthodox and Muslim East begins beyond their eastern and southern borders.

The Croats speak Croatian, formerly considered a dialect written in the Latin alphabet of the Serbo-Croatian language, but now claimed as a separate South Slav language. Substantial Croat populations live outside the republic, mostly in the neighboring areas of Bosnia.

Serb—an estimated 10.4% of the population, numbering about 480,000.

The Serbian population of Croatia is mostly descended from ethnic Serbs settled in the region by the Austro-Hungarian authorities to reinforce the frontier between the Habsburg and Ottoman empires. The majority live in the eastern region of Slavonia and the southwestern region of Dalmatia.

The mostly rural Serbs speak basically the same language as the Croats, but write in the Cyrillic alphabet. The Serbs are mostly Serbian Orthodox, and are oriented to Belgrade, not Zagreb. Many ethnic Serbs fled to Serbia during the fighting in Croatia in 1992.

Istrian (counted as ethnic Croat)—an estimated 5.3% of the population, numbering about 245,000.

The Istrians, who refer to themselves as an Istro-Romanic people, are a subgroup of the Croatians with a unique culture that has developed over centuries with mixed Slav, Germanic, and Latin elements. The Istrians, including the Istrians of neighboring Slovenia, have a strong sense of their separate identity, which embraces the three main Istrian national groups, the Croats, Slovenes, and Italians.

In 1990, even before the disintegration of Yugoslavia, the Istrians had formed the Istrian Democratic Diet (DDI), which advocated autonomy for Istria. In February 1993 the Croat Istrians firmly rejected Croatia's aggressive nationalism. The Istrian nationalist party, the DDI, won 72% of the votes in local elections, as opposed to only 16% for the Croat national party. The Istrians continue to reject the virulent nationalism emanating from Zagreb and work for closer ties to the neighboring Istrian Slovenes and Italians.

Magyar (Hungarian)—an estimated 3.7% of the population, numbering about 170,000.

The Magyars or Hungarians were left outside the borders of the reduced Hungarian state after the collapse of the Austro-Hungarian Empire in 1918. Although oriented to Budapest, they have maintained good relations with the Croats, with whom they share the Roman Catholic religion.

The Magyars live mostly in the Pannonian Plain, which borders Hungary, and have retained their own Hungarian language, an Ugrian language of the Finno-Ugrian group of languages. Most of the Magyars of Croatia speak Croatian as their second language.

Italian—an estimated 2.6% of the population, numbering about 120,000.

The Italian population of Croatia is concentrated in the regions that formed part of the Italian state until the end of World War II, the Istrian Peninsula and the port cities of Dalmatia. The treatment of the Italian minority in Croatia has, in the past, threatened relations between the Italian and Croatian governments.

Many of the Croatian Italians speak the Istrian version of Venetian, a Romance language very different from standard spoken Italian. Like the Croats, the Italians are mostly Roman Catholics, with a small Protestant minority.

Muslim—an estimated 1.1% of the population, numbering about 50,000.

The Muslims of Croatia are an ancient people living in the western part of the country, particularly in Istria and Dalmatia. Called Morlakhs, the Muslims have inhabited the region traditionally since the twelfth century. The multiethnic Istria region has a history of tolerant interethnic relations.

Highly secularized and assimilated, the Croatian Muslims have escaped the interethnic strife that has swept former Yugoslavia. There are also Morlakhs living in adjacent areas of Slovenian Istria.

Bosnian—an estimated 1% of the population, numbering about 45,000.

The Bosnians, as officially counted in Croatia, are ethnic Croats that fled the fighting in Bosnia and have settled permanently in Croatia. Other Bosnians, Muslims or Serbs, are considered refugees and have only temporary residence rights.

Slovene—estimated at less than 1% of the population, numbering about 25,000.

The Slovene population of Croatia lives mostly in the border regions between Croatia and Slovenia and in Istria. Speaking a related language and sharing the

Roman Catholic faith, the Slovenes have had few problems as a national minority. Slovenians also inhabit the Prekmurje region between the eastern Slovene border and the border of Hungary in eastern Croatia.

Czech—estimated at less than 1% of the population, numbering about 14,000.

The Czechs live mostly in the fertile Pannonian Plain of northern Croatia. The majority settled in the region under Austro-Hungarian rule and are mostly farmers in the fertile river valleys and plains.

The Czechs, like the Croats, speak a Slavic language and are mostly Roman Catholic or Protestant. Since the dissolution of the Yugoslav state in 1991, the Czechs have reestablished close ties to the newly democratic government of the Czech Republic.

Albanian—estimated at less than 1% of the population, numbering about 12,000.

The Albanians, speaking an Illyrian language, are mostly Roman Catholics who fled north to escape Muslim or Serb persecutions in the eighteenth and nineteenth centuries, during the time the southern Balkan Peninsula was controlled by the Turkish Ottoman Republic.

Montenegrin—estimated at less than 1% of the population, numbering about 10,000.

The Montenegrins, like the Serbs, use the Cyrillic alphabet, and most belong to the independent Montenegrin Orthodox Church. Originally ethnic Serbs, the Montenegrins separated from the Serbs during the five centuries of Turkish rule in Serbia.

THE NATION: Little was known of the region until the imposition of Roman rule 39–34 B.C. The region's population, under Roman rule, became Latin in culture and language. The area, particularly the districts along the Adriatic Sea coastline, was a favorite of many illustrious Romans. Forming part of Illyricum, the Illyrian provinces, the region prospered under Roman rule with fine cities and a wealthy, cultured population.

The Balkan Peninsula, after centuries of Roman rule, formed the border established at the division of the Roman Empire in A.D. 395, the beginning of the historic religious and cultural divisions of the region. While most of the Balkan region went to the Eastern or Byzantine Empire, the Illyrian provinces remained part of the western empire, the Latin Empire of Rome. The Balkan region thus became divided into a western region focused on Latin Rome and an eastern region focused on Greek Constantinople.

The flourishing region remained under Roman rule until the fifth-century invasions by barbarian tribes, Huns, Ostrogoths, and Visigoths. Slavic tribes, migrating from the northwest, settled the area in the seventh century, mostly displacing the earlier inhabitants. The newcomers were converted to Christianity by Latin and Greek missionaries, already feeling the strains between Rome and Constantinople.

During the next centuries parts of the region were included in Charlemagne's empire, while most Croatian lands eventually came under the control of the expanding Hungarian kingdom. Venetians finally gained a foothold in the coastal Dalmatian districts in the 900s.

A Croat kingdom, created in 924 under Tomislav, formed a dynastic union with the Hungarian kingdom in 1102. Under Hungarian influence the Croats remained oriented to the western half of Europe, where Roman Catholicism and the Latin alphabet predominated.

Croatia lost the coastal region of Dalmatia to Venice in 1420 and lost the eastern region of Slavonia to the advancing Ottoman Turks in the sixteenth century. Although divided between three foreign empires, the majority of the Croats escaped the centuries of Turkish rule that influenced the development of the other South Slav peoples.

Along with the Hungarian kingdom, much of Croatia became part of the Habsburg Empire, ruled from Vienna after 1687. Slavonia was ceded by the Turks to Austria in 1699. Other parts of Croatia came under Habsburg rule during the reign of Maria Theresa after 1740.

Taken by the French under Napoleon, the Croat lands formed part of the Illyrian provinces from 1809 to 1815. Given some autonomy, a Croat national movement gained support in the region. With Napoleon's defeat, Austro-Hungarian rule was reimposed and harsh retribution was meted out to those Slavs who had collaborated with the French.

The major South Slav language, called Serbo-Croatian, spoken in Croatia, Serbia, Montenegro, and Bosnia-Herzegovina, remained a collection of regional dialects. Although Serb and Croat intellectuals ultimately agreed on a standard literary form, partly under the heady influence of pan-Slavism and the South Slav Illyrian movement following the Napoleonic Wars, the standard was not in fact used as such.

Croatian resistance to Hungarian rule accompanied a cultural and national revival in the mid-nineteenth century. Croat troops aided the Austrians in putting down a Hungarian uprising in 1848–49, further straining relations between the Croats and Hungarians. The imperial government rewarded the Croats for their aid by separating Croatia from Hungary as the separate crownland of Croatia-Slavonia. However, as part of the compromise of 1867, which established the Austro-Hungarian Empire, Croatia was again placed under Hungarian authority over vehement Croatian protests. Nineteenth-century Croatian nationalism focused on the creation of a separate South Slav kingdom equal to Austria and Hungary within the Austro-Hungarian Empire.

Dalmatia, taken by the Austrians from Venice in 1797, remained under direct Austrian rule. Austrian rule in Croatian-populated Dalmatia and Hungarian control of Croatia proper provoked the first calls by Croat nationalists for unification of the Croat lands of the Austro-Hungarian Empire. Dalmatia remained under Austrian rule from 1815 to the end of World War I.

The Croats played an important role in the South Slav national movement, leading the campaign for the creation of a separate South Slav state within the Austro-Hungarian Empire. Strong Hungarian opposition to the South Slav demands provoked serious nationalist disturbances in 1903. Frustrated in their attempts to win equality within the empire, in 1912 nationalists began to advocate outright independence. The national movement gained support up to the outbreak of World War I, which began with the assassination of the imperial heir in neighboring Bosnia in 1914.

South Slav representatives from the Austro-Hungarian lands of Croatia and Slovenia met with the South Slav leaders of the independent states of Serbia and Montenegro on the Greek island of Corfu in June 1917. The meeting, with Allied encouragement, put forward a plan for an independent South Slav state with substantial autonomy for each of the national groups. In 1918, with the collapse of the Austro-Hungarian Empire and the end of the war, the South Slav peoples of the Balkan Peninsula formed the Kingdom of the Serbs, Croats, and Slovenes.

Friction between the Catholic Croats and the majority Orthodox Serbs over Croat demands for the autonomy provided for in the 1917 Corfu Manifesto began soon after independence. Tensions between the two largest peoples in the kingdom plagued the new state from its inception. The throne, held by the former Serbian dynasty, and the government, disproportionately Serb in character, gradually alienated even the most ardent South Slav nationalists among the non-Serbian national groups in the country. Calls for Croatian autonomy, led by the largest political party in the Croat districts, the Croat Peasant Party, and supported by the Roman Catholic clergy, surfaced with the Serb-dominated government's passage of a constitution that denied regional rights and centralized the government.

The placement of overall political control in Serb hands, with so many Serbs outside Serbia itself, led to substantial political infighting in the early years of the reign of King Alexander. Serbs occupied virtually all positions of political power and dominated the military.

The leader of the Croatian Peasant Party, Stjepan Radic, and several other Croat leaders were assassinated in the parliament by a Montenegrin Serb in 1928. The assassinations set off a serious crisis within the country. The outraged Croats withdrew from the central government on 1 October 1928. They set up a separate Croat parliament at Zagreb and prepared to secede from the Yugoslav kingdom.

Croat demands for separation from the kingdom were blocked by the imposition of a dictatorship. King Alexander suspended the constitution in 1929 and took personal responsibility for government in a dictatorship. The name of the new country was changed to the Kingdom of Yugoslavia. Serious tensions persisted, especially between autonomist Croats and centralist Serbs, and in Croatia the Yugoslav regime was seen as fundamentally Serbian, expansionist, and hegemonic.

Ignoring historical boundaries, the kingdom, renamed Yugoslavia, was divided into nine districts. Serbian domination of the country ensured that the crisis could not be easily resolved. Radical organizations gained followers as the crisis deepened and the worldwide depression brought ever more economic hardships. The Croats became divided between the Italian-supported Ustase, led by Anton Pavelic, openly Fascist and separatist, and a moderate faction, which favored Croat autonomy within an anti-Fascist Yugoslavia.

In 1934 a Croat of the openly Fascist Ustase movement, supported by Fascist Italy, assassinated King Alexander, who was on a state visit to France. The assassination, carried out with the complicity of Macedonian nationalists, plunged the country into a renewed crisis.

Moderate Croat political parties, fearing the growth of fascism, reached an autonomy agreement with the Yugoslav government in August 1939. The autonomy agreement was loudly denounced by the Ustase, which was supported by the Fascist governments of Germany, Italy, and Hungary.

Following a protracted political crisis in which Germany and Italy pressed for Yugoslav cooperation and the Allies sought Yugoslav cooperation against the Fascists, the Yugoslav government vacillated, and the Yugoslav army finally overthrew the government, vowed to resist the Axis, and thus triggered the invasion of April 1941. Italian, Hungarian, and German troops quickly overran the country.

Backed by his Fascist allies in the occupation armies, the Ustase leader, Anton Pavelic, declared Croatia independent of Yugoslavia on 10 April 1941. The new state included within its borders the neighboring region of Bosnia and Herzegovina, with large Muslim, Croat, Serb, and Gypsy populations. The Muslims, called Croatian Muslims, were courted as allies against the Orthodox Serbs. An Axis ally as war spread across Europe, the Croatian government adopted anti-Semitic laws and persecuted the state's Jewish, Serbian, and Gypsy minorities.

Many Croats, believing that the Axis would win, or simply motivated by hate of the Orthodox Serbs, joined the government's anti-Communist and anti-Serbian campaigns. Others, opposed to fascism, joined the royalists or the Communist-led partisans headed by an ethnic Croat known as Josip Broz.

In June 1941 the Pavelic government adopted a policy for dealing with the large Serb minority within Croatia. A third was to be expelled, a third forcibly converted to Catholicism, and a third exterminated. The policy set off a vicious civil war in the state, a war within the larger conflict called World War II. Massacres, atrocities, and genocide committed by both Croats and Serbs left between 300,000 and 700,000 dead by the end of the war in 1945. Thousands of Croats fled the collapse of the Croatian state.

On 19 November 1945 the Anti-Fascist National Liberation Council (AVNOJ), which was a provisional government with Josip Broz, also known as Marshal Tito, as prime minister, abolished the monarchy and established the Federative People's Republic of Yugoslavia, which consisted of Slovenia, Croatia, Bosnia-Herzegovina, and Serbia with its semiautonomous provinces. In January 1946 a new constitution, modeled on that of the Soviet Union, was adopted, and all opposition parties were officially abolished.

After the official end of the war, bands of Croatian Ustachi, called Crusaders, continued to fight the new Tito government for the independence of Croatia. Although an ethnic Croat, Tito opposed any form of political autonomy and promoted the centralization of the country. Tito, having defeated the nationalist and anti-Communist forces, became Yugoslavia's first postwar Communist leader and imposed a strict, centralized regime on the peninsula's warring peoples. Divided into a federation of Communist republics, the various South Slav peoples enjoyed some cultural and local autonomy, but all important decisions were made by Tito and a handful of close advisors.

A postwar cultural revival culminated in renewed calls for autonomy in the 1960s. The language issue became an important rallying point for Croatian nationalists determined to establish Croatian as a literary language separate from Serbo-Croatian. The period from 1965 to 1971 saw a great flowering of culture, the so-called Croatian Spring.

The republic, one of the wealthier in Yugoslavia, accounted for 40% of Yugoslavia's foreign earnings, but received only 5 to 7% from the government. The resentment over Croatia's foreign earnings going to prestige projects in the poorer republics added to the nationalist fervor of the late 1960s and early 1970s.

The language and economic conflicts led to a serious nationalist crisis in Croatia between 1971 and 1974. In December 1971 the entire Croat leadership was dismissed and the army purged of Croatian officers. Four hundred Croatian government and student leaders were tried and imprisoned. Zagreb and other Croat cities were shaken by large demonstrations, secretly condoned by the Croatian Communist leadership, who hoped to pressure the Tito government into more concessions.

The Yugoslav government, after resisting for decades, finally gave in to the rising tide of the nationalist crisis in the country. A new 1971 Yugoslav constitution gave the constituent republics broad powers and turned Yugoslavia into a virtual confederation of sovereign republics.

Tito's death in 1980 and the collapse of communism in 1989 fatally weakened the Yugoslav federation. In the first multiparty elections in nearly fifty years, the Communist reformers lost to parties favoring national sovereignty within a reorganized Yugoslav confederation. Faced by Serbian intransigence, the new Croat nationalist government rapidly moved the republic toward secession, vehemently opposed by the Serbian-dominated neo-Communist Yugoslav federal government and Croatia's own Serb minority.

Unwilling to accept direct Croat rule, Serbian insurgents in the districts with large Serb populations, particularly in the southwestern Krajina region, organized autonomous districts with their own Serbian army and police forces. During the spring of 1991, while delicate negotiations were taking place among the republican governments over the future of Yugoslavia, armed guerrillas and agitators, with aid from the Serb-dominated Yugoslav army, took over village after village. The Yugoslav federal army, led by an officer corps that was 80%

Serbian, then entered the rebellious regions under the pretext of preventing ethnic violence. Long before the final breakup of Yugoslavia, the federal army had
already occupied up to a quarter of Croatian national territory.

In May 1991, as the Yugoslav crisis deepened, the European Community and
the United States pressed the factions to continue negotiations toward a democ-
ratized and reformed Yugoslavia, with unchanged internal and external borders.
As soon as the constitutional crisis was ended, the European Community announced that it was prepared to start talks on Yugoslavia's associate membership.

The Yugoslav government and military leadership flatly rejected joint Slovenian and Croatian proposals for a looser federation or union of sovereign Yugoslav states. The crisis deepened when the Serbs and Montenegrins blocked
the confirmation of the moderate Croatian Stipe Mesic as chairman of the rotating federal presidency. According to the post-Tito constitutional arrangement,
the chairmanship of the federal presidency, the highest executive body in the
country, was to pass each year to the representative of a different republic, who
was to be chosen by his republic's parliament. It was Croatia's turn to select
the federal president, and Stipe Mesic was the first non-Communist ever to be
nominated to head the federal presidency. The Croatians responded to Serbian
refusals with a plebiscite in which the vast majority voted to authorize the Croatian parliament to declare independence at the end of June 1991 in the event
that the ongoing negotiations proved futile.

Supported by the referendum showing overwhelming support, the Croat government, in tandem with neighboring Slovenia, declared Croatia independent of
Yugoslavia on 25 June 1991. The major Western powers split over the question
of recognition of the new states. Local Serb militias, with increasing support
from the Serb-controlled Yugoslav army, attacked across the new state. The
Croatian military, poorly armed, and crippled by an arms embargo imposed by
the UN, fell back as the Serbs took control of the Krajina region adjoining
Bosnia—which nearly severed the southern Dalmatia region from contact with
Zagreb and the north—as well as the important eastern Slavonia region adjoining Serbia.

In July 1991, as fighting between Serbs and Croats intensified, Croat President
Franjo Tudjman announced that legislation had been prepared to offer home rule
to the Serbs of the self-proclaimed Autonomous Republic of Krajina. On 8
October 1991, when negotiations broke down, President Tudjman severed relations with rump Yugoslavia and declared the Yugoslav army an invading
force. He went on to declare Yugoslav law null and void on Croatian territory.

The victorious Serbs, intent on reunion with Yugoslavia in a "Greater Serbia," on 9 December declared all the Serb-held regions in Slavonia in the east
and Krajina in the west part of a newly constituted Serbian Republic of Krajina.
The two enclaves did not share a common border; but combined, they occupied
about a third of Croat territory and included some 300,000 people.

In the course of their war against the Croats, local Serbian militias and the

Yugoslav armed forces not merely entered Serbian-populated areas to protect Serbs, but seized wide stretches of territory where Croatians formed a majority. In such regions, they began a systematic effort to terrorize and expel the Croatian population.

In late December 1991 the government of Germany, which had championed Croatian independence, recognized the independence of Croatia and Slovenia and promised that diplomatic relations would be established on 15 January 1992. Other European Community governments quickly followed suit.

The so-called Homeland War, leaving over 10,000 dead and over 600,000 refugees, was tentatively brought to an end in early 1992 with the United Nations intervention. However, a tentative truce left Slavonia and Krajina in Serb hands.

In January 1995 the rearmed and reorganized Croatian military forces launched a ten-day offensive in Krajina that allowed Croat control of key installations. In July 1995 the Croatian army, in a lightning campaign, rolled over the Serb enclave of Krajina, sending 180,000 Serb refugees fleeing into Serb-held areas of neighboring Bosnia.

In April 1997 elections were held in Eastern Slavonia, which has been under Serb control since the war in 1991. The region is to be reintegrated into the Croat republic with autonomy for the local Serb population. The return of the Serbs who fled the fighting in Slavonia and Krajina, and the status of the Serb minority that fought against the Croatian government forces, are problems that remain to be resolved.

On 15 June 1997 Franjo Tudjman, the self-proclaimed "Father of the Nation," was elected for another five-year term as president with 61% of the vote. The election was denounced by the European Union and other observers as below minimum democratic standards. The Tudjman regime, in spite of its desire to draw Croatia into the European Union and other Western alliances, has become increasingly authoritarian.

SELECTED BIBLIOGRAPHY:
Banac, Ivo. *The National Question in Yugoslavia: Origins, History, Politics.* 1984.
McAdams, Michael C. *Croatia: Myth and Reality.* 1994.
Stallearts, Robert, and Jeannine Laurens. *Historical Dictionary of the Republic of Croatia.* 1995.
Tanner, Marcus. *Croatia: A Nation Forged in War.* 1997.
Vladovich, Simon. *Croatia: The Making of a Nation.* 1994.

CZECH REPUBLIC

Czechia; Cechy; Ceská Republika

CAPITAL: Prague (Praha)

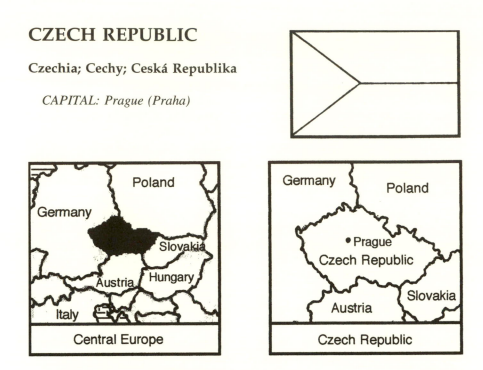

Central Europe

Czech Republic

POPULATION: (98e) 10,481,000 : 8,498,000 Czechs in the Czech Republic. MAJOR NATIONAL GROUPS: (98e) Czech (including Moravians and Silesians) 94.5%, Slovak 3.6%, Pole, German, Rom (Gypsy), Magyar (Hungarian), Ukrainian and Ruthenian, Russian. MAJOR LANGUAGES: Czech, Slovak, German, Polish. MAJOR RELIGIONS: Protestant 43.6%, Roman Catholic 39.2%, Orthodox 3%, other 13.4%. MAJOR CITIES: (98e) Prague (Praha) 1,213,000 (1,303,000), Brno 388,000, Ostrava 331,000 (805,000), Plzen 181,000, Liberec 111,000 (161,000), Olomouc 108,000, Hradec Králové 106,000, Ceské Budejovice 105,000, Pardubice 98,000, Usti nad Labem 94,000 (110,000), Havirov 92,000, Banská Bystrica 90,000, Zlín (Gottwaldov) 89,000, Kladno 72,000 (94,000), Most 67,000, Opava 62,000, Chomutov 60,000, Karlovy Vary 58,000, Decin 54,000, Jihlava 53,000, Prostejov 52,000, Prerov 50,000.

GEOGRAPHY: AREA: 30,449 sq.mi.-78,883 sq.km. LOCATION: The Czech Republic is a landlocked state lying in central Europe, bordering Poland on the north, Germany on the northwest, Austria on the south, and Slovakia* on the east. PHYSICAL GEOGRAPHY: Bohemia, in the west, is a hilly region of flat plateaus and rolling plains called the Czech Highlands, surrounded by low mountains, the Bohemian Forest in the southwest, the Erzgebirge in the northwest, and the Sudetic Mountains, which also extend into Moravia. The chief rivers are the Labe (Elbe) and the Vltava (Moldau). The Czech Highlands extend east to become part of the Bohemian-Moravian Highlands. Moravia, with part of Silesia, in the east, is a high plain characterized by rolling hills, and is crossed by several ranges, especially the Bohemian-Moravian Highlands on the border between Bohemia and Moravia. Moravia is drained by the Danube and Morava Rivers. ADMINISTRATIVE DIVISIONS: The Czech Republic is divided into eight regions or kraje (singular—kraj), six in Bohemia and two in Moravia and Silesia. POLITICAL STATUS: The Czech Republic was recognized as an independent state in 1993.

INDEPENDENCE DECLARATIONS: 28 October 1918 (from Austria); 1 January 1993 (from Czechoslovakia).

FLAG: The Czech flag is white over red with a blue trapezoid at the hoist.

PEOPLE: Many different ethnic groups are represented in the republic, but the Czech peoples—the Czechs, Moravians, and Silesians—form the overall majority in all areas. Through the centuries Austrian German influence has been a factor in the development of the region and its cultures. Until World War II the regions on the German and Austrian borders, plus many of the larger Moravian cities and towns, were predominantly German-speaking.

Czech—an estimated 81.1% of the population, numbering about 8,498,000.

The Czechs, living in the western region of Bohemia, are a Western Slav people related to the Poles, the Slovaks, and the Sorbs of Germany. The Czech culture, influenced by German and Austrian traditions and customs, is oriented to the West, and the majority of the Czechs are Protestants, with a large Roman Catholic minority.

The Czech language, formerly called Bohemian, spoken in a number of dialects, is second in importance among the Western Slav languages. It has a long literary tradition centered on Prague, and the Czech literary language is based on the dialect spoken in the city and its immediate region.

Moravian (counted as ethnic Czech)—an estimated 13.2% of the population, numbering about 1,388,000.

The Moravians, closely related to the Czechs, inhabit the eastern region of Moravia. In government censuses and official figures the Moravians are usually counted as ethnic Czechs. Culturally, the Moravians developed somewhat separately, with more Austrian influence in the region. In Moravia Czecho-Moravian dialects are spoken, along with the standard Czech, based on the dialect of Prague.

In 1989 and 1990 the Moravians, led by moderate nationalist groups, demanded autonomy. Large demonstrations were held in Brno and other cities in support of political and economic autonomy for the Moravia-Silesia region.

Slovak—an estimated 3.6% of the population, numbering about 377,000.

The Slovaks, a Western Slav people, are closely related to the Czech peoples, but are divided by over a thousand years of history. While Bohemia and Moravia were under Austrian rule, Slovakia formed part of the Hungarian kingdom. In 1994, 300,000 Slovaks opted for Czech citizenship rather than move east to the new Slovak republic.

The Slovak language, a Western Slav language, is close to Czech but differs in pronunciation and grammar and has a marked Hungarian admixture. Unlike the more secular Czechs, the Slovaks are intensely Roman Catholic.

Pole—estimated at less than 1% of the population, numbering about 63,000.

The Poles, mostly living in the border regions in the north, are the remnant of a larger Polish population that lived in the region under the rule of the Austro-Hungarian Empire. The majority moved north across the new border following the dissolution of the empire in 1918.

The Poles speak a related Western Slav language and are mostly bilingual in Czech. Intensely Roman Catholic, the Poles have often been at odds with the Czechs' traditionally anticlerical stance.

German—estimated at less than 1% of the population, numbering about 52,000.

The German Czechs are a remnant of a once very large German-speaking population that inhabited the borderlands, called Sudetenlands, of Bohemia and formed large urban populations in Prague and the Moravian cities.

The majority of the Germans were expelled after World War II. In the 1980s German claims against the Czech government for compensation for suffering and confiscated properties became a serious question in Czech-German relations and continue to overshadow relations between the new Czech Republic and Germany. German sources claim a population of around 200,000 ethnic Germans in the Czech Republic. The majority of the ethnic Germans in the region are Roman Catholics.

Silesian (counted as ethnic Czech)—estimated at less than 1% of the population, numbering about 45,000.

The Silesians live in the region of northern Moravia and Silesia around the city of Opava, their major cultural and political center. Related to the Polish Silesians across the border in Poland, the Silesians see themselves as a separate Western Slav people.

The Silesians speak a Czech dialect that is comprehensible to their Polish and Moravian neighbors, and some Silesian dialects are transitional to both. The mostly Roman Catholic Silesians tend to be more religious than their Moravian and Czech neighbors.

Rom (Gypsy)—estimated at less than 1% of the population, numbering about 32,000.

Officially, the Rom comprise .03% of the population of the Czech Republic. However, many estimates are much higher, as many Gypsies, to escape persecution, have listed themselves as ethnic Czechs or Slovaks. Estimates of the Rom population of the Czech Republic run as high as 350,000.

In September 1997 over a thousand Rom arrived in Canada seeking asylum. The wave of requests for asylum was sparked by a Czech television program that suggested that Rom asylum seekers from the Czech Republic enjoy better living conditions in Canada than in the Czech Republic.

The Rom are divided in two groups, the Sinte Rom and the Karpacky Roma or Carpathian Rom. Most of the Rom are bilingual, speaking both Czech and the Rom dialects spoken in the Czech lands.

Magyar (Hungarian)—estimated at less than 1% of the population, numbering about 21,000.

The Magyar population of the Czech Republic is mostly concentrated in southern Moravia and along the Czech-Slovak border. Most of the Roman Catholic Hungarians tend to look to Budapest, not Prague, for their cultural and political leadership. The Hungarians are mostly Roman Catholic.

Ukrainian and Ruthenian—estimated at less than 1% of the population, numbering about 11,000.

The Ukrainians and Ruthenians, mostly Uniate or Orthodox by religion, live in the eastern districts of Moravia, close to the Slovak border. Many fled west after World War II to escape the Soviet takeover of the eastern province of Czechoslovakia, Ruthenia, which now forms part of Ukraine.* The Ruthenes consider themselves distinct from the Ukrainians, although they speak a Ukrainian dialect.

Russian—estimated at less than 1% of the population, numbering about 6,000.

The small Russian population is mostly concentrated in Prague. Most of the ethnic Russians settled in the region after World War I. The majority of the Russian population is bilingual and is assimilating.

THE NATION: The region formed part of the area called Germania by the Romans, a frontier area lying north of the Alps, the limit of Roman control. With the decline of Roman power in the fifth century A.D., the region was overrun by Huns and Vandals moving into the Roman provinces.

In the fifth century Slavic tribes, moving from the east, settled in Bohemia, and from the end of the sixth century took control of Moravia. The tribes became tributary to the empire of Charlemagne, who ruled from Aachen in western Germany.

Subjugated by the Avars, the various Slavic tribes united under the leadership of a merchant named Samo. He unified the Slavonic tribes into a protective league against the Avars. However, his state, traditionally the forerunner of later Czech states, lasted only about thirty-five years.

In the eighth century the Premsyl dynasty was established in Bohemia. Its semilegendary founder, a peasant named Premsyl, was chosen as husband by Princess Libussa. Their successors united the Bohemian tribes into a single duchy.

The Moravians were first mentioned in historical documents in 822 as a powerful Slavic people straddling several of central Europe's major rivers. The Moravian lands marked the limits of the Germanic empire called the Holy Roman Empire.

In A.D. 870 the western Slavic tribes revolted against the German emperor and formed a protective alliance, later called the Great Moravian Empire. Germans and Jews, merchants and adventurers, settled in the cities, forming a powerful commercial class. German missionaries, St. Cyril and St. Methodius, converted the Slavs to Christianity, traditionally beginning with the Moravians in 863.

The Moravian empire fell apart in the early tenth century under attacks by Germans and Magyars and an invasion by migrating Huns. In 906 the Magyars conquered Moravia, which became part of the Hungarian kingdom in 955.

Bohemia became a duchy under Wenceslaus (Vaclav in Czech), the first of the great Czech rulers. He completed the Christianization of Bohemia and negotiated a peace with the German king. Assassinated by his brother, Wenceslaus was soon recognized as the patron saint of the Czechs. Under his brother's rule, Bohemia was forced to acknowledge the rule of the German emperor and become part of the Holy Roman Empire.

Under the rule of the Premsyl family, Bohemia expanded, in 1029, to include Moravia, parts of Silesia, Slovakia, and territory in Poland. In the twelfth century Bohemia was raised to the rank of electorate and in 1212 became a hereditary kingdom within the Holy Roman Empire. At the height of its power, in the thirteenth century, the Bohemian kingdom expanded into traditionally Austrian and Hungarian lands, but was defeated by Rudolph of Habsburg in 1278.

The kingdom revived in the fourteenth century and under the rule of Charles I entered a golden age of culture, art, and power. The flowering of Czech literature and art paralleled increasing national consciousness. The golden age ended when the religious wars erupted in central Europe. With the election of the Austrian Ferdinand as king of Bohemia in 1526, Bohemia and Moravia became integral parts of the Habsburg empire.

Germanization proceeded rapidly in Moravia from the thirteenth century. By the sixteenth century the Moravian middle and upper classes were thoroughly Germanized. Culturally and linguistically, German cities were surrounded by a rural Czech-speaking peasant population.

The Reformation and Renaissance saw a revival of religious writing and the development of liberal ideals and thinking. Publishing in the Czech language, begun with the Bible, was followed by works on history, science, and medicine. Religious strife between Protestant and Catholic nobles foreshadowed the later wars of religion.

The deposition of the Habsburg ruler by the Czech nobles, in 1618, inaugurated the Thirty Years' War, which devastated the region. The Czechs lost their remaining independence with the defeat of the Protestant forces at the battle of White Mountain in 1620. In 1627 Bohemia was formally declared a Habsburg crownland. The war, fought from 1618 to 1648, brought the wholesale destruction of Czech literary and artistic works, followed by the repression of Czech national life. Many Czechs fled abroad to escape oppressive taxes, religious persecution, and absentee landlords.

By the eighteenth century the Czech lands were completely incorporated in the Austrian Empire. Under Empress Maria Theresa and Emperor Joseph II, the Czechs were subjected to a program of intense Germanization. The majority of the Czech cultural leaders worked abroad, and the Czech language was gradually reduced to little more than a peasant dialect.

The oppression of the Czech culture and language continued into the nineteenth century, but at the same time a national revival took hold, with new interest in the Czechs' separate traditions, language, and history. Prague became the center of Czech nationalism in the late nineteenth century. Led by Protestant intellectuals, a great revival of the Czech language and culture spread through the Czech lands as a rejection of the Germanization pressed by the Habsburg authorities.

The Czechs led the movement for the equal rights of the Slavs of the Austrian Empire. During the Revolution of 1848 the Czechs convened a congress of Slavic leaders in Prague, but by early 1849 absolute Austrian domination had been restored and Moravia was made a separate Austrian crownland.

The establishment of the Dual Monarchy in 1867, which gave the Hungarians rights within the empire equal to those of the Austrians, gravely disappointed the Czechs. In spite of some concessions to the Czechs in 1879, when Czech delegates entered the parliament at Vienna, the Czechs and other Slavs of the empire remained unsatisfied that a third Slav kingdom had not been created within the dual empire.

Stirred by immigrant Czechs in the United States and Canada, support for autonomy within the empire grew in the first years of the twentieth century. A Czech National Council formed by exiles in the United States began to coordinate efforts with exile Slovak and Moravian groups. The Czech leader, Thomas Masaryk, joined by Slovak leader Milan Stefanik and supported by the U.S. government, began to press for independence for the region.

The defeat of Austro-Hungary, in October 1918, opened the way for Czech and Slovak independence. On 28 October 1918 the Czech leaders declared Bohemia and Moravia independent of Austria. Two days later, on 30 October, the Slovaks declared their independence from Hungary. The union of the Czech lands and Slovakia was officially proclaimed on 14 November 1918. The September 1919 Treaty of St. Germain between the Allies and Austria paved the way for official recognition of the new state.

Of the new nations that emerged in Europe following the defeat of the Central Powers, all began with democratic governments, but only Czechoslovakia remained a democratic state, while the others succumbed to totalitarian regimes. In spite of the democratic nature of the government, the Czechs, numerically and politically dominant, quickly gained control of most ministries and set the tone of government throughout the country. The constitution of 1920, although liberal and democratic, set up a highly centralized state and failed to address the increasingly serious question of the national minorities.

The German upper and middle classes continued to dominate Moravia, while the poorer eastern regions, Slovakia and Ruthenia, were mostly governed by ethnic Czechs due to a lack of trained administrators. Although Slovakia and Ruthenia were promised autonomy, in practice it was constantly postponed.

Resentment of Czech hegemony and the antireligious stance of the Prague government grew as Europe lurched from crisis to crisis.

The most cosmopolitan of the Slavic nations between the wars, Czechoslovakia gained fame as the home of many influential writers and playwrights. Bustling Prague became one of the centers of the European post–World War I revival. Economically the most favored of the former Habsburg territories, Czechoslovakia looked forward to a bright future.

While Czech cultural life flourished, Czech political life between the wars was marked by minority demands for autonomy, particularly by the Slovaks and the Sudeten Germans, who were supported by Nazi Germany after 1933. Demands for union with Germany by the Sudeten Germans led to a serious crisis between Prague and Berlin in 1938.

In September 1938 Czechoslovakia, as part of the Munich Agreement between the European powers, was forced to cede the Sudetenland, the German majority areas, to Nazi Germany. The agreement, meant to resolve the German-Czech crisis and ensure peace in Europe, prolonged the crisis. Slovakia and Ruthenia, given autonomy in 1938, increasingly opposed Czech domination of the state. On 14 March 1939 the autonomous Slovak state declared its independence, and the following day the Nazis annexed the Czech lands of Bohemia and Moravia as a German protectorate. Germany's ally, Hungary, annexed the eastern province of Ruthenia.

The Czech government set up a government-in-exile in London, and Czech units fought with the Allies. Except for the brutalities of the German occupation, including the extermination of nearly all of the formerly large Jewish population, the Czech lands suffered little physical damage and emerged from the war with their industrial base and economy mostly intact.

Soviet troops, in April 1944, overran the region from the east while American and Allied troops moved into the Czech lands in the west. In March 1945 Edward Benes, who had been elected president of Czechoslovakia in 1935, agreed to form a National Front government with Klement Gottwald, leader of the Communist Party of Czechoslovakia (CPCz).

On 5 May 1945 the Czechs rebelled against the German occupiers. Accompanied by members of the National Front coalition government, the Allies finally took control of Prague on 12 May 1945. The fall of Prague marked the end of Allied military operations in Europe. At the Potsdam Conference of 1945 the expulsion of some 3 million ethnic Germans from the Czech lands was approved.

The Communists emerged as the strongest party in the elections of 1946 and became the leading political force in the coalition government. In 1946 Gottwald was elected prime minister. In February 1948, in a coup d'état, the Communists seized the government and forced President Benes to form a new government made up entirely of Communists. In June 1948 President Benes resigned and was succeeded by Gottwald. President Gottwald embarked on a campaign of repression of non-Communists and Czech nationalists. New legislation provided for the nationalization of nearly every part of the economy and promoted rapid industrialization.

In 1960 a new constitution, modeled on that of the Soviet Union, established a unitary state of the Czech and Slovak nations. The country's name was changed to the Czechoslovak Socialist Republic. During the 1960s Czechoslovakia's intellectuals called for more freedom of expression, and many Slovaks renewed their efforts to gain recognition for Slovak rights.

In January 1968 the Slovak Alexander Dubcek became first secretary of the Czechoslovak Communist Party and introduced a program of liberal reforms called the "Prague Spring." The reforms included freedom of the press as well as increased contact with non-Communist countries. While the Czechs tended to emphasize democratic reform, the Slovaks emphasized national advantages.

Leaders of the Soviet Union and other East European nations feared that Dubcek's program would weaken Communist control in Czechoslovakia. Under the Warsaw Pact, troops from the Soviet Union, Bulgaria, East Germany, Hungary, and Poland invaded Czechoslovakia on 20 August 1968. A third of the membership of the Communist Party was expelled. Over 40,000 Czechs fled the invasion and the repression that followed. The Red Army remained when the other national armies withdrew later the same year.

On 1 January 1969 a federal system of autonomous Czech and Slovak governments was introduced, but power remained firmly in the hands of the Communist Party. In April 1969 Dubcek was replaced, which resulted in further anti-Soviet protests. In May 1970 a new twenty-year Treaty of Friendship was signed with the Soviet Union.

In 1973, amid continuing repression, the Communist government offered an amnesty to those who had fled in 1968. Many leading Czech intellectuals returned, but the government's repressive policies remained unchanged. More than 700 leading Czech and Slovak intellectuals and former party members signed a human rights declaration in 1977. The manifesto, called Charter 77, prompted a renewed crackdown on dissident groups in the country.

During the 1980s economic stagnation threatened Czechoslovakia's position as one of the more advanced of the Communist states and fed a growing popular unrest. However, a lack of anonymity, particularly in rural areas, meant very little criticism of the Communist regime. In August 1988 only some 10,000 demonstrators braved severe repression to take part in a protest marking the twentieth anniversary of the Warsaw Pact invasion of 1968.

Reactions to the new spirit of *glasnost* coming from the Communist Jerusalem, Moscow, were cautious and defensive. The government ordered a wave of arrests of dissidents in 1988 and 1989. The then Czechoslovakia initially aligned itself with the German Democratic Republic in opposition to political and economic reform. However, during November 1989, large demonstrations took place in all of the country's major cities, culminating in the resignation of the Communist Party leadership in December. The so-called Velvet Revolution had swept the Communist government from power without bloodshed.

The government, pressed by mass demonstrations and demands for change, initiated talks with the main opposition group, Civic Forum. Civic Forum's newly found influence over the political process led to the appointment of dissident playwright Vaclav Havel as president while the country set about introducing a pluralistic political system and a market economy. Multiparty elections for a new national assembly in June 1990 were won by Civic Forum. In the east, the increasingly nationalistic Slovaks demanded autonomy, and even in the Czech lands, in Moravia and Silesia, mass demonstrations in favor of autonomy swept Brno and other cities.

Despite the firm opposition of President Havel, who considered that the country could ill afford such diversions at this critical stage in its development, negotiations opened between representatives of the two republican governments in November 1991. The talks broke down within weeks, and both sides retired to await the June 1992 national election. The two parts of the country voted for nationalist parties, and a complete split between the Czech lands and Slovakia was quickly accepted as the only viable option. The formal division of Czechoslovakia into the Czech Republic and Slovakia took place with the formal declarations of independence of the two republics on 1 January 1993. The so-called Velvet Divorce had brought two new states into being in Europe. The Slovak residents of the Czech Republic were given until 31 December 1993 to apply for Czech citizenship.

The Czech lands, more advanced economically than Slovakia, looked to the West for expertise and aid. The Czech economy, freed of the less prosperous Slovak economy, became one of the strongest in the former Communist bloc and was dubbed the Czech Miracle. Only in mid-1997 did the economy begin to show signs of weakening.

The Czech government, dominated by reformers and former dissidents, moved the Czech Republic into line to join NATO and the European Union. After decades of Communist repression, the Czechs see their future security linked to a network of alliances with the most powerful states in the West. The Czech Republic has been invited to join NATO, and negotiations to join the European Union began in 1998.

President Vaclav Havel narrowly won reelection to a new five-year term following two rounds of voting by the Czech Parliament in January 1998. His challengers, representing the Communist Party and the ultra-right Republican Party, failed to win enough votes to proceed to the second round, leaving President Havel as the only candidate.

SELECTED BIBLIOGRAPHY:
Dedek, Oldrich, ed. *The Break-up of Czechoslovakia*. 1996.
Hochman, Jiri. *Historical Dictionary of the Czech Republic*. 1997.
Klaus, Vaclav. *Renaissance: The Rebirth of Liberty in the Heart of Europe*. 1997.
Leff, Carol Skalnik. *The Czech and Slovak Republics: Nation Versus State*. 1996.
Otfinoski, Steven. *The Czech Republic*. 1997.

ERITREA

State of Eritrea

CAPITAL: Asmara

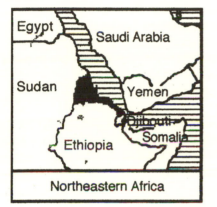

Northeastern Africa

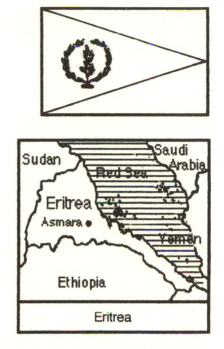

Eritrea

POPULATION: (98e) 3,621,000. MAJOR NATIONAL GROUPS: Tigrinya 43.8%, Tigré 31.2%, Afar 7.3%, Kunama 4%, Saho 4%, Bedawi (Beja, Hidareb) 3.3%, Bilen 1.9%, Nara (Baria) 1.7%, Raishada Arab 1%. MAJOR LANGUAGES: Tigrinya, Tigré, Arabic, Afar-Saho, Bedawie (Beja), Italian, English, Amharic. MAJOR RELIGIONS: Sunni Islam 52%, Christian 46%, animist. MAJOR CITIES: (98e) Asmara 609,000, Keren (Cheren) 123,000, Massawa (Mitsawa) 105,000, Assab (Aseb) 77,000, Ak'orodat 56,000, Naf'ka 55,000, Tessenei 45,000, Dekemhare 30,000, Adi Ugri 20,000.

GEOGRAPHY: AREA: 46,829 sq.mi.-121,320 sq.km. LOCATION: Eritrea lies on the Red Sea in northeastern Africa on the Horn of Africa, bordering Sudan on the north, Djibouti on the southeast, and Ethiopia* on the south. PHYSICAL GEOGRAPHY: Eritrea lies on the Red Sea with a broad coastal plain of more than 600 miles. The country includes the important Dahlak Archipelago and the Zuqar Islands farther south. The Danakil Depression in the southeast falls below sea level and has been the site of some of the highest temperatures recorded on earth. To the west the coastal plain rises sharply to the highland plateau and mountains, the northern extension of the Ethiopian Plateau. To the north and west of the central plateau ranges the land is generally hilly and drier. In the northwest, near the Sudanese border, lie the broad plains west of the Baraka River and north of the Setit River. ADMINISTRATIVE DIVISIONS: Six regions (singular—awraja) plus the capital city of Asmara. POLITICAL STATUS: Eritrea was recognized as an independent state in 1993.

INDEPENDENCE DECLARATION: 24 May 1993.

FLAG: The Eritrean state flag has a red isosceles triangle, based on the hoist side, dividing the flag into two right triangles; the upper triangle is green, the lower one is blue; a gold wreath encircling a gold olive branch is centered on the hoist side of the red triangle.

PEOPLE: Eritrea has a mixed Afro-Asiatic population reflecting diverse languages, religions, and cultures. The nine major national groups are the Tigrinya, the Tigré, the Afar, the Kunama, the Saho, the Bedawi, also called Beja or Hidareb, the Bilen, the Nara, and the Rashaida Arabs. Between 70 and 80% of the population is rural, mostly agriculturists and herders. Despite Eritrea's ethnic and religious diversity, friction between the various groups has not been a major problem, as the Eritrean peoples formed close bonds during the decades of war for independence from Ethiopia. The majority of the Eritreans speak Semitic or Cushitic languages of the Afro-Asiatic language group. The Kunama, Baria, and other smaller groups in the north and northwest speak Nilotic languages.

The war with Ethiopia and the famines that hit the entire region in the 1970s and 1980s caused a great deal of disruption and population movement, especially in the rural areas. At the time of independence approximately 20% of the population within Eritrea was displaced, while an estimated half million Eritreans were living as refugees in Sudan.

Tigrinya—an estimated 43.8% of the population, numbering about 1,584,000.

The largest national group, the Semitic Tigrinya or Tigrigna inhabit the core provinces of the country, the Ethiopian Plateau and the southern highlands. The majority of the Tigrinya are Christians, mostly Coptic Orthodox, but with smaller Roman Catholic and Protestant groups.

The Tigrinya are an Afro-Asian people speaking a Semitic North Ethiopian language written in the Ethiopian script. Closely related to the Tigreans of neighboring Ethiopia, the Tigrinya are separated from their Ethiopian kin by history and traditions.

Tigré—an estimated 31.2% of the population, numbering about 1,130,000.

The Tigré, also called Khasa or Xasa, inhabit the northern coastal plain, the region along the Sudanese border, and parts of the western plains. They are a Semitic Muslim people related to the Tigrinya. Converted to Islam by Arab invaders in the seventh century, they are separated by history, language, and traditions from the neighboring Semitic peoples.

The Tigrean language is a Semitic North Ethiopian language related to Tigrinya and Amharic, the most widely spoken language in neighboring Ethiopia. The Tigrean language is believed by some experts to be the direct descendant of Ge'ez, the Semitic language spoken by the original settlers from the Arabian Peninsula. Many Tigré speak Hadrami or Sudanese Arabic as a second language.

Afar—an estimated 7.3% of the population, numbering about 265,000.

The Afar, of mixed Semitic, Hamitic, and Arabic ancestry, are a mostly nomadic people who inhabit the coastal plain south of the Gulf of Zulia, the

Danakil Depression, and the important Dahlak Archipelago in the Red Sea. The Afar are closely related to the smaller Saho people, who some consider a branch of the Afar nation. The Afar language is a Cushitic language of the Hamitic group of Hamito-Semitic languages that has been considerably altered by exposure to Arabic. The name Danakil or Denakil, as some call the Afar, is considered an offensive term by the Afars.

The Muslim Afar, some inhabiting the hottest and lowest part of the earth in the Danakil Depression, are divided into tribes, subtribes, and clans and are also identified by a class system that segregates the population into two distinct divisions, the Asimara (Red) nobles, and the Adoimara (White) commoners. Large numbers of Afar also live in adjacent areas of Ethiopia and Djibouti.

Afar nationalism could become a serious problem for the new Eritrean government. Following Eritrean independence in 1993, some Afar leaders denounced the move as a further partitioning of their nation between the region's independent states.

Kunama—an estimated 4% of the population, numbering about 145,000.

The Kunama, also called Baza or Bada, live mostly in the western plains along the Gash and Setit Rivers and along the Sudanese border. The Kunama, mostly settled agriculturists, speak Nilotic or Nilo-Saharan languages unrelated to the Afro-Asiatic languages of the majority of Eritreans.

The Kunama are mostly Sunni Muslims. Their culture and language have been influenced by their Arabic and Semitic Muslim neighbors, although a minority adheres to traditional religions.

Saho—an estimated 4% of the population, numbering about 145,000.

The Saho, also called Sao or Shoho, closely related to the Afar, inhabit the foothills of the southern coastal plain and are the majority people around the port of Massawa. Some consider the Saho a branch of the Afar nation, but they retain their own hierarchy and culture. Their language, a dialect of Afar-Saho, is a Cushitic language very closely related to Afar.

Divided into ten tribes, numerous subtribes, and clans, the Saho maintain a strict social order and do not accept outsiders. Some of the Saho tribes, like their Afar neighbors, inhabit parts of the most inhospitable region on earth, the Danakil Depression.

Bedawi—an estimated 3.3% of the population, numbering about 120,000.

The Bedawi, also called Beja, Hidareb, or Beni-Amer, are mostly nomads in the northwest and northeast border regions. The Sunni Muslim Bedawi speak a Cushitic language that is also spoken in Sudan and southern Egypt. A minority, called Lobat, have adopted the Tigré language.

Moving with their herds of cattle and goats, the Bedawi mostly ignored international borders until more stringent controls were put in place since the 1960s. Traditionally, Bedawi herdsmen wandered as far north as Egypt.

Bilen—an estimated 1.9% of the population, numbering about 70,000.

The Bilen, also called Bogo or North Agaw, live in central Eritrea, in and around the city of Keren. The Bilen speak a Cushitic language, but many are bilingual in Tigrinya or Tigré. The younger generation mixes their speech with Arabic words and expressions.

Culturally, the Bilen are one people. However, there are both Christian and Muslim communities. The Christians tend to be urban and have intermingled with the Tigrinya. The Muslims tend to be rural and have mixed with the neighboring Tigré.

Nara (Baria)—an estimated 1.7% of the population, numbering about 65,000.

The Nara, also called Baria or Barya, a derogatory term, live in the northern districts close to the Kunama. The Nara language, related to Kunama, is a Nilotic language unrelated to the majority Afro-Asiatic languages of Eritrea. Tigré is widely spoken and is used for intercommunications with the neighboring Kunama and the Semitic peoples to the south. The majority of the Nara are Muslim, but with an animist minority.

The Nara nation is divided into four main tribal groups and several subtribes and clans. Most of the Nara in Eritrea are farmers or herders.

Raishada—an estimated 1% of the population, numbering about 37,000.

The Raishada are an Arab people speaking a Semitic Sudanese Arab dialect. A small part of the Arab population is descended from Arabic settlers who colonized the region in the seventh century. The majority of the Raishada live in the coastal towns along the Red Sea and traditionally formed a merchant class in Massawa and other port cities.

The Muslim Arab population has led the Eritreans' contacts with the Muslim states. Estimates of Arabic speakers in Eritrea, including the Sudanese, Hadramuti, and Adeni Arab dialects, run as high as 300,000.

Hadenoa—estimated at less than 1% of the population, numbering about 20,000.

The Hadenoa, also called Hadendowa, are a small, nomadic people in the northwest region. Closely related to the Bedawi, they are sometimes included as a Bedawi subgroup. They speak a Cushitic language that is inherently intelligible to Bedawi speakers. The Hadenoa are Sunni Muslims.

Adeni Arab—estimated at less than 1% of the population, numbering about 18,000.

The Adeni Arabs, originally from the region of Aden in southern Yemen, live mostly in the port city of Massawa. Although an Arab people, the Adenis consider themselves a separate people. They speak a distinct Arabic dialect called Ta'izzi-Adeni and are mostly Sunni Muslims.

THE NATION: The earliest inhabitants of the region are thought to have moved from the Nile valley into the Mereb-Setit lowlands around 4000 B.C. Over the next several thousand years Nilotic, Cushitic, and Semitic peoples settled in what became one of the earliest regions of crop and livestock domestication in Africa. As early as 3000 B.C. the inhabitants of the coastal plains were engaged in trade on the Red Sea.

Around 1000 B.C. Semitic migrants from the Arabian Peninsula settled the coastal regions and moved inland. The ancient Greek historian Herodotus chronicled the classical world's fascination with the Land of Punt, the present coastal areas of Eritrea, Djibouti, and Somalia. The coastal trading centers collected ostrich feathers, gemstones, and myrrh for export north to the Mediterranean. The Semitic settlers later moved inland, where they formed the kingdom of Aksum, which flourished from the fourth to the sixth centuries A.D.

Converted to Christianity in the fourth century, the region, along with ancient Ethiopia, was cut off from Christendom by the Muslim conquest of the territories to the north in the seventh century. Islam, introduced to the coastal regions by Arab traders and colonists, spread through the lowlands in the eighth to tenth centuries, but did not penetrate the more isolated Christian heartland of the Ethiopian Plateau. By A.D. 950 most of the region's Christian and Muslim peoples had been integrated into the Ethiopian empire. Eritrean ports provided the principal route of the empire's foreign trade. Due to its importance, Eritrea retained a fair degree of autonomy under the imperial government.

Egyptian troops took control of the principal offshore islands in 1557 and used them as a base to extend their rule to the mainland coastal districts. The invaders established an Egyptian administration under the nominal rule of an Ottoman Turkish governor.

From the seventeenth to the mid-nineteenth century the territory was disputed among the Ethiopians, the Ottoman Turks, the Tigreans, the Egyptians, and later the Italians. The decline of the Ottoman Empire, and the opening of the Suez Canal in 1869, greatly increased European interest in the formerly isolated region.

In 1869 the Italians established a military base at Assab, gradually extending their rule to the lowlands, their expansion contested by Egypt and Ethiopia. The Treaty of Uccialli, forced on a weakened Ethiopia by the Italians in 1889, recognized the Italian possession of territories on the Red Sea. On 1 January 1890 the coastal regions were officially proclaimed an Italian colony.

In 1890 the Italians, not satisfied with just the coastal towns, moved inland to seize the highlands from the Ethiopian kingdom of Tigre. The various territories were then consolidated, and the new colony was called Eritrea for the Red Sea, Mare Erythralum in the ancient Latin language.

The Italians attempted to expand into Ethiopia in 1896, suffering the first major defeat of a European colonial army in Africa. Restricting their attention to Eritrea, the Italians rapidly developed and modernized the colony. The majority of the inhabitants of the colony viewed Italian rule as generally beneficial, as Eritrea moved into the modern world much more rapidly than feudal Ethiopia. By the early 1930s Eritrea was one of the most advanced and industrialized territories in colonial Africa.

Italian troops, based in Eritrea, again invaded Ethiopia in 1935–37, the modern weapons of the Fascist army triumphant over the poorly armed Ethiopian army. Under Italian rule, Eritrea and Ethiopia were administered as a single Italian colony, but up to World War II Eritrea remained the most developed part of Italian East Africa.

In 1941 the Italian colonial forces were defeated by invading British troops. Under British rule Eritrea was again separated from Ethiopia, which was returned to the rule of the feudal monarchy overthrown by the Italians. At the end of the war the Ethiopian government advanced historic claims to Eritrea, but British rule was formalized under a mandate from the new United Nations in 1949.

The rise of Arab nationalism in the late 1940s spurred demands for independence, particularly among the Muslim peoples of Eritrea. Various Muslim Arab states supported the Eritreans' right to independence against Ethiopia's claims to Eritrea as a "lost province."

The Allied powers—France, Great Britain, the United States, and the Soviet Union—supported various plans for the disposition of the region. Italy asked for the return of the colony as a United Nations trust, while some officials supported the partition of Eritrea into a Christian area that would be added to Ethiopia, and a Muslim area that would become part of Sudan. After long debate a plan for some sort of association with neighboring Ethiopia was approved without the consent of the Eritrean peoples.

The United Nations, in 1950, passed a resolution that created an autonomous Eritrean state in federation with Ethiopia. The resolution, vehemently opposed by the Muslim population of Eritrea and the majority of the Arab states, gave Eritrea broad autonomy as a unit of the federation of Ethiopia and Eritrea under the Ethiopian monarchy. In September 1952 the British withdrew from the territory.

Ethiopia's Emperor Haile Selassie, ignoring Eritrea's United Nations–guaranteed autonomy, installed an Ethiopian as the state's chief executive in 1955, banned Eritrea's flag, and proclaimed Amhariya, the language of Ethiopia's majority Amhara people, the only official language of the Eritrean state. In 1962 the Eritrean Assembly, to protest the abrogation of self-rule, voted itself out of existence. With United Nations approval, Ethiopia annexed the Eritrean state, eliminating the remnants of its former autonomy, on 14 November 1962. Eritrea became just another Ethiopian province.

Muslims unreconciled to Ethiopian rule formed the Eritrean Liberation Front (ELF) in 1958 and in September 1961 proclaimed an armed struggle for independence from Ethiopia. The nationalists were soon joined by Christian Eritreans disillusioned with Christian Ethiopia's harsh, corrupt, and feudal rule. Armed and supported by the Muslim states, the ELF fought the Ethiopian army to a standstill. However, by the mid-1960s the ELF had split into two factions based among the Muslim and Christian groups. Conflicts between the two groups disrupted the fight for independence and curtailed the guerrilla war launched in 1968.

In 1970 organizational and ideological friction between the Christian and

Muslim factions finally split the organization. The Christian faction formed the rival Eritrean People's Liberation Front (EPLF). The rivalry between the two groups led to fighting that by 1972 had resulted in hundreds of casualties. Though the movement was dominated by those of Christian origin at the outset, the EPLF evolved to essentially reflect the religious and ethnic diversity of Eritrea itself. Over the next decade the EPLF mostly absorbed the ELF membership, bringing Muslims into the nationalist leadership of the group.

In 1974, Emperor Selassie was overthrown by the Derg, an Ethiopian military clique of leftist orientation. Despite initial hopes to the contrary, it soon became clear to the Eritreans that the nationalistic Derg was as opposed to a sovereign Eritrea as the Emperor had been. The new junta, soon to be headed by the brutal dictator Mengistu Haile Mariam, was committed to retaining control of Eritrea's important ports, whatever the cost in human lives and money.

From 1975 the war between the Eritrean nationalists and the Ethiopian military, backed by Cuba and the Soviet Union, escalated into a brutal war of attrition. Massive government offensives drove the majority of the Eritreans underground. Homes, schools, factories, and hospitals were carved out of hillsides. Drought and famine added to the suffering, but shared hardships and a common goal united the diverse Eritrean peoples as a nation.

Periodic peace talks, under the auspices of the United Nations or regional powers, failed to reconcile the two sides. The Ethiopian government repeatedly stated that it might accept a political arrangement for Eritrea short of independence, but rejected EPLF demands for a referendum that would have independence as one of its options. By the late 1980s most of Eritrea's nationalist organizations had accepted that a political settlement was unlikely.

In February 1989, as Soviet and Cuban support of the Mengistu dictatorship began to wane, the EPLF and other Eritrean groups joined a united command with other Ethiopian ethnic groups fighting the Communist Ethiopian government. In 1990 the Eritrean nationalists captured the important port city of Massawa, beginning a string of victories that finally left the Ethiopians holding only the Eritrean capital, Asmara. The war, which had cost over 500,000 lives, including those of 40,000 civilians, and had created over 1 million refugees, was nearly over.

In mid-1991, as the Ethiopian insurgents allied to the EPLF surrounded Addis Ababa, the EPLF defeated the remnants of Mengistu's army in Eritrea and took control of Asmara. Mengistu, defeated by the rebel coalition, finally fled Ethiopia. Upon overthrowing the Derg, the Ethiopian People's Revolutionary Democratic Front (EPRDF), the EPLF's allies, stated publicly that it did not intend to stand in the way of a United Nations–sponsored referendum in Eritrea on independence. Despite the intensity of "Greater Ethiopia" nationalism in Ethiopia, Ethiopian political movements convened at a July 1991 conference endorsed the EPRDF position rather than face a renewed war with the well-armed and dug-in EPLF.

Accepted internationally as the provisional government of Eritrea, the EPLF agreed to hold a referendum on independence after a two-year period of consolidation. The EPLF-dominated government of Eritrea held a referendum in April 1993, which resulted in over 99% in favor of independence. On 24 May 1993 the Eritrean government proclaimed Eritrea an independent state. Eritrea is the first new African nation recognized by the international community to emerge from the breakup of an existing state. The recognition of Eritrea has broken the sanctity of the borders inherited from the old colonial carve-up of Africa.

The new government of Eritrea, headed by EPLF leader and now Eritrean president Issias Afewerki, faces the daunting tasks of rehabilitating a country devastated by war while keeping its nine major ethnic groups, three major religious groups, and dozens of smaller ethnic and religious groups working together in a democratic environment. The practices that enabled the EPLF to finally triumph against the Ethiopian dictatorship could undermine attempts to establish a truly representative government. Transparency and tolerance may be unthinkable during a time of emergency and war, but are indispensable to a democratic system. The government's dedication to the establishment of a truly democratic state in Eritrea will surely be tested, not least by the expectations of Eritrea's diverse peoples.

The new state also faced confrontations outside its borders. Following Eritrean independence, the neighboring state of Sudan, which supported the Eritrean rebellion against the Ethiopian government, began to support Muslim fundamentalist groups seeking to undermine the new government. The thousands of Eritrean refugees still living in Sudan have become a source of antigovernment fighters for the Sudanese-based Jihad Eritrea group. The Eritrean government, in response, has given support to the Sudanese opposition groups.

SELECTED BIBLIOGRAPHY:

Cliffe, Lionel, and Basil Davidson, eds. *The Long Struggle of Eritrea for Independence and Constructive Peace.* 1988.

Connell, Dan. *Against All Odds: A Chronicle of the Eritrean Revolution.* 1997.

Iyob, Ruth. *The Eritrean Struggle for Independence: Domination, Resistance, Nationalism, 1941–1993.* 1995.

Killion, Tom. *Historical Dictionary of Eritrea.* 1997.

Longrigg, Stephen Hemsley. *A Short History of Eritrea.* 1955.

Papstein, Robert. *Eritrea: Revolution at Dusk.* 1990.

Tekle, Amare. *Eritrea and Ethiopia: From Conflict to Cooperation.* 1994.

ESTONIA

Eesti Vabarik; Republic of Estonia

CAPITAL: Tallinn

Northeastern Europe

Estonia

POPULATION: (98e) 1,471,000 : 940,000 Estonians in Estonia. MAJOR NATIONAL GROUPS: Estonian 64.2%, Russian 28.7%, Ukrainian 2.7%, Belarussian 1.6%, Finn 1.2%, Ingrian, Latvian, Lithuanian, Tatar, Rom, Chuvash. MAJOR LANGUAGES: Estonian, Russian. MAJOR RELIGIONS: Lutheran, Orthodox, Roman Catholic, Sunni Muslim. MAJOR CITIES: (98e) Tallinn 441,000 (561,000), Tartu 108,000, Narva 79,000 (110,000), Kohtla-Järve 75,000 (145,000), Pärnu 53,000 (70,000), Viljandi 23,000, Sillamäe 22,000, Rakvere 20,000, Valga 17,000 (30,000).

GEOGRAPHY: AREA: 17,457 sq.mi.-45,226 sq.km. LOCATION: Estonia lies in northeastern Europe, bordering Russia* on the east and Latvia* on the south, and is separated from Finland on the north by the narrow Gulf of Finland. PHYSICAL GEOGRAPHY: The republic occupies a broad, flat plain, the northwestern extension of the East European Plateau. The country, which has only slight variations in elevation, has over fourteen hundred lakes and lies on the eastern shore of the Baltic Sea. In the southwest the Estonian coast is the northern shore of the Gulf of Riga. Estonia's national territory includes four large and some fifteen hundred smaller islands in the Baltic Sea. The major rivers are the Pärnu, Kasari, and Narva. ADMINISTRATIVE DIVISIONS: Fifteen counties or maakonnad (singular—maakond). POLITICAL STATUS: Estonia was recognized as an independent state in 1991.

INDEPENDENCE DECLARATIONS: 24 February 1918 (from Russia); 20 August 1991 (from the Soviet Union).

FLAG: The Estonian national flag, the official flag of the Republic of Estonia, is a horizontal tricolor of pale blue, black, and white.

PEOPLE: Estonia is inhabited by dozens of different national groups, most having settled in the republic during the Soviet era. The two major divisions of the republic's population are the Finnic peoples—the Estonians, the Finns, and the Ingrians—and the Slavs—the Russians, Ukrainians, and Belarussians. Until 1996 Estonia was losing population as Russians and others left the republic. However, an inflow of ethnic Estonians from as far away as the United States, Australia, and South America has begun to reverse the population decline.

The Estonian population includes the descendants of the Livs or Livonians, a Finnish people historically closely related to the Estonians who inhabit the southwestern part of the country and straddle the border with Latvia. The Livs have maintained their distinct cultural traditions, although their language is rapidly disappearing.

Estonian—an estimated 64.2% of the population, numbering about 940,000.

The Estonians are a Finnic people closely related to the neighboring Finns, their Finno-Ugrian language close to that of their Finnish neighbors. Physically, religiously, and socially, the Estonians are closer to the Finns and the Scandinavian peoples than to the Slav peoples to the east. The majority of the Estonians are Lutheran, with a small minority, the Setu in the southeast, belonging to the Orthodox Church.

At independence, in 1991, some 8% of the total Estonian population—about 90,000 people—lived outside the republic, mostly in adjacent areas of Russia. Since independence over 30,000 ethnic Estonians have left Russia to live in Estonia.

The Estonian language, a Finno-Ugrian language closely related to Finnish, is spoken in a number of dialects. The standard language is based on the central dialect of North Estonian, which has assimilated most of the spoken dialects. Two dialects spoken in the south, Voru and Setu, as well as the dialect spoken in the islands, differ considerably from standard Estonian.

Russian—an estimated 28.7% of the population, numbering about 420,000.

The Russian population, concentrated in Tallinn and the northeast counties, mostly settled in Estonia following the reimposition of Soviet rule after World War II. The majority are industrial workers brought in to work in the newly industrialized northwestern cities during the 1950s and 1960s.

In some cities such as Narva and Kohtla-Järve the Russian-speaking population forms a majority. In some northwestern counties Russian speakers account for 75 to 80% of the total population.

Ukrainian—an estimated 2.7% of the population, numbering about 39,000.

The Ukrainians, settled in Estonia as part of Stalin's plan to Slavicize the Baltic states, mostly live in the northwest of the country and in the bigger cities. Most of the Ukrainian population is concentrated in the Russian-speaking northeastern districts of the republic, with a smaller number living in Tallinn. The majority of the ethnic Ukrainians use Russian as their first language.

Belarussian—an estimated 1.6% of the population, numbering about 23,000.

The third largest of the Slavic national groups in Estonia, the Belarussians mostly settled in the country after World War II and live among the large Russian-speaking population in the region from Tallinn to the Russian border. All but a small minority of the Belarussians in Estonia use Russian as their first language.

Finn—an estimated 1.2% of the population, numbering about 18,000.

The Finnish population, concentrated in Tallinn, Tartu, and the northern counties, has increased since independence in 1991 as the Finns, ethnically related to the Estonians, have sought to help the new state politically and economically. Finnish professionals, many descendants of Estonian refugees in Finland, have settled in Estonia. The Finns, like the Estonians, are mostly Lutheran.

Ingrian—estimated at less than 1% of the population, numbering about 15,000.

The Ingrians, including the Izhor, the third and smallest of the Finnish peoples in Estonia, were forcibly settled in Estonia during the 1950s. The Ingrian homeland, which lies around the city of St. Petersburg, was made a national district in 1928, but was abolished in 1938.

During World War II the Ingrians were accused of anti-Soviet sentiment, particularly as the majority of the Ingrians supported Finland during the Winter War and World War II. At the end of the war, the Ingrians lost all autonomy and thousands were deported, including over 16,000 forcibly resettled in Soviet Estonia.

Tatar—estimated at less than 1% of the population, numbering about 5,000.

The Tatar population of Estonia are the descendants of the Muslim Tatar population that settled in the region during the Middle Ages. Many Tatars were scattered when the Russians overran their homeland in the sixteenth century.

Some of the Tatars came to the region as settlers, encouraged by the Russian government to settle the newly annexed region in the eighteenth century. Others were forcibly settled in the area from their homeland in eastern European Russia. The Tatars are the only sizable Muslim national group in Estonia.

Rom (Gypsy)—estimated at less than 1% of the population, numbering about 3,000.

The Rom, mostly living in the rural areas of the northeastern districts, have been in the region since the Middle Ages. Their language, called Estonian Romani, is the first language. However, the majority also speak Russian.

Divided into two major groups, Lotfítka Romá in the western districts and Lajenge Romá in eastern Estonia, the Rom are further divided into clans and families. They have often suffered discrimination and persecution. During World War II many died in the Gypsy Holocaust.

Latvian—estimated at less than 1% of the population, numbering about 2,000.

The Latvians, a Baltic people, part of the Latvian nation just to the south, mostly live in the southern counties along the border with the Republic of Latvia. The Latvians speak a Baltic language. However, many also speak Russian. The majority of the Latvians are Lutheran, with a Roman Catholic minority.

Lithuanian—estimated at less than 1% of the population, numbering about 2,000.

The Lithuanians, closely related to the Latvians, were mostly settled in Estonia during the Soviet era. Most of the ethnic Lithuanians in the region live in rural areas, in small villages in the center and south of the republic. They constitute the largest Roman Catholic minority in the country.

Chuvash—estimated at less than 1% of the population, numbering about 1,000.

The Chuvash, forcibly resettled in Estonia from their Volga basin homeland during the Soviet era, live mostly in the northwestern counties among the large Russian population. The majority of the Chuvash in Estonia speak Russian as their first language, but have tenaciously clung to their separate culture and traditions.

THE NATION: The oldest traces of human habitation have been dated to the middle of the eighth millennium B.C. Around 3000 B.C. Finno-Ugrian tribes, migrating from the east, settled in the region and absorbed the earlier inhabitants. Around the year A.D. 100 the Roman historian Tacitus mentioned the Aestii as a tribal people living in the region.

The nomadic Finno-Ugrian tribes, originating in the Volga River basin, had migrated to northeastern Europe before the Christian era. They settled a huge area, but were later pushed west to the shores of the Baltic Sea by the Slav migrations of the sixth to the eighth centuries A.D. The Finnic tribes south of the Gulf of Finland developed as two distinct peoples, the Estonians (Esths) in the north and the Livonians (Livs) in the south.

Until the twelfth century the marshes and forests along the eastern shore of the Baltic remained the homeland of the isolated Finnic tribes. At the end of the twelfth century, armed German religious expansion began to pressure the tribes. By the first years of the thirteenth century the tribes were at war with the German invaders, and were soon engaged in fighting other European powers—Danes, Russians, and Swedes.

In 1208 the crusading German knights invaded the region, their incursions resisted by the Estonians for over two decades. The Danes, under Valdemar II, conquered the northern districts and founded Tallinn. By the year 1227 the Estonians had been defeated and converted to Christianity. Estonia was divided among the Livonian Order (until 1237 the Order of the Knights of the Sword), Denmark, and the bishops of Tartu and Saare-Lääne.

The St. George's Night Uprising, which began in 1343, was the first serious Estonian attempt to throw off foreign rule. Although the rebellion was finally put down in 1345, the Danes sold their lands to the German knights of the Livonian Order in 1346.

The German knights divided Estonia into some 600 feudal manors and formed a class of landed gentry with large estates worked by Estonian peasants. By the fourteenth century the peasants were legally attached to the estates, and by the sixteenth century serfdom had developed. Of the nine towns controlled by the Germans, four became members of the Hanseatic League.

The Reformation came to Estonia from Germany in 1523. The rapid conversion of the German-populated towns increased the tensions between the German masters and their Estonian serfs, most of whom remained Roman Catholic until much later. The first book was published in the Estonian language in 1525, but was later destroyed as heretical. A decade later, in 1535, the first catechism was published in Estonian.

The Swedes took control of northern Estonia in 1558 during the Livonian War. At the dissolution of the Livonian Order in 1561 Poland annexed Livonia, although a large part of the Livonian region was taken from the Poles by Swedish king Gustavus Adolphus in 1626. In 1645 the important Estonian island of Saaremaa also came under Swedish control.

Under the less stringent rule of Sweden the power of the German aristocracy was somewhat curbed, and limited protection was extended to the Estonian serfs. In 1632 the first university was founded in Dorpat (Tartu) and some education in the Estonian language was begun. The first Estonian grammar was published in 1686.

Sweden's expansion to the east brought the Scandinavian kingdom into open conflict with the Russian Empire. The conflict culminated in the long war called the Great Northern War, which began in 1700. By the terms of the Treaty of Nystad, in 1721, Sweden ceded Estonia and Livonia to Russia.

Like the Swedes before them, the Russians allowed the German minority to retain its privileged position. German remained the language of government in Estonia and Livonia. The power of the local German aristocracy was again strengthened over the land and the rural Estonian population. By the 1740s classical serfdom was firmly in place and peasants were treated as property of the manor.

Reforms adopted by the provincial governments of Estonia and Livonia in 1816 and 1819 gradually freed the peasants from serfdom. Counties were established as the local governments, and county schools, teaching in Estonian and German, quickly raised the educational level of the peasantry. Laws passed in 1849 and 1856 ensured that a certain amount of land would be made available to the peasants, and in 1866 the manors lost control over the peasants' governing bodies. The new land laws, which enabled peasants to acquire leased land as personal holdings, marked a radical change in the social structure.

The spread of education spurred the growth of Estonian national consciousness in the mid-nineteenth century. Estonian nationalism grew as an anti-German mass movement, inspired by the near feudal subjugation by the Baltic German nobility. The publication of the Estonians' epic poem, *Kalevipoeg*, the story of their ancient and powerful hero, along with the first of the now famous folk festivals in the 1860s, accelerated the Estonian national revival in the second half of the nineteenth century.

Industrialization, particularly textile manufacture, led to the growth of urban areas and the rise of an Estonian middle class and proletariat. Tallinn, called Reval, already more than 50% Estonian in 1870, was over 70% Estonian by the end of the century. Education in Estonian expanded rapidly with urbanization.

In the last decades of the nineteenth century Russian nationalism was strengthened in order to tie the peripheral provinces to the center. Alexander III, who came to the throne of Russia in 1881, greatly reduced the feudal privileges of the Baltic German aristocracy, but he also suppressed the activities of the Estonian awakening. Russian became the language of government and education, censorship became stricter, and conversion to Russian Orthodoxy was encouraged.

The policy of Russification ended in 1897, and the Estonian national movement gained strength. A new generation of educated, urbanized Estonians quickly restored the nationalist ideals. In 1904 Estonians for the first time gained control of a major city by constituting a majority in the municipal council of Tallinn.

The activism of the 1905 Russian Revolution accelerated the spread of nationalist ideas. Following the suppression of the revolution, reforms were introduced that allowed legal political opposition and trade unions. Estonian culture flourished and Estonian-language education became widespread. In 1909 the Estonian National Museum was founded.

Nationalist sentiment spread rapidly following the outbreak of war in 1914. The aspiration of autonomy within a more democratic Russia disposed most Estonians to support the revolution that overthrew the tsar in February 1917. Granted autonomy in April, the Estonians were still organizing when they lost control of the region to Workers' and Soldiers' Soviets following the Bolshevik takeover in nearby Petrograd in October 1917. The nationalists, in an attempt to gain support, declared Estonia independent of Soviet Russia on 17 November 1917, but were forced underground by troops of the Bolsheviks' Red Army.

In February 1918, the peace talks between Soviet Russia and Germany broke down. The Russian forces and the Bolsheviks who controlled Estonia fled as the German forces again advanced. Aided by a British naval squadron in the Baltic Sea, the Estonian nationalists emerged to defeat the remaining Bolsheviks, and again declared Estonia independent on 24 February 1918. The new state, recognized by the major world powers in May 1918, was quickly overrun and a German military government established.

An Estonian provisional government assumed control following the collapse of Germany in November 1918. The Soviet government, to conceal its attempt to regain the territory, established a Workers' Commune in Narva, and by the beginning of 1919 two-thirds of Estonia was under Soviet control. Aided by the presence of a British fleet in the Baltic and by volunteers from Finland and Scandinavia, the Estonians counterattacked and in a three-week campaign drove most of the Soviet forces from the country. In June and July 1919 the Estonians were successful against a Baltic German force that attempted to seize control of the state. In the autumn of 1919 the overextended Soviet forces were finally defeated. On 2 February 1920 the Tartu Peace Treaty was signed and the Soviet government recognized the Republic of Estonia.

During the 1920s right-wing political parties gained strength at the expense of the centrists. The illegal Estonian Communist Party attempted a coup on 1 December 1924, aided by the Soviet government. Following the failure of the coup, the Communist movement lost support as the more reactionary parties gained. In spite of the political uncertainties, Estonia prospered, and its standard of living soon equalled that of prosperous Finland.

The small republic attempted to steer a course between its powerful Soviet neighbor and a resurgent Nazi Germany in the 1930s. With the country destabilized by the worldwide depression, authoritarian rule was instituted. The Estonian orientation toward Great Britain changed in 1935 when a maritime treaty between the British and Nazi Germany placed the Baltic Sea in the German sphere of influence. Isolated from the West, the Estonians turned to Germany to offset Soviet pressure. However, in December 1938 the Estonian government declared Estonia a neutral state.

A secret protocol, the Molotov-Ribbentrop Pact, signed by Nazi Germany and the Stalinist government of the Soviet Union in August 1939, divided Europe into Fascist and Communist spheres of influence. Estonia, along with the neighboring Baltic republics, was assigned to the Soviet sphere. After months of increasing tensions, Soviet troops massed on Estonia's eastern border, their presence a forceful argument to back the Soviet demand for a more compliant Estonian government. Estonia was unable to resist the overwhelming Soviet military threat, and a pro-Soviet regime was installed in Tallinn. The new regime formally requested admission to the Soviet Union on 6 June 1940.

The Red Army quickly occupied the tiny republic and deported to Siberia and Central Asia over 70,000 Estonians deemed anti-Communist or anti-Stalin. On one night, that of 14–15 June 1941, over 60,000 Estonians were deported. Further deportations were precluded by the Nazi invasion of its Soviet ally on 22 June.

Estonia was overrun by the advancing Nazi forces on 5 July 1941. Many Estonians saw the Nazis as liberators. The Germans conscripted 45,000 Estonian soldiers, while many more volunteered, eager to avenge the Red Terror of 1940–41. The German population of Estonia, 1.5% of the total in 1939, was evacuated to Germany.

Although many Estonians supported Germany's drive against the hated Soviets, their hopes that Germany would support the restoration of the Estonian republic were quickly dimmed. Estonia became part of the Ostland province of the Reich. Anti-Semitic Estonians found employment in the Nazi concentration camps and in special units. Estonians who had fled to Finland joined the Finnish forces fighting the Soviets in Karelia.

In February 1944 the Red Army again posed a threat to German-occupied Estonia. Over 40,000 Estonians joined the army in a general mobilization, and together with the Germans, stopped the Soviet forces at the Narva River in northeastern Estonia. In August the Red Army invaded southern Estonia, driving the Estonian and German forces before it. On 18 September an Estonian provisional government was appointed and appeals were sent to the Allies. The Soviets reached Tallinn on 22 September, and by the end of November the country was again under firm Soviet rule. Over 70,000 Estonians fled, mainly to Germany and Sweden. In all some 100,000 Estonians reached the West before the Soviets closed the escape routes.

Between 1945 and 1949 another 80,000 Estonians were deported, including most farmers, breaking the Estonian resistance to Soviet collectivization. The Soviets replaced the 350,000 Estonians killed, fled, or deported since 1939 with ethnic Russians. The republic's Estonian population fell from 94% of the total in 1945 to just 72% in 1953.

Thousands of Estonians formed resistance groups in the forests to fight the Soviet occupation. Called the Forest Brethren, from 1944 to 1956, when the last of the groups were finally exterminated, they harassed the Soviet military and government, employing sabotage and raids on military targets. The groups, aided by their supporters and families in the villages and towns, while not a military threat to the Soviet occupation, were a direct challenge to Soviet propaganda about the brotherhood of Socialist nations.

The limited liberalization of Soviet life following Stalin's death in 1953 aided the economic growth of Estonia even though the Russian minority in the republic retained ultimate control. Light industry and advances in agriculture gave the tiny republic one of the highest standards of living in the Soviet Union, although still dismal in comparison to neighboring Finland. Those deportees who had survived were allowed to return from exile, and more Estonians were taken into the Communist hierarchy in the republic. The first contacts with Estonian exile groups were established, and traveling was allowed to a limited extent.

In the 1960s the Estonians achieved the highest standard of living in the Soviet Union. Called Soviet Scandinavia, Estonia led the Soviet Union in per-capita income, but the continuing Slavic influx and the suppression of their culture rekindled Estonian nationalism, which had the strong support of the large ethnic Estonian populations in Europe and North America. The economic achievements paled as the Soviet stagnation spread, and by the mid-1980s there were increasing shortages of food, industrial goods, and services.

Nationalism grew rapidly in the more liberal atmosphere introduced into the Soviet Union by Mikhail Gorbachev in 1987. The Estonian Popular Front, the first large political organization in the Soviet Union outside the Communist Party, was formed in Estonia on 13 April 1988. The unprecedented political activity during the summer of 1988 extended to all areas of Estonian life. Compromised politicians were forced to resign, and Estonian demands for autonomy, even independence, began to be voiced in public demonstrations.

Pressured by the mass nationalist movement, the Estonian Supreme Soviet passed a sovereignty declaration on 16 November 1988 that acknowledged the supremacy of Estonian laws within the republic. Between 1989 and 1991 a free press was established, political parties formed, and free elections were organized.

The idea that Estonia had never voluntarily joined the Soviet Union, and therefore could restore its sovereignty under international law, became widespread. The national movement galvanized all segments of society. On 24 December 1989 the Soviet government declared invalid the secret protocols of the Hitler-Stalin pact that had led to the Soviet takeover of Estonia. On 11 March 1990 the Congress of Estonia, representing all registered citizens of the Republic of Estonia, convened. On 30 March the new Supreme Council declared Soviet power to be illegal in Estonia and proclaimed a transition period for the restoration of the independent republic. On 8 May the symbols of the Estonian Soviet Socialist Republic were abolished, the Estonian national flag was made the flag of the republic, and the official name, the Republic of Estonia, was restored.

In January 1991 the Soviet government attempted to reassert control, but was opposed by the new Estonian government. In a referendum on 3 March 1991, 77.8% of the population, including about a third of the immigrant Slav population, supported the restoration of Estonian independence.

In the wake of the 19 August 1991 coup against Mikhail Gorbachev in the USSR, the Estonian government moved to sever all ties to the Soviet government. On 20 August the Supreme Council passed a resolution on national independence and appealed for international recognition. Boris Yeltsin, the president of the Russian Federation, acknowledged the independent republic on 24 August, setting the stage for the rapid disintegration of the multiethnic Soviet empire.

Independent Estonia has sucessfully reoriented its trade toward the West, with two-thirds now going to Western markets. The government's free trade policies and democratic institutions have pushed Estonia to the front of the line of countries seeking entry to the big Western clubs, the North Atlantic Treaty Organization (NATO) and the European Union (EU). In July 1997 Estonia was among the small group of former Communist states named by the European Union as prospective new members in the first expansion of the economic and political union into central and eastern Europe.

Estonia's large Russian population remains an obstacle to better relations with its huge neighbor to the east. In September 1997 leading Russian politicians reiterated their dissatisfaction with Estonia's citizenship laws and demanded that all inhabitants of the republic resident in 1991 be granted Estonian citizenship.

SELECTED BIBLIOGRAPHY:

Hiden, John, and Patrick Salmon. *The Baltic Nations and Europe: Estonia, Latvia and Lithuania in the Twentieth Century.* 1995.

Lieven, Anatol. *The Baltic Revolution: Estonia, Latvia, Lithuania and the Path to Independence.* 1994.

Raun, Toivo U. *Estonia and the Estonians.* 1991.

Smith, Graham, ed. *The Baltic States: The National Self-Determination of Estonia, Latvia and Lithuania.* 1994.

Taagepera, Rein. *Estonia: Return to Independence.* 1993.

ETHIOPIA

Federal Democratic Republic of
Ethiopia; Ye Etiyop'iya
Dimokrasiyawi Republek; Ityop'iya

CAPITAL: Addis Ababa

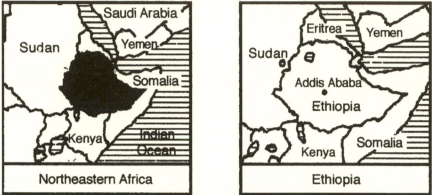

Northeastern Africa

Ethiopia

POPULATION: (98e) 57,700,000. MAJOR NATIONAL GROUPS: Oromo
(Galla) 28%, Amhara 24%, Tigrean (Tigrinya) 10%, Sidamo 9%, Somali 6%,
Wolyatta 4%, Gurage 3%, Aari (Shankilla) 2%, Agau (Agaw) 2%, Hadiyya 2%,
Kambaata 2%, Gedeo (Darassa) 1%, Kaffa, Yemma, Afar, Gamo, Bedawie,
Komso, Dawro, Libido, Alaba, Bench, Basketto, Melo, Bambala (Burji), Shak-
acho (Mocha), Xamir. MAJOR LANGUAGES: Amharic (Amharinya), Afaan
Oromo (Orominga), Tigrinya, Guaraginga, Somali, Arabic, English. MAJOR
RELIGIONS: Ethiopian Orthodox 40–45%, Muslim 40–45%, animist 10–20%,
other Christian 1%. MAJOR CITIES: (98e) Addis Ababa 3,515,000, Dire Dawa
214,000, Gonder 173,000, Nazret 155,000, Harar (Harer) 126,000 (175,000),
Jima 125,000, Dese 123,000, Debre Zeyit 118,000, Bahir Dar 100,000, Mekele
110,000, Asela 100,000, Awassa 100,000.

GEOGRAPHY: AREA: 426,002 sq.mi.-1,103,341 sq.km. LOCATION: Ethiopia is a landlocked country located in the Horn of Africa in the northeastern
part of the continent. Ethiopia is bound by Sudan to the west and northwest,
Kenya to the south, Somalia to the east and southeast, Djibouti to the east, and
Eritrea* to the northeast. PHYSICAL GEOGRAPHY: The country consists of
high, rugged mountains and isolated valleys. The Ethiopian Plateau, which occupies 66% of the land, consists of a central plateau bisected diagonally by the
Great Rift Valley to the west and the Somali Plateau to the east. The central
plateau also has a number of mountain ranges including the Chercher, Aranna,
and Chelalo. The Somali Plateau to the southeast is a flat, arid semidesert region.
The Great Rift Valley is occupied by a number of lakes in the high valleys. In

the northern and eastern parts of the country, the regions are relatively low-lying. The Danakil Depression in the northeast dips to 361 feet (116 meters) below sea level and is said to be the hottest place on the earth. In the northwest, in the highlands around Lake Tana, lies the source of the Nile River. The area, containing some of the highest regions in Africa, is known as the Amhara Highlands. ADMINISTRATIVE DIVISIONS: Nine ethnically based administrative regions or astedader akababiwach (singular—astedader akababi) and the federal capital of Addis Ababa. The Ethiopian government plans to make the nine regions into member states in the Ethiopian federation. POLITICAL STATUS: Traditionally, Ethiopia is the oldest sovereign country in Africa and one of the oldest in the world, dating back at least 2,000 years. The new, landlocked federal republic was recognized as an independent state in 1993.

INDEPENDENCE DECLARATION: 24 May 1993.

FLAG: Three equal horizontal bands of green (top), yellow, and red with a yellow pentagram and single yellow rays emanating from the angles between the points on a light blue disk centered on the three bands.

PEOPLE: Ethiopia is inhabited by over seventy different national groups. The largest are the Hamitic Oromo, and the Semitic Amhara and Tigreans, who inhabit the core regions of the high Ethiopian Plateau. At least 82 major languages are spoken in Ethiopia, along with some 200 dialects. The national language is Amharic. The population of the country includes 175,000 refugees, called Juba Somalis, who speak a Sudanese Arabic dialect and mainly live in refugee camps along the Sudanese border. Refugees are not included as official residents of Ethiopia.

The traditionally dominant religion of Ethiopia, called Ethiopian Orthodoxy, is a curious amalgam of Judaic and Christian practices and African and European religious rituals. The religion is manifestly a man's religion and only males may enter the inner sanctuary where, by tradition, Moses' Ark is hidden.

Oromo—an estimated 28% of the population, numbering about 16 million.

The Oromo, called Galla by others, are a Hamitic pastoral people related to the neighboring Somali. Some Oromo and experts in the field claim that the Oromo of Ethiopia may account for as much as 50–60% of the total population of the republic.

The Oromo have never organized in a state structure, and until the 1960s the clan system dominated Oromo life. They are broadly divided into the Southern, Eastern, and West-Central groups, made up of numerous clans and subclans. The name Galla is considered a derogatory term.

Migrating from the south, the Oromo tribes adopted the religions of the peoples they encountered; some became Muslim or Christian, while other clans retained their traditional beliefs. The clans, although divided religiously, are united by culture and kinship ties. The Oromo are estimated to be 40% Muslim, 40% animist, and 20% Christian, mostly Ethiopian Orthodox, although some evangelical sects have been gaining converts since the overthrow of the Communist dictatorship.

The Oromo peoples speak several dialects of Afaan Oromo, also called Gallinya, which is an East Cushitic language of the Afro-Asiatic language family. The language, with dozens of dialects, is spoken over a broad area of southern Ethiopia. In 1994 the Latin alphabet was adopted for use with the Oromo dialects. Many Oromo speak Amharic as a second language.

The Oromo peoples are thought to have originated in present northern Somalia, migrating to the region of Lake Rudolph in the late fifteenth or early sixteenth century. The Oromo expansion was in search of grazing lands. It was not a political movement, as the Oromo, united only by kinship and culture, migrated in independent clans. In a series of migrations from about 1550 to 1670 the Oromo occupied the rich agricultural eastern provinces of Ethiopia as far north as Harar, and into the highlands, soon coming into conflict with the Christian Amhara kingdom.

The Oromo clans that settled in the east became the Wallo Oromo, and later accepted Islam. Other Oromo groups moved into the central highlands, particularly the Mecha and Tulema, who accepted many Amhara cultural traits and mixed with the Semitic Amhara. In the south the Boran (Borana) and Bartumma settled in the less populated, drier regions. The Oromo legends tell of five fathers who established themselves in the five regions where the clans remain today.

Amhara—an estimated 24% of the population, numbering about 14 million.

The Amhara are a Semitic people descended from early Semites who migrated to the region from the Arabian Peninsula around 700 B.C. Over the centuries the Amhara have absorbed conquered peoples. The present Amhara are of mixed Semitic, Hamitic, and Black African background.

Amhara means "Mountain People" in the Amhara language, Amharinya, a Semitic language with its own distinctive script that is very complex. Estimates of the number of letters in the Amharinya alphabet vary between 247 and 259. The language is widely spoken outside the Amhara homeland and is the official language of the country.

Since the early 1990s ethnic tensions have again become serious in several areas. Amharas have charged that they have been stigmatized as *neftegna*, settlers, in regions where they have lived for centuries. Clashes between Amharas and other ethnic groups have increased since the division of the country into ethnic-based regions.

Tigrean (Tigrinya)—an estimated 10% of the population, numbering about 6 million.

The Tigreans, called Tigrinya, are a Semitic people related to the Amhara. Inhabiting the northern part of the Ethiopian Plateau, the Tigreans live on both sides of the frontier that was established between the new states of Eritrea and Ethiopia in 1993. Descendants of ancient migrants from the Arabian Peninsula, the Tigrinya separated from the Amhara and other Semitic peoples in ancient times.

The Tigrean language, Tigrinya or Tigrigna, is a Semitic language related to Amhara, a South Ethiopian language of the Afro-Asiatic language group. Tigrinya is considered the closest of all the Semitic languages spoken in northeastern Africa to old Ethiopian as spoken until the fourteenth century.

Considered the closest both ethnically and linguistically to the original Semitic settlers, the Tigreans have intermarried with other peoples less frequently than the Amhara and other Semitic peoples. Their culture retains many aspects of Middle Eastern cultures.

A minority, called the Jabarti, are ethnic Tigreans converted to Islam in the eighteenth century. The Jabarti have traditionally formed a trading class and have maintained Tigrean contacts with neighboring Muslim peoples.

Sidamo (Sidama)—an estimated 9% of the population, numbering about 5 million.

The Sidamo or Sidama are a Hamitic people inhabiting the highlands in the eastern part of the Great Rift Valley and the valley lowlands around a long string of lakes. The Sidamo heartland lies northeast of Lake Abaya and southeast of Lake Awasa.

The language of the Sidama, Sidaminya, is an East Cushitic language of the Hamitic group of Afro-Asiatic languages. The language has the status of an official literary language in Ethiopia.

Somali—an estimated 6% of the population, numbering about 3,500,000.

The ethnic Somali inhabiting the Ogaden region of Ethiopia constitute the Western Somali clans of mixed Somali and Oromo background. The most important of the clans are the Darod and the Harari around the city of Harer, the Dir around Dire Dawa, the Issa, Issak, and Gadabursi in the north, the Ogadeni in the south and southeast, and the Dolbahuna and Hawiye in the east.

The Western Somali clans speak Somali, an East Cushitic language of the Hamitic language group of the Afro-Asiatic languages. The Western Somali dialects are written in the Ethiopian alphabet, not in the Arabic used by the other Somali peoples.

The Western Somali clans are mostly herdsmen in the vast Ogaden Desert. Violent clan conflicts over water and grazing rights are common in the region. Many of the clans and subclans are nomadic or seminomadic, often moving across the international borders that divide the Somali peoples among Somalia, Ethiopia, Djibouti, and Kenya.

Wolaytta—an estimated 4% of the population, numbering about 3 million.

The Wolyatta are a Hamitic people inhabiting the part of the Great Rift Valley around Lake Abaya. The Wolyatta language, also called Wellamo or Ometo, is a North Omotic language of the Hamitic languages of the Afro-Asiatic group.

The majority of the Wolaytta continue to adhere to traditional beliefs, with a Christian, mostly Ethiopian Orthodox, minority. The rural population often professes Christianity, but mix Christian rituals with traditional beliefs.

Gurage—an estimated 3% of the population, numbering about 1,700,000.

The Gurage inhabit the upper Great Rift Valley just southwest of the Ethiopian capital, Addis Ababa. The Gurage are roughly divided into the East Gurage or Silti; the North Gurage, Kistane, or Soddo; and the West Gurage, also called Guragie or Gurague.

The Gurage peoples speak Semitic, South Ethiopian languages of the Afro-Asiatic language group. The languages, spoken in many different dialects, have diverged greatly and are not mutually intelligible. In the more accessible parts of the Gurage lands, Amharic is used as a lingua franca. However, away from the more traveled sectors very few Gurage are bilingual. The majority of the Gurage are Christian, mostly Ethiopian Orthodox, with an animist minority that has retained their traditional beliefs.

Aari (Shankilla)—an estimated 2% of the population, numbering about 1 million.

The Aari are a Hamitic people inhabiting the southern part of the Great Rift Valley in southwestern Ethiopia at the southern tip of the Ethiopian Plateau. The majority of the Aari are agriculturists and traders in the foothill regions east of the Rift Valley lakes.

The Aari speak an Omotic language of the Hamitic group of Afro-Asiatic languages. The language, spoken as the first language by 95% of the Aari population, is related to the language of the neighboring Wolaytta people. The Aari people and their language are often called Shankilla by outsiders, but the Aari consider Shankilla a derogatory term. The Aari are mostly Christian, belonging to the Ethiopian Orthodox Church. A minority in the eastern highlands has retained traditional animist beliefs.

Agaw (Agau)—an estimated 2% of the population, numbering about 1 million.

The Agaw or Awngi, also called Agau, are a Hamitic people living in several distinct areas of northern Ethiopia. The main divisions are the Agaw and the Western Agaw. The Agaw inhabit widely scattered parts of the Amhara Highlands southwest of Lake Tana. The Western Agaw, also called Qimant, live in the northwestern Amhara Region, north of Lake Tana, with several communities near Addis Ababa further south. A division of the Agaw, called Falashi or Falasha, are the Black Jews, most of whom immigrated to Israel in a widely publicized airlift mounted to save the Jews during the excesses of the Communist regime.

The Agaw speak a Cushitic language of the Hamitic group of Afro-Asiatic languages. The language, spoken in a number of separate dialects, is gradually giving way to Amharic. Only about a third of the Western Agaw use it as their first language, and the majority are bilingual, while 80% to 90% of the Agaw speakers use Amharic as their second language. The majority of the Agaw peoples are Ethiopian Orthodox, with a very small minority of the Falasha who remain in Ethiopia, adhering to an archaic form of Judaism.

Hadiyya—an estimated 2% of the population, numbering about 1 million.

The Hadiyya or Hadiya are a Hamitic people living in the southern Ethiopian Plateau southwest of Addis Ababa. The Hadiyya, mostly highland farmers, inhabit the region between the Omo and Billate Rivers centered on the town of Hosaina. The Hadiyya are often called Gudella by outsiders, a name they consider derogatory.

The Christian Hadiyya speak an East Cushitic language of the Hamitic group of Afro-Asiatic languages with two major and several minor dialects. The language is an official literary language of the Gurage, Kambaata, Hadiyya Region.

Kambaata—an estimated 2% of the population, numbering about 1 million.

The Kambaata, also Kambatta or Kambata, are a Hamitic highland people inhabiting part of the Ethiopian Plateau west of the Rift Valley lakes around the town of Durame. Their language, an East Cushitic language of the Hamitic group of Afro-Asiatic languages, is spoken in several distinct dialects. The majority of the Kambaata are Christians, mostly belonging to the Ethiopian Orthodox Church, but a minority are Sunni Muslims.

Gedeo (Darassa)—an estimated 1% of the population, numbering about 600,000.

The Gedeo, also called Darassa, are a Hamitic people living in the highlands of the Ethiopian Plateau east of Lake Abaya and southwest of the town of Dilla. The Gedeo speak an East Cushitic language of the Hamitic group of Afro-Asian languages. The Gedeo are divided into two major groups based on their religion, Ethiopian Orthodox or Sunni Muslim.

Kaffa—estimated at less than 1% of the population, numbering about 500,000.

The Kaffa or Kafa are a Hamitic people inhabiting the southwestern reaches of the Ethiopian Plateau south of the city of Jimma and around the town of Bonga. The majority of the Kaffa are agriculturists, both the Christian majority and the Muslim minority.

The Kaffa speak a North Omotic language, Kaficho, of the Hamitic group of Afro-Asiatic languages. The language has official status in the Kaffa Region along the international border with Sudan.

Yemma—estimated at less than 1% of the population, numbering about 500,000.

The Yemma are a Hamitic people inhabiting the highlands west of the Great Rift Valley in southwestern Ethiopia. Their homeland lies northeast of the city of Jimma and forms a separate district within the Oromo Region.

Their language, called Yemsa, belongs to the North Omotic branch of the Hamitic languages and has absorbed many Oromo words and forms. Many older Yemma are bilingual in Oromo. However, younger Yemsa prefer to learn Amharic. The Yemma are often called Janjero, a derogatory term. The Yemma are traditionally Christians, belonging to the Ethiopian Orthodox Church. In recent years Evangelical sects have made some inroads in the region.

Afar—estimated at less than 1% of the population, numbering about 500,000.

The Afar, of mixed Semitic, Hamitic, and Arabic ancestry, are a mostly nomadic people who inhabit the Afar Region in the northeast along the borders with Eritrea and Djibouti, which also have large Afar populations. The Afar are closely related to the smaller Saho people, considered by some a branch of the Afar nation. The Afar language is an East Cushitic language of the Hamitic group of Hamito-Semitic languages that has been considerably altered by exposure to Arabic. The name Danakil or Denakil, as some call the Afar, is considered an offensive term by the Afars.

The Muslim Afar, some inhabiting the hottest and lowest part of the earth in the Danakil Depression, are divided into tribes, subtribes, and clans and are also identified by a class system that segregates the population into two distinct divisions, the Asimara (Red) nobles, and the Adoimara (White) commoners.

Afar nationalism could become a serious problem for the new Ethiopian government. Following Eritrean independence in 1993 some Afar leaders denounced the move as a further partitioning of their nation between the region's independent states.

Gamo—estimated at less than 1% of the population, numbering about 450,000.

The Gamo are a Hamitic people living in the mountainous highlands of the Ethiopian Plateau just west of Lake Abaya. Their cultural center and major city, Abra Minch, lies at the southern tip of the lake. The Gamo are closely related to the neighboring Gofa and Dawro peoples.

The Gamo speak a North Omotic language of the Hamitic group of languages; it is intelligible to speakers of Gofa and Dawro and to the Wolayttas. The majority of the Gamo are Christian, with an animist minority.

Bedawie (Beja)—estimated at less than 1% of the population, numbering about 300,000.

The Bedawie, also called Beja, Hidareb, or Beni-Amer, are mostly nomads in the northwest border regions. The Muslim Bedawie speak a Cushitic language that is also spoken in Sudan and southern Egypt. A minority, called Lobat, have adopted the Tigré language.

Moving with their herds of cattle and goats, the Bedawie tended to ignore international borders until more stringent controls were put in place during the 1960s. Traditionally, Bedawie herdsmen wandered as far north as Egypt.

Komso—estimated at less than 1% of the population, numbering about 200,000.

The Komso live in the highlands in the southern reaches of the Ethiopian Plateau south of Lake Ciamo. The region, covered in deciduous forests, slopes down to the lowlands south of the plateau, but is intensely farmed by the Komso agriculturists. The Komso speak an East Cushitic language of the Hamitic language group. A few Komso live across the border in Kenya. The majority of the Komso adhere to traditional religions.

Dawro—estimated at less than 1% of the population, numbering about 175,000.

The Dawro, also called Dauro or Kullo, are a Hamitic people closely related to the Gamo and Gofa peoples. The Dawro inhabit the mountains west of Lake Abaya and the lowlands around the town of Arbra Minch.

The Dawro language is a North Omotic language of the Hamitic group of languages that is intelligible to Gofa and Gamo speakers. The government is developing educational materials jointly for the three closely related groups.

Gofa—estimated at less than 1% of the population, numbering about 160,000.

The Gofa are the smallest of the three related peoples living in the mountainous region west of Lake Abaya. The larger groups, the Gamo and Dawro, along with the Gofa, share many cultural traits and customs. The majority of the Gofa are Christian, with an animist minority.

The Gofa speak a North Omotic language of the Hamitic group of Afro-Asiatic languages that is intelligible to speakers of Gamo and Dawro, although their language is closer to Gamo than to Dawro.

Libido—estimated at less than 1% of the population, numbering about 120,000.

The Libido, also called Marako, inhabit the highlands of the Ethiopian Plateau in the region southwest of Addis Ababa and northeast of the town of Hosaina in an area inhabited by a number of related peoples, Hadiyya, Kambaata, and Allaba. The majority of the Libido are Sunni Muslims.

The Libido language is an East Cushitic language of the Hamitic group of Afro-Asiatic languages and is partially intelligible to speakers of neighboring Cushitic languages. The closest of the languages to spoken Libido is Hadiyya.

Basketto—estimated at less than 1% of the population, numbering about 100,000.

The Basketto, also known as Baskatta or Mesketo, inhabit a high plateau region in the southern reaches of the Ethiopian Highlands west of the Great Rift Valley. The majority of the Basketto are Christians, most belonging to the Ethiopian Orthodox Church, but with a substantial minority adhering to various Protestant sects. The language of the Basketto is a North Omotic language of the Hamitic group of languages. Most of the Basketto are monolingual, with only a few able to speak Wolaytta or Amharic.

Alaba—estimated at less than 1% of the population, numbering about 90,000.

The Alaba or Halaba live in the Rift Valley southwest of Lake Shala and south of the town of Hosaina. They are closely related to the Kambaata people, with whom they share many cultural traits and traditions. The Alaba are about 60% Muslim and 40% Christian, mostly Ethiopian Orthodox. The Alaba language, an East Cushitic language of the Hamitic language group, can be understood by speakers of Kambaata and speakers of other related languages in the region.

Bench—estimated at less than 1% of the population, numbering about 85,000.

The Bench, also called Gimira or Ghimarra, live in the southern Kafa Region close to the Sudanese border. The Bench homeland extends from Sudan through the forests and savanna around the towns of Mizan Teferi and Shewa Gimira. The majority of the Bench adhere to traditional beliefs, with a Christian minority, mostly in the towns and along the main roads.

The Bench language is a North Omotic language of the Hamitic group of Afro-Asiatic languages and is spoken in three separate dialects. About 10% of the Bench speak some Amharic.

Melo—estimated at less than 1% of the population, numbering about 80,000.

The Melo or Malo people live in the north Omo Region, in and around the town of Malo-Koza, in the highlands west of the Great Rift Valley. The majority of the Melo are Christians, mostly Ethiopian Orthodox. Their language is a

North Omotic language of the Hamitic group of Afro-Asiatic languages that is related to the Gamo-Gofa-Dawro group, but is not inherently intelligible.

Bambala (Burji)—estimated at less than 1% of the population, numbering about 80,000.

The Bambala or Burji, also called Dashi, inhabit the foothills and lowlands along the Kenyan border in southern Ethiopia south of Lake Ciamo. The majority are Christian, but there is a large and important Muslim minority. There is a Bambala population of some 10,000 across the border in Kenya.

The Bambala language is an East Cushitic language of the Hamitic language group and is believed to be related to Sidamo.

Shakacho (Mocha)—estimated at less than 1% of the population, numbering about 80,000.

The Shakacho, called Mocha by others, are a Hamitic people living in the north Kafa Region of southern Ethiopia around the town of Maasha. They are believed to be closely related to the larger Kafa tribe living in the same region. They call themselves Shakacho; however, most outsiders refer to the tribe as Mocha. The majority adhere to traditional beliefs, while a minority has adopted Christianity.

The language spoken by the Shakacho is a North Omotic language of the Hamitic group closely related to Kaficho, the language of the Kafa people. Most Shakacho are illiterate, with only a few officials able to read and write.

Xamir—estimated at less than 1% of the population, numbering about 75,000.

The Xamir, also called Xamtanga or Khamtanga, are a Hamitic people living in the northern districts of Amhara Region in the highlands at the edge of the Danakil Depression near the border of Tigray Region. The region suffered greatly during the war against the Communist dictatorship.

The Xamir language, most often called Xamtanga, is a Central Cushitic language of the Hamitic language group. The Xamir, surrounded by Semitic speakers of the Amhara and Tigrinya peoples, are often bilingual, and Amharic is used as a second language. The majority of the Xamir are Orthodox Christians.

Gawwada (Kawwada)—estimated at less than 1% of the population, numbering about 75,000.

The Gawwada or Kawwada inhabit the southern mountains of the Ethiopian Plateau in Omo Region, west of Lake Chamo. Most are peasant farmers on the rugged mountain slopes in an area of deciduous forests. The tribe includes a number of smaller subtribes, the Dihina, Geregere, Gollango, Gorose, and Harso.

The language of the Gawwada, an East Cushitic language of the Hamitic language group, is spoken in six major dialects and several subdialects. Most of the tribal leaders use Amharic, Oromo, or Komso as second languages for communicating with outsiders.

Gumuz (Shanquilla)—estimated at less than 1% of the population, numbering about 70,000.

The Gumuz, also called Gombo or Shanquilla, live in the region along the Sudanese border in northern Ethiopia. Their homeland, in the highlands west of

Lake Tana, straddles the international border, with an estimated 50,000 Gumuz living in Sudan. The Gumuz speak a Nilo-Saharan language with several major dialects. The majority of the Gumuz follow traditional religions, with Muslim and Christian minorities.

Me'en—estimated at less than 1% of the population, numbering about 60,000.

The Me'en live in southern Ethiopia in the central Kafa Region. Their homeland lies in the transition region from the highlands down to the lowlands along the Omo River. In the highlands the Tishena clans are mostly settled agriculturists. In the lowlands the Bodi clans are mostly nomadic herders.

The language of the Me'en is an Eastern Sudanic language of the Nilo-Saharan language group. Two major dialects, Bodi and Tishena, are spoken in the lowlands and highlands, respectively.

Hausa—estimated at less than 1% of the population, numbering about 55,000.

The Hausa of Ethiopia are part of a much larger Hausa population living mostly in the West African nations of Nigeria and Niger. The majority of the Hausa live in the major urban areas, particularly Addis Ababa. The Hausa language, a Niger-Congo language, is the lingua franca of much of West Africa, spoken or understood by over 40 million people.

Nuer (Naath)—estimated at less than 1% of the population, numbering about 50,000.

The Nuer or Naath live in the Gambela Region in southeastern Ethiopia. Their homeland, lying mostly in Sudan, forms part of the lowlands west of the Ethiopian Plateau. Only a minority of the Nuer live in Ethiopia. The majority, perhaps up to 1 million, live in adjacent areas of Sudan. The area has been badly disrupted by fighting in both Sudan and Ethiopia, and many Nuer refugees from Sudan live in Ethiopia. Naath is the name they use for themselves.

The Nuer speak an Eastern Sudanic language of the Nilo-Saharan language group. Their language is part of a large group of languages spoken across southern Sudan and west into Chad and the Central African Republic. The majority adhere to traditional beliefs in Ethiopia. However, in Sudan a substantial number of Nuer are Christians.

Harari (Adare)—estimated at less than 1% of the population, numbering about 50,000.

The Harari, also called Adare or Gesinan, are an ancient people, originally the inhabitants of the city of Harar in eastern Ethiopia. The majority still inhabit the town's old walled city, but large communities are also found in Addis Ababa, Nazaret, and Dire Dawa. The majority cling to traditional beliefs, with a large and influential Orthodox minority.

The Harari language, a Semitic South Ethiopian language, has a long literary tradition and is considered a language of prestige. The Harari have a higher rate of literacy than is the norm in Ethiopia.

THE NATION: In the first millennium B.C. the Sabeans of southern Arabia created a flourishing civilization. In the first and second centuries A.D. migrants from the Sabean homeland in Arabia crossed the narrow Red Sea to settle present-day northern Ethiopia. The Semitic peoples, led by Menelik, tradition-ally the son of the Hebrew King Solomon and the Queen of Sheba, according to Ethiopian legend brought the Ark of the Covenant to Ethiopia. The migrants settled the region of the Ethiopian Plateau, a region sparsely inhabited by Ha-mitic peoples.

The Semitic migrants created a new civilization in the highlands centered on Aksum in the present Tigrean homeland. The Aksumite Empire controlled the northern part of present Ethiopia from the first to the eighth centuries.

The ruler of Aksum was converted to Christianity by a Syrian, Frumentius, called Abba Salama by the Aksumites, traditionally in the year A.D. 330. Abba Salama is acknowledged as the founder of the Ethiopian church. Around A.D. 475 the Aksumites, along with the Egyptian Copts, broke with Rome.

Isolated from the rest of the Christian world by the Muslim conquest of the lands surrounding the Ethiopian Highlands in 675, the Semitic peoples of the highlands gradually split into two main branches, the Tigreans and the Amhara, and several smaller groups. In the eighth century the Christian Semitic peoples were defeated by the Bedawie moving into the highlands from the north, and by the Afar from the east. The empire split into a number of small states, and the center of Christian Ethiopia shifted away from the Tigreans of Aksum to the Amhara homeland further south.

The energetic Ethiopians, protected by mountainous terrain, soon recovered and began to spread from their highland homelands into many regions, where they mixed with the Oromo and other peoples. Gondar in the Amhara Highlands in the northwest became the center of the Abyssinian Empire, a loose confed-eration of states in the highlands of Ethiopia. The predominance of the Amhara in the empire dated from their great expansion in the fourteenth century. The Amhara incorporated subject peoples through conversion to Christianity, inter-marriage, and assimilation.

According to legend, medieval crusaders sent emissaries to the fabled land of Prester John and his Christian kingdom, now known as Ethiopia, entreating the king there to join in their war to win the Holy Land from the Muslims, but contact between Abyssinia and Europe was officially reestablished only in 1490.

By 1520 the Ethiopian peoples were engaged in long wars with the Muslims from Harar and the Somali Muslims armed and supplied by the expanding Ot-toman Turks. In 1529, led by Ahmed Gran, the Muslim peoples, mostly Somali and Oromo, launched a holy war on the Christian kingdom in the highlands. In 1541–43 the Ethiopians were saved from Muslim conquest by the intervention of Portuguese forces who came to aid their fellow Christians. The war set off centuries of sporadic warfare in the region.

The Ethiopians recovered and reconquered much of the territory lost to the Muslims. The empire consisted of a number of separate principalities ruled by a *ras* or prince, most claiming descent from Menelik. The highlands were a center of European missionary activity until the Europeans were expelled from the empire in 1633.

In the nineteenth century Tigre in the north broke away under Ras Mikail Suhul. The Tigreans were ultimately defeated by the Amharas of the central principality of Shoa under the command of Ras Theodore. In 1855 Theodore had himself crowned emperor of Ethiopia. The Tigreans and Amhara formed an alliance and jointly ruled the extensive empire. In the 1870s Egyptians invaded the empire but were unable to dislodge the Christians from their highlands and eventually withdrew.

Imperial troops had conquered many of the numerous Oromo clans in the eighteenth century. A majority of the Oromo elders accepted the authority of the emperor and often provided mercenary troops to the imperial army. The imperial capital, Addis Ababa, was founded in traditional Oromo territory in 1883, partly to ensure Oromo loyalty to the Ethiopian emperor.

In 1877 Ethiopian troops conquered Harer, the traditional capital of the Western Somali clans. Using the city as a base of operations, the Ethiopians extended their rule into the vast Ogaden as part of the colonization of the Somali lands. France, Italy, and the United Kingdom each took control of parts of the coastal Somali regions. The Western Somali clans united in 1899 to launch a twenty-one-year holy war against Christian domination.

In the late nineteenth and early twentieth centuries, the Ethiopians moved south to conquer Jimma, Kaffa, and other regions in the south. The conquests brought into the empire a large population of non-Semitic peoples, including many pagan and Muslim Oromo clans, and Black African tribes related to the peoples across the borders in Kenya and Sudan.

In the late nineteenth century the Tigreans revolted against the dominance of the Amhara and were again defeated. The Tigrean nobility was imprisoned or killed. Dominated by the Amhara clans of the central highlands, the Ethiopian empire remained static and feudal. In 1896, under Emperor Menelik, the Ethiopians rallied to defeat an army of invading Italians, the first defeat of a European colonial army in northern Africa.

The territorial integrity of Ethiopia was recognized by the European powers in 1906, leaving the Amhara the dominant people in the multiethnic empire. In the early decades of the twentieth century the majority of the Ethiopian people remained peasant farmers dominated by a feudal aristocracy.

The Oromo clans, never united politically, began to form closer ties in the early years of the twentieth century. A number of clans united, for the first time, in a widespread revolt against the imperial government in 1928–30, a forerunner of the later Oromo national movement.

The Italians, from their base in neighboring Eritrea, invaded Ethiopia without a declaration of war on 3 October 1935. The mechanized Italian forces quickly defeated the poorly armed Ethiopians and overran the entire country by early 1936. Under Italian rule the northern provinces were added to Italian Eritrea as a province of Italian East Africa. The western and southern provinces were administered as separate Italian possessions.

In 1941 Ethiopia was liberated by British troops, and Emperor Haile Selassie returned in triumph to Addis Ababa. The British turned over power to the returning imperial government in all but part of the Western Somali homeland east of Harer and Dire Dawa.

The return of the imperial government set off demands in many parts of the country for cultural or political autonomy. In the Amhara heartland in the northwest an autonomy movement began in 1942 and continued to gain strength for several years until crushed by imperial troops.

The most serious threat to the government came from the northern Tigreans. The government's refusal to allow the Tigrean prince to return, along with accusations of corruption and bad government, spurred the Tigrean national movement. In 1943 the Tigreans rebelled, destroying government installations and defeating units of the Ethiopian army sent against them. The rebel leaders proposed to separate from Ethiopia and to join neighboring Eritrea, then under British military rule. By mid-1943 the Tigrean rebels held most of Tigre province.

Citing the feudal corruption that permeated Ethiopia, the Tigrean rebels appealed to the British in Eritrea for support. The British wartime authorities, fearing that the rebellion would bring down the Ethiopian government and splinter the country, sided with the emperor. British bombers were used against the rebel positions, and in October 1943 government troops overran the remaining rebel-held districts.

As punishment for the rebellion, a large part of Tigre province was severed and added to neighboring provinces. In the 1950s and 1960s, agitation for the return of the lost territory led to the modern phase of Tigrean nationalism and to the formation of the Tigray National Organization (TNO), the forerunner of the Tigray People's Liberation Front (TPLF).

In 1946 the British government proposed to the new United Nations a plan for a trusteeship to encompass British Somaliland, former Italian Somaliland, and the part of Ethiopian Somaliland under British military rule. The plan, blocked by the Ethiopian government, was discarded, but the disposition of the Somali territories continued to be debated at the UN throughout the late 1940s.

The United Nations recommended a return to the prewar borders in 1950, including the return of British-occupied Western Somalia to Ethiopia. Vehemently opposed to Ethiopian rule, the clan elders appealed to the British authorities. The transfer of the territory was delayed until 1954, when the UN obliged the British to relinquish control. In 1955 harsh Ethiopian restrictions on the Western Somali clans provoked growing resentment and strong antiEthiopian feelings in the region.

The imperial government, faced with growing ethnic unrest in many areas of the country, instituted new measures to control the multiethnic state during the 1960s. One of the measures, which outlawed all but the official language, Amhariya, spurred the growth of nationalist movements and antigovernment sentiments throughout Ethiopia. In the late 1960s and early 1970s many Ethiopians became increasingly dissatisfied with the government and demanded better living conditions for the majority and an end to aristocratic privilege and corruption.

From 1972 to 1974 a severe drought ravaged the northeastern provinces and resulted in over 200,000 dead. In early 1974 student demonstrations and strikes rocked the country, and in September the military seized control of the government and removed Emperor Haile Selassie. The ruling military junta quickly curbed the power of the Ethiopian church and the mostly Amhara nobility. The majority of the country's numerous ethnic and cultural groups initially supported the revolution.

The Provisional Military Administration Council (PMAC) was purged by junior officers, and fifty-seven senior officers were executed in November 1974. In December, the leader of the coup, Mengistu Haile Mariam, declared Ethiopia a one-party socialist state and established close ties to the Soviet Union. The new government carried out a massive program of land reform while ruthlessly suppressing any sign of opposition or nationalist tendencies among the various national groups.

In July 1977, in support of a nationalist uprising in the Somali-inhabited Ogaden, troops from neighboring Somalia invaded Ethiopia. Initially successful, the Somali forces were gradually forced back as Soviet and Cuban arms and advisors bolstered the Ethiopian forces. By March 1978 the Somali army had been forced to withdraw, although sporadic fighting continued for another ten years.

In early 1978, in a mass purge called the Red Terror, thousands of suspected opponents of the Derg (Dergue), the ruling clique, were tortured and killed. The purge, which extended to every province, was designed to eliminate any opposition, but instead stimulated the growth of ethnically based nationalist groups, particularly in the north of the country.

The Derg eventually alienated most support outside the central Shoa Region. Serious ethnic insurgencies were active in Eritrea, Tigray, and the Ogaden, and among the Oromo clans in the east and south. By 1979 most opposition groups had broken with the Derg, and many supported the growing insurgencies. A Communist reign of terror extended to every part of the country, with tens of thousands of suspected political opponents killed or imprisoned while a convenient civil war served as a pretext to suspend civil liberties. In the early 1980s famine again stalked the country. In 1984 the government curbed international aid efforts, claiming that foreign governments were supporting the rebel armies.

In 1987 a new constitution provided for a return to civilian government, but the Derg retained all power. In March 1988 the Eritrean and Tigrean rebels launched a coordinated offensive and by mid-1989 had won control of most of Eritrea. By the end of 1989 the rebels had driven the government troops from all but a few garrison towns in Tigray. In May 1991 a coalition of several regional armed groups, the Ethiopian People's Revolutionary Democratic Forces (EPRDF), marched into Addis Ababa and liberated the country from seventeen years of one of the most brutal dictatorships in modern history.

The EPRDF—dominated by the Tigreans of the Tigrean People's Liberation Front (TPLF), but also including the Oromo Liberation Front (OLF), several Amhara groups, and other groups representing the country's largest ethnic groups—inherited a country devastated by war and totalitarian excesses. The TPLF, headed by Meles Zenawi, oversaw the transition from a Communist dictatorship to a multiethnic democracy. Zenawi became Ethiopia's first post-Communist prime minister in 1995, after a four-year interim period.

Several months after taking power, the EPRDF convened a conference of twenty-six groups that had opposed Mengistu's rule. The conference established democratic norms for the country while agreeing to the division of Ethiopia into two separate states, a new landlocked Ethiopian republic and an independent Eritrean state in the northeast.

The new government, in the hope that the splintered country might be held together, gave more power to largely self-governing regions that were created to match Ethiopia's patchwork of national groups. In spite of efforts to decentralize, conflicts between the Tigreans, who hold the major share of power in the government, and their partners, particularly the Oromo, erupted in several areas. In June 1992 several Oromo political groups pulled out of the government.

On 24 May 1993, after a two-year transition period, the Federal Democratic Republic of Ethiopia and the State of Eritrea were proclaimed. The government, the first elected government in Ethiopia's history, has begun the reconstruction and democratization of the country, Africa's oldest and one of its newest.

The Muslim peoples, often at odds with the Christian Tigreans and Amhara, have demanded greater autonomy for their regions. In 1993 the OLF left the government. Several antigovernment guerrilla Muslim political groups have been fighting the Tigrean-dominated government of President Zenawi.

Zenawi's policy of promoting regional autonomy and ethnic identity has generated much animosity from the formerly dominant Amhara, who traditionally held centralized power in Ethiopia. In spite of powerful opposition and grave problems maintaining its high ideals, the Ethiopian government has instituted a democratic regime with respect for human and national rights.

In 1996–97 several journalists were jailed for writing articles the government objected to, particularly articles about the continuing ethnic insurgencies. The lack of journalistic freedom has been protested by many international organizations as a holdover from the former Communist regime. Fighting continues to be reported in the Oromo, Somali, and Sidamo regions in the east and south.

The poor rains that affected the country in 1996–97 have again raised the fear of famine in the region. The deficit in the agricultural output of Ethiopia, a legacy of the imperial and later Communist regimes, has been the underlying cause of severe famines during the 1980s and early 1990s. In spite of the many problems facing the government, Ethiopia remains remarkably free of the corruption that permeates much of Africa.

The excesses of the Marxist regime still hang over the country. Ethiopian authorities are still looking for 2,480 suspects who allegedly committed genocide and other crimes during the military administration of Col. Mengistu Haile Mariam, who now lives in comfortable exile in Zimbabwe.

SELECTED BIBLIOGRAPHY:

Beckwith, Carol, ed. *African Ark: People and Ancient Cultures of Ethiopia and the Horn of Africa.* 1990.

Gish, Steven. *Ethiopia.* 1996.

Levine, Donald H., and Donald N. Levine. *Greater Ethiopia: The Evolution of a Multi-ethnic Society.* 1977.

Nahum, Fasil. *Constitution for a Nation of Nations: The Ethiopian Prospect.* 1997.

Tibebu, Teshale. *Ethiopia: 1896–1974.* 1995.

GEORGIA

Republic of Georgia; Sak'art'velo;
Sak'art'velos Respublika

CAPITAL: Tbilisi

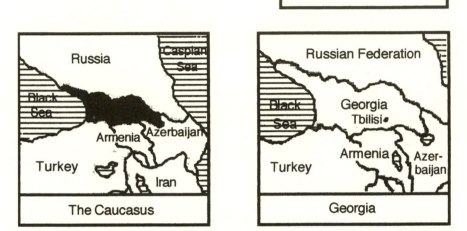

The Caucasus

Georgia

POPULATION: (98e) 5,638,000 : 3,990,000 Georgians in Georgia and another 220,000 in adjacent areas of Russia,* Armenia,* and Azerbaijan,* and up to 200,000, called Laz, in northeastern Turkey. MAJOR NATIONAL GROUPS: (98e) Georgian 70.8% (including Ajars), Armenian 7.1%, Azeri 6.3%, Russian 4.8%, Ossetian 3%, Greek 1.9%, Abkhaz 1.9%, Ukrainian, Kurd, Jew, Assyrian, Belarussian, Tatar. MAJOR LANGUAGES: Georgian, Russian, Armenian, Azeri, Ossetian, Abkhaz. MAJOR RELIGIONS: Georgian Orthodox 65%, Sunni Islam 12%, Russian Orthodox 8%, Armenian Orthodox 7%, Roman Catholic 2%, Shi'a Islam, Jewish, Protestant, Yezid. MAJOR CITIES: (98e) Tbilisi 1,273,000 (1,550,000), Kutaisi 241,000 (305,000), Rustavi 161,000, Batumi 136,000 (169,000), Sukhumi (92e) 136,000 (175,000), Gori 73,000, Poti 62,000, Zugdidi 53,000, Tskhinvali 43,000.

GEOGRAPHY: AREA: 26,911 sq.mi.-69,717 sq.km. LOCATION: Georgia is bordered by the Russian Federation to the north and east, Azerbaijan to the southeast, Armenia to the south, Turkey to the southwest, and the Black Sea to the west. PHYSICAL GEOGRAPHY: Slightly smaller than South Carolina, Georgia lies in southeastern Europe, a mountainous region on the southern slopes of the Caucasus Mountains behind a narrow coastal plain on the Black Sea. Essentially part of an isthmus between the Black and Caspian Seas, Georgia is bounded on the north by the Greater Caucasus Ranges, which include Mt. Kazbek (16,558 ft.), one of the highest points in Europe, and on the south by the Lesser Caucasus Ranges and the Armenian Highlands. Georgia's mountainous plateaus and river valleys contrast with lowland areas lying to either side of the Surami mountain range, which bisects the country along a northeast-southwest axis. In between these ranges lie a series of fertile plains and valleys. The principal rivers are the Kura and Rioni. ADMINISTRATIVE DIVISIONS: Two autonomous republics, sixty-three districts, and eight urban zones. POLITICAL STATUS: Georgia was recognized as an independent state in 1991.

INDEPENDENCE DECLARATIONS: 26 May 1918 (from Russia); 9 April 1991 (from the Soviet Union).

FLAG: The Georgian national flag, the official flag of the Republic of Georgia, is a scarlet field bearing a bicolor canton on the upper hoist, black over white.

PEOPLE: Historically, Georgia has always been a multinational country due to its geopolitical situation at the crossroads of Europe and Asia. Today some one hundred ethnic groups are represented in the republic. For centuries, Georgia's geographic position has opened it to religious and cultural influences from the West, Persia, Turkey, and Russia. The resultant diversity continues to characterize the cultural, ethnic, and religious life of modern Georgia.

Georgian—an estimated 70.8% of the population, numbering about 3,990,000.

The largest and the titular ethnic group in the republic, the Georgians are an ancient Caucasian people known for their beauty and longevity. Georgians are thought to derive from early indigenous inhabitants of the Caucasus region. Historical and archeological records reveal evidence of agricultural activity in eastern Georgia as early as the fifth century B.C. Georgians identify themselves as Kartveli, Russians use the name Gruziny, and Turks employ the term Gurcu. English usage of the term Georgia comes from the Turkish Gurcu.

The Georgian nation unites a number of closely related Kartalian peoples speaking major dialects of the Georgian language. The largest group, the Georgians, also known as Kartalians or Gruzians, inhabit the upper reaches of the Kura River from Akhaltsikhe to below Tbilisi and the Yora and Alazan plains as far east as Zakatali in neighboring Azerbaijan. The Imeritians live around the city of Kutaisi in the region west of the Surami Mountains. The Gurians inhabit the lowlands between the Rioni and Chorokh Rivers in western Georgia. The Mingrelians live in the Black Sea lowlands between the Rioni, Inguri, and Tskhenis Tskhali Rivers. The Svanetians live in the high valleys of the upper Inguri and Tskhenis Tskhali Rivers. The Kabuletians and Ajarians inhabit the Tskhali Valley and the Black Sea coast in the southwest.

The Georgian language, the official language of the republic, belongs to the southern or Kartvelian branch of the Caucasian language family. Although Georgia has known many conquerors, the language displays unique qualities that cannot be attributed to any outside influence. The alphabet, written in a beautiful script dating to the fourth century or before, has undergone several modifications or reforms, but remains, like the language itself, a cherished part of Georgia's culture. The Mingrelians, Svans, and Laz, although assimilating into the greater

Georgian culture, continue to speak separate dialects of the Georgian language. Many Georgians also speak Russian, the dominant language of the former Soviet Union.

Over 90% of the world's Georgians live in the Republic of Georgia. Very few have emigrated beyond the borders of their homeland, although a few Georgian émigré enclaves exist in western Europe and North America. Because of the existence of numerous minority groups within Georgia, however, the percentage of Georgians as part of the country's total population stands at around 70%.

The majority of the Georgians belong to the independent Georgian Church under the authority of the Catholicos at Tbilisi. The church is very closely tied to Georgia's culture and history as a separate Christian nation.

Armenian—an estimated 7.1% of the population, numbering about 398,000.

The largest of the many ethnic minorities represented in the republic are the Armenians. Apart from Tbilisi, where 200,000 Armenians lived at the time of the last official census in 1989, and where they formed the largest minority in the Georgian capital, they are mainly found in the Akhalkalaki, Ninotsminda, and Dmanisi regions in southern Georgia bordering the Republic of Armenia. One hundred thousand Armenians lived in Abkhazia before the recent war there, especially in the district of Gagra, where they formed the relative majority. Smaller numbers of Armenians live in almost every lowland region of Georgia. The majority of the Armenian population in Georgia settled in the region during the Turkish-Russian wars of the nineteenth century and during the upheavals before and after World War I.

The overwhelming majority of Armenians are Gregorian Christians, with their religious center at Echmiadzin, near the Armenian capital city of Yerevan. A small number of Armenians belong to the Roman Catholic Church. The small Muslim Armenian minority, called Khemshins, is also represented (see Meskhtekian, pp. 114–16).

The relative underdevelopment of southern Georgia, where the majority of the Armenian population lives, is a serious problem. The weak economic ties of the Armenians in southern Georgia with other parts of Georgia, due in part to the lack of transport links, has tended to economically orient the Armenians toward northern Armenia rather than to the Georgian heartland.

An unknown number of Georgian Armenians have emigrated since the last Soviet census in 1989. However, the majority have shunned Armenia, with its political and economic chaos, in favor of southern Russia. Armenians have also emigrated in significant numbers from Tbilisi, mainly to central Russia or the United States, but Tbilisi remains a traditional center of Armenian culture.

Azeri (Azerbaijani)—an estimated 6.3% of the population, numbering about 355,000.

The fastest-growing of the major national groups living in Georgia, the Azeris are concentrated mainly in the southeastern districts of Marneuli, Bolnisi, Dmanisi, and Gardabani, with smaller numbers in the Tsalka district, in the cities of Tbilisi and Rustavi, and elsewhere in eastern Georgia. The Azeri population in Georgia, other than the substantial numbers in the cities of Tbilisi and Rustavi, is mostly rural.

Although the Turkic population in Georgia is of varied origin, the majority now identify themselves as Azeris. Most of the Georgian Azeris are Shi'a Muslims, with a small Sunni Muslim minority. The intermingling of the Azeri and Armenian populations in rural southern Georgia has meant shared economic concerns, but little of the bitter struggle between Armenia and Azerbaijan has spilled across the borders into Georgia.

Ajar (Ajarian) (counted as ethnic Georgian)—an estimated 4.9% of the population, numbering about 275,000.

The Ajar population figure is based on population figures from the 1930s, estimated growth patterns, and statistics pertaining to the Georgian Muslim minority. Although the Ajar consider themselves a separate national group, they have not been counted as a distinct group in census figures since the 1930s and are included in official statistics as ethnic Georgians. The majority adhere to the Hanafite rite of Sunni Islam and are officially counted as ethnic Georgians of the Muslim faith.

The Ajars are concentrated in the southwestern region, Ajaristan. The Ajar nation is traditionally divided into the Ajars in the southern part of their homeland and the Kabuletians in the north and west.

The Ajarian culture, influenced by neighboring Turkey and closely tied to their Muslim religion, has long separated them from their Georgian neighbors even though they speak a Gurian dialect of Georgian called Guruli, which incorporates considerable borrowing from Turkish. The mainly Muslim Ajar population is growing more quickly than the Georgian population as a whole. Estimates of the Ajar population run to over 350,000.

The Ajarian Autonomous Soviet Socialist Republic in southwest Georgia was renamed the Ajarian Autonomous Republic in 1992. The continued existence of that republic reflects the religious and cultural differences that developed when the Ottoman Empire occupied part of Georgia in the sixteenth century and converted the local population to Islam. The Ajarian region was not included in Georgia until the Treaty of Berlin separated it from the Ottoman Empire in 1878. An autonomous republic within Georgia was declared in 1921.

During World War II Stalin drew up a plan for the deportation of the Muslim Ajars, but the plan was postponed and finally abandoned at his death in 1953. Spared by Stalin's death, the Ajars experienced a modest cultural and national revival that reinforced their determination to resist the Soviet Georgian government's attempts to eliminate their autonomy and to promote assimilation during the 1960s and 1970s.

The only area of Georgia not to have experienced violent confrontations since the collapse of the Soviet Union in 1991, Ajaristan remained an island of relative calm during the upheavals that shook Abkhazia, South Ossetia, and central Georgia. Ajaristan's leaders continue to vehemently resist any interference by the Georgian government in the region's autonomy.

Russian—an estimated 4.8% of the population, numbering about 270,000.

The Russian-speaking population is not concentrated geographically in Georgia, except in small areas in the Samtskhe-Javakheti and Kakheti regions where religious dissident groups like the Molokans and Dukhobors settled or where Cossack military settlements were established in the nineteenth century. However, most Russians immigrated to Georgia during the Soviet period, and these formed significant minorities in most urban areas, especially Rustavi and Tbilisi, as well as the towns along the Black Sea coast in Abkhazia.

The majority of the Russian population does not speak Georgian, which has become a serious problem. A very low birthrate and migration to central Russia or North America have greatly reduced the Russian-speaking portion of the population, a process accelerated by the conflict in Abkhazia, where they formed a significant part of the population. Most of the Russians are Orthodox, but tend to be less religious than their kin in Russia. However, dissident religious communities such as Molokans, Dukhobors, and Starovers have retained their firm religious beliefs along with traditions and dialects that have disappeared elsewhere.

Ossetian—an estimated 3% of the population, numbering about 170,000.

The Ossetians, calling themselves Iristi and their homeland Iryston, are an Iranian people speaking an East Iranian language. They are the descendants of the ancient Alans or Alani, who according to Ossetian tradition settled in the Caucasus in the fifth century B.C. In the thirteenth century, Ossetians arrived on the south side of the Caucasus Mountains when the Mongols drove them from what is now the North Ossetian Republic of the Russian Federation. The Ossetian homeland lies on the slopes of the Caucasus Mountains west of the pass where the Georgian Military Highway crosses into Russian North Ossetia, home to the majority of the Ossetian nation.

Most of the Ossetians are concentrated in the highlands, particularly the Tskhinvali region, although some live around Tbilisi as well as in rural areas in the Gori, Khashuri, and Borjomi regions. South Ossetia includes many all-Georgian villages, while the Ossetian population is concentrated in the cities of Tskhinvali and Java. Overall, in 1989 the population in South Ossetia was 66% Ossetian and 29% Georgian, while more than 60% of the Ossetian population of Georgia lived outside the Autonomous Region of South Ossetia.

In spite of the considerable mixing between the Ossetian and Georgian populations in the region, relations between the two peoples are considerably weaker than during the Soviet era. The South Ossetian autonomous region was created in 1922, following the Soviet invasion of independent Georgia. The autonomous region was abolished officially by the Georgian government in 1990, but was reinstated following the cease-fire brokered by Russia in 1992. Since the civil war in the region there has been considerable immigration to North Ossetia in the Russian Federation.

Greek—an estimated 1.9% of the population, numbering about 112,000.

The majority of the Georgian Greeks inhabit the Black Sea coast in Abkhazia and Georgia proper. The descendants of ancient Greek-speaking peoples, they belong to the Greek subgroup called Pontian Greeks or Greeks descended from the ancient Greek empire of Pontus, which once held sway over much of the Black Sea region.

Since Georgian independence in 1991 many Greeks have immigrated to Greece, helped by Greek government subsidies. Because the Georgian Greeks speak an antiquated form of the language, the Greek government has financed schools in Georgia to teach them modern spoken Greek.

Abkhaz (Abkhazian)—an estimated 1.9% of the population, numbering about 110,000.

The Abkhazians are a North Caucasian people who call themselves Apsua and speak a Caucasian language of the Abkhazo-Adygheian group. The language, a complicated mixture of Caucasian and archaic Latin elements, has its own alphabet and is the first language of over 95% of the Abkhaz population. Mostly converted to Islam following the conquest of the region by the Ottoman Turks in 1578, the Abkhaz nation is divided into four major divisions: the Muslim Gudauta, Abzhui, and Abaza, and the Orthodox Christian Samurzakan.

The Abkhazian homeland, designated an autonomous republic within Georgia in 1930, had, when fighting broke out in 1992, a mixed population of 544,000, 44% Georgian, 20% Abkhaz, 16% Russian, 6% Armenian, 2% Ukrainian, 2% Greek, and smaller percentages of other nationalities.

Massive Georgian immigration, undertaken during Stalin's rule, had reduced the Abkhaz to minority status in their homeland by the end of World War II. Stalin, himself a Georgian, and particularly suspicious of the Muslim peoples of the Caucasus, prepared a plan for the deportation of the Abkhaz in 1943. The plan, later postponed, was finally abandoned at Stalin's death in 1953.

Resentment of their minority status in Abkhazia fanned the growth of Abkhaz nationalism in the decades since World War II. The liberalization of Soviet life in the late 1980s accelerated the growth of Abkhaz nationalism. In 1989 a newly convened Abkhaz National Council called for Abkhaz secession from Georgia, provoking a strong Georgian nationalist backlash and violent confrontations between the two peoples.

Georgia's independence, following the collapse of the Soviet Union in 1991, was marked by the dominance of an ethnocentric, nationalist government determined to subdue Georgia's restive minorities. Amid growing confrontation, the Abkhaz legislature declared the autonomous republic independent of Georgia in 1992, setting off a bitter war of secession.

The separatist Abkhaz forces slowly forced the disorganized Georgian military to retreat, and in 1993 the separatists overran the Abkhaz capital, Sukhumi.

Over 200,000 Georgians fled from Abkhazia into western Georgia. In 1994 the Georgian government of Eduard Shevardnadze reluctantly accepted Russian peacekeeping troops on the Abkhaz border, effectively placing separatist Abkhazia under de facto Russian protection.

Ukrainian—estimated at less than 1% of the population, numbering about 45,000.

The majority of those claiming Ukrainian nationality in Georgia are of Kuban Cossack descent, descendants of the inhabitants of Cossack military colonies established in the newly acquired Georgian territories in the nineteenth century. Most of the Ukrainians speak Russian as their first language, but very few speak Georgian. During the Soviet era some Ukrainians were settled in the industrial towns and cities.

As with their Russian counterparts, the birthrate among Ukrainians is low and immigration is high; some have gone to Ukraine, but the majority to Canada and the United States or Russia. The total Ukrainian population of Georgia is thought to be considerably lower than the 1989 census figure of 52,000.

Kurd—estimated at less than 1% of the population, numbering about 40,000.

The Kurds, part of the large Kurdish population spread across many parts of the Middle East, are the descendants of the ancient Medes and speak a West Iranian language. However, unlike the majority of the Kurdish population, most Kurds living in Georgia are not Sunni Muslims, but Yezids. At the beginning of the twentieth century the Kurdish Yezids fled religious persecution in the Ottoman Empire to settle in the Russian Empire.

Most of the Georgian Kurds live in the large cities, Tbilisi and Rustavi, where they have retained their language and culture, and unlike some other national groups, show little interest in emigration. Many of the rural Kurds living in southern Georgia were deported in 1944 along with the other Meskhtekian peoples. Between 1979 and 1989 the Kurdish population grew the fastest of any in Georgia, increasing by some 30%.

Jew—estimated at less than 1% of the population, numbering about 18,000.

The most ancient ethnic minority living in Georgia, the Judeo-Georgians have inhabited the region for over twenty centuries. The Georgian Jews, except for those who settled in Georgia under Russian or Soviet rule, practice an archaic form of Sefardic Judaism, while over half still use a dialect called Judeo-Georgian, which combines old forms of the Georgian language with even older Caucasian and Hebrew words and influences.

The majority of the Jews live in the urban areas of Tbilisi, Kutaisi, and Oni. Although no figures are available, many of the 25,000 Jews counted in the 1989 Soviet census have since left Georgia, immigrating to Israel or the United States.

Meskhtekian—estimated at less than 1% of the population. About 15,000 of the estimated 265,000 Meskhtekians in the former Soviet Union have returned to Georgia.

The Meskhtekians are the remnants and descendants of various Muslim peoples deported from the Turkish border region of Georgia in 1944. Called Meskhtekian Turks for the region of Meskhtekistan, where they originated, the deported Muslim groups included Georgian Muslims called Meskhi, Armenian Muslims called Khemsils, Shi'a Muslim Ajars, Kurds, Karapapakh Turks, Tarakama Turks, and several smaller groups.

United by their common experience and their Muslim religion, the majority being Shi'a Muslims, these diverse peoples formed a separate national group in their exile in Siberia and Central Asia, including standardizing their own dialect, a hybrid combining the Laz dialect of Georgian with admixtures from several Turkic languages. The Meskhtekians call themselves Yerli, but in neighboring Turkey, where many of them live, namely, in the southern part of the region of Meskheti, they are called Ahska Turkery, meaning Turks from Akhaltsikhe. In Russia and the central Asian regions where they were deported, the commonly used term is Meskhtekian Turks, a name coined by the People's Commissariat of Interior Affairs during the deportations.

The problem of the Meskhtekian Diaspora began with the deportations of the small national groups from the Caucasus during World War II. Unknown in the West, the Islamic population of southern Georgia, called the Meskheti or Meskhtekian Turks, was also deported to Central Asia, supposedly for harboring pro-Turkish sentiments. The plan of deportation was prepared by the head of the Commissariat of Internal Affairs, Lavrenty Beria, and signed by Joseph Stalin, both ethnic Georgians who considered neutral Turkey an enemy state.

The Meskhtekian peoples were locked into railway cattle wagons for the long journey into exile; many of them died before arriving. There was more suffering at their destination in Central Asia, so different from their native Meskheti. In 1956 things began to change, but unlike most other deported peoples, the Meskhtekians were not allowed to return to their homeland on the sensitive Turkish border. The Meskhtekians were finally freed from humiliating KGB supervision in 1968, but remained in exile. Details of the Meskhtekian deportation began to leak out to the West only in 1969.

The great majority of the more than 130,000 Muslims deported from Georgia were women and children, since most of the men were fighting with the Soviet military forces. Another 4,000 Meskhtekians, mostly soldiers, were shipped east to exile following Germany's defeat. The Meskhtekians claim that 50,000 of their people died as a direct result of the deportations and the deprivations suffered in exile.

Having overcome the original hostility of the local population and the natural environment, Meskhtekians achieved relative prosperity while slowly forming their dispersed groups into a viable nation in exile. However, in 1989 an Uzbek nationalist demonstration turned into a pogrom. The Sunni Uzbeks turned on the mostly Shi'a Meskhtekians living in the Fergana Valley during a week of violence, rape, and murder. Over a hundred Meskhtekians were murdered and 500 were injured before the Soviet military evacuated them to guarded camps outside the Uzbek cities.

Following the breakup of the Soviet Union and the independence of the Central Asian republics in 1991, most Meskhtekians left the region, hoping to return to their homeland in southern Georgia, but the vast majority were refused entry by the radical nationalist government of newly independent Georgia. Many Georgians argued that the Meskhtekian Turks had lost their links to Georgia and hence had no rights that would justify the large-scale upheaval resettlement would cause. However, since 1992 President Shevardnadze has argued that Georgians have a moral obligation to allow this group of exiles to return. They are now concentrated in neighboring areas in Azerbaijan and the North Caucasus region of Russia waiting to return to their homeland.

Assyrian—estimated at less than 1% of the population, numbering about 7,000.

The Assyrians are adherents of various Christian sects, the largest of which are the Chaldeans and Nestorians. Like the Armenians, the Assyrians mostly arrived in Russian Georgia fleeing anti-Christian persecutions in the Arab provinces of the Ottoman Empire up to and during World War I. The Assyrians of Georgia speak the Urmiye dialect of Assyrian, a Semitic language with its roots in the biblical Middle East.

Tatar—estimated at less than 1% of the population, numbering about 5,000.

The Tatars are a Turkic group, part of the large Tatar populations that inhabit the Tatarstan Republic of the Russian Federation. They are related to the Tatars who originated in the nearby Crimean Peninsula region of Ukraine.

The Tatars, the most advanced of Russia's Muslim peoples, mainly settled in the region after the Russian conquest. The majority came as skilled administrators or workers recruited in their homeland to occupy positions in the newly conquered regions of the Caucasus in the nineteenth century.

Belarussian—estimated at less than 1% of the population, numbering about 4,000.

Often counted as ethnic Russians, as most are Russian-speaking, the Belarussians mostly settled in Georgia during the Soviet era. Many ethnic Belarussians immigrated to newly independent Belarus* following the breakup of the Soviet Union in 1991.

THE NATION: Considered by some scientists to be the earliest home of the Caucasian race, the region has been known since ancient times. For over two millennia during the formation of the Georgian nation, ethnically related groups inhabiting the mountains of the Caucasus region and speaking distinct Kartvelian dialects gradually came together under a series of different rulers.

Archeological evidence indicates a Neolithic culture in the area of modern Georgia as early as the fifth millennium B.C. During the Bronze Age large tribal confederations were formed in the region, forming the basis for the first Georgian states—Colchis, in the sixth century B.C. in western Georgia, and Kartli (Iberia) in the inland regions in the fourth century B.C. Mtskheta, ancient capital of the Kartli or eastern Georgians, existed as early as the third century B.C., but by the reign of Vakhtang in the late fifth century A.D. a new capital had been established at Tbilisi.

The early Georgian kingdoms were greatly influenced by the peoples who controlled or traded in the Black Sea region. In the last centuries of the pre-Christian era, Georgia, in the form of the kingdom of Kartli-Iberia, was strongly influenced by Greece to the west and Persia to the east. After the Roman Empire completed its conquest of the Caucasus region in 66 B.C., the kingdom was a Roman client state, called Iberia, and a Roman ally for some 400 years. In A.D. 330 King Marian III of Kartli-Iberia accepted Christianity for the Georgian people.

The tradition of the unified state was preserved in subsequent centuries, all through the Middle Ages. Even before 337, when Christianity was made the official religion in the kingdom of Kartli, and subsequently in the entire territory of Georgia, an alphabet had been developed and a written language had appeared. Christianity ultimately tied Georgia to the neighboring Byzantine Empire, which exerted a strong cultural influence for several centuries.

Included in the Armenian kingdom in the sixth century, Georgia later split into several rival states, reunited under the Bagratid dynasty in 571. Weakened by the Arab invasion of 645, the Georgian lands again increasingly came under Armenian influence. In 813 Armenian prince Ashot I began 1,000 years of rule in Georgia by the Georgian branch of the Bagratid dynasty. Western and eastern Georgia were finally united under Bagrat V in the eleventh century.

In the next century, David IV, called the Builder, initiated a golden age by driving the Turks from the country and expanding Georgian cultural and political influence southward into Armenia and eastward to the Caspian Sea. That era of unparalleled power and prestige for the Georgian monarchy concluded with the great literary flowering of Queen Tamar's reign (1184–1212). At the end of that period, Georgia was well known in the Christian West and was valued as an ally by the Christian Crusaders.

Peace did not last. In 1236 the Mongol hordes invaded Georgia, beginning a century of fragmentation and decline. A brief resurgence of Georgian power in the fourteenth century ended when the Turkic conqueror Timur (Tamerlane) destroyed Tbilisi in 1386. The capture of Constantinople by the Ottoman Turks in 1453 began three centuries of domination by the militant Ottoman and Persian empires, which divided Georgia into spheres of influence in 1553 and subsequently redistributed Georgian territory between them. By the eighteenth century, however, the Bagratid line again had achieved substantial independence under nominal Persian rule.

In 1762 Herekle II was able to unite the east Georgian regions of Kartli and Kakhetia under his independent but tenuous rule. In this period of renewed unity, trade increased and feudal institutions lost influence in Georgia. In 1773 Herekle began efforts to gain Russian protection against the Turks, who were threatening to retake his kingdom. In this period, Russian troops intermittently occupied parts of Georgia, making the country a pawn in the explosive Russian-Turkish rivalry of the last three decades of the eighteenth century.

The Persians sacked Tbilisi in 1795, and Herekle again sought the protection of Orthodox Russia against his Muslim neighbors. The last Georgian king, Peter XIII, abdicated in 1801, placing central Georgia under Russian protection. Contrary to the expectations of the Georgian aristocracy and other national leaders, the autonomous protectorate was not long honored by the tsar. Between 1803 and 1829 Russia acquired the remainder of the Georgian lands.

In 1811 the Georgian Orthodox Church lost its independent status as part of the Russification process. Annexation by the Russian Empire began a new stage of Georgian history, in which security was achieved by linking Georgia more closely than ever with Russia. This subordinate relationship would last nearly two centuries. A large and powerful Russified aristocracy, accounting for one of every seven Georgians, gained fame for its wealth and extravagance.

The economy of the country stabilized, however, under the rule of its northern neighbor, and Russian and European ideas came to influence the educated class of Georgians. Forbidden their language, and with their cherished church absorbed by the empire's official Russian Orthodox Church, the Georgians reacted by supporting a modest cultural revival that began to take hold in the 1840s, a reaction to the attempts to Russify their ancient culture.

The cultural revival evolved a strong nationalist sentiment in the 1880s and 1890s. Spurred on by the ideals of the 1905 Russian Revolution, the Mensheviks, the moderate wing of the Social Revolutionary Party, the largest of Georgia's fledgling political groups, demanded linguistic and cultural rights, a democratic government, and a free enterprise system like those of France and the United Kingdom. Georgian political radicals participated within wider Russian revolutionary circles, in which Georgian Marxists were largely Menshevik, as opposed to Bolshevik, in their sympathies.

Threatened by the Muslim Turks to the south, the Georgians initially supported the Russian government when war began in 1914. Because Turkey was a member of the Central Powers in World War I, the Caucasus region became a major battleground in that conflict. In 1915 and 1916, Russian forces pushed southwest into eastern Turkey from bases in the Caucasus, with limited success. As part of the Russian Empire, Georgia officially backed the Allies, although it stood to gain little from victory by either side. By 1916 economic conditions and mass immigration of war refugees had raised social discontent throughout the Caucasus, and the Russian Empire's decade-old experiment with constitutional monarchy was judged a failure.

Exhausted by three years of war, by 1917 the demoralized Georgian population enthusiastically joined the revolution that ended tsarist rule in Russia. The Menshevik faction took control of the Georgian government as the tsarist civil administration collapsed. Seeking safety for their small state, the Georgian leaders joined their new republic to a Transcaucasian Federation in partnership with neighboring Armenia and Azerbaijan. Tensions among the member states, particularly between the Armenians and Azeris, soon ended the attempt at cooperative sovereignty. On 26 May 1918 Georgia was declared a separate independent state.

To gain peasant support, Noi Zhordania's moderate new Menshevik-dominated government redistributed much of Georgia's remaining aristocratic land holdings to the peasants, eliminating the longtime privileged status of the nobility. However, the economy collapsed. The few years of postwar independence were economically disastrous as beleaguered Georgia, beset by hostile neighbors and restive minorities, failed to establish commercial relations with the West, Russia, or its smaller neighbors.

The Red Army, emerging victorious from Russia's civil war in 1920, quickly advanced south into the Caucasus, reconquering the secessionist states of the former Russian Empire. By early 1921 Georgia stood alone, surrounded by territories occupied by the Soviets and with the Red Army massed on its borders. In February 1921, less than nine months after Moscow had signed a treaty accepting the sovereignty of the Georgian Democratic Republic, the Red Army, led by a Georgian named Sergo Ordzhonikidze, secretly crossed into Georgia from Azerbaijan and quashed the young state. The Georgian government's frantic appeals for aid unanswered, the republic finally surrendered in April 1921.

In 1922 the Soviet Republic of Georgia joined the new Soviet Transcaucasus Federation as all remaining autonomy was ended by the Soviet authorities. Later in 1922, under the personal direction of Stalin, also a Georgian whose real name was Josef Dzhugashvili, Soviet Georgia was established as one of three nations, along with Armenia and Azerbaijan, making up the Soviet-created Republic of Transcaucasia. Violent resistance to Soviet power continued until 1924, when a last uprising was crushed by Bolshevik authorities. As many as 4,000 rebels were executed and countless others imprisoned. The Soviet Republic of Transcaucasia prevailed until 1936. At that time it was divided, and Georgia was declared a full union republic of the Soviet Union.

During the long period of Stalin's dictatorship, Georgia might have been expected to enjoy a special status within the Union of Soviet Socialist Republics, but the more Stalin came to identify himself as a Russian nationalist, however, the less he seemed willing to show any favoritism to Georgia. Instead, the incredible horrors of the purges of the 1930s, carried out among Georgian political leaders and the intelligentsia, took as high a toll in Georgia as elsewhere. During this time, Georgia came under the personal authority of Stalin's close associate, fellow Georgian Lavrenty Beria, who served as first secretary of the Communist Party of Georgia throughout the 1930s. Through Beria's firm grip, Georgia came to be just as tightly controlled by Moscow as were the other Soviet republics.

The last two decades of Stalin's rule saw rapid, forced urbanization and industrialization, as well as drastic reductions in illiteracy and the preferential treatment of Georgians at the expense of ethnic minorities in the republic. The full Soviet centralized economic planning structure was in place in Georgia by 1934. Between 1940 and 1958, the republic's industrial output grew by 240%. In that time, the influence of traditional village life decreased significantly for a large part of the Georgian population. In 1951 the Soviet Georgian government, exercising its right under the Soviet constitution, submitted a formal notice of Georgia's intention to secede from the union. An infuriated Stalin decimated the Georgian leadership and instituted a harsh repression that eased only with his death in 1953.

Georgia was not invaded in World War II, although it contributed more than 500,000 fighters to the Red Army and was a vital source of textiles and munitions. Stalin's successful appeal for patriotic unity eclipsed Georgian nationalism during the war and diffused it in the years following. Restoration of autonomy to the Georgian Orthodox Church in 1943 facilitated this process.

During the war, a substantial population of minority groups was transferred out of the Caucasus because Stalin feared that these minority groups would support the invading Axis powers. However, plans to deport Georgia's Abkhaz and Ajar peoples were postponed, then finally abandoned at Stalin's death. The Meskhtekian peoples were deported in 1944.

De-Stalinization, a liberalizing process originating with the new Soviet premier Nikita Khrushchev, resulted in pro-Stalin demonstrations in Tbilisi in March 1956. A large but peaceful demonstration threatened to take over the local radio station until police regained control. In the clash between police and demonstrators, several were killed. There continue to be those in Georgia who view Stalin as a positive national figure.

A modest national revival took hold during the 1970s, led by Zviad Gamsakhurdia, the son of a recognized national poet, who began to organize dissident Georgian nationalists. In 1972 Moscow named a relative moderate, Eduard Shevardnadze, first secretary of the Georgian Communist Party. Shevardnadze's policies were generally accepted until 1978, when mass demonstrations shook the republic as the Georgians protested the government's efforts to make Russian an official language in Georgia.

In March 1985, following a series of elderly heads of state, a relatively young Mikhail Gorbachev was elected in Moscow. He embarked on a program that radically changed the Soviet Union's relations with the West and began the restructuring of the rigid Soviet system. Gorbachev named the first secretary of the Georgian Communist Party, Eduard Shevardnadze, as head of the Soviet Ministry of Foreign Affairs.

Georgian nationalism reemerged with the relaxation of Soviet rule in the late 1980s. Gorbachev's reforms, introduced in 1987, fanned nationalist demands by the Georgians and by the non-Georgian national groups in the republic. Calls by the Ossetian and Abkhazian minorities for secession from Georgia sparked a Georgian nationalist backlash that mobilized public opinion. A peaceful, pro-independence demonstration in Tbilisi was attacked by Soviet soldiers on 9 April 1989, leaving twenty dead and many more injured. The attack on the peaceful marchers, carried out with sharpened shovels and poison gas, provoked a great outpouring of nationalism in the republic.

In the months that followed Bloody Sunday, Georgians responded to the pent-up frustrations of Soviet rule by challenging the authority of their own Georgian

Communist leadership. For Georgian Communist leaders, the dilemma was that they could appeal only to Moscow to reinforce their position. For at work was the classic trade-off operating in the Kremlin's relations with the outlying union republics. Moscow would provide military support to back up the power of the union republic's recognized government. But, at the same time, Moscow retained the power to undermine the credibility of that same local Communist Party leadership by appearing to support the independent initiatives of autonomous republics and oblasts operating within a union republic.

The immediate impact of the April 1989 massacre in Tbilisi was to galvanize support for those informal Georgian political and cultural groups that had been gathering widespread support since the introduction of the Gorbachev reforms. By August 1989, the Georgian Supreme Soviet, despite the dominant role of the Communist Party, had voted to declare Georgia's sovereignty. Although Eduard Shevardnadze's image in the West was that of a reformist foreign minister close to Mikhail Gorbachev, his very association with Moscow politics tended to relegate him in 1989 to outsider status in Georgian politics. The institutions and political leaders having the most to gain were those perceived to be most independent of the old Soviet-style leadership.

Zviad Gamsakhurdia, the charismatic Georgian intellectual, with useful credentials as a Soviet dissident, emerged as a popular national hero and political leader in the months following April 1989. The son of a recognized national poet, Zviad Gamsakhurdia never made a significant mark as an original writer, but he came to national attention as an outspoken opponent of Georgian Communist officialdom, having earlier served time in prison for his underground activities. Gamsakhurdia used the months following the April demonstrations to galvanize the support of a roundtable coalition of informal political groups. His coalition, called Round Table/Free Georgia, pressed for prompt parliamentary elections to the Georgian Supreme Soviet and demanded the restoration of the constitution that had governed the Georgian Democratic Republic from 1918 to the Soviet conquest of 1921.

In the elections of October 1990, Gamsakhurdia's Round Table/Free Georgia coalition won an overwhelming victory in the Georgian Supreme Soviet, securing 54% of the vote. Two weeks later, Gamsakhurdia was elected without opposition to head the new parliament. His post was initially that of chairman of the Georgian Supreme Soviet, the de facto Georgian head of state. In May 1991 Gamsakhurdia was elected to the newly created office of president.

Stating that his goals were those of liberating Georgia and restoring its state sovereignty, Gamsakhurdia appointed a collection of loyal anti-Communists to the new government, many of them without any prior professional governmental experience. Viewing himself as a moral savior of the Georgian nation, Gamsakhurdia backed ethnocentric, anti-Muslim government policies that further alienated many of the republic's non-Georgian national groups.

Gamsakhurdia's antipathy toward the republic's restive minorities was coupled with a ruthless and vindictive approach toward political opponents, fanning opposition within Georgia proper as well as in the autonomous republics and regions. In the election campaign, Gamsakhurdia had committed himself to the preservation of autonomy for the Abkhazians and Ossetians, but by the end of 1990, he had abandoned that position, arguing rather that South Ossetia should be abolished. Increasingly restrictive policies, designed to muzzle the minorities and the political opposition, were put into place.

Political moderates, increasingly alienated by Gamsakhurdia's policies, found themselves under threat of violence. Government policies restricting access to the media further eroded Gamsakhurdia's support within the republic. Government support among the general population plummeted as the promising economic program of Round Table/Free Georgia was largely abandoned while the Georgian economy suffered from high rates of inflation and chronic shortages.

While Georgia stumbled from crisis to crisis, Gamsakhurdia proceeded to blame Georgian Communists, the legacy of Soviet rule, and other parties for the failings of his new government. However, by the spring of 1991, Gamsakhurdia himself had carelessly reopened old ethnic and regional wounds without effectively securing the economic and political stability of the new Georgian government.

The Georgian parliament formally declared Georgian independence in April 1991. An earlier referendum submitted to the republic's electorate had garnered almost 100% support for the "restoration" of Georgian independence. The critical term "restoration" referred to an independence based upon the constitution of the Georgian state of 1918. Even though the declaration had widespread support, there were ominous signs of conflict and coercion. Gamsakhurdia had made it known that any district voting against the referendum would face the prospect of its voters losing citizenship, and thereby the right to land ownership. Moreover, Gamsakhurdia tended to dismiss outright the fact that the far-reaching 1918 declaration of independence had guaranteed equal rights for all citizens of Georgia without regard to nationality, religion, or sex.

In spite of a modest erosion in support for Gamsakhurdia in the first Georgian presidential elections, held in late May 1991, he still polled more than 85% of the Georgian vote. The election process, however, was tainted by threats and intimidation directed at some of Gamsakhurdia's opponents. Several opponents were kept off the ballot, and one was assaulted during the campaign. Gamsakhurdia's continuing popularity among the Georgian populace reflected the strength of the national desire for independence from Moscow. No other national figure could so charismatically draw upon the anti-Soviet feelings of the Georgian electorate. For Gamsakhurdia, the results strengthened his anti-Communist resolve.

The rapidly increasing political instability, violence, and economic hardships in Georgia quickly eroded Gamsakhurdia's support despite the clear plurality in the May 1991 elections. In December 1991 open rebellion broke out, and in January 1992 rebel forces violently ousted Gamsakhurdia from power. After holding out in the parliament building for over two weeks while fighting swept the Georgian capital, Gamsakhurdia finally fled in early 1992 beyond the Georgian border.

The violent departure of the dictatorial Gamsakhurdia from Georgia left the new state split between those who favored and those who opposed this first post-Soviet Georgian president. By forcibly ousting Gamsakhurdia, the rebel coalition had overridden the Georgian constitution. From the perspective of international law, the Georgian government faced growing charges of flagrant human rights abuses directed against not only the minority national groups but against political groups as well.

The rebel coalition, the Military Council, quickly sought new elections to add legitimacy to the political situation. In a step that would have been unthinkable just a year earlier during the first months of the Gamsakhurdia government, Eduard Shevardnadze was invited back to head a new interim State Council. Although Georgia joined the United Nations in July 1992 as the 179th member, in the republic the summer of 1992 was spent readying a complex election law in time for the scheduled October 1992 elections. A new alliance of former Communist Party figures, members of the intelligentsia, and other center-left political interests formed itself into an effective political bloc, the Mshvidoba, under whose umbrella Eduard Shevardnadze ran. The Mshvidoba bloc, buoyed by the support of a populace that was looking to the Communists to restore economic stability to Georgia, carried the largest number of seats in the October elections. Shevardnadze was elected acting head of state, winning for Georgia the long awaited international recognition.

Shevardnadze's credentials as an associate of Mikhail Gorbachev aided the return of Western recognition and aid. However, the uneasy calm that settled over the country was soon disrupted. Rebel troops still loyal to Gamsakhurdia took control of several areas in the western regions of Mingrelia and Abkhazia. Adding to Shevardnadze's problems, the chauvinist directives of the former president had added fuel to the deepening conflicts over South Ossetia, Abkhazia, Ajaristan, and other border regions. To secure the kind of Western investment that the internationally recognized Shevardnadze had promised, these troublesome domestic problems had to be solved. There was also the status of the remaining Russian military troops in Georgia awaiting bilateral agreement.

In August 1992, Eduard Shevardnadze sent loyal Georgian National Guard units into Sukhumi, the Abkhazian capital. Using as a pretext the need to secure Georgian officials abducted by Gamsakhurdia's followers, Shevardnadze's Georgian National Guard sought to capture Gamsakhurdia himself. The invading Georgian National Guard rampaged through Abkhazia, killing tourists on the beach and destroying several scientific research institutes and museums. More than fifty people were killed. Protesting this invasion of their territory by Georgian troops, the forces of the Abkhaz autonomous government fired on the Georgian National Guard. The heavy fighting of August 1992 led to a rapid deterioration in Georgian-Abkhazian relations.

Georgian forces were driven out of the Abkhaz region in September 1993 after a yearlong war with Abkhaz separatists. Nearly 160,000 refugees fled Abkhazia, adding substantially to the estimated 100,000 internally displaced persons already in Georgia, most displaced by the fighting between government forces and troops loyal to Gamsakhurdia. Pressured by the continuing economic and political crisis in the country, Shevardnadze finally agreed to Russian peacekeepers being deployed along the border of Abkhazia and Georgia, a move that effectively placed the breakaway Abkhaz republic under Russian protection. A similar conflict in South Ossetia had ended with the deployment of Russian, Georgian, and Ossetian troops in the region in June 1992.

In the autumn of 1993, the fall of Sukhumi to Abkhazian forces signaled the crumbling of the Georgian army, and the return of Gamsakhurdia to lead his rebel supporters in Mingrelia threatened to split Georgia into several parts. Shevardnadze, recognizing the necessity of outside military help to maintain his government, agreed to join the Commonwealth of Independent States (CIS) on terms dictated by Russia in return for protection of government supply lines by Russian troops. Meanwhile, despite denials by the Yeltsin government, an unknown number of Russians still gave "unofficial" military advice and material to the Abkhazian forces, which experts believed would not have posed a major threat to the Georgian army without such assistance. Shevardnadze defended CIS membership at home as an absolute necessity for Georgia's survival as well as a stimulant to increased trade with Russia.

By mid-1995 Georgia's gross domestic product was a mere 17% of what it had been in 1989. The economic decline represented the largest drop of any former Soviet republic or Warsaw Pact country. Supported by the West, Shevardnadze slowly imposed economic and political stability on the central Georgian regions, leaving the problem of the autonomous areas for the future. In elections held on November 5, 1995, Eduard Shevardnadze was chosen from a field of six candidates to take office as president of Georgia.

President Shevardnadze, despite numerous handicaps, has proved to be a democratic and impressive president and has helped keep Georgia relatively stable despite continuing ethnic conflicts and instability in the region. Under Shevardnadze's policies the Georgian government has increasingly oriented itself toward the West while seeking to maintain a necessary balance with its powerful northern neighbor, Russia.

In April 1997, the Abkhaz leader, Vladislav Ardzinba, ruled out further talks with the Georgian government on the status of the breakaway republic. The Russians, who are mediating the talks between the two sides, had proposed a federation of the two republics.

The Georgian government, in May 1997, reiterated its claim to some twenty vessels of the Black Sea fleet, which is disputed by Russia and Ukraine. The vessels, formerly based at the Poti naval base, are claimed by the Georgian government because of its contribution to the creation and upkeep of the fleet.

By the end of 1997, by some estimates, between 800,000 and 1 million people, approximately 20% of the total population, had left Georgia over the previous five years. The emigrants, leaving largely for economic reasons, were mostly workers and university graduates under thirty-five years of age.

President Eduard Shavardnadze survived an assassination attempt in February 1998 in which his motorcade was hit by anti-tank grenades. The attackers were not immediately identified. The attempt on the president's life clearly demonstrated the fragile peace that has settled on Georgia, which still faces separatist revolts among the national minorities and factional fighting among the Georgians themselves.

SELECTED BIBLIOGRAPHY:

Brook, Stephen. *Claws of the Crab: Georgia and Armenia in Crisis.* 1993.

Gachechiladze, R. G. *The New Georgia: Space, Society, Politics.* 1995.

Nasmyth, Peter. *Georgia: A Rebel in the Caucasus.* 1992.

Spilling, Michael. *Georgia.* 1997.

Suny, Ronald Grigor. *The Making of the Georgian Nation.* 1994.

KAZAKHSTAN

Republic of Kazakhstan; Qazaqstan
Respublikasy

CAPITAL: Akmola (Tselinograd)

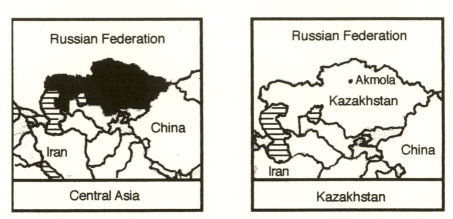

POPULATION: (98e) 17,120,000 : 7,721,000 Kazakhs in Kazakhstan, another 1,100,000 in China, and 500,000 in adjacent areas of Uzbekistan* and Russia.* MAJOR NATIONAL GROUPS: Kazakh (Qazaq) 45.1%, Russian 31.4%, Ukrainian 5.1%, German 4.7%, Tatar 2.3%, Uzbek 2.1%, Uighur 1.7%, Belarussian 1%, Korean, Azeri, Polish, Chechen, Greek, Mordvin, Moldovan, Tajik, Rom (Gypsy), Chuvash, Bashkort, Armenian, Udmurt, Lithuanian. MAJOR LANGUAGES: Russian, Kazakh, German. MAJOR RELIGIONS: Sunni Islam, Russian Orthodox, Roman Catholic, Protestant. MAJOR CITIES: (98e) Almaty (Alma-Ata) 1,230,000 (1,335,000), Qaraghandy (Karaganda) 677,000 (1,245,000), Shymkent (Chimkent) 431,000 (505,000), Pavlodar 362,000, Auliye-Ata (Dzhambul) 348,000, Semey (Semipalatinsk) 346,000, Öskemen (Ust-Kamenogorsk) 343,000, Akmola (Tselinograd) 323,000, Aqtöbe (Aktyubinsk) 276,000, Petropavl (Petropavlovsk) 251,000, Qostanay (Kustanay) 244,000, Temirtau 239,000, Oral (Uralsk) 220,000, Qyzylorda (Kyzyl-Orda) 218,000, Aqtau (Shevchenko) 190,000, Ekibastuz 185,000, Atyran (Guryev) 163,000, Aktau (Shevchenko) 158,000, Ekibastuz 156,000, Kökshetau (Kokchetav) 141,000, Rudnyy 133,000, Taldygorghan (Taldy-Kurgan) 127,000 (190,000), Zhezqazghan (Dzhezkazgan) 112,000, Turkestan 90,000, Balqash (Balkhash) 86,000 (120,000), Arqalyk (Arkalyk) 85,000, Emba 75,000 (110,000).

GEOGRAPHY: AREA: 1,048,877 sq.mi.-2,717,300 sq.km. LOCATION: Kazakhstan, located in Central Asia, is over twice the size of the other four Central

Asian republics combined, and second only to Russia among the newly independent states of the former Soviet Union. The republic is bound by Russian Siberia on the north, European Russia on the north and northwest, the Caspian Sea on the west and southwest, Turkmenistan,* Uzbekistan, and Kyrgyzstan* on the south, and China on the southeast. PHYSICAL GEOGRAPHY: Most of the country's terrain consists of vast plains, the Kazakh Steppe, which rises from the Caspian Sea to the hilly Kazakh Uplands in the east. The Uplands extend in a northwest to southwest direction to meet the Altai Mountains and the Tarbagatai Range. In the southeast are the lowlands called the Balkhash Basin and the high mountains of the Tian Shan Range. In the west and south is the Turanian Depression, an ancient seabed. The country is generally arid, with steppe or grasslands in the north, semi-desert in the center, and desert in the south. The most productive lands lie in the northern provinces bordering Russia. ADMINISTRATIVE DIVISIONS: The country is divided into nineteen provinces or oblystar (singular—oblys) and one special region, the city of Almaty. POLITICAL STATUS: Kazakhstan was recognized as an independent state in 1992.

INDEPENDENCE DECLARATIONS: 16 December 1917 (from Russia); 16 December 1991 (from the Soviet Union).

FLAG: The Kazakh national flag, the official flag of the republic, is a pale blue field with a traditional Kazakh design, in yellow, along the hoist, and a centered yellow eagle, wings spread, surmounted by a yellow multirayed sun.

PEOPLE: The Kazakh Republic is home to over a hundred distinct national groups, many of them in Central Asia due to Stalin's policy of deporting national groups from European areas of the USSR from the 1930s to the 1950s. Of the total, some 60% are Muslim, mostly Sunni. Under Soviet rule Kazakhstan was praised for being a laboratory of the friendship of peoples. An estimated 120 national groups are represented in the republic. The republic has both the largest relative percentage and the largest absolute number of ethnic Russians in Central Asia. The presence of such a large Slav population has raised considerable fervor over the question of dual citizenship and issues such as the state language, education, and the degree of local autonomy.

Kazakh—an estimated 45.1% of the population, numbering about 7,721,000.

The Kazakhs, the largest of the republic's hundred-plus national groups, are a people of mixed Turkic and Mongol ancestry. The majority of the Kazakhs physically resemble their Mongol ancestors, but they speak a Turkic language of the Kipchak (West Turkic) language group. The language, spoken in three major dialects, is written in the Cyrillic alphabet. The majority of the Kazakhs are Sunni Muslims, although the Islam practiced by the Kazakhs is mixed with earlier, non-Islamic traditions.

A majority of the Kazakhs, over 60%, live in rural villages, mostly in the southern provinces. The more developed urban Kazakhs, most of whom speak Russian and graduated from Russian schools, are spiritually integrated into Russian and European culture. The rural Kazakhs call them *mankurts*, people who have lost their roots. An estimated one-third to two-thirds of the urban Kazakhs did not know their native language when Kazakhstan became independent in 1991.

The Kazakhs, divided into *juz*, clans, have just begun to form a united ethnic and national entity. Due to the departure of large numbers of ethnic Slavs and Germans and the Kazakhs' very high birthrate, the Kazakh portion of the population has risen from about 40% in 1991 to 45.1% in 1998.

Russian—an estimated 31.4% of the population, numbering about 5,375,000.

The Russian population, concentrated in the fertile northern provinces adjoining Russia, mostly settled in the region following the completion of the Trans-Siberian Railway at the end of the nineteenth century and during the Virgin Lands scheme after World War II. The Russians are vital to the young state's economy, as they hold a disproportionate number of the scientific, technical, engineering, and administrative positions, jobs that cannot easily be filled by ethnic Kazakhs.

The majority of the Russians belong to the Russian Orthodox Church, although a substantial minority adhere to sects such as the Old Believers, who were persecuted in European Russia. A substantial minority cling to the atheism of the old Soviet state.

An unknown percentage of the Russian-speaking population are Cossacks belonging to the Siberian, Ural, and Semirechensk hordes. Although they speak dialects of Russian, culturally and historically the Cossacks are a separate people. Many of the Cossack communities are descendants of populations deported during the tsarist and Soviet eras. The Russian population has been falling due to immigration to Russia—some 614,000 people between 1989 and 1995—and the Russians' low birthrate.

Ukrainian—an estimated 5.1% of the population, numbering about 875,000.

The Ukrainians mostly settled in the northern provinces during the same period as the Russians, although a sizable number are the descendants of ethnic Ukrainians deported during the Stalin era. The majority of the Ukrainians speak Russian as their first language, while Ukrainian is spoken at home. Very few Ukrainians speak the national language, Kazakh.

The Ukrainians are mostly Orthodox, but with a large Uniate Catholic minority. Renewed ties to independent Ukraine have raised the question of religious loyalty as the Ukrainian and Russian Orthodox churches vie for prominence. Between 1989 and 1995 an estimated 82,000 Ukrainians left Kazakhstan for Ukraine and Russia.

German—an estimated 4.7% of the population, numbering about 805,000.

The German population of Kazakhstan are mostly descendants of Volga and Black Sea Germans deported from European Russia at the outbreak of World War II. The German population in Russia dates to the eighteenth century, when colonists arrived from the southern German states.

Many of the Germans still speak dialects that disappeared in Germany long ago, particularly the Low German dialect called Plautdietsch. Overall, only about half the Germans are able to speak standard German, with many using Russian as their first language. Thousands of Germans have returned to Germany since Kazakhstan gained independence in 1991. Estimates of the remaining German population are as high as 1 million and as low as 300,000.

Tatar—an estimated 2.3% of the population, numbering about 395,000.

The Tatars are a Turkic people who speak a West Turkic language of the Altaic language group. They are the most northerly of the Muslim peoples of the former Soviet Union. The Tatar homeland lies in European Russia northwest of Kazakhstan.

Many of the Tatars migrated to newly conquered Central Asia in the nineteenth century to work as administrators and teachers. The Tatars were instrumental in the conversion of the Kazakhs to Islam, the only people to adopt the Muslim religion after the Russian conquest.

Uzbek and Karakalpak—an estimated 2.1% of the population, numbering about 360,000.

The Uzbeks of Kazakhstan mostly inhabit the frontier districts along the Uzbekistan border in southern Kazakhstan. A Turkic people speaking a related language and sharing the Muslim religion with the Kazakhs, the Uzbeks have retained their distinct culture and traditions.

The language of the Uzbeks, a north Uzbek dialect, is a Turkic language of the West Turkic language group. Many of those counted as ethnic Uzbeks are actually ethnic Karakalpaks, an Uzbek nationality living in the region around the Aral Sea who are closely related ethnically and linguistically to the Kazakhs.

Uighur (Uyghur)—an estimated 1.7% of the population, numbering about 300,000.

The Uighur are mostly the descendants of refugees who fled Chinese repression in the neighboring Chinese region of Xingiang, the New Territories. The Uighur are a Sunni Muslim people speaking an East Turkic language of the Altaic language group. In Kazakhstan the Uighur population speaks the Taranchi dialect of their language, Vigus or New Uighur, which is written in the Cyrillic alphabet. The Uighurs of Kazakhstan are farmers or traders and are mostly rural. Under Soviet rule they progressed rapidly in education and culture.

Belarussian—an estimated 1% of the population, numbering about 180,000.

The Belarussians of Kazakhstan, the majority the descendants of colonists who settled in the northern provinces, are mostly Russian speakers, and most belong to the Russian Orthodox Church. A minority, mostly Roman Catholic, were deported to the region during and after World War II.

The Belarussian population, like that of the other Slav groups, is being reduced by immigration to Europe. More than 16,000 Belarussians are believed to have left Kazakhstan since the census of 1989.

Korean—estimated at less than 1% of the population, numbering about 110,000.

The Korean population lives mostly in the districts along the Syr Darya River and around Lake Balkhash in southern Kazakhstan. The majority are the descendants of populations deported from the Russian Far East during the Stalin years.

The majority of the Koreans are Buddhists, with a substantial atheist minority. Most of the Koreans live in urban areas. The government of South Korea has established contact with the scattered Korean populations since Kazakh independence in 1991 and is giving the new state substantial aid, part of which is to be used for the welfare of the ethnic Koreans.

Azeri—estimated at less than 1% of the population, numbering about 105,000.

The Azeris in Azerbaijan* across the Caspian Sea, are a Turkic people of mixed Turkic and Caucasian ancestry. Their language is a Turkic language of the West Turkic group of Altaic languages. They speak the Northern Azeri dialect of the language. The majority of the Azeris in Kazakhstan are Northern Azeris, mostly Sunni Muslims, while the majority of the population of Azerbaijan is Shi'a Muslim.

Pole—estimated at less than 1% of the population, numbering about 65,000.

The Poles in Kazakhstan, like many of the other national groups, are mostly descended from deportees from European Russia. The first Poles were exiled to newly conquered Central Asia in the latter half of the nineteenth century following the Polish uprising in the 1860s. The majority of the Poles are Roman Catholic and speak Polish, a West Slavic language. Many of the Poles are urbanized, living in the larger cities in the north of the country.

Chechen—estimated at less than 1% of the population, numbering about 55,000.

The Chechens, called Shishan or Kokhchi in Kazakhstan, are concentrated in the western provinces and along the Caspian Sea coast. They were deported during World War II, accused by Stalin of treason. They speak a Caucasian language, but the majority use Russian as their first language in Kazakhstan. Like the Kazakhs, the Chechens are Sunni Muslims.

Turk—estimated at less than 1% of the population, numbering about 53,000.

The Turks of Kazakhstan, concentrated in the southern provinces, are the descendants of the Osmanli and Seljuk Turks who later moved west to conquer Turkey and parts of the Middle East. Traditionally, the Turks have formed an urban merchant class in the southern cities. They mostly speak Kazakh as their first language, while many also speak Russian.

Greek—estimated at less than 1% of the population, numbering about 50,000.

The Greek population of Kazakhstan, Caucasian and Pontian Greeks deported from the Caucasus region of southern Russia, are mostly Greek Orthodox or Greek Catholic and speak archaic dialects of Greek. Since Kazakh independence in 1991, many have immigrated to Greece, taking advantage of subsidies offered by the Greek government.

Mordvin—estimated at less than 1% of the population, numbering about 38,000.

The Mordvin, also called Erzya in Kazakhstan, are concentrated in the northern provinces among the large Slav population. Part of the large Mordvin population of the Volga Basin of eastern European Russia, they were mostly settled in the region during the Virgin Lands campaign of the 1950s and 1960s. The Mordvin speak Erza or Erzya, one of two major Mordvin dialects, but most also speak Russian. The majority are Orthodox Christian, but they have retained many pre-Christian traditions and beliefs.

Dungan (Hui)—estimated at less than 1% of the population, numbering about 35,000.

The Dungans, also called Hui, call themselves Huizui. They are also often referred to as Chinese Muslims due to their origins in northern China. The descendants of Arab, Persian, and Central Asian Muslims who migrated to China and mixed with the local Chinese, they form part of the larger Hui nation that inhabits the region of Ningsia in China. The Dungan settled in the Kazakh Steppe region as refugees from Chinese persecution, the first arriving in the eighteenth century.

Moldovan and Romanian—estimated at less than 1% of the population, numbering about 33,000.

The Moldovan and Romanian populations are both Romanian-speaking, but their languages differ in the use of the Cyrillic and Latin alphabets. Most of the Moldovans and Romanians were deported to Kazakhstan from their homes in Moldova* and Ukraine* during and after World War II. They mostly use Russian as their first language. The majority are Orthodox Christians.

Tajik—estimated at less than 1% of the population, numbering about 30,000.

The Tajiks, living in the southwestern provinces, are part of the larger Tajik population of the Central Asian republic of Tajikistan.* Settled in Kazakhstan during the Soviet era, the majority have begun to assimilate into Kazakh culture. Their own language, an Iranian dialect, has mostly been replaced by Kazakh, with many also speaking Russian. The majority are Sunni Muslims, with a Shi'a Muslim minority.

Kurd—estimated at less than 1% of the population, numbering about 28,000.

The Kurds are part of the large Kurdish nation that straddles the borders of Turkey, Iran, Iraq, and Syria in the Middle East. They mostly settled in Russian territory to escape persecution as infidels, as their Yezid religion is not recognized as an offshoot of Islam, but is condemned as heresy. The Kurds speak Russian, but also use their own language, called Northern Kurd or Kurmanji.

Bashkort (Bashkir)—estimated at less than 1% of the population, numbering about 24,000.

The Bashkort of Kazakhstan mostly settled in the region during the conquest of their homeland, now in Orenburg Oblast of the Russian Federation, which borders Kazakhstan on the northwest. Part of the large Bashkort population of Bashkortostan, a member state of the Russian Federation, the Bashkorts in Kazakhstan mostly speak Russian, but have retained their Sunni Muslim religion.

Chavash (Chuvash)—estimated at less than 1% of the population, numbering about 22,000.

The Chavash, called Chuvash by the Russians, are a people of mixed Turkic and Finnic ancestry, although they speak a language that is considered to form a separate branch of the Turkic group of languages. They usually speak Russian as their second language. Their homeland in the Volga River region of eastern European Russia, Chavashia or Chavashstan, forms a member state of the Russian Federation. The Chavash are mostly Orthodox Christians.

Ingush—estimated at less than 1% of the population, numbering about 22,000.

The Ingush are a Caucasian people closely related to the Chechens. Their homeland, Ingushetia, a member state of the Russian Federation, lies in the North Caucasus bordering the Chechen republic. The Ingush speak a Caucasian language closely related to Chechen, and the majority are Hanafi-rite Sunni Muslims.

Jew—estimated at less than 1% of the population, numbering about 20,000.

The Jewish population of the republic, mostly living in the northern provinces, was settled in the region during the Virgin Lands campaigns after World War II. The Jews of Kazakhstan mostly speak Russian as their first language. Immigration to Israel and the United States has decreased their numbers by about two-thirds since 1991.

Lezgi (Lezgian)—estimated at less than 1% of the population, numbering about 17,000.

The Lezgi or Lezgians are a Dagestani people, Caucasians from the North Caucasus region of southern European Russia. The Lezgian population of the republic represents part of the large number deported during and after World War II. They speak a Caucasian language, but the majority use Russian as their first language. The Lezgians are Sunni Muslims.

Udmurt—estimated at less than 1% of the population, numbering about 17,000.

The Udmurts are a Finnic people from the upper Volga River basin of eastern European Russia. Settled in the region during the 1940s and 1950s, the majority now use Russian as their first language while retaining their Finno-Permian language as the group language. The majority are Orthodox Christians.

Kyrgyz—estimated at less than 1% of the population, numbering about 15,000.

The Kyrgyz of Kazakhstan live mostly along the international border with Kyrgyzstan. Closely related to the Kazakhs, the Kyrgyz speak a related language and share the Kazakhs' Sunni Muslim religion.

Lithuanian—estimated at less than 1% of the population, numbering about 10,000.

The Lithuanians, mostly deported from their homeland in Lithuania* after World War II, are concentrated in the central provinces, and most are farmers. In Kazakhstan the majority speak Russian as their first language, but have retained their Baltic language as the language of the family and group. The majority are Roman Catholics.

Mari—estimated at less than 1% of the population, numbering about 9,000.

The Mari are a Finnic people whose homeland, Mari-El, in the Volga River region, forms a member state of the Russian Federation. The Mari of Kazakhstan mostly speak Russian and are Orthodox Christians.

Georgian—estimated at less than 1% of the population, numbering about 7,000.

The Georgians of Kazakhstan, mostly living in the region around Almaty, were deported to the region during World War II. Part of the Georgian Muslim minority, most of the Kazakh Georgians are Meski or Ajar Georgians. The Georgians use Russian as their first language, but have retained Georgian dialects as intergroup languages.

Ossetian—estimated at less than 1% of the population, numbering about 4,000.

The Ossetians, also called Alans, are an Iranian people whose homeland, North Ossetia, lies in the North Caucasus region of European Russia. They mostly live in the northern provinces among the Slav population and use Russian as their first language. Many of the Ossetians are part of the Muslim minority of the Ossetian nation that was deported during World War II.

Turkmen—estimated at less than 1% of the population, numbering about 3,000.

The Turkmen, part of the Turkmen nation of Turkmenistan, live mostly in the southern provinces. Settled in the region during the colonial era in the eighteenth century, the majority of the Turkmen speak Kazakh as their second language. Like the Kazakhs, they are Sunni Muslims.

THE NATION: Nomadic Turkic tribes began to settle the vast steppe in the eighth century A.D. Influenced by the ambassadors, pilgrims, and traders crossing the region on the ancient Silk Road between China and the Mediterranean, the tribes eventually settled in communities along the important trade routes. By the tenth century the Turkic tribes had united in a powerful state called Karakan, a wealthy and cultured nation controlling the lucrative trade routes that crossed the immense plains of the Kazakh Steppe.

Invading Mongols conquered Karakan in the early thirteenth century. The invaders destroyed the sophisticated cities and irrigation systems and scattered the surviving inhabitants across the vast steppe. A division of the Mongol forces, the White Horde, began to settle the depopulated area in 1456, slowly absorbing the remaining Turkic peoples and gradually adopting their Turkic language and culture. Three new hordes, called ordas, were formed under the authority of local khans. The combining of the two peoples, Mongol and Turk, is considered the foundation of the modern Kazakh nation. Russian explorers made contact with the nomadic Kazakh tribes in the early sixteenth century, beginning the gradual Russian encroachment.

In the seventeenth century, political authority in the vast region was divided among three weak tribal states, the Great Horde, in the southern and eastern region; the Middle Horde, in the north-central region; and the Little Horde, in the northwest. The rule of Khan Teuke over the reunited Kazakh hordes lasted from 1680 to 1718, when Oirot raids on the Kazakhs disrupted life on the vast steppe.

In 1715 the first Russian expedition to the Kazakh Steppe under Peter the Great established contact with the three Kazakh hordes ruled by khans. The Oryats defeated the Middle Horde north of Lake Balkash in 1718. The three khanates, pressured militarily, accepted Russian protection, the Little Horde in 1731, the Middle Horde in 1740, and the Great Horde in 1742. In 1771 the Chinese attempted to bring the Kazakhs into a vassal relationship with their empire, raising the specter of Chinese-Russian conflicts in the region.

The Russians gradually extended their influence, and in 1822 the Khanate of the Middle Horde was abolished by the tsarist government. Two years later, in 1824, the Little Horde was abolished. Between the 1820s and the 1840s several serious Kazakh revolts broke out against widening Russian authority. The Kazakh national hero, Kenasary Kasymov, led the hordes (ordas) against the Russians in 1834, but the nomadic warriors were a poor match for the modern Russian army. In 1848 the Khanate of the Great Horde was officially ended.

The Russian military founded Fort Vernoe, later called Alma-Ata, in 1854. A year later all of Kazakhstan was fully under Russian control, with the Russian military holding the Syr Darya Line from the Aral Sea to Lake Issyk Kul. What is now called Kazakhstan was organized, in 1868, as the government-general of the Steppe Provinces, the Turgai Province, and the Ural Province.

The Kazakhs, probably as a reaction to Russian attempts to convert them to Orthodox Christianity, adopted the Islamic religion of their southern neighbors, becoming the only nation to embrace Islam after the Russian conquest. Along with their Islamic religion, the Kazakhs adopted a more political attitude toward Russian domination. In 1912 Kazakh intellectuals founded the nationalist Alash Orda Party.

The Muslim Kazakhs, exempted from military duty, were unaffected by World War I until 1916. The Russian authorities, desperate for manpower, attempted to conscript 250,000 Central Asians for noncombat labor battalions. The Kazakhs resisted, and rebellion spread rapidly across the steppe lands. Rebel forces launched attacks on Russian military garrisons and on the villages and towns of the nearly 1 million Slavs settled in their homeland between 1896 and 1911.

The Russian authorities, fearing that the rebellion would spread to neighboring Muslim peoples, hastily withdrew troops from the front, sending them against both the rebels and against peaceful Kazakh settlements. By September 1916 thousands of Kazakhs had died and over 300,000 had fled to the mountains or had crossed into Chinese Turkestan. The Slavic settlers, in revenge for earlier Kazakh attacks, joined in the massacres and seized the Kazakhs' herds and lands.

Kazakh leaders returned to the region as revolution spread across Russia in February 1917. In April the Kazakh leaders convened a congress that set up a national council called Alash Orda, the Horde of Alash, after the probably mythical ancestor of the Kazakh nation. Starving Kazakh refugees, returning to their homes during the summer, were brutally set upon by Slavic colonists unwilling to give up confiscated lands and herds. Thousands of defenseless Kazakhs were slaughtered in savage massacres carried out by the Slav colonists.

Alarmed by the antireligious rhetoric of the October 1917 Bolshevik coup, the Kazakh leaders of the Alash Orda Party severed all ties to Russia and declared an independent Kazakh republic on 16 December 1917. Allied to the anti-Bolshevik White forces, the Kazakhs valiantly resisted the advance of the Red Army, but were finally defeated and brought under Soviet rule in 1920. Under Lenin's nationalities policy Kazakhs retained many government positions and pro-government political parties were allowed to operate.

Stalin, Lenin's successor, took control of the Soviet Union in 1924. Under Stalin's rule Soviet authority became harsher. In 1927–28 the Kazakh Alash Orda Party was liquidated and most ethnic Kazakhs were eliminated from the republican government. Forced settlement of the nomadic Kazakhs, fiercely resisted, was followed by purges and the forced collectivization of the remaining Kazakh herds by the Stalinist government. Between 1916 and 1939 over 1.5 million Kazakhs died and another 1 million fled to neighboring Chinese territory.

Kazakhstan, made a separate union republic in 1936, retained a large Kazakh majority until after World War II, even though the Soviet practice of dumping unwanted and punished peoples in the region added many different national groups to the republic's population. As part of the Virgin Lands scheme of the 1950s and 1960s, millions of ethnic Slavs were transferred to the fertile northern steppe, the Kazakh population falling from 57% of the total in 1941 to just 38% in 1979. Kazakhstan became the most ethnically mixed of the union republics.

Kazakh riots broke out in 1986, protesting the replacement of the republic's Kazakh chairman with Gennadi Kolbin, a native Russian who was completely unknown in the republic. The attempt to place Kolbin in the post of first secretary of the Kazakh Communist Party presented the new Soviet leader, Mikhail Gorbachev, with his first serious ethnic challenge, helping to shape the reforms he introduced in the Soviet empire in 1987. The protests, which turned into riots by Kazakh youths, surprised the Soviet authorities and startled the complacent Kazakh Soviet elite.

Gorbachev's policies of openness and liberalization of Soviet society made little impact until 1988, when Kazakh nationalist groups began to form in reaction to the mobilization of the ethnic Russian and Cossack populations. Liberated from strict Soviet control, the Kazakh national movement grew rapidly, led by a number of unofficial groups, including organizations openly advocating independence from the Soviet Union. The population question spurred the growth of nationalism in the republic. The Kazakhs' high birthrate, as opposed to the Russians' very low birthrate, made the former the largest national group in Kazakhstan again in 1990–91.

In August 1991 factions of the KGB and military hard-liners launched a coup to preserve communism and oust Mikhail Gorbachev. The defiance of Boris Yeltsin, president of the largest of the union republics, the Russian Federation, and his subsequent recognition of the independence of Estonia,* led to the rapid breakup of the Soviet Union.

Kazakhstan became effectively independent with the disintegration of the Soviet state in August 1991. President Nursultan Nazarbayev, fearing opposition from the large non-Kazakh population, hesitated to formally declare independence until the former Soviet republics began to unite in a loose commonwealth. On 16 December 1991, exactly seventy-four years after the Kazakhs' first attempt to win freedom from Russia, Kazakhstan declared itself an independent republic, the last of the former Soviet republics to do so.

The same month, December 1991, Nursultan Nazarbayev, chairman of the Kazakh Council of Ministers since 1984, was elected president. Running unopposed because no candidates were allowed to stand against him, Nazarbayev received 95% of the vote.

The first serious challenge to the Nazarbayev government came in 1994 from the militant Cossack societies. Cossacks from the eastern oblasts called for the country to become part of the Russian Federation and demanded that a national referendum be held on the issue. The groups also called for the Russian language to be granted the status of a state language. The suspension of several Cossack organizations and the arrest of several leaders ended the crisis.

In July 1994 the leaders of Kazakhstan, Kyrgyzstan, and Uzbekistan agreed to form a comprehensive defense and economic union. The agreement will eventually coordinate the three governments' foreign affairs and military postures and provide for the creation of a Central Asian Bank for Cooperation and Development.

In 1996 the government decided to allow its six northern regions to contract directly with neighboring Russia for electricity. The decision highlights the increasing links between the Russian northern oblasts and the Russian state. The Kazakh government is also seeking Russian backing on its claim to territorial waters in the Caspian Sea, one of the most contentious issues facing the states bordering the sea, with its wealth of oil and natural gas.

The danger of ethnic violence has been used as one justification for curbing democracy in the state. Citing rising ethnic tensions, the Nazarbayev government closed the 1994–95 session of parliament and extended his presidency until the end of the decade. Balancing the contradictory goals of building a homeland for the Kazakhs that gives them priority in education and employment while developing a multiethnic state that is democratic and liberal has been the most daunting task facing the Kazakh government.

The Slav opposition to Kazakh nationalism has increased as ethnic Kazakhs take on more and more of the responsible positions in the republic's government. Slav groups, ranging from the separatist Cossack and Russian organizations not recognized by the government to the more moderate groups represented in parliament, seek to retain Slavic privileges. The most powerful Russian ethnic and cultural organization is called Lad (Republican Public Slavic Movement). The most educated and politically competent democratic organization, it includes a large number of the intelligentsia. Despite its ethnic interests, Lad is a centrist organization working to secure a place for the Kazakh Russians in the new republic. The fear is that increasing tensions between the formerly dominant Slavs and the increasingly assertive Kazakhs could lead to the secession of the northern regions.

The ethnic dimension is not the only serious problem the republic faces. It was once the testing ground for Soviet nuclear weapons, and the pollution left by the tests has caused serious health problems. An estimated 400,000 people, mostly ethnic Kazakhs, suffer the effects of radiation sickness. Added to the massive pollution of the industrial cities in the north of the country, the ecological disaster left in the wake of the Soviet disintegration will remain a serious problem for the country for decades to come.

Some positive aspects of independence concern the massive new oil finds in the republic and possibly in the Kazakh region of the disputed Caspian Sea. Western oil companies have invested heavily in the republic, particularly in the new Tengiz field, which promises to make Kazakhstan a major oil producer, perhaps rivaling the producers in the Middle East. The oil fields, being developed with American and German participation, lie in the Western provinces, however Soviet planning placed all oil refineries in the east of the country, yet another obstacle to faster development.

The Kazakh population continues to grow rapidly due to a high birthrate, but also because many of the millions of ethnic Kazakhs outside the country have begun to return to the first independent Kazakh state in modern history. In 1995 the last of some 30,000 ethnic Kazakhs arrived in the republic from the east, having trekked on foot from their former homes in Mongolia.

According to a new language law passed in July 1997, Kazakh remains the state language, but Russian has "equal status" with Kazakh at state-owned organizations and bodies of local government. The language issue, the right to use Russian, is one of the major demands of the large Russian population in the north of the republic. However, the new language law was condemned by many ethnic Russians. The Russians object to the clauses that provide for 50% of all broadcasting to be in Kazakh, and require that all ethnic Russian state officials be proficient in the Kazakh language by 2006.

Two reforms instituted by President Nazarbayev in 1997 had important consequences for the republic and for the Kazakh people. In November the capital of the state was transferred from the city of Almaty, near the Chinese border, to the mainly Russian city of Akmola, formerly Tselinograd, on the Kazakh Steppe. The transfer of the seat of power to the Russian-dominated north reinforces the Kazakh hold on the northern regions and will encourage ethnic Kazakhs to move north, changing the overwhelmingly Slav population of the area. The move will also reassure Slavs who feel they are becoming second-class citizens so far from the centers of power. The second change replaced the Cyrillic alphabet with the Latin alphabet in written Kazakh. The Latin alphabet was first introduced in Kazakhstan in 1929, when it replaced the traditional

Arabic script. However, Joseph Stalin imposed the Cyrillic alphabet on Kazakhstan in 1940, not long after forced collectivization destroyed the Kazakhs' nomadic way of life.

SELECTED BIBLIOGRAPHY:

Bradley, Catherine. *Kazakhstan.* 1992.

Curtis, Glenn E., ed. *Kazakhstan, Kyrgyzstan, Tajikistan, Turkmenistan, and Uzbekistan: Country Studies.* 1997.

Mandelbaum, Michael, ed. *Central Asia and the World: Kazakhstan, Uzbekistan, Tajikistan, Kyrgyzstan, and Turkmenistan.* 1994.

Micklin, Philip P., and William D. Williams, eds. *The Aral Sea Basin.* 1996.

Olcott, Martha Brill. *The Kazakhs.* 1995.

KYRGYZSTAN

Kirghizistan; Kirghizia; Kyrgyz
Respublikasy

CAPITAL: Bishkek (Frunze)

POPULATION: (98e) 4,535,000 : 2,410,000 Kyrgyz in Kyrgyzstan. Another 150,000 Kyrgyz live across the border in China, and 300,000 live in adjacent areas of Uzbekistan,* Tajikistan,* and Kazakhstan.* MAJOR NATIONAL GROUPS: (98e) Kyrgyz 56.1%, Russian 18.7%, Uzbek 13.2%, Ukrainian 2.2%, German 2.1%, Tatar 1.8%, Dungan (Hui) 1.6%, Uighur, Crimean Tatar, Kazakh, Tajik, Korean, Azeri, Kurmanji (Kurdish). MAJOR LANGUAGES: Kyrgyzic, Russian, Jagatai (Uzbek). MAJOR RELIGIONS: Sunni Islam, Russian Orthodox, Roman Catholic, Jewish. MAJOR CITIES: (98e) Bishkek (Frunze) 674,000 (805,000), Osh 230,000, Jalal-Abad (Dzhal-Abad) 87,000 (122,000), Tokmak 80,000, Kara-Kol (Przhevalsk) 73,000, Kara Balta 68,000 (145,000), Naryn 60,000, Talas (Talash) 56,000, Mayli Say 55,000, Ysyk-Kol (Rybachye) 53,000, Mirza-Aki (Uzgen) 52,000, Kyzyl Kiya 45,000.

GEOGRAPHY: AREA: 76,641 sq.mi.-198,391 sq.km. LOCATION: Kyrgyzstan lies in Central Asia, around Lake Issyk Kul'. Kyrgyzstan borders Kazakhstan on the north, Uzbekistan on the west, Tajikistan on the southwest, and China on the southeast and east. PHYSICAL GEOGRAPHY: The country lies between the Tien Shan Mountains to the northeast and the Pamir Alai Mountains to the southwest. Around three-quarters of the land area is mountainous, with high, broad valleys and a large salt lake, called Issyk Kul', which occupies a highland basin in the northeast. The lake is heated by volcanic action and influences the surrounding region's climatic conditions. The principal rivers are the Naryn and Chu. ADMINISTRATIVE DIVISIONS: six oblasttar (singular—

oblast) and one city, Bishkek. POLITICAL STATUS: Kyrgyzstan was recognized as an independent state in 1991.

INDEPENDENCE DECLARATION: 31 August 1991 (from the Soviet Union).

FLAG: The Kyrgyz national flag, the official flag of the republic, is a red field charged with a centered yellow sun with forty rays, representing the forty Kyrgyz tribes, and is crossed by six curving red lines, a stylized representation of the roof of a *yurt*, the traditional felt tent of the nomadic Kyrgyz.

PEOPLE: Kyrgyzstan, like the other Central Asian republics, was a dumping ground for peoples unwanted in European Russia. Thousands of people, deported from their homelands, were resettled in the region from the 1930s to the 1960s. Over fifty different national groups live in the republic, roughly divided between the Muslim peoples and the Christian European nations.

Kyrgyz (Kirghiz)—an estimated 56.1% of the population, numbering about 2,410,000.

The majority of the Kyrgyz physically resemble their Mongol ancestors, but they speak a Turkic language of the Kipchak (West Turkic) language group, and culturally they belong to the Turkic group of nations. The language, spoken in three major dialects, is written in the Cyrillic alphabet and became a modern, viable language only after the infusion of Russian words, which now constitute about 25% of the words in common use.

Former nomads, the Kyrgyz are still mainly herdsmen and farmers. The Kyrgyz percentage of the republic's population, which had fallen to just 48% in 1979, has since increased due to the very high birthrate and the departure of nearly 200,000 Slavs from the republic since 1989.

Russian—an estimated 18.7% of the population, numbering about 850,000.

The Russian population, concentrated around Bishkek, Lake Issyk Kul', and the Fergana Valley, mostly settled in the region after World War II. They came from the devastated areas of European Russia to work in the newly industrialized cities of Central Asia. Most of the ethnic Russians in the republic live in the urban areas.

Many of the Russians, seeking better economic opportunities or security, have left the republic. An estimated 296,000 Russians left Kyrgyzstan between 1989 and 1995. The departing Russians are taking their technical skills with them, skills the new republic badly needs.

The majority of the Russian population are Russian Orthodox, but with several other sects represented, particularly schismatic sects such as Dukhobors and Old Believers who left European Russia in the nineteenth century to escape persecution.

Uzbek—an estimated 13.2% of the population, numbering about 560,000.

The large Uzbek population is mostly concentrated in the Fergana Valley and the other regions that border the Republic of Uzbekistan. A Turkic people, the Uzbeks speak an East Turkic language of the Altaic language group.

The Kyrgyz government keeps a wary eye on the large Uzbek population and on the aspirations of the neighboring Republic of Uzbekistan. As the largest national group in Central Asia, the Uzbeks are not fully trusted by the other peoples of the region.

Ukrainian—an estimated 2.2% of the population, numbering about 100,000.

The Ukrainians, mostly settled in the region during the 1950s and 1960s, are concentrated around the capital and in the cities of the subtropical Fergana Valley. Like the Russians, the Ukrainians came to the region as administrators and industrial workers.

Since Ukrainian independence in 1991, and the increasingly difficult economic problems in Kyrgyzstan, over 40,000 ethnic Ukrainians have left the republic, mostly for Ukraine, but also for areas of European Russia.

German—an estimated 2.1% of the population, numbering about 95,000.

The Germans of Kyrgyzstan are mostly the descendants of the German populations of European Russia deported to Central Asia in 1941, when Stalin's ally, Hitler, launched his invasion of the Soviet Union.

Many of the Germans speak Russian as their first language while speaking archaic dialects of German brought to Russia with their ancestors in the eighteenth century. Many Germans have taken advantage of the German government's aid to return to Germany. However, many face discrimination there, as few speak modern, standard German and culturally they have absorbed many Slavic traits. Employment problems in Germany and discrimination have led to a small reverse migration as ethnic Germans return to the areas they left after Kyrgyz independence in 1991. The German government has granted financial assistance to provide employment for the Kyrgyz Germans.

Tatar—an estimated 1.8% of the population, numbering about 80,000.

The Tatar population of Kyrgyzstan are mostly the descendants of Volga Tatars sent to the region as administrators and government functionaries following the Russian conquest in the latter half of the nineteenth century.

The Tatars, who speak a West Turkic language of the Altaic language group, are the most advanced of the Muslim peoples of the former Soviet Union. The majority of the Tatars are Sunni Muslims, but with a small Christian minority called Kreschen.

Dungan (Hui)—an estimated 1.6% of the population, numbering about 75,000.

The Dungan, also called Hui or Tungan, call themselves Hui-Zu. Outside their homeland in northwestern China they are often called Chinese Muslims. They are an ancient people, the descendants of early Arab, Persian, and Turkic settlers who took Chinese wives and adopted the Chinese culture and language. The Kyrgyz Dungan live mostly in and around the city of Osh in the Fergana Valley and around Lake Issyk Kul' in the northwest.

The Sunni Muslim Dungans of Kyrgyzstan settled in the region after fleeing Chinese persecution in the nineteenth and twentieth centuries. Their language, a Chinese dialect, is spoken in three dialects, two of which are present in Kyrgyzstan. The Gansu dialect is spoken in most of Kyrgyzstan, while the Shensi dialect is spoken in the Fergana Valley. The majority speak Russian as their second language. The Dungans are Sunni Muslims.

Uighur (Uyghur)—estimated at less than 1% of the population, numbering about 45,000.

The Uighur or Uyghur are a Turkic people, part of a numerous national group in neighboring China, where they form the largest national group in the Chinese region of Xingiang. The Uighurs in Central Asia came to the area as refugees fleeing Chinese persecution.

The language spoken by the Uighurs is an East Turkic language of the Altaic language group, which in Kyrgyzstan is written in the Cyrillic alphabet. Under Soviet rule the Chinese, Arabic, and Latin alphabets used by minority peoples were forcibly replaced with the Russian Cyrillic alphabet.

Crimean Tatar—estimated at less than 1% of the population, numbering about 42,000.

The Crimean Tatar population of Kyrgyzstan is part of a larger nation deported from the Crimean Peninsula by the Stalinist government in 1944. Dumped at rail sidings across Central Asia, thousands died of hunger and exposure. The Crimean Tatars were not rehabilitated along with the other deported nations in the 1950s, but remained in exile.

The language of the Crimean Tatars is a West Turkic language related to Turkish. The Muslim Crimean Tatars have prospered in exile, but a movement to return to their homeland, now in independent Ukraine, has led to the departure of several thousand since 1991.

Kazakh—estimated at less than 1% of the population, numbering about 40,000.

The Kazakh inhabitants of Kyrgyzstan live mostly in the northern regions along the Kazakh border and around Lake Issyk Kul'. Related to the Kyrgyz, the Kazakh speak a similar West Turkic language and share many cultural traits. The Kazakhs, like the Kyrgyz, are Sunni Muslims, but retain many pre-Islamic beliefs and traditions.

Tajik—estimated at less than 1% of the population, numbering about 39,000.

The Tajiks are part of the larger nation of Tajiks just south of Kyrgyzstan in Tajikistan. An Iranian people, the Tajiks speak a West Iranian language closely related to Farsi, the language of Iran.

The Tajiks share many of the cultural traits and traditions common to all the Muslim peoples of Central Asia. Since independence in 1991, several thousand ethnic Tajiks have crossed the border fleeing the civil war in their country.

Turk—estimated at less than 1% of the population, numbering about 23,000.

The Turks of Kyrgyzstan, often called Fergana Turks, mostly live in the Fergana Valley in the southwestern part of the republic. An ancient people, the Turks claim to have lived in the oasis cities of the valley for over 2,000 years. Their language, related to the Turkish spoken in Turkey, is an archaic dialect little changed since the nineteenth century. They normally speak Russian or Uzbek for intergroup communications. The Turks are Sunni Muslims.

Korean—estimated at less than 1% of the population, numbering about 20,000.

The Koreans of Kyrgyzstan were deported from the Russian Far East during the Stalin era. Resettled in collectives across Central Asia, they were mostly forgotten until the collapse of the Soviet Union. Since 1991 they have reestablished ties to South Korea, which has provided aid to Kyrgyzstan to be used for the welfare of the Korean population. The Koreans form the largest Buddhist population in the republic.

Azeri (Azerbaijani)—estimated at less than 1% of the population, numbering about 18,000.

The Azeris living in Kyrgyzstan are concentrated in the region around Bishkek. Mostly deported to Central Asia during the Stalin era, the Azeris of the region speak North Azeri dialects of the Azeri language. Like the Kazakhs, they are Sunni Muslims.

Kurd—estimated at less than 1% of the population, numbering about 15,000.

The Kurds of Kyrgyzstan, part of the large Kurdish population of Kurdistan, which straddles the borders of Iran, Iraq, Syria, and Turkey, fled to Russian territory during the nineteenth century to escape religious persecution, as they are mostly Yezidis and are considered heretics by Sunni and Shi'a Muslims. They use Russian as their first language, but among themselves they speak Kurmanji, also called North Kurdish.

Belarussian—estimated at less than 1% of the population, numbering about 7,000.

The Belarussian population, living in the central parts of the republic, mostly settled in the region during the Soviet era. The Belarussians are the least numerous of the Slav nations living in the republic, and the majority speak Russian as their first language. They are mostly Orthodox Christians, with a small Roman Catholic minority.

Mordvin—estimated at less than 1% of the population, numbering about 5,000.

The Mordvins, part of the larger Mordvin population of the Volga River basin of eastern European Russia, are concentrated in Bishkek and the surrounding area. Mostly settled in the region during the Soviet era, the majority of the Mordvins are industrial workers or farmers.

The Mordvins of Kyrgyzstan mostly speak Erzya, one of the two dialects of the Mordvin language, a Finnic language of the Finno-Ugrian language group. The majority of the Mordvins living in Central Asia use Russian as their first language.

Armenian—estimated at less than 1% of the population, numbering about 3,000.

The Armenians, part of the Armenian nation of the Republic of Armenia,* are mostly farmers in the region around Lake Issyk Kul'. They were deported to the region during the Stalin era during the frequent purges of the Armenian Communist Party. They mostly speak Russian as their first language, and the majority belong to the Russian Orthodox Church or retain their atheist beliefs.

Bashkort (Bashkir)—estimated at less than 1% of the population, numbering about 3,000.

The Bashkort, part of the larger Bashkort nation of Bashkortostan of the Russian Federation, were settled in the region in the 1930s and 1940s. A Turkic people, the Bashkort speak a West Turkic language and, like the Kyrgyz, are mostly Sunni Muslims.

Chavash (Chuvash)—estimated at less than 1% of the population, numbering about 2,000.

The Chavash, called Chuvash by the Russians, are part of the Chavash nation of the Chavash Republic, which lies in the Volga River basin of the Russian Federation. The Chavash of Kyrgyzstan were settled in the region in the 1930s and are mostly farmers in the fertile Fergana Valley. The Chavash speak a distinct language of the Turkic language group and are mostly Orthodox Christians.

THE NATION: Central Asia was originally inhabited by Aryan peoples related to the early Europeans, and is thought to be the original home of the Aryan peoples. Experts agree that the region was one of the earliest centers of civilization in the ancient world. Archeologists have established that settlements existed in the area as early as 3000 B.C.

A Turkic people, the Kara-Kun, inhabited the valley of the Yenisei River in central Siberia as early as 400 B.C. and are mentioned in a Chinese chronicle of 201 B.C. An early feudal state was established in the fourth and fifth centuries A.D. in the Minusin Basin along the Yenisei River north of the present Kyrgyzstan Republic. The state expanded rapidly beyond southern Siberia to control the region of their present homeland. One branch of the ancient Silk Road, the Kyrgyz Way, passed through their expanded state. During that time many ethnic groups were integrated into the Kyrgyz empire.

In A.D. 840 an army of 100,000 men under the leadership of the Kyrgyz attacked the ancient Uighur capital, Orhon, located in what is now Mongolia, occupying and destroying it; the great Uighur state was defeated. A Kyrgyz khanate was created in its place, the boundaries of which extended from Lake Baikal to the Irtish River and from the present Krasnoyarsk city to the Chinese Wall.

The Kara-Kun state, in the tenth century, splintered into a number of small, weak states. In 1207 the Mongols, expanding from their homeland to the east, overran the region and conquered the southern Kyrgyz tribes and their principalities. In 1293 the Mongols moved north to destroy the Yenisei state. The Mongols destroyed the towns and irrigation systems and left the region devastated. Absorbed into the Mongol Empire, the tribes became part of the vast army that eventually conquered most of the known world.

The Kyrgyz tribes, under pressure from neighboring peoples, migrated south from Siberia to the mountains of Central Asia. Conquered by the Altai Federation of the Oirots, a Mongol people of the Altai Mountains, the Kyrgyz finally regained their freedom with the disintegration of the Oirot federation in the 1750s.

In the early nineteenth century the Kyrgyz tribes came under the rule of the powerful Uzbek khanate of Kokand. The Muslim religion and the Persianized Uzbek culture were introduced to the tribes by ethnic Uzbeks, called Sarts, who settled among the Kyrgyz tribes in the fertile Fergana Valley. The urbanized Uzbeks developed the small trading towns, which became important cities, centers of regional trade and of Muslim learning.

Russians, expanding into Central Asia in the nineteenth century, took control of the northern Kyrgyz lands in 1855. The remainder of the Kyrgyz tribes came under Russian rule with the annexation of Kokand in 1876. Slavic settlers moved into the region, aided by the completion of the rail link from European Russia in 1891. The region, forming part of the Russian government of Turkestan, by 1900 was under firm Russian control.

Their best lands taken by the Christian Slavic colonists, the Kyrgyz transferred their remaining herds to the high mountain valleys well away from the colonization areas. Seeking to escape the colonial rule of the Russians, the majority of the nomadic Kyrgyz tribes moved into the more remote districts of their mountains, shunning the Slav-populated cities of the lowlands. In their isolation, the Kyrgyz remained feudal and backward, economically exploited, and dominated by Islam.

The isolated Kyrgyz were virtually unaware of Russia's war in the west until 1916. Desperate for food and manpower, the Russian authorities attempted to confiscate the Kyrgyz herds and to conscript the Kyrgyz men into labor battalions. Paid in meaningless paper money, the Kyrgyz saw only that their herds had been stolen and their people left to starve.

A tsarist decree, signed on 25 June 1916, authorized the conscription of 250,000 formerly exempt Central Asians for unarmed labor duty at the front. Anti-Russian feelings, fanned by the forced conscription of Kyrgyz men, spread rapidly across the region. In August 1916, as tsarist officials attempted to carry out the edict, rebellion broke out among the Kyrgyz tribes.

The rebels defeated the meager Russian forces in the region and turned on the Slavic colonists, burning villages and slaughtering as many as 10,000. Troops, hastily withdrawn from the front, were sent against the rebels and unarmed Kyrgyz villagers, forcing thousands to flee into Chinese territory. The Kyrgyz rebellion, overtaken by the revolution that swept across Russia in February 1917, spawned a strong sense of unity among the diverse tribal groups. The rebel leaders formed a Kara-Kyrgyz government as civil government in the region collapsed. Many Kyrgyz who had fled to China returned as the revolution promised to redress the wrongs and return their stolen lands.

Calls for Muslim solidarity, and the Kyrgyz lack of trained administrators, persuaded the tribes to send delegates to an All-Muslim Congress at Kokand, attended by the various Muslim peoples of Central Asia. The Congress sent a delegation to the new Provisional Government of Russia seeking autonomy for Turkestan within a democratic Russian federation.

Local Bolsheviks, loyal to the leaders of the coup that ended Russia's experiment with democracy in October 1917, attempted to take control of Kyrghizia as rival governments competed for power in the region. The All-Muslim government in Kokand sought to create a European-style democracy as the chaos of the collapsing empire engulfed the region. A rival government set up by local Bolsheviks in the mainly Russian city of Tashkent disputed the Muslim claim to power in the vast Turkestan region.

Pressed by the Bolsheviks, the All-Muslim government severed its ties to Russia and proclaimed the independent Republic of Turkestan on 16 December 1917. In January 1918 fighting broke out between Bolshevik troops and Muslim nationalists. The poorly equipped Muslims were routed, and in February Kokand fell to the advancing Bolshevik forces. Thousands of Kyrgyz fled into their mountains to escape the fighting.

Conquered by the Red Army in 1919, the Kyrgyz were forced to abandon their traditional nomadic way of life. Thousands joined nationalist guerrilla groups, the Basmachi, which continued to harass the new Soviet authorities from mountain bases. Their herds gone and their homeland in ruins, an estimated half million Kyrgyz perished in the famine that devastated the region in 1921–22. Many fled to Chinese territory to escape the harsh Communist rule of the new Soviet state.

The new nationality policies of the Bolsheviks brought many benefits. Education became available to the former nomads, women were given status equal to men, and the language was given official sanction.

The Bolsheviks organized Turkestan as the Turkestan Autonomous Soviet Socialist Republic within the Russian Soviet Federated Socialist Republic on 11 April 1921, even though many areas, particularly the high mountains, remained outside government control. The final pacification of the region was accomplished with great brutality. The Muslim religion was suppressed and mosques were turned into storage barns or factories.

The collectivization of Kyrgyzstan was disastrous for the Kyrgyz. The tribes, forced to settle in permanent villages, resisted, and fighting erupted. In the ensuing conflict thousands of Kyrgyz died, were imprisoned, or were driven across the border into China. An estimated three-fourths of their herds were destroyed. The Kyrgyz began a long decline in population and culture. Alcohol and other Western vices took their toll on the tribes. Under Soviet rule the region remained isolated from the outside world.

Kyrghizia was organized as a separate autonomous province within the Russian Federation in 1924 and was raised to the status of an autonomous republic in 1926. Separated from the Russian Federation and made a separate constituent republic, Kyrghizia joined the Soviet Union in 1936 as a member state. Kyrgyz history as rewritten by Soviet historians was imposed as the official history.

During the Stalinist era, from the 1930s to the early 1950s, Slavic settlement in the republic was encouraged and became government policy. The Kyrgyz towns and new towns founded by the colonists became identical to towns in European Russia. Russification of the Kyrgyz language accompanied a marked increase in education. The Cyrillic alphabet was forced on the Kyrgyz in 1939, replacing the Latin they had used since the Revolution.

The Soviet plan for educating a generation of Kyrgyz as Soviets largely failed, mostly because educated Kyrgyz often became dissidents or leaders of nationalist or religious organizations. Agitation in the region was met with periodic purges of local government officials and show trials of prominent anti-Soviet figures.

During World War II many Kyrgyz supported the Turkestan National Committee, which supported Germany and all enemies of the hated Soviet government. In September 1942 the Turkic Legion was formed from Muslim units fighting in alliance with the Axis powers.

Following World War II, the region was given more resources. Education and material advances that outstripped those of kinsmen across the border in China turned the Kyrgyz leadership into a modern, Westernized elite. However, the Kyrgyz majority remained undereducated and clung to ancient customs and Islamic traditions.

In 1952 the banning of the great Kyrgyz national epic *Manas* sparked demands for the revision of their distorted and falsified history. The episode marked the beginning of the cultural revival and the nationalist movement that gained strength in the 1960s. Suppressed by national show trials and intense assimilation pressure, the movement reemerged with the liberalization of Soviet society by Mikhail Gorbachev in the late 1980s.

The Kyrgyz population, a minority in their own republic, began to recover their overall majority by the early 1980s. Between the 1979 and 1989 Soviet censuses the Kyrgyz population grew by 32%. A very high birthrate is common in the region, where contraception and family planning give way to Allah's will. Families of eight to ten children became the norm.

Mikhail Gorbachev, after coming to power in Moscow in 1985, brought in or promoted new people in order to impose his reform policies on recalcitrant party machines in the republics. Absamat Masaliev, his appointee in Kyrgyzstan, tried to implement limited reforms while preserving Communist Party control. The effects of nationalism and democratization came late to Kyrgyzstan, but when they arrived events unfolded with remarkable speed, pushing the republic far ahead of similar, but still hesitant, movements in neighboring republics.

In 1990 democratic opposition groups voted Masaliev out of office, electing as president Askar Akayev, a proponent of radical economic change and the Kyrgyzization of the republic. Akayev's policy of de-Russification has since been tempered by the need to accommodate the large Russian-Ukrainian element in Kyrgyzstan's population, and a solution reflecting mutual ethnic tolerance has become a model for other Central Asian states facing the exodus of the most advanced and skilled segment of the population.

Ethnic violence, aggravated by land and water rights disputes, sparked a rapid growth of nationalist sentiment in 1989–90. In spite of this new spurt of nationalist feeling, the Kyrgyz produced nothing to compare to the Popular Front groups in the western republics of the Soviet Union. The largest of several unofficial organizations, Askar (Living Space), openly espoused separatism in 1990. Pressed by the nationalists, the republican government declared the Soviet republic a sovereign state on 12 December 1990.

President Askar Akayev, one of the few Central Asian leaders to condemn the attempted Soviet coup in August 1991, declared the republic, renamed Kyrgyzstan, independent of the crumbling Soviet Union on 31 August 1991, the first independent Kyrgyz state in modern history. The nationalists quickly took control of the parliament and other branches of the former Soviet government.

The new republican government, although poorly prepared for independence, began to apply democratic and economic reform programs. The republic quickly became the most successful of the new Central Asian nations. Although old authoritarian habits remain, Kyrgyzstan has developed the most democratic and open society in the region.

The Kyrgyz government, in March 1996, amended the constitution to make Russian an official language, along with Kyrgyz, in regions and workplaces where Russian-speaking citizens form the majority. The move, part of a comprehensive government program, is designed to reassure the skilled Russians that they have a future in the Kazakh state. The government has also introduced a new passport that does not require that a person's ethnic origins be listed.

In 1994 the republic joined Kazakhstan and Uzbekistan to form the Central Asian Union, an economic and political union loosely modeled on the European Union. The union, still in its infancy, by 1997 had nearly foundered over the question of access to water. The question of water rights is likely to increasingly divide the republic in the future, as Uzbekistan and Kazakhstan need the water Kyrgzstan is unwilling to share.

The task of forming a united Kyrgyz nation after decades of Soviet domination has drawn on history, particularly the legendary *Manas*. In August 1995 the whole republic feted 1,000 years of its epic poem about the warrior-king. The poem, of up to 500,000 lines, is at least twenty times longer than the *Iliad* and the *Odyssey* combined. It tells how Manas led his people back to their homeland in the Tien Shan Mountains after they had been driven out by the Chinese. The history and culture of the Kyrgyz people are preserved and conveyed in the epic *Manas*. An oral encyclopedia, the epic has been the spiritual backbone of the nation during the darkest years of Soviet rule. The United Nations, in recognition of the importance of the epic in human history, declared 1995 the Year of the Manas Millennium.

Kyrgyzstan is one of the smallest and poorest states of the former Soviet Union. Its economy, heavily agricultural, produces cotton and tobacco on irrigated and heavily polluted lands in the southern regions. The small and obsolescent industrial sector, concentrated in Bishkek and the region around the capital, is heavily dependent on Russia and other former Soviet republics for fuel and customers. Between 1990 and 1997 the economy contracted by nearly 40%. The republic began showing signs of renewed economic growth only in late 1997.

President Akayev, the only Central Asian leader who is not a neo–Communist Party boss, has attempted to make his small country a democratic, market-oriented modern state. In spite of many successes, the economic hardships and a lack of democratic experience have left the president under strong political pressure to backtrack on some of his reform measures.

When the Soviet Union broke up in 1991, Kyrgyzstan quickly became known as the "crown jewel" of Central Asia. By 1997 the image had tarnished, as journalists were harassed and imprisoned, and popular protests against their treatment took place in the streets of Bishkek. The old authoritarian habits continue to surface in spite of the need to build a modern, multiethnic state in Kyrgyzstan.

Kyrgyzstan, although without the natural resources, such as oil and natural gas, that hold the promise of economic growth in the neighboring Central Asian states, does have abundant water, a resource that could become more important than oil within a generation. The Kyrgyz state, through its customs and economic union with Kazakhstan and Uzbekistan, may soon be in a position to trade water for the goods and services it needs to develop.

SELECTED BIBLIOGRAPHY:

Bacon, Elizabeth E. *Central Asia under Russian Rule: A Study in Cultural Change.* 1980.
Bradley, Pamela J., ed. *Kyrgyzstan.* 1992.
Curtis, Glenn E. *Kazakhstan, Kyrgyzstan, Tajikistan, Turkmenistan, and Uzbekistan: Country Studies.* 1997.
Mandelbaum, Michael, ed. *Central Asia and the World: Kazakhstan, Uzbekistan, Tajikistan, Kyrgyzstan, and Turkmenistan.* 1994.
Thomas, Paul. *The Central Asian States: Tajikistan, Uzbekistan, Kyrgyzstan, Turkmenistan.* 1992.

LATVIA

Republic of Latvia; Latvija; Latvijas Republika

CAPITAL: Riga

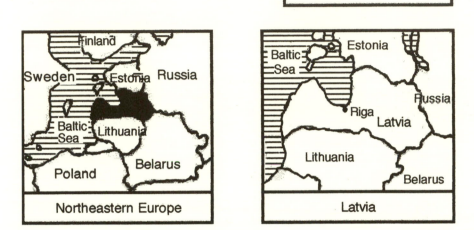

POPULATION: (98e) 2,498,000 : 1,420,000 Latvians in Latvia. MAJOR NATIONAL GROUPS: (95e) Latvian 56.8%, Russian 30.6%, Belarussian 4.2%, Ukrainian 2.7%, Polish 2.5%, Lithuanian 1.2%, Jew, Rom (Gypsy), German. MAJOR LANGUAGES: Latvian, Russian. MAJOR RELIGIONS: Lutheran, Russian Orthodox, Roman Catholic, Protestant, Jewish. MAJOR CITIES: (98e) Riga 878,000 (1,032,000), Daugavpils 127,000, Liepája 113,000, Jelgava 72,000 (111,000), Jurmala 60,000, Ventpils 48,000, Rézekne 43,000, Jekabpils 30,000, Valmiera 21,000.

GEOGRAPHY: AREA: 24,931 sq.mi.-64,589 sq.km. LOCATION: Latvia occupies a region of flat plains in northeastern Europe, bordering the Baltic Sea on the west, Estonia* on the north, Russia* on the east, and Lithuania* and Belarus* on the south. PHYSICAL GEOGRAPHY: The republic is divided into four historic regions, Kurzeme in western Latvia, Zemgale in southern Latvia, Vidzeme in the north, and Latgale in eastern Latvia. Most of Latvia is situated on a flat coastal plain, a fertile lowland, rising inland to a hilly region of forests and lakes in the east. About 20% of the country is forested, and it is drained by many rivers, the largest the Western Dvina or Daugava. Other important rivers are the Venta, Lielupe, and Gauja. The northern half of the Latvian coastline is indented by the Gulf of Riga, a large inlet of the Baltic Sea. ADMINISTRATIVE DIVISIONS: Twenty-six rajons or counties and seven independent municipalities. POLITICAL STATUS: Latvia was recognized as an independent state in 1991.

INDEPENDENCE DECLARATIONS: 18 November 1918 (from Russia); 21 August 1991 (from the Soviet Union).

FLAG: The Latvian national flag, the official flag of the republic, is a maroon field divided by a centered, horizontal white stripe.

PEOPLE: The inhabitants of the republic are broadly split between the Baltic peoples, the Latvians and the closely related Lithuanians, and the Slavs, the Russians, Ukrainians, and Belarussians that mostly settled in the republic after World War II. Dozens of different national groups are represented in the republic, a result of Soviet policies that encouraged or forcibly carried out resettlements of whole populations. Since Latvian independence in 1991 thousands of Latvians, mostly deportees, have returned to the republic from their places of exile in Central Asia and Siberia.

Latvian—an estimated 56.8% of the population, numbering about 1,420,000.

The Latvians are a Baltic people, generally tall and fair, with two major cultural and religious divisions, the mostly Lutheran Letts and the Roman Catholic Latgalians, who number some 500,000 in the Latgale region of the southeast. The Latvians and the neighboring Lithuanians make up the Baltic branch of the European peoples. The Latvians object to the name Lettish.

Language is one of the determining factors of Latvian national identity. The Latvian language is one of only two in the Baltic language group, along with Lithuanian. The language, which has absorbed more Slav influences than neighboring Lithuanian, has many features in common with the ancient Indo-European family of languages. Spoken in two major dialects, Central or Western Latvian and Eastern Latvian or Latgalian, the language is written in the Roman alphabet. Central Latvian is the basis of the Latvian literary language. Latgalian, which nearly died out in western Latvia, has had a vigorous revival since 1988. The two dialects are similar, but have separate literary traditions.

Russian—an estimated 30.6% of the population, numbering about 765,000.

The large, urbanized Slav population mostly settled in Latvia after the imposition of Soviet rule in 1940. Russians form a majority in many urban areas, including the capital, Riga. The presence of a large Russian minority in the country is one of the major problems facing the Latvian government. How to accommodate the Slav minority while building a secure homeland for the Latvians presents special problems and colors Latvia's relations with neighboring Russia.

The Russian language, which serves as a lingua franca, is the major language of business and international relations. Since independence English has become the preferred second language of many non-Russian Latvians.

Belarussian—an estimated 4.2% of the population, numbering about 105,000.

The Belarussians in Latvia live mostly in the southeast of the country in the region around the city of Daugavpils. The smallest of the Eastern Slav peoples, the Belarussians of Latvia speak Russian as their first language while speaking Belarussian at home. The Belarussians living in Latvia are mostly Roman Catholic, with a substantial Orthodox minority. The southeastern region of Latvia, the Daugavpils district, is claimed by some Belarussian national groups as part of historic Belarus.

Ukrainian—an estimated 2.7% of the population, numbering about 67,000.

The Ukrainian population of Latvia is concentrated in Riga and the other large towns and port cities. The majority of the Ukrainians settled in the republic after World War II as part of the Sovietization of Latvia. The Ukrainian language has begun to make inroads among the ethnic Ukrainians since Ukrainian and Latvian independence in 1991. However, the majority continue to speak Russian as their first language.

Pole—an estimated 2.5% of the population, numbering about 60,000.

The ethnic Poles living in Latvia are concentrated in the eastern Latgale region among their fellow Roman Catholic Latgalians, and there is a substantial Polish population in the Riga area. The Poles speak a Western Slav language, but many also speak Russian, the language of the former Soviet Union.

Lithuanian—an estimated 1.2% of the population, numbering about 30,000.

The Lithuanian population, concentrated in the southern counties along the Lithuanian border, is closely related to the Latvians. Their language, related to Latvian, can be understood by their Latvian neighbors. The Lithuanians, like the Latgalians and Poles, are Roman Catholics.

Jew—estimated at less than 1% of the population, numbering about 13,000.

The Jewish population of Latvia are the descendants of survivors of the Holocaust, Jews that returned to Latvia from abroad after the war, or Russian Jews settled in the republic during the Stalinist years.

The Jews, some native Russian speakers, normally speak Russian, at least as a second language. The Yiddish language, formerly spoken by the Jews of eastern Europe, has mostly given way to national languages.

Rom (Gypsy)—estimated at less than 1% of the population, numbering about 8,000.

The Rom or Gypsies of Latvia speak a Northern Romani language in a number of separate dialects—Latvian Romani, North Russian Romani, White Russian Romani, and so on—depending on where the Rom originated.

The Gypsies, known by the name of their ethnic group, Lotfítka Romá, are mostly rural, although in recent years a substantial number have settled in towns and cities, particularly Riga and Daugavpils. They have often suffered discrimination in housing, education, and employment.

Tatar—estimated at less than 1% of the population, numbering about 6,000.

The Tatars, a Muslim people originally from the Crimea and southern Ukraine, settled in the region under Polish rule in the fifteenth and sixteenth centuries. The Tatars speak a West Turkic language along with a second language, usually Polish or Russian. The Tatars form the only large Muslim population in the country.

Armenian—estimated at less than 1% of the population, numbering about 3,000.

The Armenians of Latvia, mostly concentrated in Riga, settled in the republic after World War II. The majority came to Latvia as part of the Soviet population exchanges. The Latvian Armenians have established ties to the Republic of Armenia,* and some have left the republic to live in Armenia. Most of the Armenians speak Russian as their first language.

Estonian—estimated at less than 1% of the population, numbering about 3,000.

The Estonian population, which was larger under Soviet rule, has diminished due to immigration to Estonia after independence in 1991. The Estonians speak a Finno-Ugrian language related to Finnish and Livonian, spoken in northwestern Latvia. The Estonians, like the Latvian majority, are mostly Lutherans.

Liv (Livonian)—estimated at less than 1% of the population, numbering about 1,500.

The Liv are concentrated in the northwest of the country. Overall numbers of ethnic Livonians are thought to be much higher. However, although the Livs or Livonians have retained many Finnic cultural traditions, only those that speak Livonian exclusively are considered ethnic Livs. The number of active speakers of the Liv language is estimated at only 15 to 20, with 1,500 possessing some knowledge of the language.

THE NATION: The region, populated since the end of the last glacial era, about 10,000 B.C., was settled by Finnic peoples moving from the east around 3000 B.C. The settlers, the ancestors of the Finns, Estonians, and Livonians, spread out across the flat plains along the Baltic Sea. Around a thousand years later, Baltic tribes moved into Latvia, and are regarded as the ancestors of the present-day Latvians and Lithuanians.

The Baltic tribes, coming from the south, were stopped by the Finnic peoples in present Latvia. The Baltic tribes first appear in written records of the Roman historian Cornelius Tacitus, in approximately 100 B.C. Tacitus referred to the Balts as farmers living on the coasts of the Amber Sea. Around the same time the Balts split into tribal groups—the Latgalians, Zemgalians, Kurzemians (Couronians), and Selonians. The tribes, straddling the major trade route between Scandinavia and the Mediterranean, developed as traders and maintained contacts with many distant nations. An important export was jewelry, made from the amber found in large quantities in the region.

Until the twelfth century the marshes and forest lands along the eastern coast of the Baltic Sea remained the undisturbed homelands of various pagan tribes. The Esths and Livs, Finnish peoples, dominated the northern coast. Farther south the Indo-European Baltic tribes lived in the heavily forested regions. The Borussians, the third of the three major Baltic peoples, moved southward, where they were early subdued and assimilated or exterminated by the Germanic peoples.

Christianity arrived in Latvia with German missionaries and armed crusaders in the twelfth and thirteenth centuries. The German crusaders, intent on spreading Christianity and the feudal traditions of the German lands, founded Riga in 1201. By the 1270s, the crusaders had established a feudal state in present Latvia and Estonia dominated by the German Knights of the Livonian Order and the Roman Catholic Church. Regular economic and cultural ties were established with neighboring areas of Europe. In 1282 Riga became part of the Hanseatic League of northern Germany, a vast network of trading cities in the regions around the Baltic Sea. The city rapidly assumed a central role in the growing east-west trade.

At the same time that the political and economic unity of the lands controlled by the knights was being consolidated, the land was parcelled out to individual knights in large feudal holdings and the Latvian peoples were reduced to a class of peasant serfs. The imposition of a feudal system stimulated the unification of the various Latvian tribes into a closer linguistic and cultural entity.

The sixteenth-century Reformation had a significant impact, except in the eastern part of the region, which at the time was part of Catholic Poland. The Lutheran creed appealed to the Latvian serfs oppressed by the small German Catholic aristocracy. Peasant uprisings against the Baltic German landlords spread rapidly, often spurred by religious zeal.

In 1554, the Master of Order, Walter von Plettenberg, fearing a wider uprising, declared Protestantism the official religion. The decision weakened the medieval state and allowed the expanding Russians to gain influence. The Livonian Wars, fought from 1558 to 1583, were partly due to Moscow's desire for a warm-water port on the Baltic Sea.

To prevent a Russian conquest of the region, the German aristocrats dissolved the Teutonic Order, except in Kurzeme and Riga, and placed their vast estates under the protection of the powerful Roman Catholic Lithuanian-Polish state in 1561. The remains of the Protestant Order were secularized, and Catholicism was again proclaimed the state religion.

The German barons west of the Daugava River formed a separate duchy, in 1561, called Kurzeme or Courland. The privileges of the German lords were preserved on both banks of the Daugava, and the Latvian serfs became even more dependent on the feudal manors. The duchy, which remained semi-independent while paying tribute to the Poles, became so successful that for a short while it held colonies in Gambia and on the Caribbean island of Tobago.

The Swedish kingdom, which had controlled Estonia from 1521, wrested most of Livonia from Poland between 1621 and 1626. Swedish rule reinforced Lutheranism as the predominant religion. In 1689 the first bible was printed, with the support of the Swedish crown, in the Latvian language. Only Latgale, which was retained by Catholic Poland, continued to adhere to the Church of Rome.

Swedish rule brought essential political and cultural changes to the region. Due to the more liberal Swedish laws, the rights of the German feudal lords were curtailed and serfdom abolished. The Latvian farmers were given representation in the Swedish parliament and could lodge complaints directly with the Swedish king. Schools were established in the rural areas, and the first books in Latvian were printed.

In the eastern region, under Polish rule, the German aristocracy was assimilated by the Poles. Culturally and politically, the Roman Catholic Latgalians remained a separate people, with their own books printed in the Latgalian dialect.

The eighteenth century opened with yet another war in the region. In 1700 the army of tsarist Russia confronted the Swedes for the purpose of winning access to the ice-free ports on the Baltic Sea. The Nordic War devastated the prosperous region and lasted for twenty-one years. During the war plagues further diminished the population and several regions became virtually depopulated. In 1710 the northern provinces of Latvia, Vidzeme, and Riga came under Russian rule. By the Treaty of Nystad, in 1721, Sweden ceded Livonia, while Poland retained control of Latgale and Courland. In the Polish partitions of 1772 and 1795 Latgale and Courland also passed to Russian rule.

The imposition of Russian rule was welcomed by the Baltic German aristocrats, whose privileges, lost under Swedish rule, were quickly restored. The return of feudalism and the miserable state of the Latvian serfs marked the first decades of Russian rule. The government policy of Russification further suppressed the Latvian language and culture. Russian Orthodoxy was imposed as the state religion, although the most ancient parish of the Old Believers, a schismatic Orthodox sect, was established in Latvia in the eighteenth century.

Suppressed by the feudal regime of the German barons, the Latvians were unable to express their identity politically or culturally. Only after the period of change from feudalism to capitalist industrialism began at the end of the eighteenth century did circumstances begin to change for the average Latvian. The abolition of serfdom, 1817–19, stimulated the growth of industry, which began to develop rapidly, absorbing the excess workers of an expanding population.

The formation of the modern nation began only at the beginning of the nineteenth century, much later than for most European national groups. Education became more widespread, including university education in the German language, fostering the formation of a nationalist Latvian elite by the mid-nineteenth century. Reforms that allowed peasants to acquire land led to developments in the Baltic provinces that differentiated them from the rest of the Russian Empire.

An urban middle class, which emerged between the 1840s and 1860s, began to challenge both the Russian civil government and the feudal Baltic German aristocracy. The Latvian national movement grew out of an anti-German movement, only later developing with the consolidation of the Latvian nation. The national awakening of the Latvian people grew with efforts to secure for their nation the same rights other European nations enjoyed. In the 1880s the tsarist government stepped up its program of Russification, threatening the autonomy of the Baltic German-dominated province and the newly emerged Latvian national movement. In 1885 Russian replaced German as the official language. Latvian worker movements, organized in the 1890s, espoused a radical form of nationalism, advocating a complete break with the Russian Empire.

The social democrats set up a party faction in Latvia in 1904. Their ideas spread rapidly, attracting support for Latvian demands during the Russian Revolution of 1905. In Latvia the uprising took on the character of a national liberation movement, an attempt to free the Latvians from both their German overlords and the Russian bureaucracy. The uprising was brutally suppressed by the Russian army.

Heavy fighting spread across Latvia soon after war was declared in 1914, with the western districts of the province soon occupied by advancing German troops. One-fifth of Latvia's population of 2.5 million became refugees. Much of Latvia's industry was transferred to the Russian interior.

In the region not occupied by the Germans, effectively independent following the 1917 Russian Revolution, nationalists proclaimed Latvia a sovereign state in November 1917, soon after the Bolshevik coup in Petrograd. Many Latvians believed in the Bolshevik promises of freedom for Latvia, and in elections in unoccupied Latvia the Bolsheviks received 72% of the votes. A Bolshevik government was proclaimed in December to rival the previously proclaimed nationalist government. German troops occupied the remainder of Latvia in February 1918, suppressing both the nationalist and Bolshevik governments.

Pro-Soviet groups took control of Latvia as the Germans withdrew, but were soon ousted by nationalists supported by a British naval squadron in the Baltic Sea. A democratic Latvian government, formed by a coalition of a number of political groups, declared Latvia independent of Russia on 18 November 1918. After the declaration of independence, the fight against Bolshevik troops, as well as against German forces and Russian monarchists, lasted for two years. The first free elections were held in April 1920.

In 1920 the Soviet Union grudgingly recognized the independence of the Latvian state, but restricted contacts and trade with the non-Communist Latvians. Cut off from Soviet raw materials, industrialized Latvia quickly reverted to an essentially agrarian economy. Agrarian reform and new property rights laws aided the success of an economy based on agriculture and light manufacturing.

The prosperous republic, in spite of impressive cultural and economic achievements, with dozens of political parties and an ethnically mixed population, failed to achieve political stability. The situation was aggravated in the 1930s by Latvia's position between the hostile Soviet Union and a rearmed and aggressive Nazi Germany. The threat of civil war hung over the republic as antidemocratic groups formed that were hostile to the Russian, German, or Jewish minorities.

In 1934, in an attempt to strengthen the Latvian government and end communal disputes, Latvia's president, Karlis Ulmanis, suspended the parliament, assumed dictatorial powers, and banned all political party activity. The slogan of the Ulmanis government, ''Latvia for the Latvians,'' highlighted the exclusion of the Baltic German and other minorities from the new government. In 1935 the composition of Latvia's population was Letts 61%, Latgalians 16%, Russians 12%, Jews 4.5%, Germans 4%, and smaller Polish, Belarussian, and Lithuanian minorities.

The Soviet Union and Nazi Germany signed a secret protocol on 23 August 1939, effectively dividing the small states on their borders into spheres of influence. Latvia was assigned to the Soviet sphere, and Soviet military pressure increased dramatically. Demands for a less nationalistic and more pro-Soviet Latvian government precipitated a severe crisis. The government, its appeals to the world unanswered, was forced to allow the stationing of Soviet forces on Latvian soil.

With Soviet troops massed on the border, the neutral Latvian nationalist government was replaced with a pro-Communist regime. On 17 June 1940 Soviet troops occupied the country, and the puppet Latvian government applied for membership in the Soviet Union. Latvia was annexed on 22 July 1940, and over 35,000 Latvians, particularly from Roman Catholic Latgale, were deported. The deportations stopped when the Soviet Union was attacked by its erstwhile Nazi ally. In July 1941 advancing Nazi forces overran the republic.

Thousands of Latvians eagerly joined the Nazis' anti-Communist crusade, some even participating in the massacre of Latvia's Jewish minority. Many Latvians took advantage of the Nazi occupation to flee to the West, often ending up in displaced persons camps at the end of the war in 1945. Thousands refused repatriation to Soviet Latvia and gradually settled in the United States, Canada, and western Europe. An estimated 130,000 fled the advance of the Red Army to reach the West. The Red Army executed thousands of anti-Communists and deported between 100,000 and 120,000 between 1945 and 1953. To maintain Latvia's productivity the Stalinist Soviet government replaced the Latvians with more reliable Slavs.

The annexation of the Baltic countries was never officially recognized by the international community. During talks between the Allied leaders and Joseph Stalin in Teheran in 1944 and in Yalta in 1945, the issue of the illegal annexations was never publicly discussed. By 1949 the Latvian portion of the population, 75% of the total in 1940, had fallen to just 56%.

The substitution of Soviet culture for the historically formed culture in Latvia was implemented by armed strength. Fellow Soviet citizens, workers from other areas of the vast Soviet empire, were sent to Latvia to man the new heavy industries dictated by government.

During the so-called thaw of the 1950s, the survivors of the Gulag and the deportations of 1940–41 as well as the postwar persecutions began to return to the republic. An estimated 20% had survived the ordeal. In spite of the massive influx of non-Latvians, Latvian culture slowly began to revive, aided by the return of a portion of the prewar intelligentsia. When attempts to gain more independence for the Latvian Soviet Socialist Republic failed, a new wave of deportations followed in 1959.

The massive Slavic influx raised Latvian fears of cultural genocide, fueling the national and cultural revival that began in the 1960s as Latvia attained one of the Soviet Union's most prosperous economies. The revival, gaining strength in the 1970s and 1980s, was the target of a crackdown in 1983. Hundreds of dissidents were arrested as part of a concerted effort to stamp out illegal groups operating in Latvia. Four years later the republic experienced a great explosion of nationalist sentiment with the introduction of reforms by the Soviet leader Mikhail Gorbachev in 1987.

In the more relaxed atmosphere initiated by Gorbachev, nationalist organizations proliferated, many demanding the reversal of the illegal 1940 annexation. Massive nationalist demonstrations swept the republic as the Latvians increasingly excised the Communist hierarchy imposed from Moscow. The fight for the survival of the Latvian language was a rallying point for many in the country, and in a petition, 354,000 residents demanded that Latvian be once again officially named the state language. On 5 May 1989 the Language Law was passed and Latvian was declared the state language.

Campaigning for democracy and independence did not begin in earnest until October 1988 with the formation of the Popular Front of Latvia (LTF). In contrast to neighboring Estonia, the Latvian Communist Party adopted an antireform stance and called for the establishment of presidential rule. At elections to the Supreme Soviet in March 1990, the Popular Front won a convincing victory with the support of the majority of the Latvian population and many of the non-Latvians in the republic. A new Latvian parliament proclaimed the restoration of Latvia's former independence on 4 May 1990 and demanded negotiations on Latvia's peaceful secession from the Soviet Union.

An alliance of the Latvian Communist Party and the Russian-dominated anti-independence group, Interfront, emerged as the strongest opposition bloc in the republic. Despite demonstrations organized by Interfront, the new Latvian Supreme Soviet adopted a series of resolutions to prepare the republic for the transition to full independence. Mikhail Gorbachev and the Soviet government strongly objected to the Latvian reforms, and official harassment of the new Latvian government became policy. After bloody assaults by Soviet forces in Riga in January 1991, a general referendum was organized in which 87.6% of the eligible voters took part. Of those who voted, 73.7% supported independence from the USSR.

In June 1991 the republic held its first free and fair elections since 1931 with the participation of twenty-three political parties representing a broad political spectrum. Eight parties won seats in the Saeima, and 90% of eligible voters participated, using a secret ballot. As citizenship and naturalization questions were not resolved before the elections, there was no mechanism for residents of Latvia who were not citizens to participate in the elections, which effectively excluded a large portion of the Slavic population.

The attempted coup against Mikhail Gorbachev in Moscow, in August 1991, presented the Latvians with an unprecedented opportunity. The Latvian parliament proclaimed Latvia's independence from the Soviet Union on 21 August 1991, the second Latvian republic quickly receiving international recognition.

Other than a crumbling post-Soviet economy, the new republic's major chal-

lenge is to reach a workable accommodation with its large non-Latvian populations. Relations with the Russian Federation have been soured by the argument
over the status of ethnic Russians resident in Latvia. The Russians have been
subjected to discrimination, and the majority are not allowed to vote in general
elections. On 5 May 1992 the language laws were put into full force, with
employment, citizenship, and passports dependent on proficiency in the Latvian
language. Hundreds of thousands of non-Latvians were classed as noncitizens
and denied many of the rights enjoyed by the Latvians. Many Slavs left the
country to return to Russia or the newly independent Ukraine* and Belarus. The
nationalities question remains in the forefront of national politics. Citizenship is
automatically granted to anyone whose family was resident in the republic prior
to 1940.

The Latvian language, according to linguists, had reached the second stage
of language extinction by the mid-1980s. Since independence the language has
again flourished and the threat of extinction has receded. However, less than a
quarter of the non-Latvians living in the republic spoke the language six years
after independence.

In November 1995 the Latvian government radically changed the government
pension system. The country, with about a quarter of the population already
drawing pensions—the highest level in the world—will now index pensions to
contributions and the years of expected life. The reforms brought a renewed
outcry from the non-Latvian population.

A decided swing to the right by the majority of the country's political parties,
even those with a more liberal past, has marked national politics since 1991. In
the September 1995 elections two populist parties took the most votes. However,
centrists and leftist groups in parliament ensure that they do not control the
government.

Latvia's economic transformation to a modern market economy, rivaled only
by Estonia among the former Soviet states, faltered in 1995 due to banking and
budget crises. Latvia's largely unregulated financial sector suffered a series of
bank failures, including the collapse of the republic's largest commercial bank,
Bank Baltija, due to the criminal activity of its owners.

The Latvian state, along with the neighboring Baltic republics, has sought
membership in the large economic and military alliances, the European Union
(EU) and NATO. On 27 October 1995, Latvia submitted its application for full
European Union membership. However, in 1997, the EU, citing the treatment
of non-Latvian residents and government failure to fully implement a market
economy, did not invite Latvia to join talks for the first expansion of the union
into eastern Europe.

In January 1997 a Russian official announced that the Russian Federation was
continuing talks with the Latvian government on the purchase of the former
naval base at Liepaja. The base, formerly the largest Soviet base on the Baltic
Sea, was abandoned in 1994 when Russian troops withdrew from the republic.

SELECTED BIBLIOGRAPHY:

Dreifelds, Juris. *Latvia in Transition*. 1996.

Hiden, John, and Patrick Salmon. *The Baltic Nations and Europe: Estonia, Latvia and Lithuania in the Twentieth Century*. 1995.

Lieven, Anatol. *The Baltic Revolution: Estonia, Latvia, Lithuania and the Path to Independence*. 1994.

Penkis, Janis J., and Andrejs Penkis. *Latvia: Independence Renewed*. 1997.

Plakans, Andrejs. *Historical Dictionary of Latvia*. 1997.

LITHUANIA

Republic of Lithuania; Lietuva;
Lietuvos Respublika

CAPITAL: Vilnius

POPULATION: (98e) 3,754,000 : 3,055,000 Lithuanians in Lithuania. MA-
JOR NATIONAL GROUPS: Lithuanian 81.4%, Russian 8.2%, Polish 6.9%,
Belarussian 1.2%, Ukrainian 1%, Jew, Latvian, Tatar, Karaim, German. MAJOR
LANGUAGES: Lithuanian, Russian, Polish. MAJOR RELIGIONS: Roman
Catholic, Russian Orthodox, Lutheran, Sunni Muslim. MAJOR CITIES: (98e)
Vilnius 602,000 (648,000), Kaunas 438,000 (477,000), Klaipeda 214,000
(240,000), Siauliai 151,000 (185,000), Panezevys 133,000, Alytus 85,000, Mar-
ijampole (Kapsukas) 54,000, Taurage 32,000, Druskininkai 26,000, Palanga
23,000.

GEOGRAPHY: AREA: 25,174 sq.mi.-65,217 sq.km. LOCATION: Lithuania
lies in northeastern Europe, bordering on the Baltic Sea. The country borders
Latvia* on the north, Belarus* on the south and east, and Poland and the Russian
oblast of Kaliningrad on the south. PHYSICAL GEOGRAPHY: Lithuania has
very few natural resources other than agricultural land, which makes up about
two-thirds of the land area, and forests, about a quarter of the territory. Lying
on the rim of the Russian Plain, the country has only two elevated regions,
separated by the Lithuanian Lowlands: a hilly country of lakes and bogs in the
east, and the Samogitian Hills in the west. The principal river is the Nemunas
or Niemen, with its two main tributaries. Neither of the upland regions reaches
over 1,000 feet. Over 2,800 lakes are included in Lithuania's national territory.
ADMINISTRATIVE DIVISIONS: Forty-four rural regions or rajonai (singular—

rajonas) and eleven municipalities. POLITICAL STATUS: Lithuania was recognized as an independent state in 1991.

INDEPENDENCE DECLARATIONS: 16 February 1918 (from Russia); 11 March 1990 (from the Soviet Union).

FLAG: The Lithuanian national flag, the official flag of the republic, is a horizontal tricolor of yellow, green, and red.

PEOPLE: The country is the most homogeneous of the three Baltic States, with the Lithuanian people making up about 80% of the total population. The Slavic community, made up mostly of Russians and Poles, also includes minorities of Ukrainians and Belarussians. A high proportion of the population, about 33%, lives in rural areas. As in Estonia and Latvia, immigration from other parts of the Soviet Union after the Soviet annexation of Lithuania in 1940 became government policy, leading to a very mixed population in the region.

Lithuanian—an estimated 81.4% of the population, numbering about 3,055,000.

The Lithuanians are a Baltic people closely related to the neighboring Latvians, the languages of the two peoples forming the Baltic branch of the Indo-European languages. The Lithuanians are the most numerous of the so-called Baltic peoples. They are devoutly Roman Catholic, with a small Lutheran minority in the north and an Orthodox minority concentrated in the cities.

The Lithuanian nation has historically been divided into four major groups and a number of subgroups that inhabited the national territory. The major groups, speaking dialects of the Lithuanian language, are the Aukstaiciai in the northeast, the Zemaiciai in the west, the Dzukai in the southeast, and the Suvalkieciai in the south.

The Lithuanian language is considered the closest to ancient Sanskrit, the basis of all the modern Indo-European languages. Written in the Roman alphabet, Lithuanian has a large number of dialects for such a small territory, including High Lithuanian, known as Aukshtaitish or Aukstaichiai, and Low Lithuanian, Shamaitish, also known as Samogotian or Zemaiciai. The Lithuanian language still retains the original sound system and morphological peculiarities of the ancient Indo-European language.

Russian—an estimated 8.2% of the population, numbering about 300,000.

The Russian population of Lithuania is concentrated in the industrial areas of the larger cities. Settled in the region mostly after World War II, the Russians came as workers in government-sponsored migrations, many from areas devastated in the fighting.

Only a small percentage of the Slav population speaks Lithuanian, as Russian had been the lingua franca of the Soviet Union. New language laws, which are tied to citizenship, have led to claims that the Lithuanian government discriminates against the Slav population. The majority of the Russians are Russian Orthodox, although several schismatic sects are represented.

Pole—an estimated 6.9% of the population, numbering about 250,000.

The Lithuanian Poles live mostly in the east and southeast of the country, around the capital, Vilnius, a part of Lithuania that belonged to Poland in the years between the wars. The Poles, like the Lithuanians, are devoutly Roman Catholic and speak a Western Slav language.

Poland's control of the Vilnius region from 1922 until World War II remains a sensitive issue in the region. Some Polish groups continue to claim Vilnius as traditionally Polish territory.

Belarussian—an estimated 1.2% of the population, numbering about 45,000.

The Belarussian population of Lithuania is concentrated in the eastern districts of the country along the border with Belarus. The region, long claimed by Belarussians as national territory, includes the capital city of Vilnius, sometimes referred to as the Belarussian Jerusalem. The Belarussians in the region are mostly Roman Catholic, with a large Orthodox minority. Many of the Belarussians speak Russian as their first language.

Ukrainian—an estimated 1% of the population, numbering about 35,000.

The Ukrainians, mostly settled in the republic after World War II, are concentrated in the larger towns and cities, particularly Vilnius and Kaunas. The Ukrainians include both Roman Catholic (Uniate) and Orthodox groups, plus some schismatic groups that migrated to the region in the eighteenth century.

The Ukrainians speak an Eastern Slavic language related to Russian and Belarussian. In Lithuania the majority of the Ukrainian population speak Russian as the language of work, business, and intergroup communications. The Ukrainian language has revived somewhat following Ukrainian independence in 1991.

Jew—estimated at less than 1% of the population, numbering about 6,000.

The Jews of Lithuania are mostly those that returned from exile after Lithuanian independence, or are Russian speakers settled in the region after World War II. The original Jewish population was massacred during World War II.

The Jewish population is mostly urban, living in the two largest cities, Vilnius and Kaunas, where they have moved into the ancient Jewish quarters. Another Jewish group, not officially counted as Jews, are the Karaim.

Tatar—estimated at less than 1% of the population, numbering about 5,000.

The Tatars of Lithuania are the descendants of Tatars settled in Lithuania between the thirteenth and fifteenth centuries. Prisoners of war or refugees, the Tatars of the Golden Horde were given land and privileges in exchange for military service.

The only sizable Muslim population in Lithuania, the Tatars have lost their original language and are almost all Lithuanian speakers. There are Muslim mosques in a number of Lithuanian towns and cities.

Latvian—estimated at less than 1% of the population, numbering about 4,000.

The Latvians, mostly living in the northern districts along the Latvian border, are closely related to the Lithuanians and speak a Baltic language that can be understood by Lithuanian speakers. The Latvians, including both Roman Catholic and Lutheran groups, have maintained their separate culture and language, although they have few problems assimilating into Lithuanian society.

Karaim (Karaite)—estimated at less than 1% of the population, numbering about 3,000.

The Karaim or Karaites are a Tatar people originally from the Crimean Peninsula on the Black Sea. Settled in Lithuania as refugees or captives during the wars of the thirteenth to fifteenth centuries, the Karaim have maintained their separate culture and language, a Ponto-Caspian dialect of Tatar, a Western Turkic language, written in either the Cyrillic or Hebrew alphabet. However, only about 15% use the language as their first language; the majority use Lithuanian or Russian.

The Karaim practice an archaic form of Judaism and have avoided mixing with the Muslim Tatar community or the so-called Rabbinical Jews. Traditions and customs brought from the Crimea centuries ago continue among the Karaim people.

THE NATION: Thought to have originated far to the east, the Baltic tribes arrived in northeastern Europe around 2000 B.C. Pushed west by the Slav migrations of the eighth and ninth centuries A.D. the tribes eventually settled along the eastern shore of the Baltic Sea, their fierce resistance halting the westward expansion of the Slavs. The Baltic tribes split into two groups. The ancestors of the Lithuanians and Latvians moved north into the lands of the Finnic peoples. The other group, the Borussians, moved south, where they were eliminated or assimilated by the Germans, leaving behind only a version of their name, Prussia.

Lithuania was first mentioned in written records in the Quedinburg Annals in 1009, although centuries earlier the Roman historian Tacitus wrote of the tribes as an agricultural people. Inhabited by pagan tribes, the forested region was not well known to the rest of medieval Europe until the thirteenth century.

Under Grand Duke Gediminas, who is recognized as the founder of modern Lithuania in the early fourteenth century, the territory of the Lithuanian state began to expand, eventually to take in territories as far away as the coast of the Black Sea. In the mid-thirteenth century, Duke Mindaugas united the lands inhabited by the Lithuanians, Samogitians, Yotvingians, and Couranians into the Grand Duchy of Lithuania. Mindaugas adopted Christianity in 1251 and was acknowledged as the head of the united Lithuanian state two years later.

In 1385, Duke Jagiello—surrounded by German Livonian and Teutonic crusaders on the north and west, and by the Muscovites and Tatars on the east—married a Polish princess and joined Lithuania to Poland in a dynastic union. Jagiello agreed to accept Catholicism and baptized the remaining pagan tribes in Lithuania, traditionally converting Lithuania to a Catholic country in 1387.

The conversion of the pagan Lithuanians invalidated claims by the German Crusaders and temporarily ended the support by the Christian states and the Pope for their campaign against the pagan peoples. Peace between the Lithuanians and the Teutonic Knights allowed the Christian peoples of northeastern Europe to unite to face a new threat.

Under a descendant of Gediminas the Lithuanians led a great Christian army against Timur (Tamerlane) in Ukraine in 1399. The battle ended without a clear victor, but so weakened Timur's forces that he eventually returned to Asia.

Following the indecisive conflict with the Tatars, the German knights returned to the offensive. In spite of appeals to the Pope that the Germans sought land,

not converts, in Christian Lithuania, the war intensified. The power of the medieval Lithuanian state, in alliance with Poland, finally defeated the crusading
German Teutonic Knights at the Battle of Tannenberg in 1410. After the decisive
defeat of the German knights, which ended the German expansion to the east,
Lithuania extended its borders to the Baltic Sea and became the most powerful
state in northeastern Europe.

The population of the Lithuanian-Polish state belonged to three groups,
shlakhta (aristocracy), merchants and artisans, and peasants. The conditions of
the groups on the lower rungs of society were generally better than in territories
under the rule of the Moscow principality or in Poland. In addition to the Lithuanians, Belarussians, Ukrainians, and other peoples living in the region, new
migrants entered the empire: Tatars and Karaites from the Golden Horde, Jews
fleeing persecution in Germany and other European countries, and Slavs belonging to sects persecuted by the Orthodox authorities farther east.

To the east, Moscow's Prince Ivan III united the surrounding territories and
proclaimed himself head of all Orthodox people in Europe after marrying the
daughter of the last Byzantine emperor. In 1480 Ivan III liberated Moscow from
the Tatars, and in 1499 war broke out between Moscow and Lithuania. The
conflict continued sporadically for the next seventy years.

In 1558 Tsar Ivan IV attacked the Livonian Order, the Crusader state neighboring Lithuania. Great Prince Zhyhimont August of Lithuania offered to come
to the aid of the Crusaders, but on the condition that the Crusader state unite
with Lithuania. The alliance marked the beginning of the twenty-year Livonian
War. Victories in 1564 and 1568 finally forced Ivan the Terrible to agree to a
truce, which left Russia with the newly conquered territories in Belarus and
Livonia.

In 1569 the Poles raised the recurrent question of the unification of Poland
and Lithuania. The two states, joined under the same ruler since 1385, were
beset by wars with Moscow as well as by attacks by Swedes in Livonia and
renewed attacks by the Crimean Tatars in southern Ukraine. In Lublin, Poland,
the state union was signed and the two states united into one. The Lithuanian
aristocracy gradually became Polish in language and culture, the Lithuanian
language and traditions surviving only in rural areas.

The Polish-Lithuanian commonwealth, ruled by an elected king, who was also
Grand Duke of Lithuania, was a multiethnic empire embracing dozens of separate peoples and cultures. Over the years the Polish-Lithuanian state became
dominated by the more numerous Poles and the Lithuanian nobility, who were
Polish in language and culture.

The sixteenth century saw a rapid development of agriculture, the growth of
towns, and the spread of ideas of humanism and the Reformation. In Lithuania
book printing expanded the dissemination of knowledge, as did the emergence
of Vilnius University in 1579. The liberal Lithuanian code of law, the Statutes
of Lithuania, stimulated the development of culture in Lithuania and other parts
of the Polish-Lithuanian state.

In 1648, in the empire's southern Ukraine provinces, the Cossacks started revolts against the Poles and against Polish and Catholic influence. Under the command of Bohdan Khmelnitski, a huge army of Cossacks defeated the Catholic troops in several battles. In 1654 Khmelnitski turned to Moscow for help. The Russians quickly established control over most of Ukraine, Belarus, and part of Lithuania. At the same time, the Swedes renewed their war against Poland and quickly occupied the western part of the empire. The Poles and Lithuanians eventually drove the Swedes and Russians from their lands, but the wars critically weakened the state.

Pressured by the expanding Russian state, the Polish-Lithuanian empire declined in the late seventeenth century. Between 1772 and 1795 the weakened state was partitioned by Austria, Prussia, and Russia, with most of Lithuania coming under the authority of the Russian Empire. Attempts to throw off Russian rule spurred uprisings in 1794 and 1830–31. In 1832 the Russian authorities closed Vilnius University.

Subjected to intense pressures to assimilate, the Lithuanians began to embrace nationalism in the mid-nineteenth century. The abolition of serfdom in 1861 stimulated the development of a market economy. As Lithuanian farmers grew stronger, an increasing number received an education, which led to the growth of the national movement. Rejecting Russification, the Lithuanians joined the Poles in open rebellion in 1863, the severe Russian reprisals and repression provoking the rapid spread of modern Lithuanian nationalist sentiment. In 1864 the authorities banned the printing of Lithuanian books in the traditional Latin alphabet.

In German-controlled Memel (Klaipeda), called Lithuania Minor by the nationalists, Lithuanian publications were produced in large numbers, then smuggled into Russian-ruled Lithuania. The national movement, suppressed in Russia, continued among the Lithuanian minority in neighboring German East Prussia. The first Lithuanian newspaper was founded in Memel in 1883.

The Lithuanians' Roman Catholic religion, closely tied to the national movement, came under sustained attack in Russia in the 1890s. In 1894 all Roman Catholics were excluded from local government positions. The ban on the Lithuanian press in Russia was not lifted until 1904.

During World War I, German troops from East Prussia occupied Lithuania in 1915. In September 1917 after the revolution of February 1917 in Russia, the Germans allowed a nationalist conference to convene in Vilnius. The conference demanded the restoration of an independent Lithuanian state and elected the Lithuanian Council, chaired by Antanas Smetona.

In the wake of the Bolshevik takeover of Russia in October 1917, the Lithuanian Council, with German support, declared an independent kingdom on 16 February 1918 and designated Duke William of Wurttemburg as their king. When the war turned against their German allies, the Lithuanians renounced the monarchy and just before the German withdrawal proclaimed Lithuania a republic on 30 November 1918.

Local Bolsheviks, encouraged by the events in Russia, overthrew the nationalist government in December 1918. The Lithuanian Bolsheviks soon lost support due to the continuing attacks on the Lithuanians' cherished Catholic religion. A force of Lithuanian nationalists, Poles, and German Free Corps, supported by the Allies, drove the Soviet government from power in Lithuania in January 1919. The Lithuanian forces occupied the region claimed as national territory, including the important cities of Vilnius and Gardinas (Grodno), claimed by Lithuania's newly independent neighbors, Poland and Belarus.

Recognized as an independent state in July 1920, the new republic was quickly embroiled in a crisis brought on by territorial disputes with neighboring Poland. When Polish troops invaded in October 1920, the Lithuanian army fell back, losing the historically and economically important cities and provinces of Vilnius and Gardinas to the victorious Poles. The Lithuanian government, transferred from Vilnius to the city of Kaunas, continued to claim Vilnius, inciting renewed fighting between the Lithuanian army and the Poles in 1922.

The territorial dispute, taken to the new League of Nations, was finally settled in Poland's favor. The disgruntled Lithuanians then turned on Memel (Klaipeda), an area long claimed as historically Lithuanian territory. They expelled the French forces that had occupied the German city at the end of the war and annexed Memel and the surrounding territory to the Lithuanian state.

By the mid-1920s the majority of the international community had recognized Lithuania's independence, but the prosperous state remained isolated between the Soviet Union and the turmoil in defeated Germany. On 17 December 1926 a military coup overthrew the government. The leader of the Nationalist Party, Antanas Smetona, became president and gradually introduced an authoritarian regime.

The state's stability, undermined by the ongoing territorial dispute with Poland, declined in the 1930s as pressure increased from both the Stalinist Soviet Union and a resurgent Nazi Germany. In March 1939 Germany forced Lithuania to surrender the Memel (Klaipeda) region, which was annexed by the Nazi government.

A secret pact between Germany and the Soviet Union, in August 1939, placed Lithuania in the so-called Soviet sphere. Soviet troops massed on the border, forcing the Lithuanian government to resign and hand power to a pro-Soviet clique that requested incorporation of Lithuania in the Soviet Union. The next day 100,000 Soviet troops occupied the country. In July 1940 the Soviet Union formally annexed the republic, the move denounced by Lithuanian nationalists and much of the West as illegal. On 3 August 1940 Lithuania was proclaimed a member state of the USSR.

The Soviets held Lithuania for about one year. Only days before the Germans invaded and occupied the region, the Soviet government began deporting large numbers of Lithuanians deemed anti-Communist or anti-Stalin. Between 14 and 18 June 1941, an estimated 16,000 people were arrested and transported east, without food or water, mostly to prison camps beyond the Urals to join the 5,000 already deported.

The Lithuanians rebelled when Germany turned on its Soviet ally in June 1941. Over 100,000 Lithuanians took up arms, many joining the Nazi forces that occupied Lithuania soon after. In spite of the support given the Nazi anti-Communist crusade by many Lithuanians, the Germans refused to support an independent Lithuania. Many Lithuanians were rounded up and taken to forced labor camps in Germany. Others volunteered for duty with the Nazi forces. The Nazis and local Lithuanian collaborators deprived all Lithuanian Jews of their civil rights, implemented the anti-Jewish laws of the Third Reich, and eventually massacred about 200,000 Lithuanian Jews.

Aided by Soviet partisan groups, groups of various political views formed an anti-Nazi underground, and armed groups took to the forest. Supporters of the Lithuanian nationalists worked particularly to deflect Nazi recruitment of Lithuanians to the German army. Some of the Lithuanian recruits participated in the Jewish Holocaust outside Lithuania, serving as guards at concentration camps or in special units that rounded up Jews in areas of the Soviet Union taken by the German military.

In 1944 the Red Army drove the last German units from Lithuania. The Sovietization begun in 1940–41 was continued. The political police, the MVD, and special screening commissions investigated the past and political views of every inhabitant over the age of twelve. Formal charges fell into two categories, war criminal or enemy of the people. Official statistics state that over 120,000 Lithuanians were deported during the period 1945–52, but many Lithuanian sources estimated the number to be as high as 300,000. The deportees included a majority of the republic's surviving national, cultural, and religious leaders.

A resistance movement known as the Forest Brethren formed as soon as the Soviet forces arrived and continued to fight Soviet control of Lithuania. As many as 100,000 Lithuanians, both forest fighters and civilian supporters, may have participated. The last of these resistance fighters were exterminated in 1953.

Lithuanian nationalism, kept alive by underground and exile groups, grew dramatically in the late 1980s, quickly pushing far beyond the modest reforms instituted by the Soviet leader Mikhail Gorbachev in 1987. In mid-1988 the Lithuanian reform movement, called Sajudis, was formed and proclaimed a program of democratic and national rights. The popular front group won nationwide popularity with their calls for the reestablishment of an independent Lithuania.

Pressured by Sajudis, the Lithuanian Supreme Soviet passed constitutional amendments on the supremacy of Lithuanian laws over Soviet legislation, annulled the 1940 decisions on proclaiming Lithuania part of the Soviet Union, and legalized a multiparty political system. Many members of the Lithuanian Communist Party supported Sajudis and calls for democracy and independence. In December 1989 the local Communist Party split from the Communist Party of the Soviet Union and became independent, renaming itself the Lithuanian Democratic Labor Party in 1990. In January 1990 Mikhail Gorbachev visited the republic, where he was greeted by a crowd of thousands demanding immediate independence.

Sajudis candidates won elections to the Lithuanian Supreme Soviet in February 1990. On 11 March 1990, its chairman, Vytautas Landsbergis, proclaimed the restoration of Lithuanian independence. The Soviet government immediately demanded revocation of the act and applied political and economic sanctions against the republic. The defiant nationalists refused to back down to Soviet pressure despite a crippling oil embargo and threatened military action. The oil embargo, put in place in April, was lifted in June following an agreement by Vytautas Landsbergis, as head of the Lithuanian parliament, to suspend the independence declaration while negotiations were undertaken.

On 10 January 1991, Landsbergis declared the suspension of the independence declaration at an end. Soviet authorities seized the central publishing house and other public buildings in Vilnius in an unsuccessful bid to overthrow the elected government. Three days later military forces seized the TV tower over the resistance of a crowd of civilians. The confrontation left fourteen dead and several hundred wounded.

To demonstrate popular support for independence, the Lithuanian government organized a national referendum. On 9 February, over 90% of those who voted—76% of all eligible voters—backed Landsbergis and his bid for independence. He continued to seek Western diplomatic recognition, while Soviet forces remained in control of many important buildings and installations.

The attempted coup against Mikhail Gorbachev on 19 August 1991 dramatically ended the standoff. Soviet troops took over several communications and other government facilities, but returned to their barracks when the coup failed. The Lithuanian government banned the Communist Party and ordered the confiscation of its properties. On 6 September 1991 President Landsbergis formally reinstated the March 1990 declaration, formally proclaiming Lithuania independent of the disintegrating Soviet Union.

The long-running border dispute between Lithuania and Poland over the Vilnius region was finally settled with the signing of a friendship and cooperation treaty in January 1992. In the agreement the Lithuanian government committed itself to safeguarding the rights of the large Polish minority.

Lengthy negotiations with Russia finally achieved an agreement for the withdrawal of the former Soviet forces, now part of the Russian military, that remained in Lithuania. In March 1992 the first units returned to Russia. The withdrawal was completed in August 1993, ending fifty-two years of harsh occupation.

In October 1992, Lithuanian voters, alarmed by the rapidly deteriorating economy, chose ex-Communist candidates over the nationalists who had led the state to independence. In December, in presidential elections, the ex-Communist Party chief of the 1980s was elected to replace Vytautas Landsbergis. In February 1993, following new elections, a former Sajudis leader became the head of state. The instability of the government continued into the late 1990s, with resignations, dismissals, and scandals involving official corruption.

The precarious economic position and the government's hesitation on implementing the reforms demanded for entry led to Lithuania's exclusion from the list of candidate countries issued by the European Union in 1997. The Lithuanian government, still wary of its Russian neighbors, is intent on membership in the union and in the Western military alliance, NATO, but in spite of the aid and support of the large Lithuanian diaspora, mostly in the United States, the country's economic situation continues to hinder progress toward its goal of financial and military security within the Western alliances.

In early January 1997, the United States overtook Germany as Lithuania's largest foreign investor. Germany remains the second largest investor, while Sweden has become the third. The investment patterns highlight Lithuania's growing trade with the West and its decreasing ties to the states of the former Soviet Union.

In September 1997, in Vilnius, Lithuanian president Algirdas Brazauskas hosted the presidents of ten countries in the region between the Baltic and Black Seas. The meeting, which should help the countries integrate into the West and smooth their relations with each other and with Moscow, marked Lithuania's new confidence as the economy began to turn around and political stability began to benefit the entire population. The conference reiterated the determination of the former Communist republics not to choose between East and West.

SELECTED BIBLIOGRAPHY:

Brooke, Rupert, and William-Alan Landes. *Lithuania*. 1997.

Chicoine, Stephen, and Brent K. Ashabranner. *Lithuania: The Nation that Would Be Free*. 1995.

Krickus, Richard J. *Showdown: The Lithuanian Rebellion and the Breakup of the Soviet Empire*. 1997.

Suziedelis, Saulius. *Historical Dictionary of Lithuania*. 1997.

Vardys, Stanley V. *Lithuania: The Rebel Nation*. 1996.

MACEDONIA

Makedonija; Makedonia; The
Former Yugoslav Republic of
Macedonia; Republika Makedonija

CAPITAL: Skopje

Southeastern Europe

Macedonia

POPULATION: (98e) 2,118,000 : 1,400,000 Macedonians in Macedonia, and
another 150,000 in adjacent areas of Yugoslavia and Albania. "GREATER
MACEDONIA" (98e) 4,563,000. Greater Macedonia is the region claimed by
militant Macedonian nationalists, who project ethnic Macedonian populations of
over 1 million in northern Greece and half a million in southwestern Bulgaria.
MAJOR NATIONAL GROUPS: (98e) Macedonian 66.1%, Albanian 22.4%,
Turk 4%, Rom (Gypsy) 2.2%, Serb 2.1%, Muslim 1.5%, Greek 1%, Bulgarian,
Vlach, Croat, Jew. MAJOR LANGUAGES: Macedonian, Albanian, Serbian,
Turkish. MAJOR RELIGIONS: Orthodox 67%, Sunni Islam 30%, Roman Catholic, Jewish. MAJOR CITIES: (98e) MACEDONIA (Vardar Macedonia):
Skopje 553,000 (620,000), Bitola (Bitolj) 81,000 (138,000), Prilep 75,000, Ku-
manovo 68,000, Veles 52,000, Tetovo 44,000, Okhrida (Ohrid) 41,000, Strumica
36,000, Gostivar 35,000, Kavadarci 28,000; GREECE (Aegean Macedonia): So-
lun (Thessaloniki) 720,000 (1,040,000), Kabala (Kavalla) 67,000, Serra (Serrai)
55,000, Drama 40,000, Berea (Veroia) 40,000, Kastur (Kastoria) 31,000, Lerin
(Florina) 26,000, Vodena (Edessa) 22,000; BULGARIA (Pirin Macedonia):
Dyumala (Blagoevgrad) 88,000, Pirin (Petrich) 36,000, Goce Delchev (Gotse
Delchev) 23,000, Sveti Vrach (Sandanski) 22,000.

GEOGRAPHY: AREA: Republic of Macedonia 9,925 sq.mi.-25,713 sq.km.
"Greater Macedonia" 25,633 sq.mi.-66,407 sq.mi. LOCATION: The Republic
of Macedonia occupies a mountainous region, traversed by the Vardar River, in
the southern Balkan Peninsula, bordering Albania on the west, Greece on the
south, Bulgaria on the east, and Yugoslavia on the north. PHYSICAL GEOG-

RAPHY: The Former Yugoslav Republic of Macedonia (FYROM) is a land-locked country of high mountain ranges and vast fertile river valleys. The Skopska Tsrna Gora Range lies in the north, the Pindus Ranges to the west, and the Western Rhodope Mountains in the east, interspersed by the valleys of the two major rivers, the Vardar and the Strumitsa. There are three large lakes, each divided by a frontier line: Lake Ohrid on the Albanian border, Lake Prespa on the Albanian and Greek borders, and Lake Dorjan on the southeastern border with Greece. "Greater Macedonia" includes, along with Vardar Macedonia, Aegean Macedonia in northern Greece at the northern end of the Aegean Sea, and Pirin Macedonia in southwestern Bulgaria, the region west of the Rhodope Mountains. The three regions make up the historic region of Macedonia. AD-MINISTRATIVE DIVISIONS: Thirty-four counties or opstinas (singular—op-stina). POLITICAL STATUS: Macedonia was recognized as an independent state under the name Former Yugoslav Republic of Macedonia (FYROM) in 1993. "Greater Macedonia," the region claimed by some nationalist groups, also includes the major portion of Greek Macedonia, the prefectures of Chalcidice, Drama, Florina, Hematheia, Kastoria, Kavalla, Kilkís, Pella, Serrai, and Thessalonike, and Pirin Macedonia, the district of Blagoevgrad and the western part of the district of Kyustendil of Sofia Province of Bulgaria.

INDEPENDENCE DECLARATIONS: 2 August 1903 (from the Ottoman Empire); 8 September 1944 (from Yugoslavia); 17 September 1991 (from Yugoslavia).

FLAG: The Macedonian national flag is a red field with a centered yellow sun and eight yellow rays extending to the edges. OTHER FLAGS: The Macedonian flag used by some nationalist groups, the former official flag of the republic, is a red field charged with a centered, sixteen-point gold star, the Star of Vergina. The traditional Macedonian flag, used outside the republic and by some nationalist groups, is a horizontal bicolor of red over black.

PEOPLE: Traditionally a crossroads region between Europe and Asia Minor, Macedonia is home to many diverse nations. The small former Yugoslav republic of Macedonia is inhabited by twenty-six different national groups. The Macedonian people are roughly divided between the mostly Christian South Slav peoples—the Macedonians, Serbs, Croats, Montenegrins, and Bulgarians—and the Islamic peoples—the Albanians, Turks, Muslims, and Gypsies, with smaller numbers of Greeks, Jews, and Vlach.

Macedonian—an estimated 66.1% of the population, numbering about 1,400,000.

The Macedonians are a Slavic people, a mixture of South Slav, Bulgarian Slav, and Greek strains. Until the latter part of the nineteenth century the Macedonians had little sense of being a separate nation, but called themselves Bulgarians, Serbs, or Greek Slavs.

The standard Macedonian language developed after World War II and is written in the Cyrillic alphabet with the addition of two letters not utilized by any other Slav language. The major dialects are Northern Macedonian, spoken in the Kumanovo-Kratovo region, Southeastern Macedonian, and Western Macedonian, which has two subdialects. Standard Macedonian was developed from the Western Macedonian spoken in the southwestern districts. In Greece the language is called simply Slavic.

The majority of the Macedonians belong to the independent Macedonian Orthodox Church, with minorities adhering to Orthodox sects or Sunni Islam. The largest non-Macedonian national groups in the republic are the Albanians in the northwest, the Turks in the south, and the Serbs in the north. The number of Macedonians outside the republic is very difficult to estimate, as the Greek government denies the existence of a Macedonian population in Greek Macedonia and the Bulgarian government does not count the Macedonian population in Pirin Macedonia separately in national censuses.

Albanian—an estimated 22.4% of the population, numbering about 475,000.

The Albanian population of Macedonia is almost evenly divided between the Gheg in the northern districts and the Tosk in south, a division that parallels the ethnic division in neighboring Albania. The Albanians dispute the latest census findings (which are thought to include a number of Rom who identify themselves as ethnic Albanians), claiming that they account for between 33% and 40% of the total population. However, international observers have certified the census figures as credible. The Albanians predominate in the western and northwestern regions, along the borders of Albania and the Albanian-populated Kosovo region of Yugoslavia. In the Tetovo and Gostivar districts they form a majority of the population.

Most of the Albanians in Macedonia are Sunni or Bektashi Muslims, but with Orthodox and Roman Catholic minorities, mostly among the Tosk population. The Albanians complain of religious discrimination, along with a lack of education and economic opportunities.

Turk—an estimated 4% of the population, numbering about 85,000.

The Macedonian Turks, also called Osmanli Turks, are part of the Turkish people that once dominated the Balkans as part of the Ottoman Empire. Most of the Turks settled in the region during the Ottoman period and are Sunni or Bektashi Muslims. The Turkish language is spoken in two dialects in Macedonia. The dialects, called Macedonian Turkish and Dinler, are basically Turkish with Slavic and Greek admixtures.

The Macedonian government has been tolerant of the Turkish community, which it hopes will not make common cause with the Muslim Albanians. The Macedonian authorities are also eager not to alienate the Turkish government, which represents a welcome counterweight to Greece.

Rom (Gypsy)—an estimated 2.2% of the population, numbering about 47,000.

The majority of the Rom or Gypsies of Macedonia belong to the Arlija people, with a smaller number of Dzambazi. Both groups belong to the Jerlídes ethnic group. The division corresponds to the two major dialects of Balkan Romani spoken in the region, Arlija and Dzambazi, along with a dialect called Tinners Romani. Most of the Rom in Macedonia are Sunni or Bektashi Muslims, but with an important Orthodox Christian minority.

The Rom originated in present Pakistan and reached the Balkans by the tenth century. Throughout the centuries they have remained outside the mainstream society and were often persecuted. In Macedonia they are often called Cigan, a pejorative term. Although the official numbers are from the latest census, many Rom are reluctant to register and still identify themselves as Macedonians or Albanians. Some Rom leaders claim there are 220,000 Rom in Macedonia.

Serb and Montenegrin—an estimated 2.1% of the population, numbering about 45,000.

The Serbs and Montenegrins in Macedonia live mainly in the northeastern part of the country near the Yugoslav border in the Skopska Tsrna Gora and Kumanovo regions. The closely related Montenegrins in the country mostly identified themselves as ethnic Serbs during the last censuses. Most of the ethnic Serbs in Macedonia belong to the Serbian Orthodox Church. The number of ethnic Serbs in the country is still a matter of dispute. Some Serb leaders claim an ethnic Serb population of up to 300,000 in Macedonia.

Muslim—an estimated 1.5% of the population, numbering about 31,000.

The Muslim Slavs, related to the Bosnian Muslims of Bosnia and Herzegovina and the Sanjak Muslims of Yugoslavia, are concentrated in Skopje and other towns in the central part of the country. The Slav Muslims in Macedonia are known by many different names, including Torbeshes, Pomaks, and Poturs. Muslim groups claim that some 70,000 of their number have been assimilated by other Muslim groups, mainly Albanian, since World War II. Thousands of Bosnian Muslim refugees have settled in the republic since 1992, but are not counted as official residents of the republic.

Almost evenly divided between the Sunni and Bektashi branches of Islam, the Muslims tend to be urbanized and secular in outlook. Muslim traditions and customs are observed, but women generally enjoy the same personal freedoms as their Christian neighbors.

Greek—an estimated 1% of the population, numbering about 21,000.

The Greeks of Macedonia live mostly in the south, near the international border with Greece, particularly in the southeastern districts of the country. Mostly Greek Orthodox and rural, the Greek population is oriented to the nearby Greek towns and has little to do with the Macedonian bureaucracy or its Slavic neighbors.

Bulgarian—estimated at less than 1% of the population, numbering about 11,000.

The ethnic Bulgarian population is concentrated in the southeastern districts along the Bulgarian border. Speaking a South Slav language closely related to Macedonian, the Bulgarians are nearly indistinguishable from the Macedonians. Like the Macedonians, they belong to the Orthodox faith, mostly to the Macedonian Orthodox Church.

Many Bulgarians continue to deny the very existence of a Macedonian nation. Some Bulgarian nationalist groups assert the Bulgarian ethnicity of all Macedonians in FYROM, Greece, and Bulgaria.

Vlach—estimated at less than 1% of the population, numbering about 10,000.

The Vlach are a Latin people, belonging to one of the three branches of the

Romanian nation. The Macedonian Vlach are also known as Koustovlahs, Aromani, or Cincari. Concentrated in the southern districts, they live around Bitolj, Resen, and Krusevo, in the Osgovo Mountains and the Kriva Valley. The number of Vlach has been falling due to assimilation into the Macedonian majority, but in recent years many more have registered as ethnic Vlach with newly formed groups calling for improved language and educational rights.

The Vlach language, also called Macedo-Rumanian or Aromunian, is a Southeastern Romance language that split from the Romanian language between A.D. 500 and 1000. The Vlach are mainly Orthodox Christians.

Croat—estimated at less than 1% of the population, numbering about 3,000.

The Croat population, living mostly in Skopje, were settled in the region as administrators and bureaucrats during the Communist era. The Croats speak a South Slav language and are mainly Roman Catholic, with a Protestant minority. Many Croats have left the republic since the breakup of the Yugoslav state.

Jew—estimated at less than 1% of the population, numbering about 2,000.

The Jews of Macedonia are primarily urban, living mostly in the capital city, Skopje. The majority are descendants of Jews expelled from Spain in 1492 and allowed to settle in the Ottoman Empire. Since the breakup of the Yugoslav state many Jews have immigrated to the United States or Israel.

THE NATION: A meeting place for the various peoples of the Balkan Peninsula for thousands of years, modern Macedonia roughly corresponds to the ancient Macedonian kingdom founded in the seventh century B.C. Under the guidance of Philip II, in the fourth century B.C., Macedonia became a prosperous, expanding state. Under his son, Alexander III, called Alexander the Great, Macedonia's military conquered the entire Greek world, the Persian Empire, and territories as far east as India. In the third century B.C., Macedonia was one of the most powerful empires in the known world.

Macedonia's empire was divided between Alexander's generals after his death in 323 B.C. and its power was weakened by the expanding Roman Republic. In 148 B.C. Macedonia became a Roman province. In A.D. 395, with the division of the Roman Empire into east and west, Macedonia was included in the Eastern or Byzantine Empire.

In the sixth and seventh centuries migrating Slavs from the north occupied most of the region, pushing south to the Aegean Sea and temporarily disrupting the Byzantine administration of the region. The Slavs settled the region and gradually assimilated the Illyrian peoples. Having become the dominant people in the region, the Slavs eventually acknowledged Byzantine rule and adopted Orthodox Christianity. The expanding Bulgarian kingdom conquered Macedonia from the Byzantines in the ninth century.

A western Bulgarian kingdom emerged in the region at the breakup of Bulgaria in the tenth century. The kingdom, with its capital at Okhrida (Ohrid), is considered by nationalists as the first Macedonian Slav state. According to nationalist tradition, the first Slavonic university in the Balkans was founded at Okhrida in the year 893.

With the decline of Byzantine power, Macedonia was the center of both Serb and Bulgarian kingdoms. In 1018 Byzantine authority was restored, and in 1204 the Bulgarians took control of the region, followed by the Serbs in 1334. Sixty years later, in 1394, Macedonia came under the control of the Turkish Ottoman Empire.

The Turks' imposition of Islam spurred a mass emigration from the region of Orthodox Slavs. They were mostly replaced by Turks from Anatolia, Albanians, and Ladino Jews expelled from the Spanish kingdom and welcomed to the Ottoman Empire as a much needed merchant and professional class.

The Albanian population, in the north and west of Ottoman Macedonia, less attached to Christianity than the neighboring Slavs, mostly converted to Islam. The Albanians formed a favored class of landowners and administrators under Turkish rule. Much of the present enmity between the Slavs and the Albanians has its roots in the Ottoman period. In the early 1800s ethnic Albanians began to settle in the western districts of present Macedonia, their land claims given precedence on the basis of their Islamic religion.

By the nineteenth century most of the Slav population of the region had lost its separate identity, considering themselves either ethnic Bulgarians, or to a lesser extent ethnic Serbs or Slav-language Macedonian Greeks. The rise of Bulgarian nationalism, with claims to Macedonia as part of the territory populated by ethnic Bulgarians, led to counterclaims by Serbia and Greece. At the end of the Russo-Turkish War, in 1878, a Bulgarian principality, which included most of Macedonia, was created. The inclusion of Macedonian territory in Bulgaria was opposed by some European powers, and the principality was divided, at the Congress of Berlin, with Macedonia being returned to direct Turkish rule.

The idea that Macedonia might have a future independent of the Bulgarians had already been voiced as early as 1876, when schemes for a separate Macedonian province had been promoted. Not until 1885, when relations between Bulgaria and Serbia became strained over the Macedonian question, did the idea of a separate Macedonian identity begin to gain support.

At the end of the nineteenth century, it became apparent that the end of the Ottoman Empire was inevitable. During the 1880s, Greece, Serbia, and Bulgaria, all former Ottoman territories, increased their efforts to assimilate the Macedonian Slavs and gain influence in the remaining European territories controlled from Constantinople. The so-called Macedonian Question was one of the most serious diplomatic problems that confronted the major European powers.

The three Balkan states, using their respective Orthodox churches, along with funding for education and charities, sought to sway the sentiments of the Macedonian Slavs. The Bulgarians concentrated their efforts in the eastern Mesta region, while the Serbs did the same in the Vardar region, and the Greeks in the southern Struma region. In spite of their efforts, a national revival, beginning in the 1870s, fostered a renewed national awareness as the Macedonians slowly began to reverse centuries of assimilation into neighboring cultures.

In the 1890s several nationalist organizations were formed to work for the separation of Macedonia from the Ottoman Empire. Some of the groups were backed by Bulgaria, Serbia, or Greece, but the Internal Macedonian Revolutionary Organization (IMRO), founded in Salonika (Thessaloniki) in 1893, rejected claims by neighboring states and worked for Macedonian independence. Nationalist guerrillas harassed the weakening Turkish administration and skirmished with rival groups and armed bands of Greeks, Serbs, and Bulgarians seeking to establish a foothold in the disputed province.

The Graeco-Turkish War of 1897 spurred the growth of anti-Turkish sentiment in the territory. The IMRO, headed by Gotse Delchev, now a national hero, gained support among the population, which increasingly rejected claims by the neighboring states. The assimilation efforts of the neighboring states highlighted the fact that Macedonia lacked a fundamental ethnic identity. The realization by some Macedonians that this deficiency left them vulnerable to outside assimilation led to the formation of the Macedonian independence faction of the Internal Macedonian Revolutionary Organization. This nationalist organization used terrorist tactics against the ruling Turks and was committed to the formation of an independent Macedonian nation and nationality.

The Macedonians of the IMRO, led by Delchev, rebelled against the Turkish authorities in Salonika in 1902. The ill-equipped rebels overran northern Macedonia and on 2 August 1903 declared the province independent of the Ottoman Empire. Threatened by a Turkish army of 40,000 dispatched to the rebellious province, the Macedonian rebels, numbering 15,000, held the Turks at bay in a vicious seven-week war that was brought to an end only by the intervention of the major European powers. A political compromise placed Macedonia under the control of a five-power European force. In 1908 the Europeans returned the turbulent province to Turkish rule. A renewed Macedonian rebellion was crushed, with incredible cruelty, by the returning Turkish authorities.

When Italy attacked the Ottoman province of Libya in 1911, the Balkan states took the opportunity to mount their own attack on the crumbling empire. In 1912, Serbia, Greece, and Bulgaria united in the First Balkan War. Victorious over the Ottoman forces, the victors took control of all the remaining Ottoman territory in Europe, except for the Constantinople area.

Serbia, its planned annexation of Albania blocked by Italy and Austria-Hungary, demanded a greater part of Macedonia as compensation. The Bulgarians, unwilling to cede territory to Serbia, attacked the Serbs, setting off the Second Balkan War in 1913. By the terms of the Treaty of Bucharest, Bulgaria lost most of its Macedonian lands. Serbia annexed Vardar Macedonia, and Greece took Aegean Macedonia, leaving a disgruntled Bulgaria with the small Pirin territory.

The Balkan wars of 1912–13, which whetted Serbian appetites for additional territories, particularly the South Slav territories of the Austro-Hungarian Empire, eventually led to the outbreak of World War I in 1914. The disappointed Bulgarians joined the Central Powers, and Bulgarian forces occupied and administered the Macedonian territories until the Bulgarians were expelled at the end of the war.

Greek persecution of its Macedonian minority in the early 1920s forced thousands to flee, with many more expelled from Aegean Macedonia to make way for ethnic Greeks evacuated from Asia Minor between 1922 and 1924. Macedonian demands for reunification and independence brought Greece and Bulgaria close to war in 1925, and provoked serious nationalist violence in Bulgarian Macedonia in 1933–35 as well as a widespread nationalist uprising in northern Greece in 1935.

In Yugoslavia, the Macedonians were called Southern Serbs, and an oppressive authority promoted assimilation. The IMRO, supported by the Bulgarians, remained an active terrorist organization in Yugoslavia. In 1934 King Alexander of Yugoslavia was assassinated in Marseilles by a Croatian, with the assistance of Macedonian nationalists.

Bulgaria joined the Axis in 1941, primarily to regain the Macedonian territory it lost in the Second Balkan War and World War I. Bulgarians, aided by the Germans and Italians, occupied and annexed Yugoslav and Greek Macedonia. The occupation of Bulgaria by advancing Soviet forces in 1944 ended the country's attempt to regain permanent control of Macedonia. The armistice of 1944 restored the former international borders.

The promise of an autonomous Macedonian republic rallied many Macedonians to Tito's Communist Yugoslav partisans during the war. He promised to unite Vadar, Aegean, and Pirin Macedonia in a separate state within a Communist South Slav Federation, a promise he was never able to keep.

German troops occupied Macedonia in 1944, and the Germans actively supported the Macedonian nationalists. On 8 September 1944 nationalist leaders declared the independence of a united Macedonian republic, but the evacuation of the German troops, in November, left the self-proclaimed republic virtually defenseless. Greek and Yugoslav troops overran the republic soon after, and Macedonia was again divided.

Vadar Macedonia was established as a separate Yugoslav republic, but without Pirin or Aegean Macedonia as promised by Tito. Under the terms of the Communist constitution adopted in 1946, the Macedonian republic was utilized to press Yugoslav claims to both Aegean and Pirin Macedonia. Thousands of ethnic Slavs fled from Greek territory during the civil war that raged from the end of World War II until the Yugoslav-backed Communist rebels were finally routed in 1950.

In 1948 Tito, the Yugoslav Communist leader, split with Moscow. All contact between Yugoslavia and Moscow's ally, Bulgaria, was immediately severed, including the ties between the peoples of Yugoslav and Bulgarian Macedonia. Until 1948 both Yugoslavia and Bulgaria had supported a unified Macedonian state in a Balkan federation of Communist states.

The Bulgarian Communist government, which had reversed earlier Bulgarian government denials of the existence of the Macedonian nation, counted the Macedonian population separately in the 1956 census. At that time 187,729 were counted as ethnic Macedonians in Bulgaria, about 95% living in Pirin Macedonia.

The creation of a standard Macedonian language, clearly distinct from Bulgarian, and the reinterpreted history of the region gave the Yugoslav Macedonians an ethnic identity equal to that of the other Yugoslav peoples. Religion, which forms an integral part of Balkan identities, was used by the government in a unique partnership between church and state in a Communist country. The establishment of a separate Macedonian Orthodox Church, in 1958, served the purpose of developing the Macedonian national consciousness. The formation of the Macedonian identity was seen as a bulwark against future Greek and Bulgarian claims. The Macedonian republic, although one of the poorest and least developed in Yugoslavia, made impressive educational and economic gains.

The Communist Bulgarian government again denied the existence of a separate Macedonian identity in 1958, raising tensions in the area that eased only with the normalization of relations between Bulgaria and Yugoslavia in the 1970s. According to the 1965 Bulgarian census, there were only 8,750 Macedonians in the country, and according to the 1975 census there were none. In spite of improved relations between Bulgaria and Yugoslavia, cross-border ties between the Macedonians were severely restricted.

The policy of promoting a separate Macedonian identity antagonized not only Bulgaria, but also Greece, which controlled the southern part of historic Macedonia, and feared claims to its territory by Macedonian nationalists. The Greeks had always refused to recognize the Slavs living in Greece as Macedonians. The government refers to them as Slavophone Greeks. The Greek stance on its Slav minority has remained consistent since the annexation of Aegean Macedonia in 1913. Following the Greek Civil War (1946–1949), an estimated 80,000 to 100,000 Slavs left Greek Macedonia, many for Yugoslav Macedonia, but with substantial numbers leaving Europe for the United States, Canada, and Australia.

The Yugoslav government's promotion of Macedonian identity also raised tensions between the Macedonian Slavs and the large Albanian population in the region. The Albanians, who resented Slav domination of the Macedonian republic, were mostly excluded from local government and education.

The collapse of communism, in 1989, resulted in the holding of free elections in the Yugoslav republics in 1990. The new government, dominated by Macedonian nationalists and led by Kiro Gligorov, attempted to curb the activities of the more militant groups that published claims to Aegean and Pirin Macedonia as part of the national territory. The adoption of the name ''Republic of Macedonia'' and the design of a new flag, based on an ancient Macedonian symbol, led the Greek government to accuse the new state of irredentist claims to Greek Macedonian territory. In August 1991 the Greek government closed the border, cutting off Macedonia from its major trade route to the Aegean, and imposed a crippling oil embargo.

As Yugoslavia disintegrated, a nationalist coalition organized a referendum on Macedonian independence. The referendum, held on 8 September, was boycotted by the Serbian and Montenegrin voters. Assured of overwhelming voter support, Gligorov declared Macedonia independent of Yugoslavia on 17 September 1991 amid widespread fears that the war and ethnic fighting extending across much of former Yugoslavia would spread to Macedonia.

In late December 1991 the new Macedonian government, along with Croatia,* Slovenia,* and Bosnia-Herzegovina, requested recognition from the European Union. On 15 January 1992, Germany recognized the independence of Slovenia and Croatia, but not Macedonia or Bosnia. On 26 December the Macedonian parliament drafted constitutional changes to fit the European Community's conditions for recognition.

The Macedonian constitution, amended in January 1992 to fall in line with EC criteria for recognition, stated that Macedonia had no territorial claims on other countries, and renounced interference in the affairs of neighboring states. The amendments also abolished Macedonian representation in the Yugoslav Assembly and presidency. However, Macedonia's internal divisions were highlighted by a referendum held by the ethnic Albanian minority on 11–12 January 1992. The Albanians voted overwhelmingly for territorial and political autonomy. On 15 January the presidency of the EC announced that its member states had decided to recognize only Croatia and Slovenia. Greece, one of the member states, blocked recognition of Macedonia because of the Skopje government's refusal to change the name of the republic or to adopt a different flag.

The landlocked republic, already suffering the loss of trade with Yugoslavia, which had been placed under United Nations sanctions due to its part in the wars in Croatia and Bosnia, was brought to the brink of collapse by the Greek embargo. Although criticized by other European states for selling oil to Serbia while slowly strangling tiny Macedonia, the Greek government remained adamant. On 10 December 1992 over a million Greeks demonstrated in Athens against the recognition of the republic under the name Macedonia. On 11 December, fearing the spread of the Balkan war to the new republic, the United Nations Security Council authorized the dispatch to Macedonia of peacekeeping forces.

The republic, under the provisional name "Former Yugoslav Republic of Macedonia" (FYROM), was finally admitted to the United Nations on 8 April 1993 over the strident objections of the Greek and Yugoslav governments. Three hundred American troops and 150 Canadians, as part of the United Nations forces, took up positions along the international borders. The European Community, under its new name, the European Union, also extended recognition to the state.

The Greek government, in September 1995, finally recognized the republic, ending a four-year quarrel over the republic's name and flag. Greek recognition ended the economic blockade and released European Union financial aid, which the Greeks had blocked. The Macedonian government, in turn, redesigned its flag and changed two articles of the constitution that, according to Greece, hinted at territorial claims to Aegean Macedonia. The matter of the official name of the republic was put off until a later date, with FYROM continuing to be used officially.

In June 1997 representatives of Macedonia, Greece, and the United Nations again met in an effort to find a permanent name for the republic acceptable to both Macedonia and Greece. The Greek government continues to insist that the republic be called the Former Yugoslav Republic of Macedonia because ''Macedonia'' alone implies territorial claims on Greek Macedonia in spite of Macedonian government denials of irredentist claims on Greek or Bulgarian territory.

When Macedonia broke away from disintegrating Yugoslavia in 1991, it luckily survived without the ethnic fighting suffered by Bosnia and Croatia. However, by 1997 tensions between the Macedonian Slav majority and the Albanian minority had become a serious threat to the stability of the state. In July 1997 violence between the two groups broke out in the town of Gostivar over the flying of the Albanian flag.

The increasing tension in the Kosovo region of neighboring Serbia, where ethnic Albanians are demanding independence from the Yugoslav Federation, has increased the tensions between the Macedonian majority and the Albanian minority in Macedonia. The increase in tensions comes at a bad time for the republic, as the economy is in poor shape and shows few signs of improving soon.

SELECTED BIBLIOGRAPHY:

Danforth, Loring M. *The Macedonian Conflict: Ethnic Nationalism in a Transnational World.* 1995.

Georgieva, Valentina, and Sasha Konechni. *Historical Dictionary of Macedonia.* 1997.

Poulton, Hugh. *The Balkans: Minorities and States in Conflict.* 1991.

Privichevich, S. *Macedonia: Its People and History.* 1982.

Shea, John. *Macedonia and Greece: The Struggle to Define a New Balkan Nation.* 1997.

MOLDOVA

Moldavia; Republica Moldova; Republica Moldoveneasca

CAPITAL: Chisinau (Kishinev)

POPULATION: (98e) 4,452,000: 2,832,000 Moldovans in Moldova and another 600,000 to 1 million in adjacent areas of Ukraine,* the regions of North Bukovina and Eastern Bessarabia, which are claimed by some nationalist groups. The population of "Greater Moldova" is 6,150,000. MAJOR NATIONAL GROUPS: (Moldova) (98e) Moldovan 63.6%, Ukrainian 12.4%, Russian 12.1%, Gagauz 4%, Rom 3.1%, Bulgarian 1.9%, Jew, German, Belarussian, Tatar, Pole. MAJOR LANGUAGES: Romanian (Moldovan dialect), Russian, Ukrainian, Gagauz. MAJOR RELIGIONS: Orthodox, Roman Catholic, Jewish, Muslim. MAJOR CITIES: (98e) MOLDOVA: Chisinau (Kishinev) 667,000 (764,000), Tyraspil (Tiraspol) 191,000, Balti (Beltsy) 172,000, Tighina (Bendery) 138,000, Ribnita (Rybnitsa) 57,000, Orhei (Orgeyev) 45,000, Kagul 45,000, Komrat 35,000, Dubäsari (Dubossary) 31,000, Soroca (Soroki) 28,000, Chadyr-Lunga 27,000. UKRAINE: Cernauti (Chernivtsi) 285,000, Ismail (Izmayil) 94,000, Cetatea (Bilhorod) 38,000, Chilia-Noua (Kiliya) 32,000, Renia (Reni) 28,000, Hotin (Khotin) 22,000.

GEOGRAPHY: AREA: 13,012 sq.mi.-33,709 sq.km. "Greater Moldova" 20,286 sq.mi.-52,813 sq.km. LOCATION: Moldova lies in eastern Europe, occupying the southwestern part of the East European Plain, east of the Prut River between Romania on the southwest and Ukraine on the north and east. PHYSICAL GEOGRAPHY: The country is generally comprised of rolling hills that slope from the northwest to the southeast and is dissected by many streams and deep river valleys. The Moldovan Uplands or Kodry are located in the center of the country, which also contains the broad flat valleys along the western bank of the Dniester (Dnestr) River, the Dnestr Uplands. In the south, Moldova is separated from the Black Sea by the so-called Budshak, which is Turkish for "angle," the part of the plains between the Dniester and Danube Rivers that was transferred to Ukraine in 1945. The region, with its gentle climate, is mainly agricultural. Moldovan wines are becoming a major export item, and vineyards account for one of the major successes of the post-Soviet economy. The national drink of Moldova is a dry white wine. ADMINISTRATIVE DIVISIONS: Forty rayons or counties. POLITICAL STATUS: Moldova was recognized as an independent state in 1991. "Greater Moldova," as defined by some nationalist groups, also includes the regions transferred to Ukraine in 1945, the oblast of Chernivtsi and the southern districts of the oblast of Odesa (Odessa).

INDEPENDENCE DECLARATIONS: 23 December 1917 (from Russia); 27 August 1991 (from the Soviet Union).

FLAG: The Moldovan national flag, the official flag of the republic, is a vertical tricolor of pale blue, yellow, and red bearing a centered gold eagle and shield charged with the national symbols, a Roman eagle in gold outlined in black, with a red beak and talons, and a yellow scepter in its left talon; on its breast is a shield divided horizontally red over blue with a stylized ox head, star, rose, and crescent, all in black-outlined yellow.

PEOPLE: Of the fifty ethnic groups represented in the republic, the largest non-Moldovan national groups are the Slavs and the Gagauz. The major ethnic groups in the republic are geographically separated, the Slavs generally living in the urban areas or east of the Dniester River, the Moldovans in the west and central regions, and the Gagauz in the southern districts. The Moldovans are ethnically and culturally Romanian, but historically they have developed separately so that there are now cultural and linguistic differences.

Moldovan—an estimated 63.6% of the population, numbering about 2,832,000.

The Moldovans are a Romanian people, one of the three divisions of the Romanian peoples. They are descendants of early Latin peoples and Bessi Slavs, who settled in the region in the seventh century and gave their name to the republic's former designation, Bessarabia.

The Moldovans speak a dialect of Romanian with a considerable Slavic admixture. Soviet linguists claimed that the Moldovan language diverged from standard Romanian in the sixteenth century. Under Soviet rule the Moldovan language was written in the Cyrillic script, but since the late 1980s it has been written in the Latin alphabet. The language is the most easterly of the Romance languages, and there is little dialectal variation in the spoken form. The proposed change from the Cyrillic to the Latin alphabet, which was initially postponed from 1994 to 1997, has yet to be fully implemented.

According to the 1979 Soviet census, 129,000 ethnic Romanians lived in the republic. They are now counted as ethnic Moldovans, as they share a common heritage and language.

Ukrainian—an estimated 12.4% of the population, numbering about 552,000.

The Ukrainian population, mostly concentrated in the larger cities and in the Dniestria region adjacent to Ukraine, is generally Russian-speaking, although Ukrainian has gained in acceptance since the breakup of the Soviet Union in 1991. Moldova is the only former Soviet republic where the Ukrainians form the largest minority national group. The Ukrainians and Russians living east of the Dniester River declared the independence of the region on 2 September 1991.

The majority of the Ukrainian population belong to the Orthodox churches, although many are Uniate Catholics, who are generally more nationalistic than the Orthodox majority.

Russian—an estimated 12.1% of the population, numbering about 538,000.

The Russian population of Moldova includes many Cossacks, descendants of the communities founded on the new frontier in the early 1800s. The Russians live mainly in the large cities and the urban areas in central Moldova and the majority Slav region east of the Dniester River. Most are Orthodox, including a minority belonging to schismatic sects.

Moldova's proposed language laws and a loss of dominant status have spurred Russian nationalism in the republic and fueled the separatist movement in Dniestria. The Russians, supported by the former Soviet 14th Army, declared the independence of Dniestria, the region east of the Dniester River, on 2 September 1991.

Gagauz—an estimated 4% of the population, numbering about 179,000.

The Gagauz are thought to be of Bulgarian or unknown origin, although culturally and linguistically they are a Turkic people. Their language is a Turkish dialect with substantial Romanian and Russian borrowings. The majority of the Gagauz speak both Gagauzi and Russian, with a growing number learning Moldovan. The language has two dialects, Bulgar Gagauzi, spoken mainly in southern Moldova, and Maritime Gagauzi, spoken by the Gagauzi minority in the southern districts of Odessa Oblast of Ukraine, territory that was formerly part of historic Bessarabia.

Wine production, the major economic activity of the Gagauz, is closely tied to their culture and traditions, which revolve around the yearly growing and production periods. The Gagauz nation, although divided by the transfer of part of its homeland to Ukraine in 1945, has maintained close ties and has developed a strong sense of its separate identity.

The Gagauz, unlike most other Turkish peoples, are overwhelmingly Orthodox Christians. Although formerly ruled by the Ottoman Turks, whose language and culture they adopted, the Gagauz have for centuries stubbornly clung to their religion.

Rom (Gypsy)—an estimated 3.1% of the population, numbering about 138,000.

The Rom of Moldova, belonging to the Ursári and Karamíta ethnic groups, live mostly in the central and eastern districts of the country, around Chisinau and the other large cities on both banks of the Dniester. As in many other newly independent European states, the Rom have suffered discrimination and persecution in Moldova.

The majority of the Rom, who speak a Balkan Romani dialect, are Muslims, although there are Orthodox and Uniate Catholic minorities.

Bulgarian—an estimated 1.9% of the population, numbering about 85,000.

The Bulgarians, living mainly in the central and southern districts, mostly settled in the region in Russian government–sponsored migrations in the early and middle nineteenth centuries. Brought to the Bessarabian territory as part of a plan to dilute the majority Romanian population, Slavs from several different areas of Europe were encouraged to take advantage of generous settlement incentives.

Speaking an eastern language of the South Slav group, the Bulgarians are the largest South Slav national group in the republic. The majority belong to the separate Bulgarian Orthodox Church.

Jew—estimated at less than 1% of the population, numbering about 35,000.

The Jews of Moldova, mostly concentrated in the larger cities and towns, have lived in the region since the fifteenth and sixteenth centuries. Historically, Bessarabia has been a stronghold of Chassidism.

The survivors of the World War II massacres, in which many ethnic Moldovans participated, have mostly immigrated to Israel and the United States. The Jewish population of the new Moldovan state formed about 2% of the population in 1991, but during and after the civil war that tore the country apart beginning in 1992, the majority of the Jews have also emigrated.

Belarussian—estimated at less than 1% of the population, numbering about 20,000.

The Belarussians, like the other Slavs, are the descendants of Slav colonists settled in the newly conquered region after 1812. Some Belarussians were settled in the republic after World War II, particularly those from devastated regions of Belarus. The majority live in the eastern districts along the Dniester River.

The Belarussians are mostly Russian speakers and, like their Russian neighbors, belong to the Russian Orthodox Church, although a minority are Roman Catholics. The Belarussians in Moldova are mostly indistinguishable from the larger Russian population.

German—estimated at less than 1% of the population, numbering about 7,000.

The German population of Moldova are mostly rural, living in the western, central, and southern districts of the republic. Settled in the region in government-sponsored colonies in the nineteenth century, many were deported in 1941 to Siberia and Central Asia.

Many of the Germans are Roman Catholic or Protestant, but very few speak German as their first language, having adopted Russian during the Soviet period. Immigration to Germany has depleted the German population since Moldovan independence in 1991.

Tatar—estimated at less than 1% of the population, numbering about 2,000.

The Moldovan Tatars are the descendants of Crimean Tatars who settled in the region following the Turkish conquest of the sixteenth century. Most of the small Tatar population lives in the capital, Chisinau, and in the wine-growing regions of the central plains.

The Tatars speak Russian as their first language, although many speak a dialect of Turkish in their homes. They constitute, along with the Rom, the only sizable Muslim population in the republic.

THE NATION: The original inhabitants of the region, called Getae by the Greeks and Daci by the Romans, came under Roman rule with Trajan's conquest of their homeland in A.D. 107. Colonized and fortified, the region formed part of Rome's trans-Danube frontier. Roman colonists, encouraged to settle in the region, imposed their language and culture on the original inhabitants.

Overrun by barbarian tribes, Visigoths and Ostrogoths, around A.D. 250, the province was finally abandoned to the Goths when the Roman colonists withdrew to south of the Danube in 270. The Romans' Latin language and the fortifications called Trajan's Walls are the only lasting legacies of Roman rule. A succession of invaders followed the Goths. Avars, Bulgars, Magyars, Pechenegs, and Cumans overran the region, each leaving an imprint on its population.

Named for the Slavic Bessi tribe that settled the area during the great Slav migrations of the seventh century, Bessarabia constituted part of the huge territory conquered by the Slavs. The region formed part of the first great Slav state, Kievan Rus, from the ninth to the eleventh centuries, laying the basis for the later Russian claims to the area.

Devastated by the Mongol invasion in 1242, Bessarabia recovered under the rule of Stephen the Great, the creator of the first Moldovan principality in 1359, with the historic nucleus of the state in northern Bukovina, now the Ukrainian oblast of Chernivtsi.

The principality fell to the Ottoman Turks and Crimean Tatars in 1513, the conquest marking the northern limit of Turkish rule. The Ottoman bureaucracy ruled through local officials, leaving the Moldovans to look after their own affairs to a great extent. Only when taxes were not paid or disturbances erupted did the strong hand of the empire descend on the region.

The Austrians wrested control of the western district, Bukovina, from Turkey in 1774, and the Ottoman Empire formally ceded the region to the Austrian Empire in 1777. Bukovina was added to Austrian Galicia as a separate district.

An expanding Russia contested Turkish control of Moldavia from 1711, finally annexing Bessarabia following the Russo-Turkish War of 1806–12. The Treaty of Bucharest transferred the Moldovan territory east of the Prut River to the Russian Empire. The newly annexed territory, 86% Romanian-speaking, was subjected to intense Russification and opened to settlement by non-Romanian colonists in order to dilute the Romanian-speaking majority. Thousands of Gagauz, Bulgarians, Ukrainians, Russians, and Poles settled in the newly conquered territory.

The Russian tsar, Alexander I, granted cultural and linguistic autonomy to the new territories, allowing each national group the same rights and privileges. The administration remained in the hands of the local aristocracy, and the administrative system continued virtually unchanged. In 1818 Moldova was given the status of an autonomous area and Romanian was given the status of the second national language, after Russian, in the region.

In 1825 Alexander I died, and Nicholas I became tsar. Step by step the Moldovans lost their privileges. In 1828 the autonomous status of the region was revoked, and Moldovans occupying posts in the administration were replaced by Russians. The Russian legal and administrative systems were introduced, and most Romanian-language schools were closed.

Anti-Russian sentiment incited the growth of Bessarabian nationalism in the 1840s. Nationalism was crushed during the severe disturbances that erupted in 1848, only to surface again in the 1870s and 1880s with the support of the neighboring Romanian kingdom. The Romanians, seeking to recover lands they claimed were part of the ethnic Romanian homeland, supported the growth of Moldovan nationalism as an anti-Russian movement.

The western region of Bessarabia, Bukovina, was made a separate Austrian crownland in 1849, following severe disturbances the year before. As part of the Roman Catholic Habsburg empire, Bukovina became the most advanced and prosperous of the Moldovan territories. Moldovan nationalist organizations, suppressed in Bessarabia, were allowed to function in Austrian Bukovina, but only as anti-Russian movements. Political newspapers and pamphlets were smuggled from Bukovina into Bessarabia for distribution by underground nationalist organizations.

Russian government attempts to channel Moldovan nationalist sentiment into the region's traditional anti-Semitism led to horrible pogroms, particularly awful during the attack on Kishinev's Jewish quarters in 1903. However, anti-Semitism proved a temporary distraction, and Moldovan nationalism continued to gather strength, culminating in widespread disturbances during the Russian Revolution of 1905 and during a futile revolt in March and April 1907. The revolt, brutally crushed by tsarist troops, drove the emerging national movement underground.

Devastated by nearly three years of war, the tsarist government collapsed in revolution in February 1917, leaving Bessarabia effectively independent as civil government disappeared. In May the Moldovan nationalists formed a government, but gave their qualified support to Russia's new democratic government. The Moldovans demanded political, linguistic, and ecclesiastical autonomy for the province and for the estimated 1 million Moldovans living in the Kherson and Podolia provinces of Ukraine. The Moldovans raised an army of 40,000 under their own officers to fight the Central Powers in support of the Provisional Government of Russia.

Following the October 1917 Bolshevik coup, the alarmed nationalists declared the region's autonomy and formed the Sfatul Tarii (Council of the Land), inviting participation by all of Bessarabia's national groups. On 7 December 1917 the Moldovans rose against the imposition of Bolshevik rule, and on 12 December the Council proclaimed autonomy and renounced all ties to the new Soviet government.

No demand for union with Romania was put forward, as the Moldovans believed there was more hope of securing free and full development within a restored federal, democratic Russia than as part of backward, feudal Romania. The Council decreed the use of the Moldovan language, with the Latin alphabet, and newspapers and other publications began to publish using the Roman script in place of Russia's Cyrillic alphabet.

Pressed by Ukrainian nationalists seeking to annex the region to newly independent Ukraine, and under a growing Bolshevik military threat, the Sfatul Tarii declared the independence of the Democratic Republic of Moldova, including Bukovina, on 23 December 1917.

The new republic, menaced by the advancing Red Army, voted for union with neighboring Romania in April 1918. Romanian troops crossed the Prut River and halted the Bolshevik advance at the Dniester. In November 1918 the region held by Romanian and Moldovan troops was formally joined to the Romanian kingdom.

The collapse of defeated Austria-Hungary in November 1918 left Bukovina virtually independent. The Ukrainians, dominant in the north of the region, voted for union with the Western Ukrainian Republic, the state set up in the former Austrian Galicia, but the Romanians, in the south, refused to become part of a Ukrainian nation. The Treaty of St. Germain, in 1919, gave only the southern districts of Bukovina to Romania, but the subsequent Treaty of Sèvres transferred the entire Bukovina territory to Romania.

Moldova was virtually colonized by the Romanian boyars, landlords given large tracts of Moldovan land who moved north into former Russian and Austrian territories. Initial enthusiasm for union with Romania quickly gave way to indignation and disgust with the corrupt, feudal Romanian system. In 1919 the Moldovan protests and demonstrations turned into serious antiroyalist and anti-Romanian riots, cruelly put down by Romanian troops. Moldova's inclusion in the Romanian kingdom, over growing Moldovan objections, was recognized by the Treaty of Paris in 1920.

The new Soviet government refused to recognize the separation of Moldova or the Romanian annexation. On 12 September 1921 the Soviets declared war on Bessarabia, which led to skirmishing along the Dniester River frontier. The region east of the Dniester, conquered by the Red Army in 1918, was organized as an autonomous Moldovan republic within Ukraine in 1924, with Tiraspol as its capital.

Bessarabia and Bukovina, as Romanian provinces, were treated as semi-agricultural colonies virtually ruled by the powerful landowners. There was much dissatisfaction with Romanian rule in the 1920s and 1930s. The provinces, more developed than most of Romania in 1918, became one of the more backward regions in Romania, and the most corrupt. The union of Moldova and Romania from 1918 to 1940 was an economic disaster for the region.

On 23 August 1939 the Soviet and Nazi German governments signed the Molotov-Ribbentrop Pact, a nonaggression agreement that virtually divided eastern Europe into Nazi and Soviet spheres of influence. The pact, assuring noninterference in Soviet actions, allowed the Soviet government to send troops into several adjoining territories, including the Romanian province of Bessarabia and the northern part of Bukovina.

The territories taken from Romania were formally ceded by the weak Romanian government in June 1940. Added to Soviet Moldova north of the Dniester River, an enlarged Moldovan republic was admitted to the Soviet Union as a union republic. Thousands of Moldovans, considered anti-Communist or potential troublemakers, were deported, most to bleak work camps in Siberia and Central Asia. The deported Moldovans were replaced by more reliable Slavs, Russians, Ukrainians, and Belarussians.

Romania joined the Axis, partly to recover the lost territories, and in June 1941 the Romanian military joined the German attack on the Soviet Union and quickly overran the disputed territories. The Romanians promoted the Romanian language and culture in the region. In 1940, when the territories were formally ceded to the Soviet Union, an estimated 65% of all men, and 85% of women, were illiterate. By 1941, when the Romanians returned as conquerors, even the small Romanian-speaking intelligentsia had been devastated by a year of Soviet rule.

The region, part of the so-called Pale of Settlement in tsarist Russia, had a very large Jewish population on the eve of the Romanian-German invasion, estimated at about 250,000. Most of the Jewish population of the territories was massacred by the Romanian Fascists and their Nazi German allies between 1941 and 1944, often with the support and participation of the local Moldovan population.

Moldova was retaken by invading Soviets in 1944, following Romania's defeat along with the rest of the Axis powers. The region was forcibly collectivized, and many Moldovans were resettled within the republic.The returning Soviet authorities forbade all contact with Romania, and a separate Moldovan culture and language were imposed, which stressed the region's historic Slavic influences and excised the Latin Romanian elements. Northern Bukovina and the Black Sea districts of eastern Bessarabia, areas with large non-Moldovan populations, were transferred to the Soviet Ukraine. Thousands of Moldovans were transported east to join those deported in 1940–41. In all, an estimated 80,000 Moldovans were deported in three mass movements between 1940 and 1949.

Romania, under a Stalinist regime, was increasingly at odds with its Soviet ally after the death of Stalin in 1953. However, cultural and student exchanges were again permitted. Moldovan intellectuals learned to read the Latin alphabet used in Romanian publications and participated in the general cultural life shared by Romania and Moldova. The Soviet reaction to the ties between the two varied with the relations between Romania and the USSR. In the mid-1960s a freeze in relations led to renewed restrictions on Moldovan ties to Romania.

In 1964 and 1966 the Romanian government accused the Soviets of manufacturing the Moldovan ethnic group out of a branch of the Romanian nation. To underline its accusations, the Romanian Communist government put forward claims to the republic on historic and ethnic grounds. The claims were rejected by the USSR.

By the early 1970s the Soviet intent to separate the Moldovans from the Romanians had succeeded too well. The Moldovan nationalism fostered by the Soviet government after World War II had slowly moved from government policy to a popular Moldovan movement. In the 1980s a specifically Moldovan nationalism began to gain support, until suppressed as part of a new government policy stressing Russification in the guise of Soviet nationalism.

Moldovan nationalism quickly gained support as the Gorbachev reforms, introduced in 1987, reduced the pressure to conform to the Soviet ideals of nationhood and brotherly unity. The Moldovan popular front (Frontul Popular al Moldovei) was formed in early 1988 and held its first congress in May of that year.

In March and April 1989 thousands took to the streets to protest the Russification of their language and culture since the reimposition of Soviet rule in 1944. The huge demonstrations, led by the newly formed nationalist organizations, demanded the return of the Latin alphabet and that Moldovan be made the official language of the republic. A plan was put forward to replace Russian and the Cyrillic alphabet with Moldovan (Romanian) and the Latin alphabet within five years. The proposed changes to the language laws were met with strikes and demonstrations by the large Slavic population, particularly in the heavily Slav region east of the Dniester River. Finally two laws were passed in August 1989 that declared Moldovan the state language, but retained Russian as the lingua franca.

A nationalist government, elected in February 1990, continued to stress the predominance of the Romanian language. Proposals to restrict the use of Russian after independence exacerbated tensions between the Moldovan majority and the Slav minority. The alleged degradation of Russian quickly alienated the republic's large non-Moldovan minorities. Among the Slav population the new government was seen as trying to impose a new culture and language on the Soviet peoples of the region. Even among the smaller nationalities, such as the Gagauz, who were mostly bilingual in their own language and Russian, resistance to the need to learn yet another language fueled the nascent national movements.

The Soviet government, in 1990, in an effort to stave off total collapse, focused on preserving the unitary state by creating a new Soviet structure. A proposal to set up a union of thirty-five republics was drafted. Fifteen of the republics were to replace the union republics, sixteen were to be created within the Russian Federation, and four were to be created within other republics. Two of the new formations were planned for the Moldovan Soviet Socialist Republic, Dniestria and Gagauzia. The plan was set aside as the Soviet Union rapidly disintegrated.

The government passed a proclamation of state sovereignty on 23 June 1990. In August 1990 the Gagauz proclaimed their homeland in the south an autonomous republic, and in September the Slavs, who controlled the region east of the Dniester, unilaterally proclaimed the autonomy of the Transdniestria region under an unreformed Communist government.

Effectively independent following the abortive coup and the subsequent disintegration of the Soviet Union in August 1991, the Moldovan government formally declared independence on 27 August. The declaration, greeted with mass rallies and enthusiasm by the Moldovans, was rejected by the Slavic population concentrated north of the Dniester River, who feared that Moldova would unite with neighboring Romania. Some national groups demanded that the new government begin immediate negotiations with neighboring Ukraine to recover the territories transferred to Ukraine by Stalin.

Demands for separation of the Transdniestria region from newly independent Moldova escalated tensions between the Moldovan majority and the large Slav minority. Even many anti-Communist Slavs supported the hard-line Communists of the Transdniestria region, who claimed to protect the Slavs against inclusion in an expanded Romanian state. Some nationalist groups called for an exchange of territory with neighboring Ukraine, ceding the Transdniestria region of Moldova to Ukraine in exchange for the territories transferred to Ukraine by Stalin in 1945, the historic regions of North Bukovina and Eastern Bessarabia.

The Russian 14th Army, which had formerly policed the southwestern Soviet Union, supported the secession of Transdniestria from Moldova. Backed by the Russian military, the Dniestrian leaders defied the new Moldovan government. The Slav leaders denounced the Moldovan declaration of independence, and on 2 September 1991 the regional parliament declared the independence of the region as the Dniester Moldavian Republic. In December 1991 armed conflict broke out, pitting the secessionists, backed by the Soviet 14th Army, against the new Moldovan army. By June 1992 over 700 people had died in the fighting and 50,000 had fled the escalating conflict.

In the southeast, the leaders of the Gagauz nation resisted the Moldovan government's efforts to assert control in their homeland. However, fearing the ethnic violence that had broken out in a number of former Soviet republics, the Gagauz leaders, in March 1992, accepted a government offer of self-government within the new Moldovan republic. The agreement was accepted with the stipulation that should Moldova decide to reunite with neighboring Romania, Gagauzia would be allowed to peacefully secede from the republic.

On 21 June 1992, following a series of meetings with the participation of Moldova, Russia, Romania, Ukraine, and the Dniestrian leaders, the Transdniestria region was accorded a special status within Moldova. The accords also included a clause that the region will be granted the right to determine its own future should Moldova decide to merge with Romania.

In January 1993 the Moldovan parliament narrowly defeated a proposition to hold a referendum on reunification with Romania. In elections, held in early 1994, the Moldovan nationalists won greater support than those favoring unification with Romania. The Moldovan government, in March 1994, rescinded the language law that began the alienation of the non-Moldovan national groups in the republic in 1989. In May 1994 a draft constitution provided for a special legal status and broad powers of self-government for the autonomous republics of Gagauzia and Dniestria.

In 1995 the nonviolent conflict with the Gagauz was finally settled by a formal grant of autonomy to the Gagauz republic, which now forms a self-governing republic within Moldova. The Gagauz, whose lands are given over to Moldova's world-class wines, have aided the transition to a market economy. Also in 1995, Moldova became the first of the newly independent states in Europe to join the Council of Europe.

In May 1996, Moldovan and Russian officials agreed to establish a joint commission on procedures and deadlines for withdrawing the former Soviet and now Russian 14th Army from eastern Moldova. The accord, protested by the Dniester separatists, calls for the phased withdrawal to Russia of the mostly ethnic Russian military units.

The Moldovan government, firmly rejecting any suggestion that Moldova and Romania may merge, has applied for both European Union and NATO membership and has joined many international organizations. Romania, the first country to extend diplomatic recognition, having had second thoughts on Moldovan independence, maintained only low-level representation in Chisinau until 1994. Since 1996 relations between the two Romanian nations have been arranged to suit their status as independent states.

In presidential elections, in November 1996, the chairman of the parliament, Petru Lucinschi, was elected. In February 1991, a pro-Lucinschi political group, the Movement for a Democratic and Prosperous Moldova, was formed as a centrist party, with affinities to both the moderate left and right. The move to centrist politics should aid the Moldovan government's campaign to negotiate the final autonomy agreements with both the Dniester Republic (Dniestria) and the Gagauz Republic (Gagauzia).

SELECTED BIBLIOGRAPHY:

Applebaum, Anne. *Ukraine, Moldova, Belarus: Between East and West.* 1995.
Dailey, Erika, ed. *Human Rights in Moldova: The Turbulent Dniester.* 1993.
Dima, Nicholas. *From Moldavia to Moldova: The Soviet-Romanian Territorial Dispute.* 1991.
Dyer, Donald L. *Studies in Moldovan: The History, Culture, Language and Contemporary Politics of the People of Moldova.* 1996.
Jewsbury, George F. *The Russian Annexation of Bessarabia.* 1976.

NAMIBIA

Republic of Namibia

CAPITAL: Windhoek

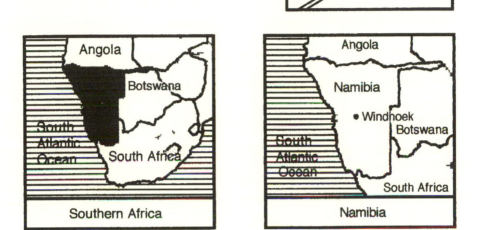

POPULATION: (98e) 1,730,000. MAJOR NATIONAL GROUPS: (98e) Ovambo 48.5%, Kavango (Okavango) 8.8%, Herero 8.1%, Damara 7%, White (Afrikaans, German, English) 6.8%, Colored 5.2%, Nama 4.9%, Caprivian 4.3%, San (Bushmen) 2.8%, Baster 2.2%, Tswana, Kwambi, Mbukushu, Kwangali, Diriku. MAJOR LANGUAGES: Ovambo, Afrikaans, Kavango, English, Herero. MAJOR RELIGIONS: Lutheran 50%, Other Christian (Dutch Reformed, Roman Catholic, Baptist, Methodist) 30%, animist. MAJOR CITIES: (98e) Windhoek 174,000 (203,000), Walvis Bay 40,000 (54,000), Swakomund 22,000, Luderitz 18,000, Rehoboth 16,000, Rundu 16,000, Keetmanshoop 15,000, Tsumeb 15,000.

GEOGRAPHY: AREA: total area: 318,416 sq.mi.-824,212 sq.km. LOCATION: Namibia lies in southwestern Africa, bordering the South Atlantic Ocean on the west, Angola on the north, Zambia on the northeast, South Africa on the south and southeast, and Botswana on the east. PHYSICAL GEOGRAPHY: Most of Namibia consists of high plateaus and deserts, the Namib Desert along the coast and the Kalahari Desert in the east. The country is roughly divided into four distinct regions: the coastal desert region, which includes the Namib Desert and follows the entire length of Namibia's coastline; the inland plateau, which also contains the isolated peaks of the Tsaris Mountains in the southwest, the Anas Mountains in the center, and the Erongo Mountains in the west; the Etosha Pan, an enormous alluvial basin that was once a huge lake; and the dune and grass region of the Kalahari Desert in the east and south of the central plateau. The country, one of the driest on earth, has little fertile land that can be used to grow crops, estimated at about 1% of the total land area. Most of the country is pasture and herd lands, with forest regions in the higher elevations. The principal rivers are the Orange, the Rio Okavango, and the Fish or Vis. The only year-round rivers are on the country's borders.

ADMINISTRATIVE DIVISIONS: Thirteen districts. POLITICAL STATUS: Namibia was recognized as an independent state in 1990.

FLAG: A large blue triangle with a yellow sunburst fills the upper left section, and an equal green triangle (solid) fills the lower right section; the triangles are separated by a red stripe that is outlined in white.

INDEPENDENCE DECLARATION: 21 March 1990 (from South Africa).

PEOPLE: Namibia, with a large territory, is sparsely populated, but those few constitute an unusually diverse group of peoples and cultures. The country's predominant Black African population, about 86% of the total, is composed of several different ethnic groups. The so-called Colored population is mostly of mixed Afrikaner and Black derivation. The small but economically important White population is comprised mostly of Afrikaners, Germans, and English. There is also a significant Asian population. The majority of the population lives in the north, where the climate is less arid.

English, the mother tongue of about 7% of the population, is the official language of the country. Afrikaans, the official language under the apartheid regime and the mother language of about 60% of the White and Colored populations, is spoken widely and is the language of intergroup communications. Some 32% of the White population speaks German. The most important of the indigenous languages are Oshvambo, Herero, and Nama.

Ovambo—an estimated 48.5% of the population, numbering about 840,000.

The largest of the national groups of Namibia, the Ovambo inhabit the northern region, called Ovamboland. The Ovambo tribe straddles the border, with substantial numbers of ethnic Ovambo also living in adjacent areas of Angola, where they are known as the Ovimbandu. Most Ovambo are agriculturists and herders. They are mainly Christian, with a minority adhering to traditional religions.

The Ovambo are a Bantu people speaking a Southern Bantu language, Owambo or Otjiwambo, of the Niger-Congo group of languages. The language, spoken in several distinct dialects such as Ndonga, Ngandyera, and Kwanyama, is spoken throughout northern Namibia.

Kavango—an estimated 8.8% of the population, numbering about 152,000.

The Kavango or Okavango, mostly living in the northeast, are a Bantu people closely related to the Ovambo. The second largest of the Bantu nations in Namibia, they are concentrated in the northern region of Okavango or Kavangoland near the Angolan border.

The Kavango speak a Southern Bantu language related to Ovambo. The language is spoken in several major dialects, some of which are spoken only in

Angola. The majority of the Kavango also speak the Ovambo language, the lingua franca of northern Namibia.

Herero (Herrero)—an estimated 8.1% of the population, numbering about 140,000.

The Herrero are a cattle-herding people living in the north and northwest of the country. Former aristocrats who own enormous herds of longhorn cattle, the Herrero are a Bantu people speaking a Southern Bantu language.

At times erroneously called Damara, the Herrero are the former masters of the Damara, who were serfs and herdsmen dominated by the Herrero aristocracy. The Herrero are mainly Christian, with an animist minority.

Damara (Demara)—an estimated 7% of the population, numbering about 120,000.

The Damara or Demara live in the northwest, in the region between the Namib Desert and the Etosha Pan. The ethnic origins of the Damara are unknown. Historically, they were alternatively the slaves of the Nama and the Herrero.

The Damara speak the Nama language, probably adopted during their period of slavery under the Nama aristocracy. The dialect spoken by the Damara is called Dama or Damaqua.

White—an estimated 6.8% of the population, numbering about 117,000.

The White population of Namibia is made up of three distinct groups. The largest group, the Afrikaans, mostly settlers from South Africa, account for about 60% of the total White population. The second group, the Germans, about 32% of the total, are the descendants of the European settlers who came to the German colony in the late nineteenth and early twentieth centuries. The third group, the English, about 7% of the total White population, mostly settled in the region under South African rule.

Colored—an estimated 5.2% of the population, numbering about 90,000.

The Colored population of Namibia is of mixed European and Black background. A number of separate groups are considered Colored, the most important being the Kaokovelders and Koisan. The largest group, the Koisan, live throughout the country, but are concentrated in Windhoek and the central regions.

The language of the Colored population is Afrikaans, and most belong to the Dutch Reformed or Lutheran churches. Although the Coloreds are counted as one group, the different groups have never united and consider themselves distinct national groups.

Nama—an estimated 4.9% of the population, numbering about 85,000.

The Nama, also called Hottentot, are the descendants of the original Bantu peoples. The Nama nation is made up of two branches, one the original Hottentots, the other, often called Koisan, of mixed European and Nama background. Most Nama live in the south-central area of the country in the region called Great Namaland. The language of the Nama is a Koisan language also spoken in neighboring South Africa and Botswana. Most Nama are Christians, mainly Lutheran.

Caprivian—an estimated 4.3% of the population, numbering about 75,000.

The Caprivians or East Caprivians inhabit the long finger of land known as the Caprivi Strip in the northeast of the country. The largest of the groups known as Caprivians are the Mafwe, who make up about half the Caprivian population and speak Fwe, a Central Bantu language. The other tribal group is the Rotse or Barotse, more numerous in neighboring Zambia, who speak a Southern Bantu language, which is the lingua franca of the region.

The Caprivians are mostly Christian, primarily Roman Catholic, the religion brought to the region by missionaries in 1936. Under South African rule, the area known as the Caprivi Strip was separate from the rest of Namibia under its own administration.

San (Bushmen)—an estimated 2.8% of the population, numbering about 48,000.

The San, more commonly known as Bushmen, belong to a number of separate tribal and linguistic groups. The original inhabitants of the region, the Bushmen have been pushed into the least fertile regions by more powerful invaders.

The major San languages are Aukwe or Akhoe, Kung-Ekoka, Xun, and Kung-Tsumkwe. The languages are the major dialects of the Koisan group of languages spoken in southern Africa. The Vasekela Bushmen, mostly in the Caprivi region, migrated there to escape the civil war in neighboring Angola. Most of the San adhere to traditional beliefs, with a Christian, mostly Protestant, minority.

Baster—an estimated 2.2% of the population, numbering about 38,000.

The Basters, meaning Bastards, take pride in their name. The descendants of Dutch and French settlers and Khoi women, originally in the Cape of Good Hope area of South Africa, the Basters, rejected by both the White and Black populations, left the Cape for Southwest Africa.

The language of the Basters, a dialect of Afrikaans, is spoken as the national language and as a means to communicate with other national groups in Namibia. Many Basters live outside the Rehoboth region, formerly the official homeland of the Basters. Most of the Basters, like their Afrikaans kin, belong to the Protestant Dutch Reformed Church.

Tswana—estimated at less than 1% of the population, numbering about 8,000.

The Tswana population of Namibia, mostly concentrated in the northwest, are more numerous in neighboring Botswana, South Africa, and Zimbabwe. The Tswana speak a Sotho-Tswana language of the Niger-Congo group of Bantu languages. The majority of the Tswana are Christians, with an animist minority.

Kwambi—estimated at less than 1% of the population, numbering about 6,000.

The Kwambi are a Bantu people, part of the large Bantu group that inhabits the northern districts of Namibia. They are part of a larger group of Kwambi living across the international border in Angola. The majority are herders and adhere to traditional religions.

Mbukushu—estimated at less than 1% of the population, numbering about 6,000.

The Mbukushu, concentrated in northern Namibia, are a Bantu people closely related to the Kwangali and the Ovambo and are also herders and farmers. Most adhere to traditional beliefs, with a Christian minority.

Kwangali—estimated at less than 1% of the population, numbering about 5,000.

The Kwangali, also called Kwangare or Sikwangali, are a Bantu people living in the northern part of Namibia. Related to the dominant Ovambo, the Kwangali are mostly herders and farmers. Their language, Rukwangali, is a Southern Bantu language of the Niger-Congo group of languages.

Diriku—estimated at less than 1% of the population, numbering about 5,000.

The Diriku are a Bantu people living in the northern districts of Nambia near the Angolan border. The Diriku are mostly herders in the dry lands east of the coastal desert. Their language is a Southern Bantu language of the Niger-Congo language group.

THE NATION: The San or Bushmen, who have inhabited the region for at least 2,000 years, were the first people to live in the region now known as Namibia. Hunters and gatherers, the San roamed the dry plateaus, living in concert with nature and the seasons.

Between the thirteenth and sixteenth centuries Bantu tribes, migrating from the north, settled in the region. The tribes, more powerful than the gentle San, took possession of the most fertile lands and drove the surviving Bushmen into the less hospitable deserts. The Bantu peoples lived in tribal territories, with frequent wars over land, water, and women.

In the fifteenth century Portuguese seamen sailed along the coast, but the forbidding Namib Desert and the warlike tribes discouraged exploration. For several hundred years the region remained virtually unknown, until the early 1800s, when a German merchant, F.A.W. Luderitz, purchased much of the coastal area from the Hottentots.

European explorers from several nations crossed the region in the nineteenth century, including David Livingston in the late 1840s. In 1851 Livingston discovered the Zambezi River, which flows through the Caprivi Strip region of Namibia.

In the 1840s German colonists, arriving from Europe, settled the more fertile regions along the coast and founded a number of inland settlements. In 1868, to escape persecution by both Blacks and Whites in the Cape Colony, the Basters trekked north to settle the area just south of the present capital, Windhoek. The Basters established a self-governing district, the Baster Gebiet of Rehoboth, in 1872.

In 1878 the British took control of Walvis Bay, the region's only deep-water port. The port and its hinterland were added to British Cape Colony in 1884. Walvis Bay became an important military base for the British navy in the South Atlantic.

In 1885 German trading rights were extended over most of the territory, then known as South-West Africa. The German Empire, in 1892, formally proclaimed the region a German colony, German Southwest Africa. Walvis Bay remained under British authority.

The British South Africa Company, in the interior, established a protectorate in Barotseland, around the Zambezi River, in 1889. Two years later, in an agreement with German count Georg Leo von Caprivi, the Company ceded the so-called Caprivi Strip to the German Empire. The new strip of territory gave German Southwest Africa access to the important Zambezi River.

German colonial troops garrisoned the inland settlements and dealt harshly with the native peoples. The endemic wars between the tribes were ended, although the warlike Herrero, who had conquered the Hottentot peoples, remained in a state of war with the German authorities. In 1903 the cattle-herding aristocrats rebelled against German rule. So ruthless was the German response that the Herrero were reduced from more than 80,000 people to less than 15,000 impoverished refugees in less than one year.

Diamonds, discovered on the coast in 1908, set off a diamond rush, bringing thousands more Europeans to the region, including many Germans from Europe. During the same period, many German families arrived to take up farming in the inland plateaus.

During World War I, South African troops, part of the Allied forces, invaded German Southwest Africa. In June 1915, the German authorities in the colony were forced to surrender. The South Africans set up a provisional administration to govern the huge territory. Unhappy under South African rule, many Germans returned to Europe, while White South Africans settled in the region to exploit its natural resources and to farm.

In 1919 the new League of Nations formally placed the territory under South African administration. In December 1920, the territory was given to South Africa as a class ''C'' mandate under the auspices of the League. Class ''C'' mandates were to be governed as an integral part of the countries receiving the mandates. However, the agreement called for the eventual self-government of the territory when it was sufficiently developed.

The South African government extended South African laws, including the country's racial laws, to the new territory. In 1922 the South African government annexed Walvis Bay to Cape Province, ensuring future South African control of the vital deep-water port.

After World War II all countries holding former League of Nations mandates turned the mandated territories over to the jurisdiction of the new United Nations. The South African government, in 1946, put forward a plan to annex Southwest Africa rather than place the territory under UN control. The UN rejected the plan, insisting that South Africa submit the territory to the UN Trusteeship Council.

The South African government vacillated, while in South Africa proper, in 1948, the Afrikaners gained power and instituted a series of harsh and discriminatory racial laws. The new racial laws were also applied to Southwest Africa in 1949. The application of the racial laws caused some unrest in the territory, which was put down by South African police and military units. In 1950 the International Court of Justice declared South Africa's control of the territory illegal.

Several Ovambo groups, in 1958, formed the South West African People's Organization (SWAPO). They began to launch guerrilla attacks on South African security forces in October 1966, the same year the racially discriminatory apartheid laws were extended to the territory. The United Nations, in response to the extension of apartheid to Southwest Africa, passed a resolution stating that South Africa had forfeited its mandatory rights. The South African government rejected the resolution. Two years later the UN officially changed the name of the territory from Southwest Africa to Namibia, after the Namib Desert.

The World Court, in 1971, handed down an advisory opinion that South Africa had no legal jurisdiction over the territory and should withdraw its administration. The South African government rejected the opinion, but various countries, including many in Europe, accepted that South Africa's administration was illegal and openly aided the SWAPO rebels in the growing guerrilla war.

The South African government moved thousands of troops into the territory and, as in South Africa, set up autonomous bantustans (tribal homelands). The Ovambo Legislative Council was set up in 1968, Kavango in 1970, Caprivi in 1973. Eventually nine homelands were erected, leaving over two-thirds of the territory in the hands of the small White minority.

Neighboring Angola became independent in 1975 under a Marxist regime that offered aid and sanctuary to the SWAPO rebels. The UN General Assembly voted unanimously in January 1976 to approve a resolution calling for UN-supervised elections. In December the General Assembly endorsed the "armed struggle" of the people for independence and recognized the Marxist SWAPO as the legitimate representative of the Namibian people.

The failure of SWAPO to drive the South Africans from Namibia set off a backlash among SWAPO supporters. Vicious infighting and purges in the guerrilla camps in Angola and Zambia outraged many of SWAPO's overseas supporters. Many non-Ovambo nationalists were killed or disappeared along with Ovambo leaders opposed to Sam Nujoma's autocratic rule of the organization.

In 1977 South Africa was preparing to grant Namibia independence under a plan that would give local political leadership to an assembly dominated by White Namibians, which the UN strongly opposed. In 1978 the UN passed a resolution that called for UN-supervised elections before independence for Namibia could be discussed.

South African–supervised elections were held in December 1978, but were boycotted by SWAPO and other nationalist organizations. The Democratic Turnhalle Alliance (DTA), a multiethnic political party supported by South Africa, won the elections, which the UN refused to recognize. Throughout 1979–80 talks were held between the representatives of the UN and the South African government in an effort to reach agreement on an acceptable plan for future Namibian independence.

The South African government refused to allow free elections, assuming that SWAPO, supported by the largest tribes, the Ovambo and Kavango, would easily win. While South Africa continued to press for assurances for the White minority, violence escalated in the territory. In June 1983 a state council made up of representatives of the territory's political parties was formed to erect an interim government. The council was boycotted by SWAPO and some other groups, and, like earlier initiatives, collapsed. As no settlement was possible without SWAPO, all the South African plans foundered.

The guerrilla war continued to grow during the 1980s, with the Angolan government and its Cuban allies aiding the SWAPO rebels. In 1983–84 South African forces crossed into Angola to attack SWAPO bases. The South African government announced that no solution would be possible until all Cuban troops left Angola. In January 1983, the South African government resumed direct control of the territorial government.

In 1984 the South Africans and the Angolan government signed an interim agreement on several issues. The most important agreement called for Angola to curb the activities of the SWAPO rebels on its territory.

Within the territory, opposition to SWAPO was also evident. Several of the ethnic groups, other than the Whites, particularly the Herrero, were not enthusiastic about an independent Namibia dominated by the Ovambos and the Marxist SWAPO. The South Africans, through the territorial administration, continued to stress the divisions between the many national groups in Namibia.

Progress toward a settlement was very slow, but liberalization and reforms in South Africa finally broke the deadlock. In 1988 the South Africans and Cubans agreed to a mutual withdrawal of their troops from Angola, an essential step toward a solution to the Namibian problem. Following the withdrawal of the troops, elections were planned, and the peace process proceeded according to a UN plan. On 22 December 1988 South Africa agreed to the terms that were initiated in April 1989. In the same month clashes with the South African forces broke out as SWAPO guerrillas returned to Namibia; a cease-fire was arranged so that elections could take place.

Elections, held under UN auspices in November 1989, gave SWAPO 57% of the vote, sufficient for an overall majority, but less than the two-thirds needed to enable SWAPO to rewrite the UN-sponsored constitution. The main rival of SWAPO, the Democratic Turnhalle Alliance, made a strong showing among Whites and in areas populated by groups nervous about the Ovambo dominance of SWAPO. In February 1990, Sam Nujoma, the leader of SWAPO, was elected president of Namibia.

On 21 March 1990, President Nujoma formally proclaimed the independence of the Republic of Namibia, the first new state to emerge from the control of a totalitarian regime. Namibian independence terminated seventy-four years of South African rule and formally ended the apartheid laws, the harsh and discriminatory racial laws. The new state became a model for nations seeking independence in other parts of the world, particularly in the collapsing Communist bloc.

The portion of the Baster population led by Kaptein Diergaardt refused to accept inclusion in an independent Namibia dominated by the large Ovambo tribe or to give up their special status, which predated the establishment of German power in the region. Following government refusal to grant Rehoboth special status within Namibia, Diergaardt convened the Volksraad, the national assembly of the Basters, on 20 March 1990. The assembly voted a unilateral declaration of independence for the district. The Namibian authorities ignored the declaration, and eventually support for secession melted away.

The new government, dominated by SWAPO, which became the largest political party in the country, quickly jettisoned its former Marxist rhetoric and adopted a conciliatory attitude toward its political opponents and the country's formerly predominant White minority. The economy remained largely in the hands of its previous owners, although a popular land reform program redistributed much of the farmland.

The outstanding post-independence territorial issue between Namibia and South Africa was the status of Walvis Bay. The port, which handled 90% of Namibia's international trade, remained under South African jurisdiction at independence. However, the change from a totalitarian White minority government to a majority government in South Africa greatly eased relations between the two countries. On 1 March 1994 the South Africans turned over the administration of Walvis Bay and a dozen offshore islands to the Namibian government.

Sam Nujoma, with widespread support, was again elected president in December 1994. His second term, begun in March 1995, is still dominated by Namibia's dependence on neighboring South Africa. His government is seeking to limit its dependence on South Africa by extending trade ties to neighboring states and abroad, but the major exports—diamonds, gold, and uranium—are all commodities dominated by the huge South African output.

The legacy of South African rule remains both a boon and a problem. The excellent road system and infrastructure have aided the growth of the economy, but the continuing control of the economy by the White minority also remains. According to UN experts, only 5% of the population controls some 72% of the economy.

The government's policy of reconciliation is not without political risk. Some SWAPO activists are bewildered by the government's generous attitude toward White privilege. Although opposition remains disorganized and isolated, the continuing control of the Namibian economy and many government ministries by Whites could lead to problems for Nujoma's plans for an equitable, multiracial society in Namibia.

In August 1997 Sam Nujoma announced his intention to run for a third term as president. A third term would entail changing the independence constitution, which has led to objections and alarm among many democratic and national groups in the country. The erosion of the freedom of the press has also become a serious issue.

The huge country, with its relatively small population, has become a magnet for immigrants from the less developed regions, particularly neighboring Angola. In September 1997 the government expelled 750 Angolans who had entered the republic illegally. The expulsions have raised tensions between the Ovambo, who straddle the Namibia-Angola border, and the other Namibian peoples, who support the expulsions.

SELECTED BIBLIOGRAPHY:

Cooper, Allan D., ed. *Allies in Apartheid: Western Capitalism in Occupied Namibia.* 1988.

Deutschmann, David, ed. *Changing the History of Africa: Angola and Namibia.* 1991.

Grotpeter, John J. *Historical Dictionary of Namibia.* 1992.

Kaela, Laurent C.W. *Question of Namibia.* 1992.

Sparks, Donald L. *Namibia: The Nation after Independence.* 1992.

RUSSIA

Russian Federation; Rossiyskaya Federatsiya; Rossija

CAPITAL: Moscow

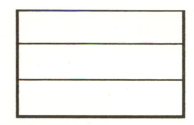

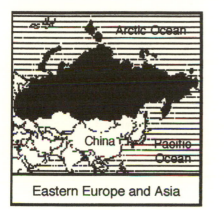

Eastern Europe and Asia

European Russia

POPULATION: (98e) 148,177,000 : 115,502,000 Russians in Russia and another 23 million in the other states of the former Soviet Union. MAJOR ETHNIC GROUPS: (98e) Russian 77.9%, Tatar 4.5%, Ukrainian 2.9%, Bashkort (Bashkir) 1.6%, Chavash (Chuvash) 1.5%, Dagestani Peoples 1.4%, Mordvin 1.2%, Belarussian, Udmurt, Moldovan and Romanian, Chechen, German, Jew, Mari, Kazakh, Avar, Komi, Armenian, Sakha (Yakut), Ossetian, Buryat, Kabardin, Rom (Gypsy), Azeri, Korean, Ingush, Karel, Tuvan, Kalmyk, Karachai, Georgian, Adygei, Finn, Greek, Pole, Balkar, Khakas, Ingrian, Circassian (Cherkess), Lithuanian, Uzbek, Estonian. MAJOR LANGUAGES: Russian, Tatar, Ukrainian, Chavash, Dagestani languages, Mordvin, Ukrainian, Belarussian. MAJOR RELIGIONS: Russian Orthodox, Sunni Islam, Roman Catholic, Protestant, Shi'a Islam, Jewish, animist. MAJOR CITIES: (98e) Moscow 8,514,000 (13,583,000), Sankt-Peterburg (St. Petersburg) 4,693,000 (6,374,000), Nizhniy Novgorod 1,342,000 (2,102,000), Novosibirsk 1,345,000 (1,597,000), Yekaterinburg 1,273,000 (1,577,000), Samara 1,172,000 (1,304,000), Omsk 1,171,000 (1,235,000), Ufa 1,102,000 (1,223,000), Chelyabinsk 1,078,000 (1,319,000), Kazan 1,074,000 (1,202,000), Perm 1,028,000 (1,116,000), Rostov-na-Donu 1,028,000 (1,228,000), Volgograd 1,008,000 (1,412,000), Voronezh 922,000, Saratov 886,000 (1,188,000), Krasnoyarsk 868,000, Tolyatti 721,000 (837,000), Ulyanovsk 720,000, Krasnodar 663,000 (758,000), Izhevsk 661,000, Vladivostok 631,000 (805,000), Yaroslavl 622,000, Khabarovsk 621,000 (702,000), Barnaul 593,000 (681,000), Irkutsk 592,000 (704,000), Novokuznetsk 567,000

(814,000), Ryazan 546,000, Penza 538,000, Orenburg 537,000, Tula 530,000 (648,000), Naberezhnye Chelny 529,000 (764,000), Tyumen 503,000, Kemerovo 498,000 (722,000), Astrakhan 482,000, Lipetsk 480,000, Ivanovo 471,000, Kirov 470,000 (622,000), Tomsk 467,000, Bryansk 465,000, Tver 459,000, Cheboksary 454,000 (591,000), Kursk 451,000, Magnitogorsk 424,000, Kaliningrad 422,000, Nizhniy Tagil 403,000, Murmansk 397,000 (582,000), Arkhangelsk 371,000 (678,000), Ulan-Ude 369,000, Makhachkala 366,000 (464,000), Sochi 362,000 (457,000), Kaluga 361,000, Smolensk 360,000, Kurgan 358,000, Orel 353,000, Stavropol 352,000, Vladimir 343,000, Belgorod 340,000, Cherepovets 325,000, Saransk 324,000, Chita 321,000, Tambov 320,000, Vladikavkaz 319,000, Vologda 318,000, Komsomolsk-na-Amure 308,000, Volzhskiy 306,000, Orsk 279,000 (416,000), Prokopyevsk 245,000 (421,000), Shakhty 233,000 (394,000), Novomoskovsk 142,000 (386,000), Pyatiagorsk 137,000 (313,000).

GEOGRAPHY: AREA: 6,592,812 sq. mi.-17,079,823 sq.km. LOCATION: Russia is the world's largest country in area, covering a large part of both Europe and Asia and accounting for about an eighth of the earth's surface. Russia extends from northeastern Europe to Asia and is bordered by the Arctic Ocean to the north; Norway, Finland, Latvia,* and Estonia* to the northwest; Belarus* and Ukraine* to the west; Georgia,* Azerbaijan,* Kazakhstan,* the Black Sea, the Caspian Sea, China, Mongolia, and North Korea to the south; and the Sea of Japan, the Pacific Ocean, the Barents Sea, and the Okhotsk Sea to the east. The Baltic region of Kaliningrad is separated from the rest of Russia by Belarus and Lithuania.* PHYSICAL GEOGRAPHY: Vast plains cover most of Russia's territory, around 70% of the total land area. European Russia is essentially a lowland area dominated by the East European Plain, sometimes called the Russian Plain. Beyond the Urals is the flat and broad West Siberian Plain, a marshy lowland that climbs to the Middle Siberian Plateau and the Central Yakut Plain. The mountainous regions predominate in the east and south. The ranges of the Greater Caucasus Mountains, which include the country's highest point, separate European Russia from Turkey and the Middle East. The Ural Mountains constitute a natural backbone from north to south separating European and Asian Russia east of the East European Plain. Many active volcanoes are found along the Pacific coast of the Far East and throughout the Kuril Islands. Russia also contains over 2 million fresh and saltwater lakes as well as many glaciers in the Arctic region and the high mountains. The major rivers include the Dnieper (Dnepr), Don, and Volga in European Russia, and the Ob and its tributaries, Yenisei, and Lena in Siberia and the Far East. ADMINISTRATIVE DIVISIONS: Twenty-one autonomous republics (avtomnykh respublik, singular—avtomnaya respublika); forty-nine oblasts (oblastey, singular—oblast'); six krays (krayev, singular—kray); ten autonomous okrugs; one autonomous oblast; and the cities of Moscow and St. Petersburg, which are governed as federal cities. POLITICAL STATUS: The Russian Federation was recognized as an independent state in 1991.

INDEPENDENCE DECLARATION: 24 August 1991 (from the Soviet Union).

FLAG: The flag of the federation is a horizontal tricolor of white (top), blue, and red.

PEOPLE: According to the latest surveys, 176 distinct national groups inhabit the territory of the Russian Federation. (The 1989 census reported only 128, because many national groups or subgroups were either included as ethnic Russians or counted as part of other officially recognized nationalities.) The process of de-Russification has accelerated since 1991, and the percentage of those who counted themselves ethnic Russians or declared Russian to be their first language has substantially decreased.

Russian—an estimated 77.9% of the population, numbering about 115,502,000.

The Russians are the largest of the East Slav peoples, whose original homeland is thought to have been in present Poland. The Russian population is decreasing due to a drastic drop in the birthrate and an increase in mortality (the average lifespan for a Russian man is only fifty-eight years). Even with the large number of ethnic Russians returning to Russia from the other states of the former Soviet Union, the population of the Russian Federation is shrinking, which is considered a demographic disaster by Russian nationalists.

Russian, the most important of the East Slav languages, is spoken by an estimated 300 million as a first or second language. The official language of the Russian Federation, Russian is the lingua franca used for intergroup communications in most of the newly independent states of the former Soviet Union. As the language of renowned writers such as Tolstoy, Dostoyevsky, Chekov, Pushkin, and Solzhenitsyn, Russian has great importance in world literature.

The peoples counted as ethnic Russian include a number of national groups of diverse histories and cultures, but that are ethnically and linguistically Russian. The groups include the Siberiaks, the inhabitants of the vast lands east of the Ural Mountains; the Far Easterners, who inhabit eastern Siberia along the Pacific Ocean; along with various Cossack groups, the largest of which are the Don, Kuban, Terek, Ural, and Transbaikal Cossacks. These groups, suppressed during the decades of Communist rule, have begun to assert their distinct cultures, histories, and dialects since Russian independence in 1991.

Tatar—an estimated 4.5% of the population, numbering about 6,621,000.

The largest of the non-Russian nations of the federation, the Tatars are also among the most dispersed, with large numbers beyond the federation borders in Central Asia, Ukraine, and the Baltic States. In Russia there are Tatar populations in European Russia, Siberia, and the Far East, with the largest concentrations in Tatarstan, their national republic, the neighboring republics of Bashkortostan and Udmurtia, and in the regions of Tyumen, Chelyabinsk, Yekaterinburg, Ulyanovsk, Orenburg, Moscow, Perm, and Samara.

The Tatars, the most northerly of the Sunni Muslim peoples of the Russian Federation, are a Turkic people speaking a West Turkic language of the Turkic groups of Altaic languages. The language is spoken in three major dialects,

Middle Tatar or Kazan, Western Tatar or Misher, and Eastern Tatar or Siberian Tatar. The literary language is based on the Kazan dialect spoken in the Tatar heartland in Tatarstan. The Tatars include several subgroups: the closely related Mishar or Misher; the Kreshen or Kerashen, who are Orthodox Christians and speak a distinct dialect called Uralian Tatar; and the Karatai, originally ethnic Mordvins, but now mostly assimilated into the Tatar language and culture. Some 375,000 ethnic Bashkort also speak Tatar as their mother tongue.

Ukrainian—an estimated 2.9% of the population, numbering about 4,297,000.

The Ukrainians living in the Russian Federation represent the second largest of the East Slav nations, more numerous in neighboring Ukraine. Like the Tatars, the Ukrainians are dispersed throughout the Russian, later Soviet, territory, with large numbers in many oblasts of Russia's European and Asian regions. The largest concentrations of ethnic Ukrainians live in Western Siberia, the Northern Caucasus, the Urals, and northern European Russia. Over 250,000 ethnic Ukrainians live in the Moscow region, and 150,000 live in St. Petersburg.

The majority of the Ukrainians are Orthodox Christians, mostly belonging to the Russian Orthodox Church, but in recent years many congregations have established ties to the Ukrainian Orthodox churches that were banned during the Soviet era. A minority, including many Ukrainians deported to Siberia during the Stalin years, belong to the Byzantine rite Uniate Church affiliated with the Roman Catholic Church.

Bashkort (Bashkir)—an estimated 1.6% of the population, numbering about 2,310,000.

The Bashkort, called Bashkir by the Russians, are a Turkic people related to the neighboring Tatars. Of mixed Finnic, Turkic, and Mongol ancestry, the Bashkort are traditionally divided into seven clans and numerous subclans. The majority of the Bashkort live in their traditional homeland between the Volga River and the Ural Mountains, mostly in the Bashkortostan Republic, but with substantial numbers in the Chelyabinsk, Orenburg, Yekaterinburg, Perm, and Tyumen oblasts.

The language of the Bashkort, a Uralian language of the West Turkic language group, is the mother tongue of about three-quarters of the ethnic Bashkort. About a quarter of the total Bashkort population speak Tatar or Russian as their first language. The Bashkort language, which is close to Tatar, is spoken in three major dialects, Kuvakan or Mountain Bashkort, Yurmaty or Steppe Bashkort, and Burzhan or Western Bashkort.

Chavash (Chuvash)—an estimated 1.5% of the population, numbering about 2,255,000.

The Chavash, called Chuvash by the Russians, are the descendants of the medieval Bulgar people with later admixtures of Turkic and Finnic strains. The Chavash nation comprises two major divisions, Anatri and Viryal, both represented in their national republic, Chavashia, in the Volga River basin. Even though more than half the Chavash live outside their national republic, Chavashia or Chavashstan, they have proved less susceptible to assimilation than many larger national groups and have preserved their unique culture intact. In contrast to most of the other Turkic peoples of the Russian Federation, the majority of the Chavash are Orthodox Christians.

Culturally a Turkic people, the Chavash speak the only extant language of the Bolgar branch of the Turkic languages. The language differs considerably from the other Turkic languages, and its exact place in the Uralo-Altaic language family is still debated. The language is spoken in two major dialects corresponding to the two divisions of the Chavash nation, Anatri or Lower Chavash and Viryal or Upper Chavash.

Mordvin (Mordvinian)—an estimated 1.2% of the population, numbering about 1,842,000.

The Mordvins are a Finnic people, the descendants of the pre-Slav population of the Volga basin. Traditionally divided into two distinct groups, the Moksha and Erza (Erzya), the Mordvins had been assimilating into Russian culture before the collapse of the Soviet Union and the nationalist reawakening that swept the Russian Federation beginning in 1989. The large Mordvin population inhabits their national republic, Mordvinia or Mordovia. However, the republic has a Russian majority, and over half the Mordvin nation lives outside the republic, with large concentrations in Samara, Penza, Orenburg, and Ulyanovsk oblasts and farther west; over 60,000 live in Moscow and its surrounding area. The Mordvin are traditionally Orthodox Christians.

The Mordvin language, a Finnic language of the Finno-Ugrian group of Uralic languages, is actually two closely related but distinct languages, Moksha and Erzya. Moksha, spoken in the southern regions, is considerably different from Erzya, which is spoken in northern Mordvinia. The majority of the Mordvin are bilingual and use Russian as a second language. The Erzya Mordvin include two subgroups, the Meshcheryak and the Teryukhan, that are ethnically and culturally Mordvin, but their first language is Russian. A third subgroup, the Tengushen, are ethnically Erzya, but speak Moksha.

Belarussian—estimated at less than 1% of the population, numbering about 1,185,000.

The Belarussians, the third largest of the major East Slav nations, inhabit widespread areas of the Russian Federation. The majority were settled in Russia during the Soviet era, many during and after World War II, when Belarus was devastated. Although Belarus borders Russia on the west, the major concentrations of ethnic Belarussians are in Moscow and its environs, St. Petersburg, Kaliningrad Oblast on the Baltic Sea, Rostov Oblast in the North Caucasus, the Republic of Karelia and Murmansk in the north, and Tyumen in Western Siberia.

The majority of the Belarussians living in Russia speak Russian as their first language, although interest in their own East Slav language has grown since the dissolution of the Soviet Union. Most Belarussians belong to the Russian Orthodox Church, with minorities of Greek and Roman Catholics.

Udmurt—estimated at less than 1% of the population, numbering about 1,120,000.

The Udmurt are a nation of the eastern or Permian branch of the Finno-Ugrian peoples. Their homeland, the Udmurt Republic, a member state of the Russian Federation, lies between the Kama and Cheptsa Rivers near the Ural Mountains in eastern European Russia. The majority of the Udmurts live in the republic, but substantial numbers also inhabit other parts of Russia, particularly neighboring Tatarstan, the Kirov and Perm oblasts of European Russia, and Irkutsk Oblast of Siberia.

The Udmurt speak a Permian language of the Finno-Ugrian languages. The language, spoken in two major dialects, North Udmurt or Vesermyan and South Udmurt, corresponds to the two major divisions of the Udmurt nation, the Udmurt and the Besmerians or Besermyan, originally ethnic Tatars, but now culturally and linguistically Udmurt. Most Udmurts speak Russian as their second language. The majority are Orthodox Christian, with a minority that have retained their traditional beliefs.

Chechen—estimated at less than 1% of the population, numbering about 924,000.

The Chechen are the most numerous of the North Caucasian peoples. The Chechen nation is comprised of 128 distinct clans. Their homeland, the Republic of Chechnya, nominally a member of the Russian Federation, lies in the North Caucasus bordering the Republic of Georgia. The majority of the Chechen population of Russia lives within the republic. However, a substantial population, including many refugees, live in the neighboring Dagestan Republic and other regions of the North Caucasus.

The Chechen language, a Vienakh or Northeastern Caucasian language, is spoken in six major dialects: Ploskost, Itumkala, Melkhin, Kistin, Cheberloi, and Akkin. Melkin is the transitional dialect to the closely related language of the neighboring Ingush. The language developed as a literary language in the nineteenth century.

Thought to be descended from the ancient Scythian tribes, the Sunni Muslim Chechen are a fiercely independent people. In 1991 the leader of the Chechen Republic, General Dzhokar Dudayev, declared Chechnya independent of the Russian Federation, setting off a long and bitter conflict with the federal government. Fighting broke out in the region in 1994 as the Chechens fought to free their small nation from Russian domination.

German—estimated at less than 1% of the population, numbering about 894,000.

The German population of Russia, the descendants of eighteenth-century settlers from the southern German states, is widely dispersed throughout the regions of the Russian Federation. The largest concentrations are in the Urals, Western Siberia, and the North Caucasus. Speaking dialects that long ago disappeared from Germany, the Russian German culture has absorbed many Slavic traits, setting them apart from the modern Germans of Western Europe.

The majority of the Germans are Roman Catholic or Lutheran, although other Protestant sects have made inroads in recent years. Deported from European

Russia in 1941, the dispersed Germans have begun to succumb to assimilation into Russian culture.

Jew—estimated at less than 1% of the population, numbering about 833,000.

The Russian Jews, mostly concentrated in Moscow, St. Petersburg, and the Northern Caucasus, are also represented in many other regions of the federation, particularly in Siberia and the Far East. However, only about 8,000 live in the officially designated Jewish Autonomous Oblast in the Russian Far East.

Often persecuted, many Jews do not register, but list themselves as ethnic Russians. The majority speak Russian as their first language, while some can still speak the traditional Jewish dialect, Yiddish, the Jewish-German language of Eastern Europe, which is written in the Hebrew script. The Russian Jews tend to be more secular than their kin in other parts of the world.

Mari—estimated at less than 1% of the population, numbering about 765,000.

The Mari are a Finnic people of the Volga River basin. Many experts believe they represent the region's earliest inhabitants. The majority live in Mari-El, a member state of the Russian Federation, with large numbers also living in Bashkortostan farther east in the Volga Valley, and in the Urals and other regions of the Volga basin.

Divided into two distinct groups, the Olyk or Volga Mari and the Kuryk or Vetluga Mari, the Mari speak a Finnic language of the Finno-Ugrian group of languages, with two major dialects responding to the two national divisions. The Mari have successfully resisted assimilation, and over 90% continue to use their national language as their first language. Some experts count a third group, the Grassland Mari, as a major subgroup.

The majority of the Mari are nominally Orthodox Christians. However, a substantial number continue to practice a set of animist beliefs called Kugu Sorta, which combines shamanism with Islamic and Orthodox traditions. The religion is an integral part of the Mari culture.

Kazakh—estimated at less than 1% of the population, numbering about 649,000.

The Kazakhs of Russia, part of the larger Kazakh population of neighboring Kazakhstan, mostly live in regions bordering Kazakhstan, Astrakhan, and Orenburg oblasts. However, some live as far away from the border regions as Moscow and St. Petersburg.

The language of the Kazakhs, a West Turkic language, is still the first language of the majority. However, most now speak Russian as the language of interethnic communications. The Kazakhs are mostly Sunni Muslims, with a small Orthodox minority.

Avar—estimated at less than 1% of the population, numbering about 572,000.

The Avars are Caucasians, the second largest of the Caucasian peoples of the North Caucasus and the most numerous of the various Dagestani peoples. The majority live in the mountainous Dagestan Republic, a member state of the Russian Federation, with smaller numbers living in the neighboring republics of Chechnya and Kalmykia.

The descendants of the Huns who invaded the Black Sea region in the sixth century, they moved east following their defeat by Charlemagne in 796. Threatened by neighboring nations, they retreated into the Caucasus Mountains, their present homeland.

The Sunni Muslim Avars speak a language of the Avaro-Andi-Dido group of Northeast Caucasian languages. The language is spoken in at least thirteen major dialects, corresponding to the seventeen distinct subgroups that form the Avar nation. The language is written in the Cyrillic alphabet. The Avar nation includes various peoples who were once considered distinct ethnic groups. Each distinct language is now considered a dialect of Avar.

Armenian—estimated at less than 1% of the population, numbering about 528,000.

The Armenians, Russian subjects since 1828, live mostly in the North Caucasus regions of the Russian Federation, with smaller numbers in Moscow and scattered across Siberia and the Far East. Many were deported from their Transcaucasus homeland during the Stalin era. Some Armenians have left Russia for the newly independent Republic of Armenia* since the dissolution of the Soviet Union in 1991.

The Christian Armenians mostly belong to the independent Armenian Orthodox Church, with smaller numbers of Russian Orthodox and Roman Catholics. The Armenian language, the only extant language of the Thraco-Phrygian branch of the Indo-European languages, is spoken mostly as a second language by the Armenians in Russia, whose first language is usually Russian. The Russian Armenians form part of the large Armenian Diaspora.

Sakha (Yakut)—estimated at less than 1% of the population, numbering about 520,000.

The Sakha or Sakhalar, called Yakut by the Russians, are considered the largest group of the Altaic branch of the Turkic peoples. However, the Sakha are actually of mixed Turkic, Mongol, and Paleo-Siberian origins, and the population displays two distinct physical types, Turkic and Mongol. The Sakha homeland, the Sakha Republic or Sakha Omuk, a member state of the Russian Federation, covers a vast area of the Russian Far East on the Arctic Ocean. About 40% of the Sakha homeland lies within the Arctic Circle.

The Sakha language, without dialects and with few regional differences, is related to the Turkic languages, but its roots are about a third Turkic, a third Mongol, and a third unknown, probably adopted from the earlier Paleo-Asiatic peoples of the Arctic region. The language is used by some neighboring peoples as a regional lingua franca.

Traditionally nomadic fishermen and hunters, the majority of the Sakha now live in villages and are farmers or herders. Most are Orthodox Christians, but in the more remote areas of their huge homeland, a minority retain their ancient shamanistic beliefs.

Ossetian (Alan)—estimated at less than 1% of the population, numbering about 503,000.

The Ossetians or Alans are a North Caucasian people related to the Iranians and Tajiks. Most Russian Ossetians live in North Ossetia, a member state of the Russian Federation, with only a small minority outside the republic, mostly in Moscow and the neighboring republic of Kabardino-Balkaria.

There are three culturally and linguistically distinct divisions of the Ossetians. The largest, the Iron, live mostly in North Ossetia in Russia. The Tuallag inhabit the South Ossetia region of the neighboring Republic of Georgia. Both are Eastern Orthodox Christians. The third group, the Digor, were converted to Sunni Islam in the seventeenth and eighteenth centuries and speak an archaic form of Ossetian. Many of the Digor were deported to Central Asia in the 1940s.

The Ossetian language is an East Iranian language, the only Iranian language native to Europe. The language is spoken in two major dialects, I'iron and Digor.

Buryat—estimated at less than 1% of the population, numbering about 455,000.

The Buryats are a Mongol people whose homeland, the Buryat Republic, a member of the Russian Federation, lies in the area of Lake Baikal north of Mongolia in Eastern Siberia. Of disputed origins, the Buryats physically resemble the Mongols, but their culture is a mixture of Mongol, Turkic, and Evenki elements. The majority live within their national republic or in the neighboring Russian oblasts of Irkutsk and Chita, particularly in the Buryat autonomous regions of Agün Buryatia and Ust-Ordün Buryatia.

The Buryat population east of Lake Baikal is less influenced by the Russians and is more closely related to the Mongols of Mongolia. Their language forms a separate branch of the Mongol languages and is spoken in several distinct dialects. Most Buryats, particularly the younger generations, are also fluent in Russian. The two parts of the Buryat nation, divided by Lake Baikal, tend to speak different dialects, and traditionally those west of the lake are farmers and agriculturists, while east of the lake the majority are cattle and horse herders.

The largest Buddhist nation in the Russian Federation, the Buryat practice the Tibetan form of Buddhism, Lamaism. A small portion of the population is Orthodox Christian, while in more remote areas some Buryats have retained their traditional shamanistic beliefs.

Kabardin—estimated at less than 1% of the population, numbering about 443,000.

The largest and most easterly of the Circassian peoples of the North Caucasus region, the Kabardin are a Caucasian people who share the Kabardino-Balkar Republic, a member state of the Russian Federation, with the Turkic Balkars. An estimated 94% of the Kabardins live in their national republic, with the remainder in adjacent areas of Krasnodar and Stavropol krays.

The language of the Kabardin, also called Upper Circassian or East Circassian, belongs to the Abkhazo-Adygheian branch of the Caucasian languages. It is spoken in at least seven major dialects and subdialects and is written in the Cyrillic alphabet. The Kabardins are Sunni Muslims.

Komi—estimated at less than 1% of the population, numbering about 432,000.

The Komi, also called Komi-Zyrian, are a Permian people related to the Komi-Permyak and Udmurt peoples. Their homeland, the Komi Republic, a member of the Russian Federation, lies in northern European Russia in the basins of the Pechora, Vychegda, and upper Kama Rivers. The Komi are the most northerly of the Finnic peoples, and their culture has absorbed influences from the neighboring non-Finnic peoples. Most of the Komi are reindeer herders, hunters, fishermen, or loggers.

The language of the Komi, a Permian language of the Finno-Ugrian language group, has one major dialect, Yazva, and is the major language of the republic, although the majority speak Russian as a second language. In 1989, 42.8% of the Komi living in their republic reported Russian as their first language. In a 1994 survey, this percentage had dropped to just 26.3% of the total Komi population. Most of the Komi belong to the Russian Orthodox Church.

Dargin—estimated at less than 1% of the population, numbering about 373,000.

The Dargin, the second largest of the Caucasian Dagestani peoples, live in the central mountains of the Republic of Dagestan, with only small numbers living outside the republic, mostly in the neighboring Stavropol Kray and the Republic of Kalmykia. The Dargins are subdivided into three groups, Dargins, Kubachins, and Kaitags.

Their language, Dargwa, is a Lak-Dargwa language of the Northeast Caucasian languages and is spoken in at least nine separate dialects. The majority of the Dargins are Sunni Muslims, with a Shi'a Muslim minority. Culturally and linguistically, the Dargins are very close to the neighboring Laks.

Rom (Gypsy)—estimated at less than 1% of the population, numbering about 345,000.

The majority of the Rom in the Russian Federation live in the North Caucasus region in southern European Russia. Although historically the Rom have suffered persecution in Russia, their culture and music have influenced Russian culture. The number of ethnic Rom in the federation is disputed, with many Rom groups claiming numbers three and four times the official estimates.

The major Rom language spoken in Russia is Domari, an Indo-Aryan language mixed with Slav and Caucasian elements. Of the several dialects of the spoken language, the most important in Russia is Karachi. The majority of the Rom are Sunni Muslim. A minority, the Kalderash, speak Vlach Romani and are mostly Orthodox Christian.

Azeri (Azerbaijani)—estimated at less than 1% of the population, numbering about 342,000.

The Azeri population of the Russian Federation mostly belong to the Northern Azeri subgroups, Ayrumy, Afshary, Karapapakhi, Padary, and Shakhseveny, and are Sunni Muslim. Their kin in the Republic of Azerbaijan are mostly Southern Azeri, and the majority are Shi'a Muslims. The majority of the Russian Azeris live in the Dagestan Republic adjacent to Azerbaijan, with smaller numbers living in Moscow, St. Petersburg, and the oblasts of Western Siberia.

The Azeri language, an Oghuz or South Turkic language, is written in the Cyrillic alphabet in Russia and is spoken in several distinct dialects. The dialects spoken in Dagestan have acquired many Russian and Dagestani borrowings.

Korean—estimated at less than 1% of the population, numbering about 312,000.

The Korean population of the Russian Federation mostly lives on Sakhalin Island and in Primorski Kray in Russia's Far East. Many of the Koreans, brought to Sakhalin before World War II as slave labor by the Japanese, who controlled the southern part of the island, were left behind when the Japanese ceded the colony to the Soviet Union in 1945. Others were deported from the Ussuri region of the Far East to Central Asia between 1928 and 1937. Following the dissolution of the Soviet Union many have left the Central Asian republics to return to their homeland in the Far East.

The Koreans mostly speak Russian as their first language, with Korean remaining the language of the home. Until 1980 there were no schools teaching in the Korean language. The majority of the Koreans are Buddhists, with a minority that has converted to Orthodox Christianity.

Ingush—estimated at less than 1% of the population, numbering about 287,000.

The Ingush, calling themselves Galgai or Ghalghay, are a Caucasian people closely related to the neighboring Chechen in the North Caucasus region of southern European Russia. The majority of the Ingush live in the Republic of Ingushetia, a member state of the Russian Federation, with smaller numbers in the neighboring Chechen Republic and North Ossetia. Many of the Ingush living in North Ossetia fled the region following severe ethnic violence between the Ingush and Ossetians over territorial claims.

The language of the Ingush, a North Central Caucasian language closely related to Chechen, is the mother tongue of over 95% of the small nation, although many speak Russian as a second language. Overall the Ingush have been less hostile to the Russians than the Chechens, with whom they shared an autonomous republic until 1991. The Ingush are Sunni Muslims adhering to the Hanafi rite.

Kumyk—estimated at less than 1% of the population, numbering about 267,000.

The Kumyk are a Turkic people living in the northern and eastern Caucasian Plain in the northern districts of the Republic of Dagestan. The origin of the Kumyks is not clear, but it seems probable that they are rooted in an intermingling of indigenous Caucasian peoples with Turkic tribes who migrated to the region in the tenth century. Since 1990 there has been an active movement for the separation of the Kumyk homeland from the Dagestan Republic, which is dominated by the Dagestani Caucasian peoples.

The Kumyk speak a Ponto-Caspian language of the West Turkic languages. The language, spoken in three major dialects, Khasavyurt, Buinaksk, and Khaikent, is written in the Cyrillic alphabet. The three dialects are quite divergent. The Kumyk are Sunni Muslims.

Lezgin—estimated at less than 1% of the population, numbering about 258,000.

The Lezgins are a Dagestani people, a Caucasian nation inhabiting the high Caucasus Mountains that straddle the border between the Russian Federation and the Republic of Azerbaijan. Lezgin nationalists have proposed the unification of the Lezgin territories on both sides of the border, which they claim has an ethnic population of 1.2 million. The disparity between nationalist claims and official estimates is explained by the fact that many ethnic Lezgins formerly registered as ethnic Azeris. The Azerbaijani government claims that the Russian government supports separatism among the Azeri Lezgin.

The Lezgin language, a Northeastern Caucasian language, is spoken in seven major dialects, some not inherently intelligible with others. The majority are Sunni Muslims, with a Shi'a Muslim minority, mostly in Azerbaijan.

Karel—estimated at less than 1% of the population, numbering about 250,000.

The Karel or Karelians are a Finnic people closely related to the Finns of Finland and form a major branch of the Finnic peoples. The true number of ethnic Karels in the Russian Federation is a matter of dispute, as during the Soviet era many registered as ethnic Russians. The historic boundary between Karelia, which forms a member state of the Russian Federation, and Finland reflected the religious division between the Orthodox Karels and the Lutheran Finns.

The Karels speak a Balto-Finnic language divided into four regional dialects, which reflects the major divisions within the Karel nation, Northern Karelian, Southern Karelian (St. Petersburg), Novgorod, and Tver. Livvi or Olonetsian, also spoken in Karelia, is considered a separate language, although the Karels claim it is a transition dialect to Ingrian.

Tuvan—estimated at less than 1% of the population, numbering about 245,000.

The Tuvans, also called Tuvin or Uriankhai, are a Northern Turkic people living in Tuva Ulus, a member state of the Russian Federation that borders Mongolia in Eastern Siberia. Of mixed Turkic and Mongol background, the Tuvin nation is made up of two major divisions, Western and Eastern, and a number of subgroups, one of which, the Urjankhai, inhabits adjoining areas of Mongolia.

The Tuvan language, a North Turkic language, is spoken in five distinct dialects and is written in the Cyrillic script. The Tuvans are Buddhists, belonging to the Tibetan branch, Lamaism. The Dalai Lama of Tibet is revered as the spiritual leader of the Tuvan nation.

Kalmyk—estimated at less than 1% of the population, numbering about 210,000.

The Kalmyk, also called Kalmyk-Oirat or Kalmuck, are a branch of the Oirat

Mongols. Most of the Russian Kalmyk live in the Republic of Kalmykia, a member state of the federation, in the North Caucasus region of southern European Russia. The descendants of nomadic migrants, the Kalmyk are the only large Buddhist nation in Europe.

Most Kalmyk belong to the Tibetan branch of Buddhism, Lamaism, although traces of their pre-Buddhist shamanism are still evident. The Kalmyk speak a Western Mongol language sometimes called European Oirat that is divided into at least five major dialects. Tibetan is used as the religious language.

Moldovan and Romanian—estimated at less than 1% of the population, numbering about 182,000.

The Moldovan and Romanian population of the Russian Federation, part of the larger Romanian nations in Moldova* and Romania, are concentrated in Moscow and St. Petersburg and in the southern oblasts of Siberia. The Moldovans and Romanians in Siberia are mostly those deported from their homeland during the Stalin era. The distinction between the two peoples is mostly a question of tradition and alphabet.

The majority of the Moldovan-Romanian population in Russia speak their own Romance language as a second language, using Russian as their first language. Traditionally, the Moldovans use the Cyrillic alphabet, imposed during the Stalin era, while the Romanians use the Latin alphabet. Most belong to the Orthodox churches, with a minority belonging to the Catholic Uniate churches.

Komi-Permyak—estimated at less than 1% of the population, numbering about 175,000.

The Komi-Permyak, also called Komi Otir, live in eastern European Russia just south of the Komi Republic. Their homeland, the Komi-Permyak Autonomous Region, has the largest Komi-Permyak population in the federation. The only other sizable concentration is in neighboring parts of Perm Oblast. The small nation is made up of two distinct groups, the Yazvin and Zyuzdin, and is closely related to the Komi nation just to the north.

The national language is a Permian language of the Finno-Ugrian language group closely related to Komi. The major dialects, Zyudin, Kochin-Kam or North Permyak, and Inyven or South Permyak, are quite divergent and form transition dialects to Komi and Udmurt. Most Komi-Permyak are Orthodox Christian, with a small minority retaining traditional beliefs.

Karachai—estimated at less than 1% of the population, numbering about 159,000.

The Karachai are of mixed Caucasian and Turkic ancestry, although culturally and linguistically they are a Turkic people. Their homeland, part of the Karachai-Circassia Republic, is in the valley of the upper Kuban River in Russia's North Caucasus region. The Karachai share the republic with the Caucasian Circassians.

The language of the Karachai is a Ponto-Caspian language of the West Turkic language group. The language is almost identical to Balkar, and the two are considered dialects of the same language. The two peoples, although they share the same language and culture, have been separated by decades of Communist rule. The Karachai are Sunni Muslims.

Georgian (Gruzian)—estimated at less than 1% of the population, numbering about 130,000.

The Georgian population of Russia, part of the larger population in the Republic of Georgia, are often called Gruzians. Although the majority live in the North Caucasus region, there are also concentrations of ethnic Georgians in Moscow and St. Petersburg.

Russian is the first language of many of the Russian Georgians, while their own language, a Kartvelian language of the Caucasian language group, remains the language of the home. The majority of the Georgians belong to the independent Georgian Orthodox Church. However, there are also Georgian Muslims and Roman Catholics.

Adygei (Adyge)—estimated at less than 1% of the population, numbering about 129,000.

The Adygei are a Caucasian people, the most westerly of the Circassian peoples of the North Caucasus region. Representing a nation formed by the unification of as many as ten Circassian tribes, the Adygei mostly live in the Adyge Republic, which is a member state of the federation, although it is surrounded by territory of Krasnodar Kray, also called the Kuban. The Adygei are closely related to the Circassians and Kabardins, and all three peoples refer to themselves as Adygei or Adyge.

The Adygei language, also called Lower Circassian, is a Kiakh language of the Abkhazo-Adygheian group of Caucasian languages. Spoken in as many as four major dialects, the language has been an official literary language since 1994. The Adygei are Sunni Muslims.

Tabasaran—estimated at less than 1% of the population, numbering about 110,000.

The Tabasaran are a Caucasian people, one of the Dagestani nations of the Dagestan Republic in southern European Russia. Closely related to the neighboring Avar, Dargin, Lezgin, and other Caucasian Dagestani peoples, the Tabasaran are among the most numerous of the smaller Dagestani nations.

Their language, a Northeastern Caucasian language related to Lezgian, is spoken in two distinct dialects, South Tabasaran and Khanag or North Tabasaran. The literary language is based on the southern dialect. The Tabasaran, like the other Dagestani peoples, are Sunni Muslims.

Lak—estimated at less than 1% of the population, numbering about 107,000.

The Lak are a Caucasian people, one of the Dagestani nations living in the Dagestan Republic of southern European Russia. They traditionally live in the mountainous Koshu region and use lands in the northern steppe and the region north of Makhachkala as winter pastures. The most educated and advanced of the Dagestani peoples, many Lak speak Russian as their first language, which has raised fears that they could lose their ethnic identity.

The language spoken by the Lak is a Lak-Dargwa language of the Northeast Caucasian language group. Spoken in five major dialects, all of which are mutually intelligible, the language is written in the Cyrillic alphabet. The Lak are Sunni Muslims.

Finn—estimated at less than 1% of the population, numbering about 106,000.

The Russian Finns, living mostly in the St. Petersburg region and southern Karelia, are part of the Finnish nation of neighboring Finland. They are the remnant of the large Finnish population that mostly fled the region during World War II.

The Finns speak a Balto-Finnic language of the Finno-Ugrian languages. Several dialects are present among the Russian Finns, with the eastern dialects merging gradually into Karelian. Many of the ethnic Finns are bilingual in Russian and during the Soviet era registered as ethnic Russians. The majority of the Finns are Lutheran Christians.

Greek—estimated at less than 1% of the population, numbering about 105,000.

The Greek population of the Russian Federation is concentrated in the North Caucasus, in Krasnodar and Stavropol krays. Deported from the Mariupol region of Ukraine in 1944, they were forcibly settled in the region of the Sea of Azov. Since the dissolution of the Soviet Union in 1991 many have returned to their homeland in Ukraine or have immigrated to Greece.

A Pontian dialect of the Greek language, mostly used in religious ceremonies, has been preserved, but the majority now speak Russian as their first language and speak a dialect of Crimean Tatar in the home. The Greeks mainly belong to the Greek Orthodox Church.

Pole—estimated at less than 1% of the population, numbering about 97,000.

The Russian Poles are scattered over a huge area of the Russian Federation, with the most important concentrations in Moscow and St. Petersburg and in the region of Western Siberia, Tomsk, Irkutsk, and Omsk oblasts, and Altay Kray. Many of the Poles were deported from European Russia during the imperial and Soviet eras.

The Roman Catholic Poles speak a West Slav language. However, the majority in Russia speak Russian as their first language. The Poles in European Russia have reestablished ties to Poland since the collapse of the Soviet Union.

Balkar—estimated at less than 1% of the population, numbering about 91,000.

The Balkar, calling themselves Malkar, are a Turkic people living in the North Caucasus region of southern European Russia. The Balkar and the closely related Karachai constitute the two parts of a single nation although they have been divided by decades of Soviet rule. The two peoples speak dialects of the same language and share their culture and history. The Balkar inhabit the southern part of the Republic of Kabardino-Balkaria, which they share with the Caucasian Kabardins. They mostly live in the mountains and in the valley of the Baksan

River. Since 1991 many Balkar have supported a movement to separate from the joint republic and establish a sovereign Balkar republic within the Russian Federation.

The Balkar language, a West Turkic language, is a dialect of the language they share with the Karachai. There are only small differences between the two dialects. The Balkar are Sunni Muslims.

Khakas—estimated at less than 1% of the population, numbering about 87,000.

The Khakas, also called Abakan or Yenisei Tatar, are a North Turkic people living in the Abakan Steppe and the basin of the Yenisei River north of the Altai Mountains in Eastern Siberia. Their homeland forms the Republic of Khakassia, a member state of the Russian Federation, although they are a minority in the region. The Khakas are of mixed Turkic and Mongol ancestry, although culturally and linguistically they are a Turkic people. The majority of the Khakas are herders of sheep, goats, cattle, and horses, although since World War II many have gone to work in the region's newly industrialized towns.

The Khakas language is a North Turkic language of the West Altaic language group. Spoken in six major dialects, it is a literary language based on the Sagai or Sagaj dialect. The majority of the Khakas are now Russian Orthodox, but a substantial portion of the population has retained many of their original shamanistic beliefs.

Ingrian—estimated at less than 1% of the population, numbering about 85,000.

The Ingrians are a Finnic people who call their small nation Inkeri. The remnant of a much larger pre–World War II population, the majority of the Ingrians, until recent years, had registered as ethnic Russians for political reasons. Most of the Ingrians live in the Kingisepp and Lomsonsov areas of St. Petersburg Oblast.

The Ingrian language, which is close to Karelian, is spoken in four dialects in Russia: Soykin, Khava, Lower Luzh, and Oredezh or Upper Luzh. The majority of the Ingrians are Lutheran, but a large number, to escape persecution, converted to Russian Orthodoxy during the Stalin era.

Nogai—estimated at less than 1% of the population, numbering about 81,000.

The Nogai are a nomadic Turkic people living in the steppe lands north of the Caucasus Mountains in the North Caucasus region of southern European Russia. Their historical territory, the once huge Nogai Steppe, is included in the northern part of the Republic of Dagestan and the eastern region of Stavropol Kray. The majority of the Nogai live in the northern districts of Dagestan and the adjoining Neftekumsky district of Stavropol, but with important concentrations in the neighboring Chechen Republic and in Karachai-Circassia farther west. The majority live in rural areas as herdsmen. Since 1991 Nogai nationalists have worked for the unification of the Nogai lands in a separate Nogai republic.

The Nogai speak an Aralo-Caspian language of the West Turkic languages related to the Turkic languages of Central Asia, where the Nogai originated.

Traditionally, the Nogai have been divided into three groups speaking dialects of the language, White Nogai, Black Nogai, and Central Nogai. The majority speak Russian as a second language. The Nogai are Sunni Muslims, with admixtures of their earlier beliefs.

Circassian (Cherkess)—estimated at less than 1% of the population, numbering about 76,000.

The Circassians, called Cherkess by the Russians, are a Caucasian people who share the Karachai-Circassia Republic, a member state of the federation, with the Turkic Karachai. Closely related to the Adygei and Kabardin nations, the Circassians are the remnant of a much larger population that mostly migrated or were expelled to Turkish territory in the nineteenth century.

The Circassian language, a Northwestern Caucasian or Kiakh language of the Abkhazo-Adygeian language group, is spoken in as many as four major dialects and is often called Lower Circassian. The Circassians are Sunni Muslims.

Ajai—estimated at less than 1% of the population, numbering about 76,000.

The Ajai are a Caucasian people, part of the Dagestani nations living in the Dagestan Republic of Russia's southern North Caucasus region. Most of the Ajai live in the high valleys in the Caucasus Mountains. The majority are herdsmen of sheep and horses.

The Ajai language is a Dagestani language of the Caucasian language group. The Ajai are fervently Sunni Muslim, mostly belonging to the Shafi rite.

Altai—estimated at less than 1% of the population, numbering about 73,000.

The Altai are a Turkic people of mixed Turkic and Mongol background. Although physically resembling the Mongols, the Altai are culturally and linguistically Turkic. The Altai consist of two groups with distinct languages, a northern group including the Tabulars, Chelkans, and Kumandas, and a southern group comprising the Telengits, Telesy, Teleuts, and Altai.

The Altai speak two separate Turkic dialects, Northern Altai or Teleut and Southern Altai or Oirot. The two languages are not inherently intelligible, although some dialects are bridge dialects. The written language is based on Southern Altai, although some Northern Altai speakers reject it as their literary language.

The Altai peoples mostly adhere to a traditional religion called Burkhanism, which combines aspects of their earlier shamanistic beliefs with later Christian and Buddhist influences. In rural areas many Altaians, mostly sheepherders, still revere fire and milk and continue to respect the wisdom of the traditional shamans.

Lithuanian—estimated at less than 1% of the population, numbering about 64,000.

The Lithuanians in Russia are a Baltic people whose homeland, Lithuania, formed part of the Soviet Union until 1991. Most of the Lithuanians live in the southern Siberian provinces, where they were exiled during the Stalin era, although there are also Lithuanian populations in Moscow and St. Petersburg.

The Lithuanians speak a Baltic language, but most use Russian in daily life.

They are mostly Roman Catholic. Since the disintegration of the Soviet Union many Lithuanians have returned to newly independent Lithuania.

Uzbek—estimated at less than 1% of the population, numbering about 63,000.

The Uzbeks of the Russian Federation are concentrated in Moscow, St. Petersburg, the southern oblasts of Siberia, and the Urals. The Uzbeks are a Turkic people, and most are Sunni Muslims. Many of the Uzbeks in Russia were resettled in government-sponsored population exchanges or were deported from their homeland during the Soviet era.

The Uzbeks speak an East Turkic language of the Turkic language group. The Uzbeks living in the large cities of European Russia mostly use Russian as their first language. Many Uzbeks have left Russia since 1991 to return to their homeland in newly independent Uzbekistan.*

Estonian—estimated at less than 1% of the population, numbering about 55,000.

The Estonians living in the Russian Federation are mostly concentrated in the region of the international border with Estonia and in the St. Petersburg area. About 30,000 ethnic Estonians have left Russia for Estonia since 1991.

A Finnic nation closely related to the Finns of Finland, the majority of the Estonians are Lutherans, with a small minority belonging to the Russian Orthodox Church. Their language, a Finno-Baltic language closely related to Finnish, is the first language, but the majority of the Estonians in Russia are bilingual in Russian.

Tajik—estimated at less than 1% of the population, numbering about 42,000.

The Tajik, part of the Central Asian nation of Tajikistan, were resettled in the Russian Federation during the Stalin era. Some of the Tajiks formed part of a Soviet program of population exchanges; others were deported from their homeland for alleged crimes.

The Tajik language, an Iranian language, is now the second language of the Tajik population in Russia, with Russian used as the first language. The Tajiks are Sunni Muslims.

Abaza (Abazin)—estimated at less than 1% of the population, numbering about 40,000.

The Abaza, called Abazin by the Russians, are a Caucasian people living in the Karachai-Circassia Republic in southern European Russia. The Abaza are closely related to the Abkhaz people in adjacent areas of the Republic of Georgia.

The Abaza language, a Northwestern Caucasian language of the Abazo-Adygeian language group, is spoken in three major dialects and is partially intelligible with Abkhaz. Russian is also widely used, with about two-thirds of the Abaza bilingual in Russian. The Abaza are Sunni Muslims.

Nenets—estimated at less than 1% of the population, numbering about 38,000.

The Nenets, formerly called Samoyed, are traditionally nomadic reindeer hunters in the far north of European Russia and Western Siberia. Concentrated in the Nenets Autonomous Region and the northern districts of the Yamalo-Nenets and Taimyr (Dolgano-Nenets) autonomous regions, the Nenets population lives in an area with an average 260 days a year of snow and freezing temperatures.

The language of the Nenets is a Northern Samoyedic language of the Samoyedic group of Uralic languages commonly called Yurak. The language is spoken in two major dialects, Forest Yurak and Tundra Yurak. Around 80% of the Nenets population uses the language in daily life, with Russian used as a second language. The majority of the Nenets are Orthodox Christian, with a minority adhering to traditional shamanistic beliefs.

Chukot (Chukchi)—estimated at less than 1% of the population, numbering about 36,000.

The Chukot or Chukchi are a Paleo-Asiatic people ethnically related to the Native American peoples. Traditionally, the Chukot are divided into two groups, the Chauchu (those keeping reindeer) and the Ankalyn (those who live by the sea). The Chauchu are mostly nomadic reindeer herders, while the Ankalyn hunt seals and whales. Most of the ethnic Chukot, many registered as ethnic Russians during the Soviet era, live in the Chukotka Autonomous Region in the northeastern region of the Russian Far East opposite Alaska across the Bering Sea.

The Chukot language, spoken in eight dialects, is the most widely spoken of the isolated language group, the Luorawetlan languages, that includes the languages of the related Koryak and Kamchatchdal peoples. The majority of the younger Chukot speak Russian with varying proficiency. Most of the Chukots retain their traditional shamanistic beliefs.

Evenki (Evenk)—estimated at less than 1% of the population, numbering about 34,000.

The Evenki, also called Tungus, are a Tungus people spread over a large area of Siberia, from the Sea of Okhotsk to the Yenisei Valley and from Chinese Manchuria to the Arctic Ocean. The largest concentration is in the Sakha Republic in the Russian Far East, but a substantial number also live in the Evenk Autonomous Region in north-central Siberia. The northern Evenki are mostly reindeer herders and hunters; the southern groups are mostly farmers.

The Evenki language, a Tungus language of the Tungus-Manchurian group of East Altaic languages, is spoken in at least twenty-seven dialects based on geographic area. The majority of the Evenki are bilingual in Russian, Yakut, or Buryat. Some Evenki groups are Orthodox Christians. Others retain their traditional shamanistic beliefs or have adopted the Buddhist religion of the Buryats of southern Siberia.

Assyrian—estimated at less than 1% of the population, numbering about 30,000.

The Assyrian population of Russia is mostly concentrated in the North Caucasus region of southern European Russia. They are the descendants of refugees fleeing persecutions in the Moslem territories of the Middle East.

The adherents of a bewildering variety of Christian sects, the most numerous of the Assyrian peoples in Russia are the Chaldeans and the Nestorians. The majority use Russian as their first language, with the Assyrian language, Semitic in origin, used in the home. The Urmiye dialect of Assyrian is the most widely spoken in Russia.

Khanty—estimated at less than 1% of the population, numbering about 29,000.

The Khanty are an Ugrian people inhabiting the Western Siberian Plateau east of the Ural Mountains. The largest groups live in the Khanty-Mansi Autonomous Region of west-central Siberia and the Yamalo-Nenets Autonomous Region just to the north. The Khanty are divided into three distinct cultural and linguistic groups, Northern, Southern, and Eastern.

The language of the Khanty is an Ob Ugrian language of the Ugrian group of Uralic languages. The Ugrian languages also include Hungarian, the largest of the language group, which is spoken in central Europe. The majority of the Khanty have retained their traditional shamanistic beliefs.

Latvian—estimated at less than 1% of the population, numbering about 27,000.

The Latvians of Russia, mostly living in the border region with Latvia, are a Baltic people closely related to the Lithuanians. Many Latvians were deported from their homeland to various parts of Siberian Russia during the Stalin era.

The Latvians speak a Baltic language, but many use Russian as their first language. The majority of the Latvians are Lutherans, with Roman Catholic and Orthodox minorities. Many Latvians have returned to independent Latvia since the breakup of the Soviet Union.

Agul—estimated at less than 1% of the population, numbering about 24,000.

The Agul, also called Koshan, are called Aguly by the Russians. One of the smaller Caucasian peoples of the Dagestani group of the Dagestan Republic, the Agul mostly live in the canyons of southeastern Dagestan and in the Derbent region. They are an ancient people; the oldest known reference to the small nation is an Armenian manuscript of the seventh century A.D. They are Sunni Muslims of the Shafi rite.

The Sunni Muslim Agul speak a Dagestani language of the Caucasian language group that has four major dialects despite their small numbers. The language is not a literary language. The Aguls use the closely related Lezgin as their literary language.

Rutul—estimated at less than 1% of the population, numbering about 23,000.

The Rutul, called Rutultsi by the Russians, are a small Caucasian people belonging to the Dagestani peoples of the Dagestan Republic of southern European Russia. They live in the southeastern districts of Dagestan, mostly in the high valleys of the Caucasus Mountains.

The language of the Rutul, a Dagestani language of the Caucasian language group, is spoken in three dialects, although they are not sharply defined. An unusual 99% of the Rutul use their language as their first language, although the literary language is Lezgin. The Rutul are Sunni Muslims.

Crimean Tatar—estimated at less than 1% of the population, numbering about 22,000.

The Crimean Tatars are a Turkic Tatar people who originally inhabited the Crimean Peninsula, now part of Ukraine. The majority of the Crimean Tatars were deported to Central Asia during World War II, accused by Stalin of collaborating with the Nazi invaders. The Crimean Tatars in Russia are part of the Crimean Tatar nation, but live across the narrow Kerch Strait from the peninsula in the Russian Krasnodar Kray. The Crimean Tatars speak Russian as their first language, while using their Turkic language as the group language. The majority are Sunni Muslims.

Shor—estimated at less than 1% of the population, numbering about 21,000.

The Shor or Aba are a small nation of mixed Turkic and Mongol ancestry, although culturally and linguistically they are a Turkic people related to the Altai and Khakas. Most of the ethnic Shor live in the adjoining Khakas and Altai republics. The Shor are divided into two major groups, Northern or Mras and Southern or Kondoma. The Shor are sometimes called Mras and Kondoma Tatars.

The Shor language, a North Turkic language, is spoken in two major dialects that correspond to the ethnic division of the nation. The Shor are mostly Russian Orthodox.

Vep (Veps)—estimated at less than 1% of the population, numbering about 17,000.

The Vep or Veps are a Finnic people living in northwestern European Russia, mostly in the Republic of Karelia and the adjoining St. Petersburg Oblast. The Vep, who claim a much larger ethnic population in the region, mostly registered as ethnic Russians, are closely related to the Karels and the Finns of neighboring Finland. Since the dissolution of the Soviet Union the Vep have mobilized to revive their nation and language. During World War II about half their nation fled to Finland.

The language of the Vep is a Balto-Finnic language of the Finno-Ugrian language group spoken in three distinct dialects, Southern Veps, Central Veps, and Prionezh or Northern Veps. The majority of the Vep are bilingual in Russian, and many also speak Karelian or Finnish. The majority of the Vep are Orthodox Christian.

Even—estimated at less than 1% of the population, numbering about 16,000.

The Even, also called Lamut, are a Tungus people scattered across the northeastern regions of the Russian Far East from the Arctic Circle to the Kamchatka Peninsula. The majority are reindeer herders and hunters. The Even are considered the aboriginal people in the northeastern part of Siberia.

The language spoken by the Even, called Lamut or Ewen, is a Northern Tungus language of the Tungus-Manchurian group of East Altaic languages. The language is spoken in at least ten dialects that correspond to the major concentrations of ethnic Even. Most of the Even have adopted Russian Orthodox Christianity.

Mansi—estimated at less than 1% of the population, numbering about 13,000.

The Mansi or Vogul nation lives in the Khanty-Mansi Autonomous Region of Western Siberia between the Ural Mountains and the Ob River. The Mansi are traditionally hunters, fishermen, and cattle herders.

The Mansi language, an Ob Ugrian language of the Ugrian group of Finno-Ugrian languages, is the closest to spoken Hungarian. The language is spoken in four dialects and several subdialects. Mansi speakers use Russian as their second language. The majority of the Mansi have retained their traditional beliefs.

Karata—estimated at less than 1% of the population, numbering about 13,000.

The Karata are a Caucasian people of the Dagestani group of nations living in the Dagestan Republic of southern European Russia. Their language, part of the Avaro-Andi-Dido group of Northeastern Caucasian languages, is spoken in two distinct languages but is not a written language. They use Avar as their literary language. The Karata are Sunni Muslims.

Nanai (Nanay)—estimated at less than 1% of the population, numbering about 13,000.

The Nanai or Nanay, also called Gold or Hezhen, are Southern Tungus people living in the Russian Far East at the confluence of the Amur and Ussuri Rivers and in the Ussuri, Sikhote-Alin, and Amur valleys near the Chinese border.

The language spoken by the Nanai is a Southeast Tungus language of the East Altaic language group spoken in at least eight dialects, one of which is the basis of the literary language. The Nanai normally speak Russian as a second language, although many older Nanai also speak Chinese dialects. The majority of the Nanai adhere to their traditional shamanistic beliefs.

Chamalal—estimated at less than 1% of the population, numbering about 13,000.

The Chamalal are a Caucasian people, part of the Dagestani group of the Dagestan Republic of southern European Russia. The Chamalal speak an Andi language of the Avaro-Andi-Dido group of Northeastern Caucasian languages. The language is spoken in three dialects, but is not a written language. Avar is the literary language of the Chamalal. They are Sunni Muslims.

Koryak (Nymylany)—estimated at less than 1% of the population, numbering about 12,000.

The Koryak, called Nymylany by the Russians, are a Paleo-Asiatic people divided into twelve clans or tribes. The majority live in the Koryak Autonomous Region in the northeastern part of the Russian Far East and are ethnically related to the native peoples of North America. Most are fishermen and hunters along the coasts; inland most are cattle herders.

The language of the Koryak is a Paleo-Siberian or Luorawetlan language related to Chukot and Itel'men. Spoken in at least eight dialects, it is a literary language, although the Koryak use Russian as their second language. Most Koryak adhere to their traditional beliefs, with a minority belonging to the Russian Orthodox Church.

Tat—estimated at less than 1% of the population, numbering about 12,000.

The Tat are an ancient Caucasian people living in the southern regions of the North Caucasus Region of southern European Russia. The majority live in Dagestan, but there are scattered groups living in other regions of the Caucasus Mountains. The Tat are divided into two separate groups, one Jewish and the other Sunni Muslim. Traditionally, the Jewish Tat, often called Mountain Jews, have lived in the Caucasus since 722 B.C.

The language of the Tat, Tati, divided into Jewish and Muslim dialects, is a Southwestern Iranian language spoken in several subdialects. Judeo-Tat is now sometimes written in the Hebrew alphabet. Muslim Tat is written in the Cyrillic alphabet.

Botlikh—estimated at less than 1% of the population, numbering about 12,000.

The Botlikh are a Caucasian people of the Dagestani group living in the Caucasus Mountains of southern European Russia. Their language is an Andi language of the Avaro-Andi-Dido group that is very close to spoken Andi. It is not a written language. The Botlikh use Avar as their literary language and are Sunni Muslims.

Chulym—estimated at less than 1% of the population, numbering about 12,000.

The Chulym, also called Melets Tatar, are the smallest of the North Turkic peoples living in the Altai and Khakas republics of Eastern Siberia. A smaller people, the Kacik, are often considered part of the Chulym nation culturally and linguistically.

The language of the Chulym is a North Turkic language related to Khakas, Altai, and Shor, particularly the latter. It is spoken in two dialects, Lower Chulym and Middle Chulym. The majority of the Chulym retain their traditional shamanistic beliefs.

Tsakhur—estimated at less than 1% of the population, numbering about 11,000.

The Tsakhur are a Caucasian people of the Dagestani group of the Dagestan Republic in southern European Russia. They are the most widely scattered of the smaller Dagestani ethnic groups; a larger number of Tsakhur live across the border in Azerbaijan.

The language of the Tsakhur is a Lezgian language of the Northeast Caucasian languages. It is a written language, although Lezgin is also used as a literary language. The Tsakhur are Sunni Muslims.

Serb (Serbian)—estimated at less than 1% of the population, numbering about 11,000.

The Serbs of Russia, living mostly in Moscow and the regions of southwestern European Russia, are a related Slav people, part of the Serb nation of the Balkan state of Yugoslavia.* Most of the Serbs settled in Russia after World War II, when Yugoslavia's Tito broke with Stalin.

The Serbs speak the Serbian dialect of Serbo-Croatian, although the majority use Russian as their first language in Russia. The majority belong to the Russian Orthodox Church, although there are congregations affiliated with the independent Serbian Orthodox Church of Belgrade.

Andi (Qwannab)—estimated at less than 1% of the population, numbering about 11,000.

The Andi, also known as Qwannab, are a Caucasian people of the Dagestani group in the Dagestan Republic of southern European Russia. Their language, Andi, forms part of the Avaro-Andi-Dido group of Northeast Caucasian languages and is spoken in five dialects, but it is not a literary language. Avar is used as the literary language. The Andi are Sunni Muslims.

Dido—estimated at less than 1% of the population, numbering about 9,000.

The Dido are one of the Caucasian Dido peoples of the Dagestan Republic of southern European Russia. The language of the Dido, a member of the Avaro-Andi-Dido group of Northeastern Caucasian languages, is spoken in two dialects, Dido and Sagadin. The language is not a literary language. The Dido use Avar as their written language and Dido are Sunni Muslims.

Tindi—estimated at less than 1% of the population, numbering about 8,000.

The Tindi or Tindal are a Caucasian people of the Dagestani group of the Dagestan Republic in southern European Russia. They speak an Andi language of the Avaro-Andi-Dido group of Northeastern Caucasian languages that is used in daily communication but is not a written language. They use Avar as their literary language. The Tindi are Sunni Muslims.

Dolgan—estimated at less than 1% of the population, numbering about 8,000.

The Dolgan live in the Taimyr or Dolgano-Nenets Autonomous Region in northeastern Siberia. Originally a Tungus people, the Dolgan have been culturally and linguistically influenced by the neighboring Yakut people.

The Dolgan language is a North Turkic language separate from Yakut, although most experts consider it a dialect of Yakut. There are two orthographies, one based on Yakut and one based on Russian, which is spoken as a second language. Most of the Dolgan retain their traditional shamanistic beliefs.

Nivkhi—estimated at less than 1% of the population, numbering about 6,000.

The Nivkhi are an aboriginal people living in the southern Far East and on Sakhalin Island. The mainland and island groups are about the same size, each representing about half the small Nivkhi nation. Traditionally fishermen, forced resettlement has obliged some to take up farming.

The Nivkhi language, called Gilyak, is an isolated language not related to any of the neighboring language groups. It is mostly spoken by the older generations, while younger Nivkhi mostly speak Russian. The language has three major dialects that are not inherently intelligible, Amur, East Sakhalin, and North Sakhalin. The Nivkhi have retained their traditional religious beliefs.

Akhvakh—estimated at less than 1% of the population, numbering about 6,000.

The Akhvakh are a Dagestani people of the North Caucasus region of southern European Russia. One of the smallest of the Dagestani peoples, the Akhvakh speak an Andi language of the Northeast Caucasian languages. The language is not a literary language. Avar is used as the literary language. The Akhvakh are Sunni Muslims.

Selkup—estimated at less than 1% of the population, numbering about 5,000.

The Selkup, sometimes called Ostyak Samoyed, are a Samoyedic people living mostly in northwestern Siberia. The scattered Selkup groups live in Tomsk Oblast, Krasnoyarsk Kray, and the Yamalo-Nenets Autonomous Region on the Arctic Ocean. Most of the Selkup are fishermen and hunters.

The language of the Selkup is a Samoyedic language of the Uralic language group spoken in four major dialects. The northern Selkup groups, about 90%, use the language as their first language. In the south the language is disappearing in favor of Russian. About half the Selkup are Orthodox Christians. The other half are animists, following their traditional shamanistic beliefs.

Ghodoberi—estimated at less than 1% of the population, numbering about 3,000.

The Ghodoberi or Godoberi are a Dagestani Caucasian people of the southern European Dagestan Republic in the North Caucasus. The Ghodoberi speak a Dagestani language of the Avaro-Andi-Dido group of Northeast Caucasian languages that is very close to Andi and Botlikh. The language is not a written language. The Ghodoberi use the Avar language as their literary language. The majority are Sunni Muslims, with a Shi'a Muslim minority.

Ulchi—estimated at less than 1% of the population, numbering about 3,000.

The Ulchi live in the Russian Far East, in the Amur River valley and along the coast of the Tatar Channel near the Chinese border. The majority inhabit Ulchskiy rayon or county of the Khabarovsk region.

The language of the Ulchi, called Ulch or Hoche, is a Nanai language of the Southeastern Tungus languages of the Tungus-Manchurian group of East Altaic languages. Most of the Ulchi are Orthodox Christians.

Bezhta—estimated at less than 1% of the population, numbering about 3,000.

The Bezhta, also called Kapuchin, are a Caucasian people of the Dagestani group living in the Caucasus Mountains. Their language is a Dido language of the Avaro-Andi-Dido group of Northeastern Caucasian languages that is spoken in three dialects. The Bezhta language is not written, and they use Avar as their literary language. The Bezhta are Sunni Muslims.

Itel'men (Kamchadal)—estimated at less than 1% of the population, numbering about 3,000.

The Itel'men, also called Kamchadal, are a Paleo-Asiatic people closely related to the Koryak. Their homeland is the Kamchatka Peninsula of the Russian Far East. They are considered the original inhabitants of the peninsula and are related to the Native American peoples across the Bering Sea. Most of the Itel'men are now concentrated in the small Kovran district of the northern peninsula. Most work in the fish canning factories in the town of Kovran.

The Itel'men language, commonly called Kamchadal, is a Paleo-Siberian language closely tied to the language of the neighboring Koryaks. Most of the Itel'men are Orthodox Christians.

Hunzib—estimated at less than 1% of the population, numbering about 2,000.

The Hunzib, part of the Dagestani group of nations in the Dagestan Republic of southern European Russia, live in the high Caucasus Mountains of southern Dagestan. They speak a Dagestani language of the Avaro-Andi-Dido group of Northeastern Caucasian languages that is not a literary language. They use Avar as their literary language. The Hunzib are Sunni Muslims.

Sami (Lapp)—estimated at less than 1% of the population, numbering about 2,000.

The Sami or Saami, commonly called Lapp or Lap, are Finnic people living in the Kola Peninsula region of northwestern European Russia. The Sami include the Mountain or Reindeer Sami as well as the Forest, River, and Sea Sami. Most of the Sami in Russia are Reindeer Sami. Many fled to Finland during World War II.

The Sami language, a Finnic language of the Finno-Ugrian language group, is a recognized literary language that has its own writing system. The majority of the Sami are bilingual in Russian. The Sami claim that their numbers are much higher than official estimates and that Soviet censuses only counted the nomadic Sami and designated the more numerous settled Sami as ethnic Russians. The majority are Orthodox Christians.

NATION: The vast Eurasian territory that comprised historic Russia was inhabited before Paleolithic times. Written history indicates that early Greek traders conducted extensive commerce with Scythian tribes around the shores of the Black Sea and the Crimean Peninsula region. In the third century B.C., the Scythian tribes were displaced by Sarmatians, who in turn were overrun by waves of Germanic Goths in the third century A.D.

Huns from Asia overran the region, scattering the Goths, but were conquered by the Turkic Avars in the sixth century. By the ninth century Eastern Slavs, thought to have originated in present Poland, began to settle Ukraine, Belarus, and the Novgorod and Smolensk regions of Russia. Many of the Slav clans came under the rule of the Khazar nation to the south.

Viking tribes from Scandinavia, later in the ninth century, moved south along the rivers that connected the Baltic and Black seas. The Vikings mixed with the East Slavs and challenged Byzantium's hold on the Black Sea region. In 860 the East Slav forces cleared the Dnepr River region and attacked Constantinople.

In 862 the East Slav state known as Kievan Rus was established in what is now Ukraine under the rule of Rurik, traditionally the first monarch of the state. The East Slavs were united and freed from Khazar authority. Kiev became the center of the expanding East Slav empire.

The middle of the tenth century was marked by the continued expansion of the Rus state at the expense of the Khazar empire, which controlled most of the Caucasus and the steppe lands of southern Russia. In 980 Vladimir, later St. Vladimir, took the throne. Under his leadership distant Slavic tribes were brought under Kievan rule, and he waged successful wars against the Lithuanians, the Bulgars, and the Greeks of the Crimea. In 989, in order to wed Anna, the sister of the Byzantine emperor, Vladimir was baptized and made Orthodoxy the state religion. He used force to oversee the acceptance of the religion by his subjects. Byzantine forces aided the Rus in destroying Khazar power, which had blocked expansion to the south.

Following Vladimir's conversion and marriage, Byzantine culture predominated in the state, greatly influencing East Slav architecture, music, and art. The schism between the Eastern Orthodox and the Western Catholic churches in 1054 deepened the Byzantine influence in the state. Between 1054 and 1073 the Russkaia Pravda, the first Russian law, was written even as the state was divided and new centers rose to challenge Kiev's supremacy—Vladimir, Suzdal, and Novgorod.

In 1125 Yuri Dolgoruki became grand duke over a much reduced area. During his reign Novgorod, which controlled northern Russia to the Urals, became independent. In 1156 he founded Moscow as a fortified village. In 1169 Kiev was sacked by the forces of the prince of Vladimir-Suzdal and the capital of the grand duchy was moved from Kiev to Vladimir.

The Mongols invaded the East Slav lands in 1223, finally conquering all but the northwestern region between 1237 and 1242. Daniel, the son of Alexander Nevsky, who defeated the Swedes on the Neva River, founded the principality of Moscow in 1271 as a vassal state of the Mongol-Tatar Golden Horde.

The next two centuries saw the rise of Moscow as a provincial capital and the center of the Orthodox Church. Gradually Moscow became the center of the most powerful of the Russian principalities under the hegemony of the Golden Horde. The rulers of Moscow took the title of grand duke as the state expanded. Adjacent areas were subdued or united with Muscovy as the grand duchy's power continued to increase. Between 1430 and 1466 the Golden Horde, weakened by internal wars and outside pressures, disintegrated, leaving the Grand Duchy of Moscow the most powerful of the successor states in Russia.

In 1462 Ivan III became grand duke, and in 1472 he married Sofia (Zoe), the niece of the last Byzantine emperor. Ivan III, called Ivan the Great, conquered the Novgorod state in 1478, extended his authority over the other Russian principalities, and checked the eastward expansion of Lithuania. The forces of the Golden Horde, in 1480, attempted to reassert Mongol-Tatar authority over Moscow, but were defeated.

Ivan's grandson, later called Ivan the Terrible, was the first to bear the title tsar when he took the throne in 1547. Under Ivan's rule Moscow's military forces conquered Kazan and the Tatar lands to the east and Astrakhan and the shores of the Caspian Sea in the south, and fought wars with Poland and Sweden. During his reign the long struggle between the tsars and the powerful landed nobility, known as the boyars, became a serious threat to the state. Late in his reign Cossacks conquered Siberia, greatly extending the land area of his empire.

In the seventeenth and eighteenth centuries Russia remained isolated from the rest of Europe, a semi-Oriental state distrustful of foreigners and innovations. The consolidation of central power was attained only by forcibly depriving the boyars of their powers. In compensation, the boyars were granted vast estates and increasing rights over the masses of common people. Serfdom, which tied the Russian peasants to the boyar lands, approached virtual slavery and provoked serious peasant revolts. In 1613 Michael Romanov was elected tsar, and the Romanov dynasty was established in the Russian Empire.

Two outstanding rulers strengthened the Russian Empire during the late seventeenth and eighteenth centuries. Peter the Great, who ruled from 1689 to 1725, forced the boyars to accept a series of reforms and "Westernized" Russia following his conquest of the lands up to the Baltic Sea. As a symbol of Russia's new position as a European power, Peter founded St. Petersburg in the newly conquered area in 1703. The city was to become his window on Europe. The second able ruler, Catherine the Great, who ruled Russia from 1762 to 1796, pursued a policy of enlightened despotism while continuing the aggressive foreign policy initiated by Peter.

In the first quarter of the nineteenth century, under Tsar Alexander I, the first steps were taken to dismantle the system of serfdom, particularly the selling of serfs without land. The process was disrupted by Napoleon's invasion of Russia in 1812. Having burned Moscow, Napoleon was forced to retreat through the Russian winter, losing thousands of his best troops. Napoleon's defeat and the peace settlement formulated at the Congress of Vienna made Russia and Austria the leading European powers.

Under the rule of Nicholas I, Russia became the most reactionary state in Europe, acting as the policeman of the continent in combating all liberal tendencies. A clash between Russia and the Western powers in the Ottoman Empire led to the Crimean War, which revealed the inner weakness of the near-feudal Russian state.

The liberal Alexander II, who became tsar in 1855, one year before the Crimean War ended, was determined to modernize his defeated country. Among his reforms was the liberation of the serfs in 1861. His rule oversaw the territorial expansion to include the Caucasus region, Turkestan, and the southern regions of the Far East. Russia reached its greatest extent, with its borders extending to China, Afghanistan, and the Pacific Ocean.

Alexander III succeeded the assassinated Alexander II in 1881. He quickly reversed most of the earlier reforms and instituted a reactionary domestic policy that suppressed all manifestations of free thought and progress. While great social, economic, and political change swept the rest of Europe, Russia remained dominated by feudal agrarian traditions and the wasteful privilege of the aristocracy. Accomplishments such as the opening of the Trans-Siberian Railroad, in 1892, made vast frontiers available for development, but failed to resolve the fundamental problems of the mass of the Russian people. Alexander III was succeeded in 1894 by Nicholas II, the last tsar of the Russian Empire.

In 1897 the authorities carried out the first all-Russian census, which counted 128,907,692 people in the empire, making it by far the largest European power. Counting on numbers to overcome a lack of modern armament, Russia's generals blundered into the disastrous war with Japan in 1904–5, which made possible the success of the 1905 Russian Revolution. Nicholas was forced to grant a constitution and allow the formation of a parliament, the Duma, but reactionary forces soon gained control, and the new democratic freedoms were curtailed. Popular anger was channeled into anti-Semitic pogroms and other actions against non-Russian national groups.

In 1907 Russia formed the Triple Entente with France and Great Britain against the Triple Alliance of Germany, Austro-Hungary, and Italy. Russia's aid to the Slavic nations against the weakened Ottoman Empire in the Balkans in 1911–13 established the empire as the protector of Europe's Slavic peoples. A new wave of worker unrest ended with the crisis that overtook Europe in 1914.

Serbia's defiance, backed by Russia, of the Austro-Hungarian Empire in 1914 set off a continental conflict that soon drew in all the major European powers. Poorly prepared and cut off from its allies in the West, Russia suffered serious military reverses. Inflation, corruption, food shortages, and poor morale among the troops eventually provoked the February Revolution of 1917 and the abdication of Nicholas II.

A moderate, democratic regime oversaw a chaotic transfer of power, but its insistence on continuing to fight the Germans and Austrians soon undermined its support. Finally, in October 1917 (November by the Western calendar), Lenin and his small Bolshevik faction seized control of the government and negotiated a humiliating peace with the Central Powers. Regions and provinces inhabited by non-Russian populations proclaimed their independence as anti-Bolshevik White forces mobilized to defeat the Bolshevik government. The civil war between Reds and Whites and the intervention of foreign forces ended only in 1920 with the victory of the Red Army.

In 1917 Russia was officially proclaimed the Russian Soviet Federated Socialist Republic, which formed the Union of Soviet Socialist Republics with newly reconquered Ukraine, Belarus, and the Transcaucasian Federation of Armenia, Azerbaijan, and Georgia. The devastated state, controlling considerably less territory than the former empire, was isolated and feared by the West.

Vladimir Ilyich Lenin, as leader of the newly renamed Communists, was faced with a ruined economy and peasant unrest. He finally instituted the New Economic Policy, which gave peasants the right to sell their grain surpluses. His policy on nationalities, cultural independence without political independence, was applied to the numerous non-Russian national groups, giving them some control over local affairs. The fundamental policy of the Russian Communist

Party was, from its beginnings, complete state control of the economy and the redistribution of wealth.

Lenin's death in 1924 was followed by a collective leadership that was soon dominated by Josif Vissarionovich Stalin. After eliminating all rivals, Stalin began the forced collectivization and industrialization of the Soviet peoples. Millions died in political purges and the vast penal and labor system or in state-created famines. The Soviet Union proclaimed that the historic process of the drawing together of nations and nationalities gave rise to a new historical community, the Soviet people. The term "Soviet people" came into official use in the 1930s.

Stalin's distrust of any alternative power base led to waves of purges and arrests. In 1937, suspecting a plot, he had many of the Soviet army's officers executed. Two years later the Soviet Union signed a nonaggression pact with Nazi Germany that effectively divided central Europe into Nazi and Soviet spheres. Unopposed, the Soviet Union annexed the independent Baltic states and other territories that formed part of neighboring states, but in 1941 its Nazi ally turned on the Soviet Union and invaded the western republics of the union. The Nazi invasion forced the Soviet Union into an alliance with the Western powers, the United States and the United Kingdom and their allies.

The defeat of Germany and the Axis powers left the Soviet Union a leading world power despite its loss of some 20 million people during the war. Soviet authority was extended west to the central European states liberated from Nazi rule, effectively dividing Europe into two hostile camps. In 1949 the USSR became the second state to test an atomic bomb, bringing it superpower status.

Stalin's death in 1953 began a partial thaw of the Stalinist policies in Soviet society under the Khrushchev regime. The Soviet Union, determined to retain its authority in the Communist bloc, intervened against liberalization movements in Hungary in 1956 and Czechoslovakia in 1968 during the so-called Cold War. Soviet attempts to install nuclear weapons in newly Communist Cuba brought the world close to nuclear war in October 1962. While maintaining a military stance that required the focus of the national economy, Russia's citizens lived in poverty.

Between 1964 and 1985 a series of reactionary leaders did little to relieve the suffering of the Russian and Soviet peoples. Khrushchev was ousted in 1964, and Leonid Ilyich Brezhnev took power. His rule was marked by growing economic problems and unrest in the non-Russian republics. Achievements such as launching the world's first space satellite or advances in military hardware did little to offset the growing poverty of the Soviet system. Most of Russia's people lived in conditions little better than those in the poorer countries of Africa.

In 1985 Mikhail Gorbachev became president of the Union of Soviet Socialist Republics. He embarked on a program that restructured the USSR's relations with the West, easing the tensions of the decades-long Cold War. His internal reforms, *glasnost* (openness) and *perestroika* (restructuring and reform), led to profound changes within the Soviet Union as Moscow's iron grip weakened. By 1989 ethnically based national movements demanding greater autonomy had emerged in most of the union republics.

Within the Russian Federation, non-Russian nationalities also called for greater freedom from Russian domination. Ethnic Russians also rediscovered their roots and a nationalist sentiment buried under seven decades of Soviet rule. Dismay at what they saw as the ungrateful stance of the peoples they had helped lead out of poverty and ignorance led to a Russian backlash that spurred the growth of a particular Russian national movement.

In 1989 the Communist regimes of Eastern Europe, deprived of unconditional Soviet support, collapsed amid great rejoicing. The convulsions extended to the Westernized republics of the USSR in 1990, with demands for a looser union or in some cases complete independence.

The Russians, who claimed that they had suffered the most under the Soviet regime, also pressed for greater freedom. On 12 June 1990 the Congress of People's Deputies of the Russian Federation passed a declaration of state sovereignty. One year later, on 12 June 1991, Boris Yeltsin became the first democratically elected Russian president.

The spasms affecting communism reached their politically decisive climax with an attempted coup against Mikhail Gorbachev in August 1991. One day after the coup leaders announced their takeover, on 20 August, Yeltsin spoke to a large crowd from the top of a tank, then barricaded himself in the parliament building. On 24 August Gorbachev resigned as the head of the Communist Party, which was disbanded in the Russian Federation by Boris Yeltsin. On the same day, Yeltsin, on behalf of the independent Russian Federation, recognized the independence of Estonia, setting the stage for the Russian recognition of Latvia and Lithuania, and rapid disintegration of the Soviet empire. Although legally the Soviet Union lasted for another four months, as of 24 August the Russian Federation no longer recognized the authority of the Soviet government.

The failed coup brought an unexpected end to the largest extant empire, the most influential political movement, and the most powerful state political party of the twentieth century. It also marked the resurgence of the formerly quiescent Russian nation that had both created and been victimized by all three of these forces. The simultaneous collapse of communism and the Soviet Union intensified the Russian search for a new national identity.

Many Russian citizens had grown into the habit of feeling at home anywhere within the Soviet Union's frontiers. It had been a single country with a powerful center controlling an intricately linked command economy. Between 1930 and 1970, millions of Slavs had settled in other parts of the Soviet Union in search of better pay, decent housing, and higher social and professional status. Often they had been encouraged to move by the Soviet authorities, who, in addition to pursuing the political aim of strengthening control and cohesion throughout the state, also wanted to improve underdeveloped areas and boost agricultural and industrial production. These millions of ethnic Russians suddenly found themselves a diaspora of some 25 million people, often unwanted and unwelcome in the newly independent states.

On 8 December 1991 the presidents of Russia, Belarus, and Ukraine signed a treaty to officially abolish the Union of Soviet Socialist Republics and to form the new Commonwealth of Independent States (CIS). On 25 December Gorbachev formally announced his resignation, and the USSR ceased to exist. In its place fifteen new states had emerged, including the still huge Russian Republic, a multinational state of over 128 recognized national groups.

The Russian Federation, the largest of the successor states of the Soviet Union, inherited its permanent seat on the United Nations Security Council, as well as the bulk of its foreign assets and debts. In 1992 the Russian government persuaded eleven of the fifteen former Soviet republics to form the Commonwealth of Independent States. A twelfth state, Georgia, joined the group in 1993. Russian nationalist groups often look on the CIS as a tool for safeguarding the large ethnic Russian populations left behind as the empire shrank back to the historic Russian lands.

While the Soviet Union collapsed, within the Russian Federation the non-Russian regions unilaterally upgraded their status to that of full republics, member states of the renewed federation. Their new status, along with the greater powers granted the other regions, was confirmed by a federation treaty signed by all the autonomous republics except Chechnya and Tatarstan. The new Russian Federation became the most decentralized state in Russia's long history. The precise distribution of powers between the central government and the regional and local authorities was not clearly defined.

The southern republic of Chechnya, which proclaimed its independence in 1991, was the scene of a humiliating attempt to reimpose Russian rule in 1994. On 1 December 1996 the Russian troops were withdrawn, having been fought to a stand-off by the ill-equipped and much smaller Chechen forces. The Chechen rebellion, while the most far-reaching, is mirrored to some extent in many of the other republics where the process of de-Russification and autonomy movements have galvanized national movements across the vast Eurasian state.

The average Russian has a poor understanding of the benefits of democracy, often associating democratic institutions with social disorder, crime, corruption, and economic hardships. In spite of numerous setbacks in its democratic development, Russia has made some progress in governmental and human and group rights since independence in 1991.

The turbulent events of Russian history often have led Russians to scapegoat "foreigners" and "others" for their internal problems. The humiliation of losing the Soviet empire is no exception. The hard-line Russian nationalist press targets Jews as the alleged agents both of the advent of communism and of its demise. Not only Jews, but darker peoples, Armenians, Azeris, Chechens, Georgians, and Gypsies, bear the brunt of ethnic Russian suspicion and blame. A xenophobic view of non-Russian peoples has often vilified other national groups as foreigners in their native land.

Once again Russia is entering a *smula*, a time of troubles. The reemergence of a nationalist right, the first in Russia since 1920, has moved the whole spectrum of Russian politics. The reappearance of a Russian national movement, one firmly believing that Russia's rightful role as a great power can only be achieved by a strong authoritarian government, has alarmed Russia's other national groups and raised doubts about Russia's future intentions toward the other former Soviet republics.

The deadlock over economic and political control within the Russian government, particularly conflicts between the Yeltsin presidency and the parliament, has allowed local governors and presidents to go their own way. The result is a Russia much more decentralized than it ever was in the past. Many regional governments have signed treaties with Moscow that give them a greater share and greater control over their resources. Crucial decisions on reform are increasingly made at the provincial and republican level.

The continuing weakness of the central government and the strength of the republican and regional governments suggests that Russia's future may lie somewhere between the disintegration of its predecessor, the Soviet Union, and a genuine federal structure. Attempts to reassert federal government control could founder in the absence of the former levers of power, the Communist Party, the secret police, and the Red Army. New democratic levers are not yet in place, partly due to deep suspicion from the regions of any attempt by Moscow to recoup some of the enormous power it held during the Soviet era.

The humbling defeat of the Russian Army at the hands of the Chechen separatists in 1996 highlighted the decline of military power. The Russian military, by mid-1997, was in a shambles. In 1996 some 500 soldiers committed suicide due to the harsh conditions and the lack of food and resources. In July 1997, President Yeltsin signed decrees that will shrink the military from 1.8 million to 1.2 million in three years. Giant ships molder in harbors around the country, and dissatisfaction with current conditions has demoralized all branches of the military service.

Six times over the past three centuries Russia has turned toward the West, seeking to emulate the economic and social reforms there. The first five attempts, starting with Peter the Great and ending with Lenin, failed, and the autocratic Russian tradition reasserted itself. The sixth attempt, inaugurated by Boris Yeltsin in 1991, is still evolving, and Russia's future hangs in the balance.

SELECTED BIBLIOGRAPHY:

Batalden, Stephen K. *The Newly Independent States of Eurasia: Handbook of Former Soviet Republics.* 1993.

Beloff, Max, ed. *Beyond the Soviet Union: The Fragmentation of Powers.* 1997.

Gilbert, Martin. *Atlas of Russian History.* 1993.

Jacobsen, Karen. *The Russian Federation.* 1994.

Satter, David. *Age of Delirium: The Decline and Fall of the Soviet Union.* 1996.

Shlapentokh, Vladimir, ed. *The New Russian Diaspora: Russian Minorities in the Former Soviet Republics.* 1994.

SLOVAKIA

Slovenska Republika; Slovensko;
Slovak Republic

CAPITAL: Bratislava

POPULATION: (98e) 5,386,000 : 4,556,000 Slovaks in Slovakia and another 500,000 in adjoining areas of Hungary, Ukraine,* and the Czech Republic.* MAJOR NATIONAL GROUPS: (98e) Slovak 84.6%, Hungarian 10.6%, Rom (Gypsy) 1.5%, Ruthene (Carpatho-Rusyn) 1.4%, Czech 1.1%, Ukrainian, Pole, German, Russian, Serbian. MAJOR LANGUAGES: Slovak, Hungarian, Czech, Ukrainian (Carpatho-Rusyn dialect). MAJOR RELIGIONS: Roman Catholic 60.3%, Lutheran 8.4%, Orthodox 4.1%, Uniate, Jewish, Muslim. No religion 9.7%. MAJOR CITIES: (98e) Bratislava 463,000 (520,000), Kosice 248,000 (275,000), Nitra 97,000, Presov 93,000, Banská Bystrica 89,000 (155,000), Zilina 88,000 (130,000), Trnava 69,000, Martin 66,000, Trencin 62,000 (85,000), Poprad 55,000, Zvolen 44,000, Komarno 35,000 (72,000), Piestany 33,000.

GEOGRAPHY: AREA: 18,923 sq.mi.- 49,023 sq.km. LOCATION: Slovakia is a landlocked country located in the heart of Europe. The Slovak state borders Hungary on the south, Poland on the north, Austria and the Czech Republic on the west, and Ukraine on the east. PHYSICAL GEOGRAPHY: Slovakia is a mountainous country, with the Carpathian Mountains, including the High Tatra, in the north and northeast, the Low Tatra and Slovak Ore Mountains in the south, and the Eastern Carpathian Mountains in the east. Mountainous areas make up a third of the country and are usually heavily forested or wooded. The lowland area in the southwest is part of the Great Hungarian Plain. The country's principal rivers are the tributaries of the Danube River, such as the Vah, Nitra, and Hron. ADMINISTRATIVE DIVISIONS: Four departments or kraje (singular—kraj). POLITICAL STATUS: Slovakia was recognized as an independent state in 1993.

INDEPENDENCE DECLARATIONS: 30 October 1918 (from Hungary); 14 March 1939 (from Czechoslovakia); 1 January 1993 (from Czechoslovakia).

FLAG: The Slovak national flag, the official flag of the republic, is a horizontal tricolor of white, blue, and red bearing, near the hoist, a red shield, outlined in white and charged with the national symbols, three blue peaks surmounted by a white cross known as the Pribina Cross.

PEOPLE: The Slovak Republic, lying in the heart of Europe, is inhabited mostly by Slavs, including the majority Slovaks. The other Slav populations are part of larger populations living across Slovakia's international borders, Ruthenes, Ukrainians, Czechs, and Poles. The only large non-Slav population is the Magyar (Hungarian) population in the southern districts of the country that border on Hungary.

Slovak—an estimated 84.6% of the population, numbering about 4,556,000.

The Slovaks are a West Slav people closely related to the Czechs to the west, the major differences between the two West Slav peoples being a thousand years of separate history and the Slovaks' Roman Catholic religion. The Slovaks speak a West Slavic language of the Slavic group of languages that incorporates a Hungarian admixture. The Slovaks tend to be more rural and less sophisticated than their Czech cousins, a result of their particular history. While the Czechs lived in the most industrialized region of the former Austro-Hungarian Empire, the Slovaks lived as near-serfs on lands controlled by Hungarian landlords.

A substantial Slovak population lives outside the republic, in the Czech Republic, Hungary, Poland, Romania, Ukraine, and Yugoslavia. The Slovak population in the New World—the United States, Canada, and South America—has retained close ties to the country.

Magyar (Hungarian)—an estimated 10.6% of the population, numbering about 570,000.

The Magyars or Hungarians living in Slovakia are concentrated in the southern districts along the international border with Hungary. Although the Hungarians share their Roman Catholic religion with the Slovaks, language and history have separated the two peoples.

The Hungarians speak a Ugrian language of the Finno-Ugrian language group and before World War I were the predominant people in the region. Recent clashes between the Hungarian minority and the Slovak government have centered on language and political rights in the Hungarian majority regions.

Rom (Gypsy)—an estimated 1.5% of the population, numbering about 80,000.

The Rom population of Slovakia, by some estimates numbering over half a million, mostly live in the eastern part of the country. The poorest segment of the Slovak population, the Rom have historically suffered persecution and discrimination.

Two distinct ethnic groups, the Sárvika Romá in northern and eastern Slovakia, and the Ungrike Romá in southern Slovakia, are the largest of the Rom groups in the country. All Rom groups are usually called Karpacki Roma or Carpathian Rom. Their language, called Carpathian Romani or Bashaldo, is spoken in three major dialects, Moravian Romani, East Slovakian Romani, and West Slovakian Romani. The majority of the Rom are Roman Catholic, with a Protestant minority. Some Rom groups claim an ethnic population of over 300,000 in the Slovak Republic.

Ruthene (Ruthenian/Carpatho-Rusyn)—an estimated 1.4% of the population, numbering about 75,000.

The Ruthenes or Ruthenians, who call themselves Carpatho-Rusyn, are descended from Slavic migrants and early Ruthene tribes of unknown origin. The name Rusyn, an early designation for all Slavs, persisted in the isolated valleys of the Carpathian Mountains.

The language of the Ruthenes, called Rusyn or Carpatho-Rusyn, is considered a dialect of Ukrainian, an Eastern Slav language. The Ruthenes consider their dialect a separate Slav language, the national language of their small nation. The Ruthenes are mostly Uniate or Roman Catholics. In 1995–96 the Rusyn language officially became a literary language distinct from Ukrainian.

Officially, the Ruthenes account for only a small percentage of the Slovak population, but experts estimate their numbers at over 100,000, and Ruthenian nationalists claim an ethnic Ruthenian population of over 300,000. The discrepancy may arise from the fact that the Ruthene population, prior to Slovak independence in 1993, had been assimilating culturally and linguistically.

Czech—an estimated 1.1% of the population, numbering about 60,000.

The Czechs, mostly living in the large cities, particularly Bratislava, and in the western districts along the Czech border, are closely related to the Slovaks and speak a Western Slav language that can be understood by Slovaks. The majority of the Czechs settled in the region as administrators or professionals following the independence of Czechoslovakia after World War I. Most of the Czechs in the republic are Roman Catholics, with a Protestant minority.

The Czech minority is the remnant of a larger Czech population before independence in 1993. The majority returned to the Czech lands when the Czech Republic and Slovakia separated.

Ukrainian—estimated at less than 1% of the population, numbering about 22,000.

The Ukrainians, living mostly in the eastern districts along the Ukrainian border, are an Eastern Slav people more numerous in neighboring Ukraine. The majority of the Ukrainians in Slovakia are Uniate Catholics. Ukrainian nationalist groups claim an ethnic Ukrainian population of over 100,000 in the republic.

Pole—estimated at less than 1% of the population, numbering about 6,000.

The Poles, concentrated in the north along the Polish border, are a Western Slav people related to the Slovaks. Like the Slovaks, the Poles are devoutly Roman Catholic. The Poles living in Slovakia mainly use Slovak as their first language while speaking Polish, which is a related West Slav language, in the home.

Jew—estimated at less than 1% of the population, numbering about 6,000.

The Slovak Jews, the survivors of a much larger pre–World War II population, are mostly concentrated in Bratislava and the other large Slovak cities. Many of the Jews are Orthodox, retaining their traditional clothing and speaking the Yiddish language. Following independence in 1993 there have been some cases of anti-Semitic violence in the republic. Immigration to Israel and the United States has led to a decline in the Jewish population of the republic.

German—estimated at less than 1% of the population, numbering about 5,000.

The German population, also called Moravian Germans, mostly live in the western region near the Moravian region of the Czech Republic. Germans have lived in the region for over a thousand years, and during the domination of central Europe by the Habsburg empire, the German population formed the predominant ethnic group.

Russian—estimated at less than 1% of the population, numbering about 2,000.

The Russians living in Slovakia are mostly concentrated in the eastern districts and include groups of schismatic Orthodox groups such as Old Believers and Dukhobors. The majority of the Russians speak archaic dialects of Russian no longer understood by the general Russian public. They usually speak Slovak as their first language and for communicating beyond their own national group.

Serbian—estimated at less than 1% of the population, numbering about 2,000.

The Serbian population mostly settled in Slovakia during Habsburg rule, when Slovakia and parts of present Yugoslavia* formed part of the Austro-Hungarian Empire. The Orthodox Serbs are mostly urban, living in the towns and cities of eastern Slovakia. The Serbs speak a South Slav language, but most use Slovak as their first language.

THE NATION: Celtic tribes from the west settled the Carpathian highlands between 500 and 100 B.C. The Boi settled in the west, in Bohemia. The Cotini moved farther east to occupy Moravia and Slovakia. Many of the region's towns and cities began as Celtic settlements.

Slavic tribes, migrating from east of the Vistula River, settled the Danube basin in the sixth century A.D. and united under the Slovak national hero, Prince Pribina, in the early ninth century. Later in the same century the Slovak lands were included in a united West Slav state known as Great Moravia. The Christian religion spread to Slovakia through the missionary work of Czech priests moving into the pagan east.

The Magyars, originally nomadic horsemen from the region east of the Ural Mountains in Russia,* terrorized the region for half a century before destroying the Great Moravian state in 906. Their victories over the West Slav peoples brought them into conflict with the Holy Roman Empire, which controlled the territories threatened by the Magyars just to the west.

The Magyars, finally defeated near Augsburg in 955 by Emperor Otto I, were compelled to settle in the river lowlands along the Danube and Theiss Rivers. The Magyars later adopted Latin as the official and literary language of the Hungarian kingdom. Social position, not nationality, was the measure of status in the multiethnic kingdom. All power was concentrated in the hands of a clerical and secular nobility headed by the king. Slovakia was colonized by Hungarian nobles, and the Slovaks were relegated to virtual serfdom on large Hungarian estates.

The Hungarian kings, in the thirteenth century, made concessions to the powerful nobles in order to gain their support for the expansion of the kingdom. The concessions gradually reduced the kingdom to a number of distinct regions ruled by feudal lords. The most powerful of the barons in the Slovak lands was Matus Cak of Trencin, who ruled over most of Slovakia. The Arpad dynasty of Hungary died out in 1301, further weakening the kingdom.

The expanding Ottoman Empire took control of part of the Hungarian kingdom, including eastern Slovakia, in 1526. The Magyar capital, Buda, fell to the Ottoman Turks in 1541, forcing the Hungarians to transfer their administrative center to Bratislava, called Pozsony.

The Austrian Habsburg empire took control of the remaining Hungarian lands in 1687. The Habsburgs added the kingdom to their vast empire and took the title King of Hungary as yet another royal title. In the eighteenth century, under Empress Maria Theresa and Emperor Joseph II, who abolished serfdom, the Slovaks were subjected to intense Germanization.

Bratislava remained the center of the Hungarian kingdom until 1789, when the capital was returned to Budapest. However, the Habsburg Hungarian kings were crowned in Bratislava's cathedral until 1835. The city remained an important Hungarian cultural center, but at the same time became the focus of growing Slovak nationalism.

The nationalist ideal, led by the Slovak Catholic clergy, gained support during the mid-1800s, particularly during the upheavals that shook the Austrian Empire in 1848. The revival of the Slovak language and culture was paralleled by a new determination to win the right to shape their own future.

The Hungarians forced Austria to share power in the empire in 1867. The compromise between the Habsburg empire's two most powerful nations reinforced official policy aimed at assimilating the minority peoples into Austrian or Hungarian culture. The Slovaks, in the Hungarian half of the empire, reacted to renewed assimilation pressures by the Hungarian authorities by espousing nationalism. In the backward, neglected, and oppressed region, the only opportunity for education and advancement was the Catholic priesthood, which resulted in ever closer ties between the Roman Catholic Church and the growing Slovak national movement. To escape grinding poverty Slovaks began to emigrate in large numbers in the 1880s, mostly to North America.

Stirred by the large emigrant population in the United States and Canada, Slovak demands for political and cultural autonomy gained momentum up to

World War I. The Slovak National Council, formed by immigrant groups in the United States, initiated close cooperation with parallel Czech national groups.

At the outbreak of World War II in 1914, the idea that the national groups of the Habsburg empire might become free peoples became the nationalist goal. From the United States, Slovak nationalist leader Milan Stefanik joined with Czech leader Thomas Masaryk to promote Slovak-Czech independence. Thousands of Slovak conscripts in the Austro-Hungarian armies deserted to the Allies.

The collapse of the defeated Austro-Hungarian Empire gave the nationalists the opportunity they had waited for. The Czechs declared their independence from Austria on 28 October 1918. The Slovaks followed by declaring independence from Hungary on 30 October. In an attempt to prevent the Slovak secession, Hungarian troops invaded the new state on 3 November, but were forced by the Allied powers to withdraw. On 14 November 1918 the Czech lands and Slovakia united.

Roman Catholicism, the dominant religion in Slovakia, was unpopular at the time, being seen as a remaining tie to the former Austro-Hungarian Empire. Only after tensions between the Slovaks and Czechs surfaced did the Church regain its former popularity.

The new Czech and Slovak government adopted agreements drawn up by nationalists in the United States that provided for major Slovak autonomy within the new republic of Czechoslovakia. According to the pre-independence agreements, Slovakia was to be a partner, with only defense, foreign affairs, and internal security overseen by the federal government in Prague.

On 28 March 1919 a resurgent Hungary declared war and proceeded to reconquer all of Slovakia. A Hungarian minority of about 1 million inhabited southern Slovakia, one of the new state's most urgent problems. When Romanian troops invaded Hungary, Hungarian troops were forced to withdraw from Slovakia. Leftist Slovaks then proclaimed a Slovak Socialist Republic, which lasted for four weeks until overthrown by Czechs and moderate Slovaks.

The 1920 constitution, supported by the majority Czech population, set up a democratic although highly centralized government, which seriously damaged relations between the two peoples. The Slovaks, neglected under Hungarian rule, had not developed trained bureaucrats or military officers to lead Slovak regiments in the new Czecho-Slovak army, so Czechs from more advanced Bohemia were dispatched to administer Slovakia. The anticlerical stance of the Prague government caused much tension with the devoutly Roman Catholic Slovaks. The Catholic Church supported Slovak agitation for the autonomy promised in the pre-independence agreements.

Slovakia's status remained that of an ordinary province, even though the separate Slovak language was allowed. In the 1930s, as Fascist governments took power in Germany and Hungary, more radical groups emerged in Slovakia, many espousing the Fascist ideals.

Slovak nationalism, supported by Nazi Germany, veered rapidly toward fascism in 1938 following the Munich Agreement that effectively dismembered Czechoslovakia. Germany allowed its ally, Hungary, to annex the Hungarian-populated districts of southern Slovakia while promoting the Fascist Slovak nationalist movement led by a Catholic priest, Joseph Tiso. Tiso declared Slovakia independent under German protection on 14 March 1939. Tiso then appealed to Hitler, who used the crisis to occupy and annex the Czech lands of Bohemia and Moravia as a German protectorate.

Many Czechs were expelled from the new Slovak state, and all the trappings of a Fascist dictatorship were created, including anti-Semitic laws. Tiso erected a one-party authoritarian regime and allowed German troops to garrison the republic. With the outbreak of World War II, the Slovak state entered the war as a German ally, while a large anti-Fascist underground grew steadily in opposition to the Fascist regime. During the course of the war, Slovakia's 67,000 Jews were massacred with the active participation of many Slovaks.

In 1944 the Slovak underground launched a popular rebellion, paving the way for the Soviet occupation of the region. In 1945 Tiso was hanged; his state was dismantled and again integrated into a reconstituted Czecho-Slovak republic.

Slovakia was finally granted autonomy as part of the reconstituted Czecho-Slovak state in 1945. Many ethnic Hungarians were expelled, but a move to deport the remaining half million Hungarians from Slovakia was blocked by the Allies. In the 1946 elections, 66% of Slovak voters gave their support to conservative political parties supported by the Catholic Church.

The 1948 Communist takeover of Czechoslovakia again raised the old antagonism between the Czechs and Slovaks, aggravated by the new Communist regime's attacks on the Slovaks' cherished Catholic religion and the abolition of Slovakia as a separate region. Harsh repression in the 1950s targeted Slovak nationalism and the Slovak Catholic hierarchy. Thousands of priests, bishops, and nuns were herded into concentration camps amid a wave of show trials of Slovak Catholic leaders.

A Slovak national revival, beginning in 1963, gained wide expression in the late 1960s. Alexander Dubcek, an ethnic Slovak, became the Communist Party leader in Czechoslovakia. His liberalization and reforms led to the so-called Prague Spring, the flowering of the Czech and Slovak cultures. The brief liberalization, which threatened the Communist hold on eastern Europe, was crushed by invading Warsaw Pact tanks in 1968.

The reimposition of authoritarian communism was accompanied by the adoption of a new constitution. On 1 January 1969 Slovakia became a separate republic in a federal state with equal rights to the partner Czech Republic. However, the division of the country into two republics had little impact, as the Czechoslovak Communist Party continued to rule with little meaningful autonomy for Slovakia. Following the Warsaw Pact invasion and the creation of the federal republic, tensions between the Czechs and Slovaks worsened. Many Czechs accused the Slovak Communists of cooperating with the Soviets in the ''normalization'' of the republic.

In the 1970s and early 1980s the Slovaks urbanized and industrialized. By 1986 heavy industries had been established in many Slovak towns and cities and only 15% of the Slovak population tilled the land. The national revival interrupted by the 1968 invasion gradually regained support as controls relaxed in the late 1980s.

Factions of the national movement took on a vehement anti-Hungarian and anti-Semitic rhetoric that outraged moderates seeking closer ties to Western Europe. Joseph Tiso, executed as a war criminal in 1947, became a national hero to the more reactionary factions. Slovak nationalist groups, particularly those on the right, became anti-Czech and anti-Hungarian.

Thousands of Slovak Catholics marched through Bratislava in March 1988 to protest the lack of religious and political freedom. Police used riot sticks, dogs, and tear gas to break up the demonstration, the first important defiance of the Communist government in Slovakia. Loyalty to the Catholic Church became stronger than in past decades as young Slovaks saw the Church as the spearhead for increasing freedom.

In April 1988, the Czecho-Slovak government, following the Soviet lead, began a series of limited economic reforms but allowed few political reforms. The most conservative government in the Communist bloc, the government refused to institute reforms like those in neighboring Poland and Hungary and in the Soviet Union. In October 1988 the Communist leadership of Slovakia resigned amid the first tentative cultural and economic liberalizations.

The federal government reacted to the burst of political activity with a wave of police repression, using force to crush unauthorized demonstrations and raiding the homes of dozens of Slovak dissidents. The tacit agreement in the post-1968 period—material abundance in exchange for near-absolute political calm—began to disintegrate as the economic crisis worsened and shortages became common.

The overthrow of communism in Czechoslovakia in 1989, known as the Velvet Revolution, allowed nationalist sentiment to reemerge, stimulated by conflicts with the Czechs over the name of the federal state, demands for greater autonomy, and the growing economic differences between the more advanced Czech lands and the aging heavy industries situated in Slovakia by the Communists. Mass demonstrations were held in Bratislava and other Slovak cities by nationalists demanding autonomy and a new name for the country that would clearly specify their separate identity. Nationalist organizations accused the Czechs of dominating the federation and demanded greater monetary aid for the already heavily subsidized Slovak economy.

In March 1990 nationalist passions were aroused by the ongoing issue of a new name for the federal republic. The Slovaks demanded that the name clearly identify their nation as an equal partner. The final choice as the official name of Czechoslovakia, the Czech and Slovak Federal Republic, satisfied neither the Czechs nor the Slovaks.

The economic reforms set in place following the dismantling of the Communist command economy began to be felt in mid-1990. While the Slovaks demanded greater economic aid for their unprofitable heavy industries, many Czechs complained that Slovakia already received too big a share of federal revenues and jobs. Czech demands for cuts in spending further alienated many Slovak nationalists. Feelings were running so high that the federal parliament was deadlocked, delaying much-needed economic reform legislation.

President Vaclav Havel was authorized by the federal parliament, in July 1991, to call a national referendum on separation. On 17 July 1991 the Slovak parliament declared the sovereignty of the republic within the federation. Continuing disagreements over a new federal constitution deepened until Czech and Slovak leaders finally agreed to the division of the federation into two sovereign states in August 1992.

The Republic of Slovakia was declared an independent republic on 1 January 1993, quickly recognized by most European governments and the United States. The so-called Velvet Divorce between the Czech Republic and Slovakia split the former Czecho-Slovak state peacefully, although disputes over the distribution of state funds, industries, and infrastructure continued to plague relations between the two new states.

Slovakia, by 1997, had fallen behind the Czech Republic in several important areas. The Slovaks' democratic and civic rights are primitive compared with those enjoyed by the Czechs. The Slovak state increasingly interferes with the Slovak economy, which has been hit harder than the Czechs' by post-Communist economic reforms. The Slovak government has signed an array of agreements with Russia ranging from arms transfers and the sharing of intelligence to supplies of oil and gas. Should the enlargement of NATO and the European Union erect a new border between east and west, Slovakia has placed itself on the eastern side. The government, in spite of its lack of reforms, continues to measure Slovakia's progress in comparison to that of the Czech Republic.

The prime minister, Vladimir Meciar, is a heavy-handed authoritarian who depends on patronage and cronies to keep himself in office. His vicious campaign to unseat the president, Michal Kovac, has bitterly divided Slovaks. The kidnapping in 1995 of the president's son and the subsequent death of an ex-policeman who may have known too much are widely thought to be the work of the Russian-trained Slovak secret service. Strong-arm tactics against the local press, laws that discriminate against minority languages, particularly Hungarian, the cancelling of a referendum on whether the president should be directly elected, and the education ministry's use of European Union aid money to publish a school textbook that denies any Slovak complicity in the wartime murder of the Slovak Jews are among the reasons that Slovakia is not among the European states invited to join NATO or the European Union in 1997.

The office of president, left vacant after the Slovak parliament failed to elect a successor to Michal Kovac, whose term ended on 2 March 1998, has mostly been usurped by the government—in other words, Vladimir Meciar. Wasting no time, he immediately dismissed thirty-three of Slovakia's forty-two ambassadors, canceled a referendum on the direct elections for the country's president, and has granted dubious presidential amnesties, including pardoning his associates involved in the kidnapping of President Kovac's son in 1995. Slovakia's chances of soon joining the European Union or NATO would seem to depend on Mr. Meciar's continuing anti-democratic behavior.

SELECTED BIBLIOGRAPHY:

Delfiner, Henry. *Slovakia 1938–1939: A Case Study of Subversion.* 1974.

Drobna, Olga, ed. *Slovakia: The Heart of Europe.* 1996.

Kirschbaum, Stanislav J. *A History of Slovakia: The Struggle for Survival.* 1995.

Leff, Carol Skalnik. *The Czech and Slovak Republics: Nation versus State.* 1996.

Magocsi, Paul Robert. *The Rusyns of Slovakia: An Historical Survey.* 1994.

SLOVENIA

Slovenije; Republika Slovenije;
Republic of Slovenia

CAPITAL: Ljubljana

Central Europe

Slovenia

POPULATION: (98e) 1,942,000 : 1,795,000 Slovenes in Slovenia and another 125,000 in adjacent areas of Austria and Italy. MAJOR NATIONAL GROUPS: (98e) Slovene (including Istrian) 90.6%, Croat 2.5%, Serb 2.1%, Muslim 1.4%, Italian, German, Slovak, Friuli, Czech. MAJOR LANGUAGES: Slovene, Croatian, Serbian, German. MAJOR RELIGIONS: Roman Catholic 72%, Orthodox 2.5%, Uniate 2%, Muslim 1.5%, Protestant 1%. MAJOR CITIES: (98e) Ljubljana 264,000 (337,000), Maribor 116,000 (198,000), Celje 46,000, Kranj 38,000, Koper 24,000, Trbovlje 18,000, Velenje 15,000.

GEOGRAPHY: AREA: 7,817 sq.mi.-20,251 sq.km. LOCATION: Slovenia lies in south-central Europe, bordering the Gulf of Trieste on the southwest, Italy on the west, Austria on the north, Hungary on the northeast, and Croatia* on the south and southeast. PHYSICAL GEOGRAPHY: The country occupies the Karst Plateau, an area of alpine highlands in the Carnic, Karawanken, and Julian Alps that rise to Mount Triglav, Slovenia's highest point. In the south a northern spur of the Dinaric Alps, the limestone Karst Plateau, slopes down to a short coastline of about 30 miles (48 km.) on the Gulf of Trieste area of the Adriatic Sea. The Slovenian lowlands lie in the east and along the Adriatic coast in the western districts. The principal rivers are the Sava and Drava. The republic has several important *bled*, or glacial lakes, and other lakes in the Karst Plateau. ADMINISTRATIVE DIVISIONS: sixty provinces or pokajine (singular—pokajina). POLITICAL STATUS: Slovenia was recognized as an independent state in 1991.

INDEPENDENCE DECLARATION: 25 June 1991 (from Yugoslavia).

FLAG: The Slovene national flag, the official flag of the republic, is a horizontal tricolor of white, blue, and red charged with the Slovenian shield, an image of Mt. Triglav on the upper hoist, bearing three white peaks crossed by two wavy lines and surmounted by three six-pointed yellow stars.

PEOPLE: Slovenia is the most homogeneous of the former Yugoslav republics; less than 10% of the population is non-Slovene. The Slovene nation also includes sizable populations in Italy (about 120,000) and Austria (78,000), and about 25,000 in the Prekmurje region in eastern Croatia near the Hungarian border. The Slovene culture is centered on the cities of Trieste, called Trst in Slovenian, and Klagenfurt, called Celovec, which with Ljubljana historically made up the three historic centers of the Slovene culture and nation.

Slovene—an estimated 90.6% of the population, numbering about 1,795,000.

The Slovenes are a South Slav nation, the most northerly of the South Slav peoples of the Balkan Peninsula. Historically the Slovenes have been dominated by the German-speaking Austrians to the north, their basically alpine culture showing many Austrian influences. The industrious Slovenes have achieved the highest standard of living in the Balkan Peninsula.

The Slovene language, a western South Slav language showing a marked German admixture, is written in the Latin alphabet, with the exception of the letters q, w, and y. The language, spoken in two major dialects, Lower Carniola and Upper Carniola, is further divided into forty-six subdialects. Overwhelmingly Roman Catholic, the Slovenes are closely allied to the neighboring Catholic Croats, and most Slovenes are bilingual in Croatian, a closely related South Slav language.

The most Westernized and advanced of the South Slav peoples, the Slovenes have achieved the highest standard of living of the newly independent states. The inhabitants of the new country have maintained close contacts with the prosperous Slovene minorities in Italy and Austria.

Croat—an estimated 2.5% of the population, numbering about 48,000.

The Croats of Slovenia, mostly living in areas that border Croatia, are a South Slav people closely related to the Slovenes, with whom they share Westernized cultures and the Roman Catholic religion. Many Croats have moved to neighboring Croatia since independence in 1991.

The Croat language, formerly considered a dialect of Serbo-Croatian, is written in the Latin alphabet. Since independence in 1991, the Croats have emphasized the differences between the Croat and Serbian dialects and now claim that Croatian is a separate language.

Serb—an estimated 2.1% of the population, numbering about 40,000.

The Serbs, an eastern South Slav people, are related to the Slovenes, but historically have been influenced by the Turks and the Orthodox peoples of the eastern Balkan Peninsula. The majority of the Serbs live in Ljubljana and the other large cities, where they settled under Austrian rule.

The Serb language, a South Slav language written in the Cyrillic alphabet, is close to spoken Slovene, so that most Serbs are bilingual. The Serb minority is the largest Orthodox Christian group in the country.

Istrian (counted as ethnic Slovene)—an estimated 1.9% of the population, numbering about 37,000.

The Istrian Slovenes, inhabiting the southwest of the country in Slovenia's part of the Istrian Peninsula, refer to themselves as an Istro-Romanic people and have preserved a unique culture that developed over centuries of mixed Slav, Germanic, and Latin elements. The Istrians are mostly bilingual in Slovene and Croat, while many also speak Italian.

Muslim (Morlakh)—an estimated 1.4% of the population, numbering about 28,000.

The Muslim population, called Morlakh in Slovenia, has historically inhabited the western districts and the Istrian Peninsula. Although Muslim by religion, culturally the Morlakh are assimilated in the Slovene culture and speak the Slovene language.

Italian—estimated at less than 1% of the population, numbering about 20,000.

The Italians of Slovenia, concentrated in the western districts and Istria, are the remnant of a much larger Italian population that inhabited the region up to World War II, when parts of Slovenia were under Italian rule. Under Slovene authority, they have been granted the right to use their language and to form cultural and national organizations.

Mostly bilingual, speaking both Italian and Slovene, the Italians have maintained their separate culture through decades of Communist repression and persecution. The Venetian dialect is the spoken language, while standard Italian is understood and is the literary language.

German—estimated at less than 1% of the population, numbering about 20,000.

Most of the German population of Slovenia is descended from Bavarian and Austrian settlers who remained following the collapse of the Austro-Hungarian Empire in 1918. Like the Slovenes, the Germans are mostly Roman Catholic, and their alpine culture shares many traditions and traits with that of the Slovenes. The majority of the Germans live in the Alpine regions in the north of the country.

The Slovene Germans speak a South Bavarian dialect of German, which is also spoken in Austria and southern Germany. The majority of the Germans also speak Slovene or Croatian.

Hungarian—estimated at less than 1% of the population, numbering about 20,000.

The majority of the Slovene Hungarians live in the eastern districts along the Hungarian border. The Hungarians speak an Ugrian language of the Finno-Ugric languages, but are mostly bilingual, also speaking Slovene or Croatian. Most of the Hungarians are Roman Catholics, with an important Protestant minority.

Friuli—estimated at less than 1% of the population, numbering about 7,000.

The Friuli, more numerous across the Italian border, inhabit the southwestern

Slovene districts near the Italian city of Trieste. The descendants of the ancient inhabitants of the region, the Friuli are considered the oldest of the ethnic groups in the area of the northern Adriatic Sea.

The Furlan language spoken by the Friuli is a Rhaeto-Romantic language considerably influenced by the Venetian dialect of Italian.

Slovak—estimated at less than 1% of the population, numbering about 5,000.

The Slovaks, a Western Slav people, settled in the region when both Slovakia and Slovenia formed part of the multiethnic Austro-Hungarian Empire. Mostly concentrated in the larger towns and cities, the Slovaks, like the Slovenes, are predominantly Roman Catholic.

Czech—estimated at less than 1% of the population, numbering about 2,000.

The Slovene Czechs, descendants of migrants who settled in the region in the eighteenth century, are mostly concentrated in the central districts around Ljubljana. The Czechs speak a Western Slav language closely related to Slovak, and most are bilingual in Slovene. Like the Slovenes, the majority of the Czechs are Roman Catholic.

THE NATION: Originally inhabited by Illyrian and Celtic peoples, the region came under Roman rule in the first century B.C. Part of the Roman province of Illyricum, the region was a wealthy and cultured area known for the splendor of the Roman cities along the Adriatic Sea.

Slavic tribes moved into the area from the east in the sixth century A.D. The migrating Slavs reached the Karst Plateau, traditionally in A.D. 568, and settled the valleys of the Sava, Drava, and Mura Rivers. Under pressure from the Avars, the Slavic tribes spread out across the Friuli plains, north to the Danube, and along the Adriatic Sea. Historically, the ancestors of the Slovenes settled in four distinct areas, Styria, Carniola, Carinthia, and Gorizia.

The tribes formed a separate state called Karantanja, later known as Carinthia. In 745 the Slovene duchy was included in the Frankish Empire of the Carolingians, the forerunner of the Holy Roman Empire. Under Bavarian domination after 843, the Slavs converted to Christianity while gradually losing their independence. In the ninth century the German peoples took direct control of the Klagenfurt region, while most of Slovenia was ruled by a succession of German princes until its piecemeal incorporation into the Habsburg Austrian Empire between 1278 and 1335.

In 1364 the Slovene territories became hereditary possessions of the House of Habsburg. The central districts were erected as the titular Duchy of Carniola, while the eastern districts came under the authority of the Hungarian kingdom. The Habsburg empire was the first to control all the Slovene lands. Under Habsburg rule the region became Westernized and the German language was predominant.

The imperial government refused to recognize the Slovenes as a minority, and intense pressure was applied to assimilate the Slovenes into German Austrian culture. The cities and towns became Germanized, while the Slovene language and culture survived in the rural areas. In 1551 a Protestant minister published the first book written in the Slovene language, and in 1584 the first Slovene grammar was written.

Over the next centuries the Slovene culture was preserved only as rural traditions, and the Slovene language survived as a group of peasant dialects. Only in the nineteenth century did a sense of nationhood begin to appear among the various Slovene groups. In 1848, during the nationalist upheavals in the empire, a group of Slovene intellectuals issued the first political program for a united Slovenia within the Habsburg empire. The first Slovene political organizations appeared in 1860, the forerunner of the later political parties.

Increasing access to education and the spread of nationalist ideas stimulated a Slovene national revival in the 1880s and 1890s. The most advanced of the South Slav peoples of the Austro-Hungarian Empire, the Slovenes led the campaign for Slovene autonomy within the empire, only later espousing the creation of an autonomous South Slav state equal to the Austrian and Hungarian partners in the empire.

Slovene nationalism won widespread support as the Austro-Hungarian Empire slowly collapsed during World War I. At Allied urging, the Slovenes sent a delegation to a meeting of the leaders of all the South Slav peoples in 1917, where they reluctantly agreed to join a sovereign state made up of the South Slav nations of the Habsburg empire, along with the less advanced but more numerous Orthodox South Slavs of Serbia and Montenegro.

The defeat of Austria-Hungary, in November 1918, left the Slovenes effectively independent. Slovene leaders in Ljubljana proclaimed the country's independence, and although the Slovenes feared domination by the Orthodox Serbs, they feared even more the neighboring states to the east, west, and north. By the terms of the 1919 Treaty of St. Germain between Austria and the Allies, the western portions of historic Slovenia, including the city of Trieste, with an Italian majority, were transferred to Italy over Slovene protests. The territorial dispute soured relations between the South Slav state and Italy between the wars. Irredentist claims to Slovene-populated regions of Italy and Austria kept the region in turmoil.

The least enthusiastic for South Slav union, the Slovenes greatly resented the domination of the new kingdom by the Serbs. The Serb control of power in the kingdom provoked widespread discontent and demands for Slovene autonomy. The wealthier Slovenes resented having the revenue from their lumber and mining taken by the central government for projects in Serbia and the poor southern regions of the kingdom. The government of the state, renamed Yugoslavia in 1929 to blunt local nationalisms, divided the national regions into counties, effectively partitioning the various ethnic and religious groups.

In April 1941 the armies of the Axis powers invaded Yugoslavia. A pro-Fascist Slovene became the head of an Italian-occupied puppet state called the Province of Ljubljana. Other portions of Slovenia were placed under direct German and Hungarian rule.

Soon after the occupation the Slovenes under Italian authority rebelled and were joined by the Julian Slovenes under German rule. The Slovene rebels formed the Freedom Front (OF), which became the center of Slovene resistance. The Slovene uprising was the first rebellion by a national group against the Italian and German Fascists.

Italy changed sides in 1943, and German troops occupied the territories formerly held by the Italian forces. Until then the Slovene nationalist resistance had maintained their independence of the Communist partisans led by Josip Broz Tito, himself partly of Slovene origin. The Communist resistance pressed for control, and the ''Dolomite Proclamation'' was approved by the assembly of activists. The proclamation gave the Slovene Communist Party a leading role in the resistance, and many non-Communist partisan groups, called White Guards, were massacred, reportedly on Tito's direct orders.

Another 40,000 non-Communist Slovenes were massacred by the Communists at the end of World War II, including many that had fled to Allied-occupied territory. It reportedly took eight days to kill the Slovenes and dispose of their bodies in mass graves. The British military had agreed to the forced repatriation of the Slovenes in return for a Yugoslav withdrawal from Austrian Carinthia.

Tito, the Communist resistance leader, gained control of all of postwar Yugoslavia and organized the state as a federation under firm Communist control in 1946. Slovenia was joined to the new Communist federation as a constituent republic under the control of the League of Communists of Slovenia (LCS).

Yugoslav claims to the traditionally Slovene city of Trieste (Trst), also claimed by Italy, resulted in the creation of a separate Free City of Trieste under UN auspices in 1947. In 1954, after seven years of independence, the Free City was divided between Yugoslavia, which received the rural southern region— mostly populated by Slovenes—and Italy, which gained the city of Trieste and its immediate area. The border region remained a source of tension between Yugoslavia and Italy from World War II to the signing of a final agreement on Trieste in 1975.

Slovenia developed as Yugoslavia's wealthiest and most advanced republic, resentful of Yugoslav government policies that taxed the Slovenes for development projects in Serbia and the poorer southern republics of the federation. In 1962 the Slovene republican government threatened secession over the ''economic nationalism'' of the Serb-dominated federal government. Growing demands for economic and political autonomy ended with purges and arrests in 1971 and 1976. With less than 8% of the Yugoslav population, Slovenia earned between 25 and 30% of the country's foreign exchange between the 1960s and the 1980s.

Tito's death in 1980 dramatically loosened decades of centralized, firm Communist control. Fueled by a severe economic crisis, the Slovenes moved to separate their more prosperous republic both economically and politically from the Serb-dominated Yugoslav federal government.

In the summer of 1988 the military trial of three young Slovene journalists and an army officer led to the first calls for Slovene independence. Along with political unrest, economic problems mounted, and Yugoslav inflation hit 1,200%. Amid the growing economic and political crisis, in 1989 communism began to collapse and a radical Serb nationalist group took control of the federal government.

A crisis in Kosovo, an autonomous province of Serbia, where the Serbian government had ousted the provincial government and imposed military rule, further alienated the Westernized Slovene and Croat republics from the Yugoslav heartland in Serbia. In February 1989 the Slovene Communist leadership publicly protested the state of emergency imposed on Kosovo, fearing that the liberalizing Slovenia would be the next target of the Serb-dominated Yugoslav army (JNA). In late 1989 the federal government imposed an economic embargo on Slovenia because of its stand on Kosovo.

Slovenia and neighboring Croatia demanded reforms and the formation of a confederation of sovereign states in Yugoslavia, but were blocked by the Serbs. A coalition of nationalist groups, Demos, won Slovenia's first free elections in April 1990, stimulating more demands for a looser Yugoslav federation. Milan Kucan, a Communist turned nationalist, was elected president of the republic. The largest of the republics, Serbia, under a neo-Communist government, strongly resisted the decline of its traditional domination of the federation.

On 23 December 1990 a Slovene referendum on independence resulted in overwhelming support, giving the Slovene government a mandate to negotiate a less restrictive political relationship with Belgrade within six months or to complete the process that would lead to independence. Amid a continuing political crisis, the Slovene leadership declared the independence of the Republic of Slovenia on 25 June 1991.

The Yugoslav army, on June 27, picked Slovenia as an easier target than Croatia, which had also declared independence. The army moved in to secure the borders and take over important government buildings. The Slovenes resisted, setting up blockades and attacking advancing armored columns. After a ten-day war, on 7 July 1991 the army called off further intervention, and the Slovene government, acting on a European Community proposal, accepted a three-month moratorium on the country's independence.

On 7 October the Slovenes took control of their borders, and on 25 October 1991 the last Yugoslav soldier left the country. Germany promised that diplomatic relations would be established on 15 January 1992. On that date the presidency of the European Community announced that its member states had decided to recognize Croatia and Slovenia, but not the other former Yugoslav states.

The first national elections, on 6 December 1992, were a high point for newly independent Slovenia. The Slovenes bucked the trend in the former Communist states by rejecting militant nationalism and electing a liberal, democratic government. In June 1993 they celebrated two years of independence and their status as the richest, most stable state to emerge from the collapse of communism.

The new republic, with a clear Slovene majority, looked to the West for security as former Yugoslavia dissolved into war. Along with Macedonia,* in the south, Slovenia escaped the general Balkan war that convulsed neighboring Croatia and Bosnia and Herzegovina.

Relations with the other former Yugoslav republics, particularly Yugoslavia, which claims to be the sole successor to Tito's state, became increasingly tense in 1994–95. The distribution of the assets of the former Socialist Federal Republic of Yugoslavia (SFRY), which Yugoslavia claims, has become an issue for Slovenia and continues to cloud relations between the two successor states.

In March 1995 the European Union granted a mandate for negotiations to begin between the EU and Slovenia on an association agreement. Slovenia's market economy and democratic politics made the country one of few in the former Communist bloc to meet EU requirements for association.

In July 1997 Slovenia was among the countries named to take part in talks leading to the European Union's first expansion into central and eastern Europe. On 14 July the Slovene parliament voted to amend the constitution to permit foreigners to own property, an EU requirement. The property issue is politically sensitive because many Slovenes fear that lifting the ban might lead to a massive influx of foreign buyers, particularly Italians whose families left the region in the wake of World War II.

SELECTED BIBLIOGRAPHY:

Benderly, Jill, and Evan Kraft, eds. *Independent Slovenia: Origins, Movements, Prospects.* 1996.

Carmichael, Cathie. *Slovenia.* 1996.

Hafner, Danica Fink, ed. *Making a New Nation: The Formation of Slovenia.* 1997.

Plut-Pregelj, Leopoldina. *Historical Dictionary of Slovenia.* 1996.

Prunk, Janko. *A Brief History of Slovenia: Historical Background of the Republic of Slovenia.* 1993.

TAJIKISTAN

Tadzhikistan; Takikistan;
Tojikiston; Respubliki i Tojikiston

CAPITAL: Dushanbe

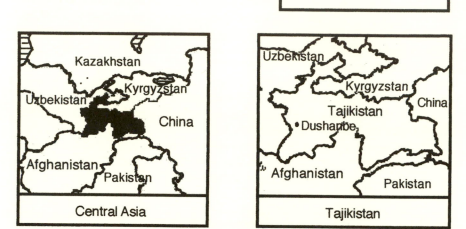

POPULATION: (98e) 6,155,000 : 3,920,000 Tajiks in Tajikistan and another 6 million in Uzbekistan,* Afghanistan, China, Iran, and the neighboring Central Asian states. MAJOR NATIONAL GROUPS: (98e) Tajik (including Yagnobi and Pamiri) 65.7%, Uzbek 24.6%, Russian 3.1%, Tatar 1.7%, Kyrgyz 1.6%, Ukrainian, Persian, Korean, Turkmen, Pashtu, Kazakh, Jew, Ossetian, Bashkort, Armenian, Baluchi, Uighur, Arab. MAJOR LANGUAGES: Tajiki, Jagatai (Uzbek), Russian, Yagnobi, Pamiri. MAJOR RELIGIONS: Sunni Islam 85%, Shi'a Islam 5%, Russian Orthodox, Ismaili Islam. MAJOR CITIES: (98e) Dushanbe 612,000 (750,000), Khujand (Leninabad) 207,000 (255,000), Kulob (Kulyab) 124,000, Qurghonteppa (Kurgan-Tyube) 89,000 (121,000), Orjonikidzeobod 76,000, Uroteppa (Ura Tyube) 53,000, Kondibodom (Kanibadam) 41,000 (69,000), Isfara 39,000 (76,000), Panjakent (Pendzikent) 34,000, Tursunzoda (Tursunzade) 28,000, Khorugh (Khorog) 23,000, Norak (Nurek) 21,000.

GEOGRAPHY: AREA: 55,251 sq.mi.-143,137 sq.km. LOCATION: Tajikistan lies in Central Asia, a landlocked country bordering Uzbekistan on the northwest and west, Afghanistan on the south, China on the east, and Kyrgyzstan* on the northeast. PHYSICAL GEOGRAPHY: Tajikistan is a mountainous country with 90% of its national territory covered by mountain ranges, including the high Pamir Mountains, with some of Asia's highest peaks, in the southeast. About 85% of the population lives in the lowland valleys. The country can be divided into four distinct regions: the Fergana Valley in the north; the Gissar and Vakhsh Valleys to the south; the Pamir Mountains in the east; and the

Turkmenistan, Zeravshan, and Gissar Ranges that run east to west in western Tajikistan. Tajikistan is a region of cotton monoculture, which in some parts of the country occupies 90% of all irrigated land. Cotton remains the most important cash crop in the mountain foothills, in the valleys, and even in mountain areas. The principal river is the Amu Darya, which is also called the Pyandzh in its upper course. ADMINISTRATIVE DIVISIONS: Three provinces or viloyotho (singular—viloyat), a central region, including the capital, which is under direct republican government authority, and an autonomous oblast, Badakshoni Kuni, in the southeast. POLITICAL STATUS: Tajikistan was recognized as an independent state in 1991.

INDEPENDENCE DECLARATION: 9 September 1991 (from the Soviet Union).

FLAG: The Tajik national flag, the official flag of the republic, is a horizontal tricolor of red, white, and green bearing a gold crown surmounted by seven five-pointed stars centered on the white stripe.

PEOPLE: Ethnically, Tajikistan occupies a kind of bridge between the Turkic and Persian worlds. While the Tajik nation is related to the Iranians, historically Tajikistan has formed part of Central Asia, where various ethnic groups occupied different economic niches. For many centuries bilingualism was seen as normal, not only among the intellectual elite but among the common people as well. Command of three or four different languages is not exceptional. An extremely high birthrate continues to rapidly increase the Tajik population, which grew 45% in the decade between the last two Soviet censuses, 1979–89.

Tajik (including Yagnobi, Pamiri)—an estimated 65.7% of the population, numbering about 4,045,000.

The Tajiks are an Iranian people believed to be descended from Central Asia's pre-Turkic inhabitants. The three major divisions—the majority Tajik, the Yagnobi in the center and east, and the Pamiri in the southeast—speak distinct languages. The Tajiks speak a West Iranian language, the Yagnobi speak an East Iranian language thought to derive from ancient Sogdian, and the Pamiris speak several different dialects collectively called the Pamiri dialects that form part of the East Iranian language group. The Tajik language, called Tajiki or Galcha, is closely related to modern Iranian, and is spoken in four groups of small dialects with no distinct boundaries. The language is written in the Russian Cyrillic alphabet. Considered the most conservative of the Central Asian peoples, the Tajiks are mostly Sunni Muslim, with smaller numbers of Shi'a and Ismaili Muslims, mostly in the Pamir Mountains in the southeast.

Uzbek—an estimated 24.6% of the population, numbering about 1,515,000.

The Uzbeks are a Turkic people, more numerous across the border in Uzbekistan. Formerly the dominant people in Central Asia, the Uzbeks live mostly in northern Tajikistan and in the Fergana Valley. The Uzbeks, formerly called Sarts, were a settled people, while the Tajiks were still nomadic herdsmen and may have been of ethnic Tajik origin. In the 1920s many ethnic Uzbeks were registered as Tajiks, and many Tajiks were forced to register as Uzbeks.

The language spoken by the Uzbeks, and by many Tajiks, is an East Turkic language of the Turkic groups of languages. The Uzbek language is used as a lingua franca throughout much of Central Asia. The Uzbeks, like the Tajiks, are generally Sunni Muslims.

Yagnobi (counted as ethnic Tajik)—an estimated 13.1% of the population, numbering about 805,000.

The Yagnobi are an ancient people thought to be the direct descendants of the ancient Sogdians. Originally the Yagnobi inhabited the high mountain valley of the Yagnob River, but in the 1960s many were resettled in southern Tajikistan, forced to leave their cool mountain valleys for the irrigated desert plains.

The language of the Yagnobi is an Eastern Iranian language, more closely related to Dari, the predominant language of Afghanistan, than to Tajiki. The language is spoken in two dialects, Western and Eastern, but the literary language of the Yagnobi is Tajiki. Unlike the majority Tajiks, the Yagnobi are mostly Shi'a Muslims.

Russian—an estimated 3.1% of the population, numbering about 190,000.

The Russian population of Tajikistan, which has fallen from some 13% of the total population in 1979, is concentrated in Dushanbe and the towns of the Fergana Valley. Mostly settled in the region during and after World War II, the Russians came to Tajikistan as administrators and workers, largely in the more industrialized cities of the northern districts.

Since independence in 1991, thousands of Russians have left the republic for Russia.* Many left during the civil war, which the ethnic Russians were not directly involved in, but which threatened their safety and economic well-being.

Pamiri (Badakshani) (counted as ethnic Tajik)—an estimated 2.8% of the population, numbering about 175,000.

The Pamiris, who inhabit the high-altitude valleys of the Pamir Mountains, are made up of a number of small tribal or clan groups, speaking different languages and with different traditions, but historically united by their isolation, their occupation as herdsmen, and their hostility to the Tajik lowlanders.

They also share their religion, Ismaili Islam, a breakaway sect of Shi'a Islam. They have no mosques, no clerics, and no weekly holy day. The spiritual leader of the Ismailis is the Aga Khan, a Swiss-born businessman and horse breeder revered by the Pamiris as a living god. The Aga Khan's charity has sustained the Pamiris and has kept starvation at bay since the Pamiris backed the losing side in the civil war that engulfed Tajikistan soon after independence.

The Pamiri dialects, the languages spoken in the Pamir valleys, include the major dialects of Shughni, Rushani, and Wakhi, each divided into a number of subdialects, all inherently intelligible. The dialects, which belong to the East Iranian group of languages, are closer to the Yagnobi language than to modern Tajiki, although Tajiki is used as the literary language.

Tatar—an estimated 1.7% of the population, numbering about 105,000.

The Tajiki Tatars, the descendants of Volga Tatars brought to the region during the colonial period as administrators and bureaucrats, mostly live in the northern districts and in the larger cities. Many Tatars still hold government positions in the national and local administrations.

The Tatars, who speak a West Turkic language, are mostly bilingual, also speaking Russian and often Uzbek or Tajik. Most are Sunni Muslims, with an Orthodox Christian minority.

Kyrgyz—an estimated 1.6% of the population, numbering about 98,000.

The Kyrgyz are concentrated in the northern districts along the border with the Kyrgyz Republic and in Tajikistan's sector of the multiethnic Fergana Valley. The Kyrgyz, part of the Kyrgyz nation of Kyrgyzstan, speak a Turkic language and are mostly Sunni Muslims.

Ukrainian—an estimated 1% of the population, numbering about 61,000.

The Ukrainian population, the second largest of the Slav groups, mostly live in Dushanbe and the larger cities. The majority came to the region as industrial workers and government employees during the Soviet period. Since independence in 1991 over 30,000 Ukrainians have left Tajikistan to return to Ukraine* or Russia.

Persian (Iranian)—estimated at less than 1% of the population, numbering about 31,000.

The Iranian population of Tajikistan is largely rural. The majority work on collective farms, mostly in the southern districts. Their language, Western Farsi, is spoken by only about 30% as the first language, as most are bilingual in Tajiki, which is closely related to the Farsi dialect. The Iranians are Shi'a Muslims, but are less religious than their kin in the Islamic Republic of Iran.

The Persians, although closely related to the Tajiks, have retained their ancient culture and dialect and have not assimilated into the larger Tajik culture. Thought to be the descendants of the ancient peoples of the region, they are among the region's least developed national groups.

Korean—estimated at less than 1% of the population, numbering about 23,000.

The Korean population, which is falling due to immigration to South Korea, is descended from Koreans deported from the border regions of the Soviet Far East during the Stalin era. Dumped at rail sidings across Central Asia, many of the Koreans perished due to hunger and exposure. The survivors make up the largest Buddhist population in Tajikistan.

Turkmen (Turkomen)—estimated at less than 1% of the population, numbering about 18,000.

The Turkmen, more numerous in the neighboring Republic of Turkmenistan,* are a Turkic people related to the other Turkic peoples of Central Asia. Noted horsemen, the Turkmen were the last to surrender to the Russian colonial forces. The Turkmen population is spread from Chinese Turkestan west to Iraq and Turkey.

The language spoken by the Turkmen, a South Turkic language of the Turkic language group, is related to Turkish and Azeri, languages spoken farther west. The Turkmen, like the Tajiks, are mostly Sunni Muslims.

Pakhtu (Pushtu)—estimated at less than 1% of the population, numbering about 13,000.

The Pakhtu or Pushtu are part of the large Pakhtu population that inhabits parts of Pakistan and Afghanistan. Their language, an East Iranian language, is used as the spoken language. However, in Tajikistan the Pakhtu use Tajiki as their literary language. The Pakhtu are Sunni Muslims.

Jew—estimated at less than 1% of the population, numbering about 11,000.

The Jews of Tajikistan, mostly living in Dushanbe, have been leaving the country in large numbers since the civil war began in 1992. The majority have immigrated to Israel or the United States.

The Jews, mostly Russian-speaking, settled in the region as workers or were deported to Central Asia during the Stalin era.

Kazakh—estimated at less than 1% of the population, numbering about 11,000.

The Kazakh population of Tajikistan, mostly living in the north of the country, is part of the larger Kazakh nation of the Republic of Kazakhstan.* A Turkic people closely related to the other Turkic peoples of Central Asia, the Kazakhs generally show more of their Mongol ancestry than the neighboring peoples. Most are Sunni Muslims.

Ossetian—estimated at less than 1% of the population, numbering about 10,000.

Deported from the North Caucasus region during World War II, the Ossetians are the descendants of the ancient Alans. The Ossetian language, an East Iranian language, is the only Iranian language spoken in the Caucasus Mountains of southern Russia. The Tajiki Ossetians are mostly Sunni Muslims, as the Muslim minority among the Ossetians was targeted for deportation during the Stalin era.

Bashkort (Bashkir)—estimated at less than 1% of the population, numbering about 7,000.

Called Bashkir by the Russians, the Bashkort are a people of mixed Finnic, Turkic, and Mongol ancestry. Part of the large Bashkort population that inhabits the Republic of Bashkortostan in the Russian Federation, most of the Bashkorts settled in the region since World War II.

A Sunni Muslim people, like the Tajiks, the Bashkorts mostly speak Russian and their own language. Many also speak Tatar. The Bashkort have retained their unique culture, although some Central Asian traditions and customs have been adopted.

Armenian—estimated at less than 1% of the population, numbering about 6,000.

The Armenians, concentrated in the Fergana Valley, are the descendants of deportees from the Caucasus during the colonial and Stalin eras. In Tajikistan the majority use Russian as their first language while maintaining their own language at home. The Armenians are Christians, mostly adhering to the separate Armenian Orthodox Church.

Baluch—estimated at less than 1% of the population, numbering about 5,000.

The Baluch or Baluchis living in Tajikistan mostly settled in the region during the colonial period, for the most part to escape persecution in Iran and Pakistan. The Baluch, part of a much larger population that straddles the borders of Iran, Pakistan, and Afghanistan, are mostly Sunni Muslims, with a Zikri Muslim minority.

Uighur—estimated at less than 1% of the population, numbering about 4,000.

More numerous across the border in Chinese Turkestan, the Uighur are a Turkic people related to the other Central Asian peoples. They speak an East Turkic language of the Turkic language group and are primarily Sunni Muslims. The majority settled in the region during the colonial era and after World War II, mostly fleeing persecution in China.

Arab—estimated at less than 1% of the population, numbering about 2,000.

The Arab population of Tajikistan live mostly in the southern part of the country, but some also live in the northern cities. They mostly speak Tajiki as their first language while retaining their traditional Arabic dialect, which is close to the Arabic spoken in Iraq and Syria. Their society tends to be very closed, and they rarely mix with other ethnic groups.

THE NATION: Inhabited as early as 3000 B.C., most of the area was included in the ancient regions of Bactria and Sogdiana. The region was conquered by the Persians between 550 and 525 B.C., and by the Greeks of Alexander the Great two centuries later. A Greco-Bactrian state emerged about 250 B.C. and expanded to eventually include parts of Afghanistan and India. Later included in successive Parthian and Persian empires, the region developed as part of the Silk Road, the ancient trade route between China and the Mediterranean.

Overrun by Muslim Arabs about A.D. 710, the population mostly adopted Islam, the earlier Persian religion, Zoroastrianism, surviving only in the high Pamir valleys. The merging of Arab and Persian cultures produced a great flowering of Tajik culture in the ninth and tenth centuries, which marked the beginning of a long Tajik literary tradition.

The Mongol and Turkic peoples of the Golden Horde conquered the region in the thirteenth century. The devastation and massacres of the Mongol conquest ended the brilliant Tajik civilization. Dominated by Turkic successor states after the disintegration of the Golden Horde, the Tajiks had degenerated to a backward, tribal existence when the Turkic Uzbeks conquered the region in the sixteenth century. The Tajik lands were divided among the rule of various Uzbek khanates.

European Russian explorers and Cossacks began to penetrate the Uzbek khanates in the seventeenth century, the forerunners of Russia's colonial expansion. A Russian army invaded Central Asia in 1865, with the Tajik lands eventually divided between annexed Russian territory and the Uzbek emirate of Bukhara, declared a Russian protectorate in 1868. The divided Tajiks remained poor, economically exploited, and dominated by religious strictures. A small, educated elite, some 2% of the population, formed the first Tajik nationalist organization after the 1905 Russian Revolution.

The area was little affected by World War I until the authorities began to conscript Muslim minorities for labor battalions in 1916. A small nationalist movement emerged to lead the resistance to military conscription. In the aftermath of the Russian Revolution, in February 1917, the Tajiks formed a national government in the regions outside Bukhara and participated in the creation of a regional Muslim government in Turkestan.

Inspired by the Bolshevik coup that ended Russia's revolutionary democratic movement in October 1917, local Bolsheviks attempted to take power in the region, fervently opposed by the Muslim religious hierarchy and the nascent national movement. On 16 December 1917 the Uzbek-dominated Muslim government at Kokand declared independence from Russia, followed by a similar declaration by the Emirate of Bukhara a day later.

In spite of the declared independence of the states in nominal control of the Tajik homelands, the political situation in the region remained confused as Tajik, Uzbek, Bolshevik, and anti-Bolshevik groups fought for control. In 1921 the Bolsheviks had gained control of all but the mountainous regions where Tajik guerrillas, called Basmachi, held out against the victorious Communist forces until 1927.

The Soviet authorities divided Central Asia, collectively called Turkestan, into ethnic based provinces in 1924, with the Tajik state made a separate union republic and a member state of the Union of Soviet Socialist Republics in 1929. Even though the Tajiks suffered severe religious repression and periodic political purges, material and educational standards in Soviet Tajikistan rapidly surpassed those of their ethnic kin in Iran and Afghanistan.

Forced Soviet collectivization in 1929–31 sparked a serious revolt of the Tajik tribes. Another revolt broke out in 1941 following the command to change the Tajik literary language from the Persian alphabet to the Russians' Cyrillic alphabet. Soviet reprisals for the revolt, which took place during the war in Europe, created a leadership vacuum in the region that lasted into the 1950s and 1960s.

Tajikistan is the only former Soviet republic where regionalism developed under the cover of the Communist Party to the level of government policy. For over a half century the Soviet government allowed power to be controlled by representatives of one area or region. The clan system was used for its political leverage to accumulate wealth and power for the leaders of its local region in the north at the expense of the rest of the republic. The northern clan leaders sustained a system called "feudal socialism," a system of nepotism and corruption.

Two events shaped Tajik national consciousness in 1979: the Soviet invasion of neighboring Afghanistan and the Islamic Revolution in Iran. Tajik units sent to fight ethnic Tajiks in Afghanistan developed fervently anti-Soviet sentiments, often refusing direct orders to fight. In 1985 some eighty Tajik soldiers were shot for refusing to fire on their Tajik Afghan kin or fellow Muslims of other Afghan ethnic groups. The Islamic Revolution that overthrew the monarchy in Iran, led by Shi'a Muslim zealots, had a lesser effect on the more secular Soviet

Tajik population; nevertheless, the revolution augmented a reculturation and a renewed interest in the long suppressed Islamic religion.

The liberalization of Soviet society begun by Mikhail Gorbachev in 1987 was slow to take hold in the republic, which was ruled in a near feudal fashion by Communist Party bosses appointed by Moscow. The growth of national sentiment was provoked by disputes over water and land rights as well as the Tajik nationalist claims to the historic cities, claimed as traditionally Tajik urban centers, of Samarkand and Bukhara in neighboring Uzbekistan. The territorial dispute and growing disputes over the dwindling water supplies led to ethnic violence between Tajiks and Uzbeks in 1989–90.

In 1990 the republic had the lowest per capita income in the USSR, the highest rate of population growth, and the lowest standard of living. The least prepared for the rapid changes that overtook the Soviet Union, the leaders of the republic fought to maintain their power. As nationalism finally took hold in the republic, led by a popular front movement, Rasto-Khez, the Communist leaders converted to nationalism as a way to survive. On 25 August 1990 the republican leaders declared Tajikistan a sovereign state within the Soviet Union.

Initially hesitating, Tajikistan's Communist leaders reluctantly declared the republic independent on 9 September 1991 following the disintegration of the Soviet Union. Growing instability in the new state divided the population along political, religious, tribal, regional, and clan lines. In an effort to form a national government, the neo-Communists formed a coalition with a number of nationalist, religious, and regional political organizations.

In December 1991 the former Communists again took power as violence and instability spread. Large nationalist demonstrations in Dushanbe, in April and May 1992, finally forced the neo-Communist Tajik government to share power with the nationalist and religious groups. The Tajik Islamic political party was the largest in Central Asia. Civil war broke out in May 1992, just nine months after the dissolution of the Soviet Union. By January 1993, more than half a million people had fled from the fighting in the southwestern region of the country. Between 20,000 and 40,000 died in the first year of the war.

In early 1993 a cease-fire and the presence of a 25,000-strong, mostly Russian, peacekeeping force ended the major battles, although sporadic fighting continued between government forces and opposition fighters in strategic areas. Real peace proved elusive, in spite of Russian, Western, and UN negotiated cease-fires and peace talks.

Most of the tension in Tajikistan continued to be fueled by regional differences and the fact that the government was dominated by two clans, those from the regions of Kulob and Khujand, the most powerful of the pro-Communist groups. At the same time, tensions between Tajiks and ethnic Uzbeks, as well as between Tajiks and Afghan refugees, have mounted in certain regions of the country. The government and the opposition had engaged in United Nations–sponsored peace negotiations since April 1994, and another agreement on cessation of hostilities was signed on 17 September 1994.

On 6 November 1994, Imomali Rakhmonov, a Kulabi, was elected president of the republic in a nationwide election marred by fear and flagrant fraud. A week later, the Tajik government and the opposition held their first meeting in Dushanbe. The government, purged of the Khujand clan, became dominated by the Kulabis, headed by the country's president.

In December 1996, under Russian auspices, the Tajik government and the opposition began a series of negotiations. The issues, including regional autonomy, power sharing, and religious and language questions, were mostly set aside in the interests of agreements that would end the fighting.

A peace accord, signed on 27 June 1997, by President Rakhmonov and the leader of the united opposition, Sayid Adbullo Nuri, created a power-sharing arrangement and legalized some of the previously banned political parties and movements that formed the Islamic Revival Movement in 1993. In 1996 the movement was renamed the United Tajik Opposition (UTO) to more clearly demonstrate its composition of both religious and secular political groups.

The country, its independence demonstrated by its own flag, a national airline, and a scattering of embassies abroad, is the least developed, politically or economically, of the former Soviet republics. The northern districts are part of Uzbekistan in all but name, the mountainous Pamir region remains virtually cut off from the rest of the country, and a hard-line Communist government remains, supported by a Soviet-style bureaucracy and military.

Tajikistan survives on the credits and loans granted it by the Russian Federation, partly to ensure the security of the large Slav population. The country has experienced three changes of government since 1991, and deeply rooted regional and clan animosities remain a powerful force. In August 1997, in spite of the new truce agreement, fighting again broke out, and for almost two weeks soldiers loyal to President Imomali Rakhmonov fought a renegade warlord and his troops. The fighting, stemming from a power struggle between feuding clans within the Tajik government, demonstrated the fragile nature of the truce.

The meetings between Tajik President Imomali Rakhmonov and the leader of the United Tajik Opposition (UTO), Said Abdullo Nuri, in Afghanistan in early December 1997, and later in Moscow, were seen as positive indications that the Tajik conflict may finally be coming to an end. However, the road to real peace will be long and difficult. Already, in early 1998, leading officials on both sides were expressing their doubts.

Arms were indiscriminately passed out to anyone willing to fight during the civil war of 1992–97, so that the country is awash with weapons. Government efforts to disarm the various groups have mostly been unsuccessful, and future political conflicts will always have the threat of armed intervention hanging over them.

SELECTED BIBLIOGRAPHY:

Atkin, Muriel. *The Subtlest Battle: Islam in Soviet Tajikistan.* 1989.
Conquest, Robert, ed. *The Last Empire: Nationality and the Soviet Future.* 1986.

Djalili, Mohammad Reza, ed. *Tajikistan: The Trials of Independence*. 1998.
Ghasimi, Reza, ed. *Tajikistan*. 1994.
Mandelbaum, Michael, ed. *Central Asia and the World: Kazakhstan, Uzbekistan, Tajikistan, Kyrgyzstan, and Turkmenistan*. 1994.

TURKMENISTAN

Turkmenia; Turkomenistan;
Republic of Turkmenistan

CAPITAL: Ashgabat (Ashkhabad)

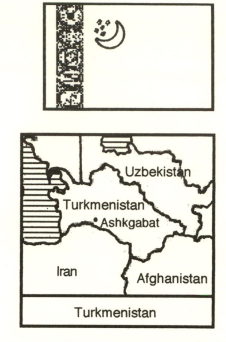

POPULATION: (98e) 4,436,000 : 3,260,000 Turkmen (Turkomen) in Turkmenistan and another 4 million in Uzbekistan,* Kazakhstan,* Iran, Afghanistan, Turkey, and Iraq. MAJOR NATIONAL GROUPS: (98e) Turkmen (Turkomen) 73.5%, Uzbek 9.9%, Russian 7.6%, Kazakh 3.1%, Tatar 1.8%, Ukrainian 1.1%, Azeri, Armenian, Baluchi, Lezgi, Belarussian, Mordvin, Karakalpak, Korean, Kurd, Jew, Bashkort. MAJOR LANGUAGES: Turkmen, Russian, Uzbek. MAJOR RELIGIONS: Sunni Islam, Shi'a Islam, Russian Orthodox, Jewish. MAJOR CITIES: (98e) Ashgabat (Ashkhabad) 427,000 (530,000), Chärjew (Chardzhou) 178,000 (220,000), Dashowuz (Tashauz) 124,000, Mary (Merv) 98,000, Nebitdag (Nebit-Dag) 95,000, Urfa (Krasnovodsk) 66,000, Bayramaly (Bayram-Ali) 57,000, Gyzylarbat (Kizyl-Arvat) 52,000, Tedzhenstroy (Tedzhen) 50,000, Kerki 35,000 (55,000), Kum Dag (Kum-Dag) 30,000, Iolotan 30,000, Chelenken 20,000 (35,000).

GEOGRAPHY: AREA: 188,455 sq.mi.-488,255 sq.km. LOCATION: Turkmenistan lies in south Central Asia, bordering the Caspian Sea on the west, Iran and Afghanistan on the south, Uzbekistan on the north, and Kazakhstan on the northwest. PHYSICAL GEOGRAPHY: Around 85% of the land area of the republic consists of the Garagum (Kara Kum) Desert, with some fertile lands and a string of oases in the south. The western and central parts of the republic are level desert lands. The eastern part of the country is a plateau region. The only significant upland areas are along the southern and eastern borders. The country's major river is the Amu Darya, which flows along the Uzbek border in the north. Other important rivers are the Murghab in the southeast and the Tedzhen. The majority of the population is concentrated in the oases at the foot of the Kopet Dagh Mountains. ADMINISTRATIVE DIVISIONS: Six provinces or welayatlar (singular—welayat). POLITICAL STATUS: Turkmenistan was recognized as an independent state in 1991.

INDEPENDENCE DECLARATION: 27 October 1991 (from the Soviet Union).

FLAG: The Turkmen national flag, the official flag of the republic, is a green field charged with a white crescent moon and five stars on the upper hoist near a vertical strip of pale red bearing five white, black, and orange *guls*, an asymmetrical carpet design, which represent the five major tribal divisions of the Turkmen nation.

PEOPLE: The majority of the population of Turkmenistan lives in the Transcaspian region in the west and in the fertile lands and oases in the south. Nearly half of the Turkmen nation lives outside the republic; large Turkmen populations are found across the republic's borders in the adjacent states and as far away as Turkey and Iraq. The largest non-Turkmen populations, with the exception of the Russians and the other Slav peoples, are related Turkic peoples, Uzbek, Kazakh, and Tatar.

Turkmen (Turkomen)—an estimated 73.5% of the population, numbering about 3,260,000.

The Turkmen, also called Turkomen, are a Central Asian people, descendants of early Caucasian tribal groups and later Orguz Turks, many retaining the light hair and light eyes of their ancient Caucasian ancestors. The Turkmen, the most traditional of the Central Asian peoples, are divided along tribal lines, the largest divisions being the Tekes of Mary, the Tekes of Attok, the Ersaris, the Yomuds, and the Goklans, all further divided into clans and family groups.

The Turkmen tribes and clans all speak dialects of the same Orguz Turkic language of the West Altaic language group. The Turkmen language is spoken in at least eleven separate dialects and is written in the Cyrillic alphabet.

The majority of the Turkmen population is Sunni Muslim, with a substantial Shi'a Muslim minority concentrated in the border regions with Iran and Afghanistan. Iran has not attempted to extend its Islamic Revolution to the new states of Central Asia.

Uzbek—an estimated 9.9% of the population, numbering about 440,000.

The Uzbek population of Turkmenistan is concentrated in the western districts of the country, particularly the region along the coast of the Caspian Sea and in the cities and towns, particularly Ashgabat. There are also large Uzbek populations in the northern region along the Uzbek border.

Speaking a Western Turkic language, the Uzbeks are mostly Sunni Muslims. Turkmen memories of Uzbek domination prior to the Russian colonial period have, at times, threatened the relations between the two largest groups in the republic.

Russian—an estimated 7.6% of the population, numbering about 337,000.

The Russians of Turkmenistan, living mainly in Ashgabat and the other large cities in the south of the country, mostly settled in the region after World War II. Brought to Turkmenistan to oversee the important cotton production and to work in the new industries, very few of the Russians bothered to learn the language or to understand Turkmen culture. The Russian population is the largest of the European peoples living in the republic.

Since 1991 thousands of ethnic Russians have left the republic to return to Russia.* However, Russian skills and technology are vitally important to the republic, and the government has begun to implement programs that will reassure the Slavs that they have a future in Turmenistan.

Kazakh—an estimated 3.1% of the population, numbering about 137,000.

The Kazakhs living in Turkmenistan are concentrated in the western part of the country. Most are herdsmen and farmers in the fertile lands east of the Caspian Sea. Many of the Kazakhs are nomadic or semi-nomadic, freely crossing the international border between Kazakhstan and Turkmenistan with their herds.

A Turkic people related to the Turkmen, the Kazakhs more closely resemble their Mongol ancestors than the Turkmens, and ethnic confrontations have increased since 1991. The Kazakhs are mostly Sunni Muslims.

Tatar—an estimated 1.8% of the population, numbering about 83,000.

The Tatars, living in the southern districts and in the fertile regions in the north, mostly settled in the region during colonial times as administrators and overseers. Sunni Muslims like the newly conquered Central Asians, the Tatars became middlemen between the Muslims and the Russian government.

Ukrainian—an estimated 1.1% of the population, numbering about 48,000.

Concentrated in the southern districts, particularly around Ashgabat, the Ukrainian population comprises the second largest Slav Christian people in the republic. The majority of the Ukrainians in the republic speak Russian as their first language, although Ukrainian has gained momentum since the independence of Ukraine* in 1991.

Azeri (Azerbaijani)—estimated at less than 1% of the population, numbering about 37,000.

Most of the Azeris in Turkmenistan live along the Caspian Sea coast in the west of the country, opposite the Republic of Azerbaijan* on the opposite shore.

The Azeris share with the Turkmen their Turkic language and culture and their Sunni Islam religion. However, disputes over Caspian Sea oil have soured relations between the two republics, and ethnic tensions are rising. The majority of the Azeris in Turkmenistan are Sunni Muslim Northern Azeris, unlike the Southern Azeris, who are mostly Shi'a Muslims.

Armenian—estimated at less than 1% of the population, numbering about 31,000.

Most of the Armenians in Turkmenistan, the majority of whom were deported to the region during the Stalin era, live in the larger towns and cities in the south and east of the country. The Armenian population, mostly belonging to the Armenian Orthodox Church, also includes a Muslim minority called Khemsils or Khemshins.

Baluch (Baluchi)—estimated at less than 1% of the population, numbering about 28,000.

The Baluch or Baluchi, living in the eastern districts of the republic, are part of a larger Baluch population that straddles the borders of Iran, Afghanistan, and Pakistan. They mostly settled in the region during the colonial period, fleeing wars and persecution in their homelands.

The Baluch of Turkmenistan are often called Western Baluch. They speak the Western Baluch dialect, and in Turkmenistan the Turkmen language is used as the literary language. The majority are Sunni Muslim, with a Zikri Muslim minority.

Lezgi (Lezgian)—estimated at less than 1% of the population, numbering about 13,000.

The Lezgi or Lezgians are a Caucasian people originally from the Dagestan Republic region of the Russian Federation. A Sunni Muslim people, the Lezgians speak a Caucasian language unrelated to either Russian or the Turkic languages of Central Asia.

The majority of the Lezgi were deported to Central Asia during World War II along with many other Muslim minorities suspected by Stalin of disloyalty. Although the whole Lezgi nation was not deported like the other peoples, many Lezgi leaders and anti-Communists were included in the brutal deportations.

Belarussian—estimated at less than 1% of the population, numbering about 5,000.

The Belarussians, the third largest of the Slav peoples in the republic, mostly live in Ashgabat and the other southern cities. Like the Russians and Ukrainians, they came to the region as workers during the postwar era. The majority of the Belarussians living in Turkmenistan speak Russian as their first language.

Mordvin—estimated at less than 1% of the population, numbering about 3,000.

The Mordvins, more numerous in the Mordvin Republic of the Russian Federation, are a Finnic people mostly settled in the region during and after World War II. Many are the descendants of anti-Communist or anti-Stalin deportees. The majority are Orthodox and speak Russian as their first language while retaining their own Finnic language as the language of the national group. Their language, Ezrya, is one of the two dialects spoken by the Mordvin nation.

Karakalpak—estimated at less than 1% of the population, numbering about 3,000.

The Karakalpak, the smallest of the Central Asian peoples, are concentrated in Uzbekistan, but with a substantial population across the border in Turkmenistan. Also called Tudzit, the Karakalpaks include in their ancestry Orguz and Kipchak Turks, Mongols, and Iranian peoples. Their language, of the West Turkic group, is classed by some scholars as a dialect of Kazakh.

Korean—estimated at less than 1% of the population, numbering about 3,000.

The Koreans of Turkmenistan, the majority of them the descendants of deportees from the Russian Far East, live mostly in the southern regions. The only large Buddhist population in the republic, the Koreans have, since independence, been useful in opening relations with South Korea and in persuading that country to grant Turkmenistan aid and to invest in its economy.

Kurd—estimated at less than 1% of the population, numbering about 3,000.

The Kurds, part of the larger Kurd nation that straddles the Turkish, Iraqi, and Iranian borders, live mostly in the western districts. A Sunni Muslim people, the Kurds speak a language that belongs to the Iranian group of languages.

Jew—estimated at less than 1% of the population, numbering about 2,000.

The Jews, part of a declining population due to emigration, live mostly in Ashgabat. They were settled in the region after World War II, and most speak Russian as their first language. Since 1991 many Jews have left the region for Russia or have immigrated to Israel or the United States.

Bashkort (Bashkir)—estimated at less than 1% of the population, numbering about 2,000.

The Bashkort, called Bashkir by the Russians, are part of the large Bashkort population of the Bashkortostan Republic of the Russian Federation. Mostly settled in the region during the colonial era, the Bashkort are a Sunni Muslim people. They speak a Turkic language and have little problem assimilating into Turkmen society.

THE NATION: The early inhabitants of the region, known in Arab and Hindu legends as the birthplace of the Aryan race, were Caucasian tribes living in the fertile oases, where a settled agricultural civilization developed. In the sixth century B.C., the territory was under the rule of the Persian dynasty of the Achaeminids, who ordered several powerful fortresses constructed in the region.

Conquered by the Greeks of Alexander the Great in the third century B.C., the region came into contact with the Mediterranean civilizations farther west. The Greeks founded cities, and Greek soldiers settled the region, taking wives from the native tribes. From about 225 B.C. most of the Turkmen lands formed part of the Greek-influenced Bactrian kingdom before again coming under the rule of the Parthian Empire of the Persians.

The Parthians, rivals of Rome for domination of the Middle East, fought long wars with the expanding Roman Empire. In 53 B.C. 10,000 Roman prisoners, captured by the Parthians during battles with the Romans, were transported to the region and settled at Merv, then called Margian. The region, forming part of the ancient Persian Empire, remained the domain of nomadic tribes, with a Persianized settled population in the oases.

Muslim Arabs, invading from the south, overran the settled communities in A.D. 651. The Caucasian population converted to Islam, and their homeland was joined to the Muslim empire, the Caliphate. Merv (Mary), the seat of Arab administration for a large part of Persia and Central Asia, became one of the major centers of Arab learning and Arab-Persian Muslim culture.

Turkish tribes of the Orguz Confederation conquered the area in 821 and took control of the important trade routes crossing the territory. In the eleventh and twelfth centuries the oasis settlements were important stops on the Silk Route. The Turks made the city of Merv the center of the Seljuk Empire from 1118 to 1157, when the majority of the Turkish tribes migrated farther west. The remaining Turkish tribes continued to dominate the region, their language and tribal system imposed on the Caucasian oasis dwellers.

The Mongol hordes invaded the area in 1219–22, destroying the extensive irrigation system and slaughtering, according to Turkmen legends, over a million people. Their agricultural civilization decimated, the survivors gathered in tribal groups that spread across the region as nomadic herders, later renowned as horsemen and warriors. Expanding from their oasis centers, the Turkmen conquered a huge area that formed a loose empire stretching as far west as Armenia and Azerbaijan from 1378 to 1502. The Turkmen populations of Turkey, Iraq, and other regions far from the Turkmen heartland date from this period.

Turkic Uzbeks subjugated all of Central Asia in the sixteenth century. Their empire soon split into several states, the most powerful the Khanate of Khiva and the Emirate of Bukhara. The Turkmen inhabiting lands claimed by the Uzbek states resisted for over two centuries, the last Turkmen tribes coming under the rule of Khiva only in the early nineteenth century.

The first Russian expedition into Turkmenistan was sent by Peter the Great. The members of the expedition, seeking a route for Russian trade with southern Asia and the Middle East, were murdered by Turkmen tribesmen near Khiva in 1716. Thirty-one years later, in 1747, the first diplomatic contacts between Moscow the Uzbek-dominated Emirate of Bukhara were finally established.

Only in 1802 did several of the Turkmen clans officially become Russian subjects. During the nineteenth century, the Turkmen tribes accepted Russian aid during their frequent rebellions against the authority of Khiva and Bukhara. In June 1865 Russian forces took control of the Uzbek city of Tashkent, and in 1867 the Governorate-General of Turkestan was created with Tashkent as its capital. In 1868 the Emirate of Bukhara became a Russian protectorate.

The Khanate of Khiva, weakened by ethnic disputes and Russian incursions, lost control of the Turkmen land in the mid-nineteenth century. Led by the powerful Teke tribes, the Turkmen began to erect an independent state in the Transcaspian region. In 1869 a Russian army invaded Turkmenistan, meeting the fiercest resistance and suffering the greatest losses of the campaign to win control of Central Asia. The Russians established a fort in Turkmen territory at Krasnovodsk on the Caspian Sea. The western clans, fearing a return of Uzbek rule, willingly accepted Russian rule, but the southern and eastern clans resisted Russian annexation. In 1880 the Khanate of Khiva also became a Russian protectorate, extending Russian claims to the remainder of the Turkmen lands.

In January 1881 the Russian slaughter of Turkmen tribesmen at the Battle of Gok-Tepe allowed the Russians to colonize much of the region and to create the Transcaspian province in the region south and west of the vassal states of Bukhara and Khiva. In 1884 Russian forces occupied the Merv oasis, officially completing the conquest of Turkmenistan. However, Turkmen warriors continued to fight the Russian conquest until finally defeated in 1895.

The turbulent Turkmen lands, added to the Russian province of Turkestan, remained the least developed, poorest, and most backward region of Central Asia. Frequent revolts and disputes over lands and water resources were endemic, Russian authority extending only to the main towns, garrisoned oases, and the strategic Russian military forts.

Virtually untouched by World War I until the attempted conscription of Muslims into labor battalions in 1916, the Turkmen rebelled rather than serve the hated Russian soldiers. Led by Dzhunaid Khan, the Turkmen took control of the vassal state of Khiva and established a national government. The Turkmen revolt, overtaken by the Russian Revolution in 1917, ended as the Russian civil government collapsed and the Turkmen were left effectively independent. Participating in a joint Muslim government of Turkestan, the Turkmen supported an autonomous Muslim state in Central Asia.

In the wake of the Bolshevik coup that overthrew Russia's brief democratic government in October 1917, the anti-Bolshevik Russian White forces formed a provisional government of Transcaspia at Ashkhabad (Ashgabat), refusing to recognize the Turkmen nationalist aspirations. Led by the Turkmen national hero, Oraz Serder, the Turkmen fought the Whites until Bolshevik troops invaded the region in 1918. Alienated by the Bolsheviks' opposition to their Muslim religion, the Turkmen reluctantly formed an alliance with the Whites. In July 1918 the soldiers of the White government of Transcaspia captured Ashkabad from the forces of the Tashkent Soviet. Threatened by the Red forces, the Whites appealed to the British forces in Persia for assistance, and a British force occupied much of the region. The British withdrew in February 1919.

The Turkmen tribes allied to the Whites shared the Whites' defeat in July 1919, and all of Turkmenistan came under Soviet rule. Unreconciled to harsh Soviet rule, the Turkmen formed guerrilla bands called Basmachi in 1921. The last of the Turkmen Basmachis were defeated and destroyed by the Red Army in 1924.

The Soviet authorities divided Central Asia along ethnic lines in October 1924. The Turkmen republic was formed from the former Transcaspian government, the Charijui vilayet of Bukhara, and part of the Khanate of Khiva. The ethnic Turkmen state was admitted to the Soviet Union as a constituent republic in 1925. In the 1930s, Turkmen nomads, labeled parasites, were forced in bloody battles to settle on Soviet collectives.

Far from the centers of Soviet power, over the next decades the republic was ruled by Communist appointees whose only qualifications were unquestioning loyalty to the Soviet hierarchy. Wielding almost feudal power, the Communist bureaucrats systematically looted the republic, earning themselves the derisive appellation "Turkmen Mafia." In 1937–38 Stalin systematically purged the Muslim Communist leaders of Central Asia.

In 1948 a massive earthquake destroyed much of the Turkmen capital, killing an estimated 110,000 people. For five years the region was closed to foreigners while bodies were recovered and the wreckage cleared. Meanwhile, the cultivation of cotton was extended to the most fertile region of the republic, ravaging the environment and endangering public health in the 1960s and 1970s.

The Communist hierarchy of the Turkmen Soviet Socialist Republic, based on clan, family, and influence ties, that dominated the republican government was notorious for corruption, but loyalty to Moscow counted for much more than capability. Saparmurad Niyazov became head of the Turkmen Communist Party in 1985 and led the republic during the era of the Gorbachev reforms of the late 1980s.

In early 1990 there was a sudden upsurge of national sentiment as the campaigns for the first open elections began. In spite of the close vigilance of the authoritarian government, open discussion of such formerly forbidden subjects as nationalism, language, environment, and social conditions animated the elections. A popular front group, Ogzibirlik (National Unity), was formed, and led a campaign to recall the entire Turkmen parliamentary delegation from Moscow for its extraordinary passivity.

The decentralization of the Soviet government, particularly in terms of giving more responsibility to the republics, only increased the hold of the Turkmen Communist government on the republic. The rapid reform of Soviet society culminated in the disintegration of the Soviet Union in August 1991. A 26 October 1991 referendum on independence, passed by 97%, pushed the reluctant Communist Turkmen government to finally declare Turkmenistan an independent republic on the following day, 27 October 1991. The head of state, Saparmurad Niyazov, became the republic's first president.

The government, as part of its Turkmenization of the republic, in 1992 changed Russian place names to Turkmen spellings and pronunciations. The status of the national language and the right to automatic citizenship are issues that still face the government. Turkmen nationalism, despite support for independence, having been dormant for decades, has only just begun to be felt in the state.

The Republic of Turkmenistan, a one-party state dominated by its president and his closest advisors, made little progress in moving from a Soviet-era authoritarian style of government to a democratic system. The Democratic Party, the renamed Communists, retained a monopoly on power and repressed all opposition political activities. Emphasizing stability and gradual reform, the efforts to construct a Turkmen nation focused on fostering nationalism and glorifying President Niyazov.

Politically, Turkmenistan has proved to be the most stable of the new Central Asian republics. The Turkmen are divided so that no credible challenge to the current leadership of the republic has formed. Although Islam is a powerful force, the Muslim clerics are not organized to a point where they might challenge the secular government, in spite of a large Shi'a Muslim minority and growing Iranian influence.

Iran is geographically very important to the republic, as it represents the only alternative land route to the West and the Persian Gulf apart from Russia. The Turkmen oil and natural gas will have to go through Iran, on the only available road and rail routes. Thus good relations with Iran will be important to Turkmenistan's future. Iran has been very cautious in attempting to export Islamic ideology to the region.

In July 1997, to diffuse a growing dispute over the oil-rich Caspian Sea, the Turkmen government proposed creating an international commission to delineate the dividing lines between the national territories. In October 1997, representatives of the two republics met to discuss dividing the Caspian Sea into national sectors. In November, international oil companies, in partnership with the Azerbaijani government, began petroleum production in the Kyapaz offshore field, which Turkmenistan claims is located in its sector.

By 1997, six years after independence, Turkmenistan's economic situation remained static. Economic reforms have made little headway, with the state continuing to dominate nearly all sectors of the economy. The country, in spite of a wealth of oil and natural gas, remains dependent on Russia for most of its trade.

SELECTED BIBLIOGRAPHY:

Allworth, Edward, ed. *Central Asia: One Hundred Thirty Years of Russian Dominance: A Historical Overview*. 1994.

Hall, Rachel A. *Turkmenistan*. 1994.

Mandelbaum, Michael, ed. *Central Asia and the World: Kazakhstan, Uzbekistan, Tajikistan, Kyrgyzstan, and Turkmenistan*. 1994.

Muller, Helga W., ed. *Turkmenistan*. 1994.

Thomas, Paul. *The Central Asian States: Tajikistan, Uzbekistan, Kyrgyzstan, Turkmenistan*. 1992.

UKRAINE

Ukrayina; Republic of Ukraine

CAPITAL: Kyyiv (Kiev)

POPULATION: (98e) 51,568,000 : 38,265,000 Ukrainians in Ukraine and another 12 million in Russia* and other former Soviet republics, Slovakia,* Poland, and Romania. MAJOR NATIONAL GROUPS: (98e) Ukrainian 74.2%, Russian 18.4%, Pole 2.4%, Jew, Belarussian, Moldovan, Rom (Gypsy), Crimean Tatar, Greek, Bulgarian, Hungarian, Romanian, Tatar, Armenian, German, Gagauz, Czech, Georgian, Slovak, Uzbek, Ossetian, Albanian. MAJOR LANGUAGES: Ukrainian, Russian, Romanian, Polish. MAJOR RELIGIONS: Ukrainian Orthodox and Ukrainian Autocephalous Orthodox 68%, Russian Orthodox 18%, Uniate 10%, Protestant 3%, Roman Catholic 1%, Jewish, Muslim. MAJOR CITIES: (98e) Kyyiv (Kiev) 2,698,000 (2,912,000), Kharkiv (Khar'kov) 1,640,000 (2,015,000), Dnipropetrovs'k (Dnepropetrovsk) 1,219,000 (1,692,000), Odesa (Odessa) 1,217,000 (1,377,000), Donecke (Donetsk) 1,120,000 (2,322,000), Zaporizhzhya (Zaporozh'ye) 902,000, L'viv (L'vov) 809,000, Kryvyy Rih (Krivoy Rog) 710,000, Mariupol' (Zhdanov) 536,000, Mykolayiv (Nikolayev) 521,000 (637,000), Luhans'k (Voroshilovgrad) 526,000, Makiyivka (Makeyevka) 462,000, Sevastopol 383,000, Kherson 367,000, Simferopol 352,000, Horlivka (Gorlovka) 347,000 (875,000), Vinnytsia (Vinnitsa) 327,000, Poltava 325,000, Cherkasy (Cherkassy) 311,000, Chernihiv (Chernigov) 310,000, Dniprodzerzyns'k (Dneprodzerzhinsk) 288,000, Kirovohrad (Kirovograd) 284,000, Sumy 276,000, Chernivtsi (Chernovsty) 269,000, Rivne (Rovno) 257,000 (322,000), Khmel'nyts'kyy (Khmelnitskiy) 254,000, Ivano-Frankivs'k (Ivano-Frankovsk) 251,000, Kremenchuk (Kremenchug) 235,000,

Ternopil' (Ternopol) 214,000, Bila Tserkva (Belaya Tserkov) 204,000, Kramators'k 203,000 (490,000).

GEOGRAPHY: AREA: 233,089 sq.mi.-603,857 sq.km. LOCATION: Ukraine lies in east-central Europe, bordering Belarus* on the northwest, Russia on the northeast and east, the Black Sea on the south, Moldova* and Romania on the southwest, and Hungary, Slovakia, and Poland on the west. PHYSICAL GEOGRAPHY: Ukraine lies in the southwestern part of the East European Plain, a vast undulating expanse bound by the Carpathian Mountains to the southwest and the Black Sea to the South. The Carpathian Mountain region is heavily forested, while the plain is sparsely wooded and the Black Sea Lowlands are completely flat steppe lands. In the northwest the country extends into the Great Pripyat Marshes. The flat plains, 95% of the total land area, have almost no natural boundaries. However, over 2,000 rivers and 3,000 lakes are included in the country's national territory. The steppe lands, the prairies, with fertile black soil, are exceptionally well suited to grain farming, which earned Ukraine the name "Breadbasket of Europe." Northern and western Ukraine are less flat, and include hilly, forested regions. The largest of the rivers are the Bug, Dnieper (Dnepr), Donets, Dniester (Dnestr), Prut, and Tisza. ADMINISTRATIVE DIVISIONS: twenty-four provinces or oblasti (singular—oblast'), one autonomous republic, the Republic of Crimea, and two independent municipalities with oblast' status, Kiev and Sevastopol. POLITICAL STATUS: Ukraine was recognized as an independent state in 1991.

INDEPENDENCE DECLARATIONS: UKRAINE: 22 January 1918 (from Russia); 24 August 1991 (from Soviet Union). WESTERN UKRAINE: 14 November 1918 (from Austria); 6 October 1941 (from the Soviet Union). CARPATHO UKRAINE: 2 March 1939 (from Czechoslovakia).

FLAG: The Ukrainian national flag, the official flag of the republic, is a horizontal bicolor of pale blue over yellow.

PEOPLE: Ukraine, which occupies the central position in the European continent, with the geographic center of Europe lying in the western Transcarpathia (Carpatho-Ukraine) region, has long been a crossroads between Europe and Asia. The mixed population of over one hundred national groups reflects Ukraine's position as a bridge between East and West. The low birthrate and small net immigration have caused a decline in the republic's population. The population is projected to continue to contract well into the twenty-first century. About two-thirds of the Ukrainian people are urban, while a third, large by European standards, remain rural.

Ukrainian—an estimated 74.2% of the population, numbering about 38,265,000.

The Ukrainians are a Slavic people, the second largest of the East Slav nations. An ancient people, for most of their history they have been under the rule of more powerful neighboring states. The Ukrainian culture and language survived in spite of intense pressure to assimilate into other cultures.

Their language, an East Slav language related to Russian and Belarussian, is spoken in three major dialects and is written in the Ukrainian Cyrillic alphabet. Although dialectical differences are slight, in the border regions the language has been influenced by neighboring languages, and most Ukrainians are bilingual in Russian.

The majority of the Ukrainians belong to the Orthodox churches, particularly the Ukrainian Orthodox churches banned from 1930 to 1990. In western Ukraine a large number are Uniate Eastern rite Catholics, or Roman Catholic.

Russian—an estimated 18.4% of the population, numbering about 9,485,000.

The largest of the republic's many non-Ukrainian national groups, the Russians are mostly urban industrial workers. The majority of the Russian population is concentrated in the eastern industrial oblasts and in the Crimean Peninsula, which formed part of Russia until 1954. Since Ukrainian independence in 1991 many people formerly counted as ethnic Russian, particularly those born of mixed marriages, now call themselves ethnic Ukrainians.

The Russian population of Ukraine, with a large number claiming no religion, is mostly Russian Orthodox. The Russian language, which is spoken throughout Ukraine as a lingua franca, is the second language of the majority of Ukraine's national groups.

Ruthene (Carpatho-Rusyn) (counted as ethnic Ukrainian)—an estimated 3% of the population, numbering about 1,550,000.

The Ruthenes, calling themselves Carpatho-Rusyn, are descended from Slavic tribes and earlier Ruthene tribes of unknown origin. The name Rusyn, an early designation for all Slavs, persisted in the isolated valleys of the Ruthenes' Carpathian Mountain homeland. Their homeland, which before World War I formed part of Hungary, was a province of Czechoslovakia from 1918 to 1945, when it was annexed by the Soviet Union and added to Soviet Ukraine.

The Rusyn language, although considered a dialect of Ukrainian, is difficult for Ukrainian speakers to understand. Standard Ukrainian is the literary language, and most Ruthenes are bilingual or trilingual, many also speaking Russian or Hungarian.

The Ruthenes, like the Western Ukrainians, are mostly Uniate Catholics, belonging to a separate Ruthene Uniate Church. Their religion forms an integral part of the Ruthenes' Carpathian culture. Since Ukrainian independence in 1991, a nationalist movement has gained support with calls for cultural, religious, and linguistic autonomy within the Ukrainian state.

Pole—an estimated 2.4% of the population, numbering about 1,237,000.

The Polish population of Ukraine, mostly concentrated in the former Polish territories in western Ukraine, is the second largest ethnic group in the western provinces, which have been contested by Russia and Poland for centuries. The Polish language, a West Slav language, as spoken in the Ukraine, has absorbed many East Slav traits and words.

The Poles form the largest Roman Catholic national group in Ukraine, although the Western Ukrainians' Uniate Church is also affiliated with Rome. The Poles, particularly since Ukrainian independence in 1991 and the loosening of restrictions, have looked to Warsaw for cultural and religious support.

Belarussian—estimated at less than 1% of the population, numbering about 360,000.

The Belarussian population, concentrated in the northwestern provinces, is part of the larger Belarussian nation in neighboring Belarus. The third largest of the East Slav peoples, the Belarussians speak a language related to Ukrainian, but many also speak Russian or Ukrainian. The majority are Orthodox, but there are also Roman Catholic and Uniate minorities.

Moldovan—estimated at less than 1% of the population, numbering about 310,000.

Officially, the Moldovans of Ukraine account for less than 1 percent of the population. However, Moldovan sources often cite figures for ethnic Moldovans and Romanians in Ukraine of up to 1 million. Living mostly in the southwestern provinces of Odesa and Chernivtsi, adjoining Moldova, the Moldovan population formed part of historic Moldova until parts of the region were transferred to Ukraine in 1945.

The Moldovan language is Romanian, although the distinction between the Romanians and Moldovans remains. In Ukraine the Moldovan language is written in the Cyrillic alphabet, although the use of the Latin alphabet is becoming more frequent.

Jew—estimated at less than 1% of the population, numbering about 265,000.

The Ukrainian Jews, mostly living in the large cities and towns in the central and southern provinces, are considered a separate national group. The majority of the Jews speak Russian as their first language. Immigration to Israel and the United States has decreased the numbers of Jews living in the state by nearly half since 1990.

Most of the Jews in the region were massacred during World War II by the Nazi occupiers and their Ukrainian allies. An estimated 750,000 Ukrainian Jews were killed in the Holocaust.

Rom (Gypsy)—estimated at less than 1% of the population, numbering about 258,000.

The Rom or Gypsies of Ukraine, often called Ungrike Romá or Hungarian Gypsies, are concentrated in the western provinces and Transcarpathia. The most prevalent dialect, called Carpathian Romani, is spoken in eastern Hungary, southern Poland, and western Ukraine. A minority belong to the Kalderash group, called Volóxuja, Kalderari, Sárvi, or Lóvari in Ukraine. Along with the Rom dialects, the majority also speak Hungarian, Russian, or Ukrainian.

The Gypsy population, usually adopting the majority religion, are mostly Uniate Christians, with an Orthodox minority. Thousands of Ukrainian Rom were massacred by the Nazis and their Ukrainian allies during World War II.

Crimean Tatar—estimated at less than 1% of the population, numbering about 185,000.

The Crimean Tatars, the original inhabitants of the Crimean Peninsula, were deported during World War II for allegedly collaborating with the Nazi invaders of the Soviet Union. Dumped at rail sidings across Central Asia, thousands died of hunger and exposure. Forbidden to return to their homeland until Ukrainian independence in 1991, by late 1996 about 5,000 a month were returning to the peninsula from Uzbekistan,* Kyrgyzstan,* and the other states of former Soviet Central Asia.

The Crimean Tatar nation includes three distinct divisions united by culture, history, and adversity. The largest, the Tatars, the descendants of the peninsula's original inhabitants, are a Sunni Muslim people speaking a Turkic language related to Turkish. The Krymchaks, numbering about 60,000, were formerly the inhabitants of the mainland region adjacent to the Crimean Peninsula. The Karaites or Karaim, numbering about 30,000, speak a distinctive dialect and practice an archaic form of Judaism.

Greek—estimated at less than 1% of the population, numbering about 226,000.

The Greek population of Ukraine are the descendants of ancient and medieval Greek colonies in the southern provinces and the Crimean Peninsula. In the latter half of the eighteenth century, following Russia's conquest of the region, most of the Greek population was uprooted and resettled in the region around the city of Mariupol, which was founded in 1778 and named for the Virgin Mary. Over half of Ukraine's Greek population still lives around the city.

The Greeks, while retaining their own archaic Greek dialects, also speak Russian or Ukrainian. The majority belong to the Greek Orthodox Church, although during the years of Soviet rule many joined the official Russian Orthodox Church.

Bulgarian—estimated at less than 1% of the population, numbering about 224,000.

The Ukrainian Bulgarians mostly live in the southern region, particularly in Odesa, Kherson, and Mykolayiv provinces. The descendants of Bulgarian Slavs invited to settle the newly conquered region in the late eighteenth and early nineteenth centuries, the Bulgarians are a South Slav people who speak a separate Slav language. However, many are bilingual in Russian or Ukrainian.

Magyar (Hungarian)—estimated at less than 1% of the population, numbering about 178,000.

The Magyar or Hungarian population of Ukraine lives mostly in the southwestern Transcarpathia region bordering Hungary and Slovakia. Mostly settled in the region when it formed part of the Austro-Hungarian Empire, the Hungarians remained after the breakup of the Hungarian kingdom after World War I.

Following independence in 1991, the Ukrainian government agreed to grant autonomy to the Magyar population, which increasingly looks west to Budapest for economic and cultural aid. The Hungarian language, a Finno-Ugrian language, is spoken in a distinct Transcarpathian dialect, but in recent years the use of standard Hungarian has increased.

Mostly Roman Catholic, but with important Uniate and Protestant minorities, the Ukrainian Hungarians have retained religion as an integral part of their separate mountain culture. There is a strong movement for Hungarian autonomy within the Ukrainian state.

Romanian—estimated at less than 1% of the population, numbering about 152,000.

The Romanian population is concentrated in the historically Romanian regions of Bukovina and southern Bessarabia, which were incorporated into the USSR in 1940. The Romanians and Moldovans form one people, but in Ukraine the Romanians have closer ties to Romania and use the Latin alphabet, while the Moldovans look to Moldova and use the Cyrillic alphabet.

Tatar—estimated at less than 1% of the population, numbering about 103,000.

The Tatars of Ukraine live mostly in the southern provinces and are the descendants of the Tatars who once controlled most of Ukraine. Like their kin, the Crimean Tatars, most are Sunni Muslims and speak a Turkish dialect.

Armenian—estimated at less than 1% of the population, numbering about 54,000.

The Armenian population, mostly living in the towns and cities of the southeastern provinces, are part of the larger Armenian nation of the Transcaucasus region. Since the dissolution of the USSR many ethnic Armenians have returned to the newly independent Republic of Armenia.*

German—estimated at less than 1% of the population, numbering about 37,000.

The Germans are the descendants of settlers who were invited to the region in the late eighteenth century. The present population are the survivors of a brutal deportation ordered by Stalin in 1941. Most of the Germans settled in Ukraine after independence, having left the more unstable Central Asian republics where they were exiled.

Gagauz—estimated at less than 1% of the population, numbering about 35,000. The Gagauz are thought to be of Bulgarian or unknown origin, although culturally and linguistically they are a Turkic people. Their language is a Turkish dialect with substantial Russian and Romanian borrowings. Unlike the majority of Turkic peoples, the Gagauz are Orthodox Christians.

The Gagauz, living in the southern districts of Odesa Oblast, are part of a nation divided when portions of their historic homeland, in Moldova, were transferred to Ukraine in 1945. Wine production is an integral part of the Gagauz culture.

Czech—estimated at less than 1% of the population, numbering about 29,000.

The Czech population mostly live in the Transcarpathian region, which formed part of the Czechoslovak republic between the world wars. Most settled in the region in the 1920s and are the remnant of a larger population that inhabited the region prior to its incorporation into the Soviet Union in 1945.

Georgian—estimated at less than 1% of the population, numbering about 25,000.

Settled in Ukraine during the Soviet era, the Georgians mostly live in Kyyiv and the other larger Ukrainian cities. Part of the larger Georgian nation of the Transcaucasus region, many have left Ukraine to return to the Republic of Georgia* since independence in 1991.

Mordvin—estimated at less than 1% of the population, numbering about 21,000.

The Mordvins are a Finnic people, originally from the region of the Volga River basin. The Mordvin population of Ukraine, settled in the region during the Soviet era, speaks Erzya, one of the two Mordvin dialects. The Mordvin dialects form a separate branch of the Volga-Baltic language group. The majority are Russian Orthodox.

Slovak—estimated at less than 1% of the population, numbering about 12,000.

The Slovak population is concentrated in the Transcarpathian region adjacent to the Slovak border. Speaking a West Slav language, the Slovaks and the Czechs of the region form the largest West Slav group in the southwest. The majority are Roman Catholic.

Uzbek—estimated at less than 1% of the population, numbering about 10,000.

Far from their homeland in Central Asia, the Uzbek population was resettled in Ukraine during the Soviet era, partly to offset Slav settlement in their homeland, Uzbekistan. They speak a Turkish dialect, Northern Uzbek, and are Sunni Muslims.

Kazakh—estimated at less than 1% of the population, numbering about 7,000.

Another Central Asian people resettled in Ukraine during the Soviet era, the Kazakhs are part of the Kazakh nation of Kazakhstan.* They speak a Turkish dialect and are Sunni Muslims.

Albanian—estimated at less than 1% of the population, numbering about 5,000.

The Albanian population of Ukraine lives mostly in the western provinces. The majority speak Tosk, one of the two major dialects of Albanian. The majority are Sunni Muslims.

Ossetian—estimated at less than 1% of the population, numbering about 5,000.

The Ossetians, part of the larger Ossetian nation of the Caucasus region, settled in Ukraine during the Soviet era. They speak an Iranian language and include both Sunni Muslims and Orthodox Christians.

Bashkort (Bashkir)—estimated at less than 1% of the population, numbering about 5,000.

The Bashkort, part of the larger Bashkort nation of Bashkortostan, a member state of the Russian Federation, live mostly in the northeastern region adjacent to Russia. The Bashkort speak a Turkish dialect and are mostly Sunni Muslim.

THE NATION: The known history of the region, inhabited in ancient times, began with the establishment of Greek cities on the Black Sea coast. Called Sarmathia, the region later formed the frontier of Roman power. The formation of the Ukrainian nation began with the great Slav migrations of the sixth and seventh centuries A.D. Tribal peoples, the Slavs slowly formed alliances and unions, the most important becoming tribal states.

Around A.D. 875 Kiev emerged as the center of the first East Slav state, a loose empire called Kievan Rus or Rus'-Ukraine. The city of Kiev, called the Mother of Cities, was the earliest center of East Slav culture and learning. The Kievan Rus state extended its authority to the Gulf of Finland and Karelia in the north, to the upper course of the Volga River in the east, to the Syan and Western Sub Rivers in the west, and to the Crimean Peninsula in the south. From the ninth to the twelfth centuries the Slav empire was the leading power in Europe.

In order to marry the sister of the Byzantine emperor, Prince Vladimir accepted Christianity in 988. On his orders his subjects were baptized in mass ceremonies in the Dnieper River, which flows through Kiev. The city became the first center of Slavic Orthodox Christianity. By the eleventh century the Slavs began to separate into national groups, with the Ukrainians, Russians, and Belarussians emerging as the largest of the East Slav groups.

In the twelfth century internal strife further separated the East Slav peoples and weakened the Kievan Rus state. In the 1130s the state began to break up into smaller feudal states. While Kiev remained the center of the most powerful of the states, other centers of power developed, the most important being the Galician and Volynian principalities in the northwest.

In 1169 the Russian prince of Suzdal seized control of Kiev, which shifted the center of power away from the Ukrainians. Overwhelmed by invading Mongols in 1237–41, the East Slav state disintegrated, most of its territory coming under the rule of the Mongol-Tatar Golden Horde. Other regions of the Slav empire were incorporated by Muscovy and Belarus.

In 1199 the Volynian prince Roman Mstyslavovych united the lands of Galicia and Volynia in a powerful medieval state. His son, Danylo, an able ruler, later inherited the throne of the principality and extended its borders. Separated from the Slav heartland by the Mongol-Tatar invasion, the Galician-Volynian principality survived as the new power center of Ukraine. The principality declined after 1349, and in 1386 was conquered by Lithuania. Other Ukrainian territories came under the rule of Poland and the Ottoman Empire.

Roman Catholic Poland and neighboring Lithuania united in 1569, bringing the northern Ukrainian territories together under Polish rule. The southern regions continued under the rule of the Tatar successor state to the Golden Horde, the Khanate of Crimea, which controlled the Crimean Peninsula and a large territory of the southern Ukrainian steppe.

The advance of serfdom and the persecution of the Ukrainian Orthodox Church sparked widespread opposition to Catholic Polish rule. Resistance centered on a warrior group called the Zaporozhan Sich, the Zaporozhye Cossacks, which formed in southern Ukraine in the early sixteenth century. Bohan Khmelnitski (Khmelnytsky), the *hetman* (chief) of the Cossacks, led a national rebellion in 1648. The Cossacks were successful and established an independent Cossack state, but, too weak to resist the powerful Polish-Lithuanian army, Khmelnitski turned to the Russians.

In 1654 Khmelnitski signed a treaty with Moscow recognizing that state's authority over the Zaporozhye Cossack territories. The Treaty of Pereyaslav, which formed a political and military alliance between the Cossack state and Moscow, was to give protection to the mostly independent Ukrainian Cossack state. Russian encroachment on Ukraine's independence alienated many Ukrainians, who signed a separate treaty with Poland in 1658. This set off a war between Russia and the Polish-Lithuanian state, which ended with the partition of Ukraine in 1667.

Hetman Mazeppa of the Zaporozhye Cossacks tried, from 1687, to break free of foreign rule. He formed an alliance with Sweden and joined the Northern War between Sweden and Russia. In 1709 the allies were defeated at Poltava by the Russians, led by Peter the Great. The defeat sealed the fate of the Ukrainian territories, as Ukrainian autonomy was further curtailed. Between 1764 and 1775 the Zaporozhyan Sich was suppressed by the tsarist government and all political autonomy was ended.

Galicia, with a mixed population of Ukrainians and Poles, became part of Austria as a result of the first Polish partition in 1772. The southeastern region around Chernivtsi, called Bukovina, was added to Austrian Galicia three years later. The revolutionary events in the Austrian Empire in 1848 gave rise to a number of reforms in Galicia. Serfdom was abolished, a parliament was created, and Galicia became a full province of the empire. Austrian rule, less oppressive than Russian, allowed the growth of Ukrainian nationalism as part of the European nationalist revival in the mid-nineteenth century.

The Ukrainian national movement in Austrian territory, based in Galicia, Ruthenia (Transcarpathia), and Bukovina, stimulated a Ukrainian cultural and political revival in Russian Ukraine. Under the influence of the romantic and liberal ideas penetrating the Austrian and Russian empires, young Ukrainians began to take a renewed interest in their particular history and traditions. Among the leading intellectuals to embrace Ukrainian nationalism was Taras Shevchenko, a poet and artist, who exercised an immense influence on the development of a Ukrainian national consciousness.

Consolidated under tsarist rule, eastern Ukraine was subjected to a policy of intense Russification in the eighteenth and nineteenth centuries. In the 1870s and 1880s, a cultural revival stimulated the spread of Ukrainian national sentiment, leading to renewed oppression and a government ban on the use of the Ukrainian language in 1876.

The Revolution of 1905 in Russia resulted in some relaxation. The ban on the Ukrainian language was abolished, and Ukrainians were allowed to form political organizations. Two major revolutionary movements gained support, one seeking to overthrow the tsarist autocracy, the other a particular Ukrainian nationalism. The first, heavily socialist in nature, saw a universal culture and remained divided among the various factions, as in Russia; the second, based on Ukraine's separate history, language, and outlook, advocated autonomy within Russia, while more militant factions demanded support for separation from the Russian Empire and the unification of all Ukrainian lands.

Millions of Ukrainians served in the tsarist armies during World War I, many of the soldiers later forming the nucleus of a Ukrainian national army when revolution swept the Russian Empire in February 1917. Nationalists formed a *rada* (parliament) in Kiev and demanded a status within democratic Russia equal to that of Finland and Poland, the two Russian possessions promised autonomy by the new Provisional Government of Russia. The demand for autonomy was refused by the government, still at war with the Central Powers, as it felt that Russia could not survive without Ukraine's grain, coal, and other natural resources. The overthrow of the Provisional Government by a small band of Bolshevik plotters in October 1917 ended efforts to win autonomy within a federal Russia.

As the defeated Austro-Hungarian Empire disintegrated at the end of the war, Ukrainian nationalists took control of Galicia and on 14 November 1918 proclaimed the independent Republic of Western Ukrainia. In the east, on 22 January 1918, with support from Germany and Austria, the Ukrainian nationalist leaders declared the independence of Russian Ukraine as the Ukrainian National Republic. In January 1919, threatened on all sides, the two Ukrainian states were merged, but they faced renewed threats from the Red and White Russian forces as well as Polish and German forces.

Invaded by Bolshevik troops in February 1918, the state faced rising turmoil as defeated Germany and Austria withdrew their troops in November. Driven from Kiev by Bolshevik soldiers, the Ukrainian government fought a multisided war as armies and guerrilla bands of every political stripe plundered the state. In late 1919 the Bolshevik Red Army won control, and on 17 February 1920 a Soviet republic was proclaimed. Newly independent Poland, at war with the Soviets, conquered the Catholic majority provinces in western Ukraine, while newly independent Czechoslovakia was awarded Ruthenia (Transcarpathia) by the Allies. Romania took control of Bessarabia and Bukovina.

Stalin, the Soviet dictator after 1924, was determined to crush the rebellious Ukrainians for all time. Over 3 million died during the collectivization of the rich Ukrainian agricultural districts in 1929–32, and another 6 to 7 million perished in a systematically planned famine in 1932–33. Uncounted millions died in labor camps and the mass executions that accompanied the periodic Stalinist purges between 1932 and 1937. In 1930 the Ukrainian Autocephalous Orthodox Church, labeled "counterrevolutionary," was officially banned and its properties confiscated by the official Russian Orthodox Church.

In the western districts, Western Ukraine and Carpatho-Ukraine (Transcarpathia), where conditions were less severe, Ukrainians under Polish and Czech rule were denied the autonomy the governments had agreed to in the post–World

War I settlements. Ruthenes and Ukrainians were mostly excluded from administrative positions and were under intense pressure to assimilate.

The rise of Nazi Germany first impacted the Ukrainian lands in Czechoslovakia. In 1938 Ruthenia, called Carpatho-Ukraine, was made an autonomous province with its own government within a federated republic. Amid the continuing Czech crisis, the government of the province declared Carpatho-Ukraine independent on 2 March 1939, but in accordance with a secret pact between Hungary and Germany, the Hungarian military occupied the small state on 14–15 March.

The Soviets, as part of a Nazi-Soviet pact signed in September 1939, occupied Polish Western Ukraine in November, and in 1940 took control of Bukovina from Romania. The region's ties to the Vatican and the West provoked severe Soviet repression. Up to a million people in the region were killed or deported, including anyone having the smooth hands of an intellectual.

The Nazis turned on their ally and invaded the Soviet Union in June 1941. On 30 June 1941, shortly before the German troops reached Lviv, the capital of Western Ukraine, nationalists proclaimed the restoration of the Western Ukrainian republic. The Nazis ignored the proclamation and arrested the nationalist leaders. The western Ukraine was turned into a German colony, and thousands were conscripted into the German army or deported as laborers to Germany.

In September 1941 the Germans entered Kiev and were welcomed by many Ukrainians as liberators from the hated Soviets. A nationalist government was formed under Stephen Bandera. The war divided the Ukrainian nation, with Ukrainians often facing each other on the battlefield. During the war the large Jewish population of over 1 million was destroyed, often in massacres with Ukrainian participation. The Ukrainian nation lost about 6 million people through death or deportation during the war.

Taken by the Red Army in 1944, thousands were arrested and deported. In 1945 the Soviet Union annexed to Soviet Ukraine the Galician region of Poland, Ruthenia from Czechoslovakia, and northern Bukovina and eastern Bessarabia from Romania. Overlooking the contribution made by millions of Ukrainians to the Soviet war effort, Stalin accused the entire nation of collaboration in 1945. Only their sheer numbers saved the majority of the Ukrainians from the mass deportations that Stalin inflicted on many smaller nations. At Stalin's insistence, the Ukrainian Soviet Socialist Republic was numbered among the founding members of the United Nations in 1945.

The Uniate Catholic Church of Western Ukraine was banned and absorbed by the Russian Orthodox Church in 1946. While the Russian Orthodox hierarchy received state subsidies, Uniate Catholic priests, nuns, and laymen filled Stalin's slave labor camps.

The state terror of the Stalin era relaxed somewhat following his death in 1953. In a conciliatory gesture, the Crimean Peninsula was transferred from the

Russian Federation to Soviet Ukraine in 1954 to mark the three hundredth anniversary of the union of Ukraine and Russia.

A modest national revival, begun in the 1960s, was ended in 1972 with the arrest of members of the Ukrainian dissident movement. Driven underground, most nationalist activity was centered in the large Ukrainian populations in Canada and the United States, and among exile groups in Western Europe.

Ukrainian nationalism, stifled for over four decades, began to resurface with the Soviet liberalization in the late 1980s, slowly gaining support from its strongholds in the western Ukraine and Kiev. Nationalists formed the Ukrainian Popular Front (RUKH), which worked for Ukrainian autonomy and later led the calls for separation and independence. Growing opposition to the republic's conservative Communist government forced a change in the leadership of the republic in 1989. The new Communist government of the republic, led by Leonid Kravchuk, rapidly took on nationalist coloring, necessary to survive in the atmosphere of renewed Ukrainian nationalism.

The nationalist groups rapidly gained support on economic and cultural platforms. Members of RUKH denounced Moscow's control of 95% of Ukrainian industry and its taking 90% of the republic's profits. The economic colonization of Ukraine, they claimed, had no historical precedent, not even in colonial Africa.

In January 1990 RUKH organized a human chain stretching 311 miles from Kiev to the western Ukrainian capital at Lviv to symbolize the unity of the historically divided Ukrainian nation. Mounting pressure on the Communist government led to increasing openness, including, after fifty years of silence, Communist officials admitting to the man-made famine of 1932–33. The Ukrainian Orthodox Church and the Ukrainian Autocephalous Orthodox churches were legalized and some properties returned. In the western province the Uniate Church was also legalized, leading to confrontations over the disposition of confiscated properties.

In March 1990, Ukrainians elected their first real parliament since 1918, in what were semi-free elections. Despite the fact that over two-thirds of the deputies in the parliament were Communist Party members, on 16 July 1990, the parliament declared Ukraine a sovereign state with only six dissenting votes. In December, the parliament declared Ukrainian the national language of the state.

In the aftermath of the abortive coup in Moscow, on 24 August 1991, the Ukrainian parliament proclaimed the independence of Ukraine. Ukraine's refusal to join a revamped union was the final blow to the disintegrating Soviet Union. On 1 December 1991 the citizens of the new state voted overwhelmingly in support of the independence declaration, and on the same day they elected Leonid Kravchuk the country's first president. The United States extended official recognition on 25 December.

The new state, determined to establish an effective independence, was increasingly at odds with the neighboring Russian Federation over the disposition of the former Soviet military assets on its territory, particularly the huge naval base at Sevastopol in the Crimea. The economy, already in crisis, contracted rapidly under the forces of a free market and the loss of many of its former sources of raw materials in Russia.

In July 1994, in free elections, Leonid Kuchma, a former Communist turned nationalist, was elected to the office of president. The democratic transfer of power was the first in Ukraine's history. Giving high priority to the division of power within the government and the revival of the economy, President Kuchma sought a wide range of political and economic ties beyond the Commonwealth of Independent States (CIS), the grouping of former Soviet republics.

In 1996 Ukraine became the third largest recipient of U.S. aid, after Egypt and Israel. At the same time the Ukrainian government attempted to settle remaining differences with the Russian Federation. On 31 May 1997 the two countries signed a treaty of friendship and settled the prickly question of Sevastopol and the Black Sea fleet.

In August 1997, President Kuchma announced two major changes in Ukraine's security policy. He stated that Ukraine did not intend to join NATO, although future cooperation was possible, and that Ukraine would no longer be bound by the provisions of the CIS, which effectively moved Ukraine farther from Moscow's influence, although Russia remains Ukraine's largest trading partner and probably the largest direct investor.

The republic, the largest state wholly within Europe, faces a continuing economic crisis, the threat of Russian separatism in the eastern provinces and the Crimea, and vast regional differences due to the separate histories and cultural development of its various regions. The republic, which began to see modest benefits from the free market only in 1997, is determined to survive as the first successful, independent Ukrainian state in modern history.

SELECTED BIBLIOGRAPHY:

Clay, Rebecca. *Ukraine: A New Independence*. 1997.

Magocsi, Paul Robert. *A History of Ukraine*. 1996.

Motyl, Alexander J. *Dilemmas of Independence: Ukraine after Totalitarianism*. 1993.

Sabrin, B. F., ed. *Alliance for Murder: The Nazi-Ukrainian Partnership in Genocide*. 1991.

Subtelny, Orest. *Ukraine: A History*. 1993.

UZBEKISTAN

Republic of Uzbekistan;
Ozbekiston Republikasy;
Uzbekiston Respublikasi;
Turkestan; Turkistan; Turan

CAPITAL: Toshkent (Tashkent)

Central Asia

Uzbekistan

POPULATION: (98e) 23,295,000 : 16,655,000 Uzbeks in Uzbekistan and another 4,500,000 in Tajikistan,* Turkmenistan,* Afghanistan, China, and Kazakhstan.* MAJOR NATIONAL GROUPS: (98e) Uzbek 71.5%, Russian 7.1%, Tajik 5.2%, Kazakh 3.6%, Karakalpak 2.1%, Tatar 1.3%, Turkmen, Korean, Kyrgyz, Crimean Tatar, Ukrainian, Meskhtekian, Jew, Fergana Turk, Armenian, Azeri, German, Bashkort, Uighur, Persian, Belarussian, Mordvin, Chavash, Ossetian, Georgian, Moldovan. MAJOR LANGUAGES: Jagatai (Uzbeki), Russian, Tajiki, Kazakh, Tatar, Karakalpak. MAJOR RELIGIONS: Sunni Islam, Russian Orthodox, Jewish. MAJOR CITIES: (98e) Toshkent (Tashkent) 2,143,000 (2,640,000), Samarqand (Samarkand) 545,000 (640,000), Namangan 331,000, Andijon (Andizhan) 318,000 (475,000), Bukhoro (Bukhara) 237,000, Farghona (Fergana) 214,000 (450,000), Quqon (Kokand) 188,000, Nukus 184,000 (230,000), Chirchik 175,000, Qarchi (Karshi) 169,000, Angren 137,000, Margilan 135,000, Urganch (Urgench) 134,000, Almalyk 127,000, Nawoiy (Navoi) 117,000, Jizzakh (Dzhizak) 115,000, Bekabad 109,000, Termiz (Termez) 83,000 (111,000), Kattakurgan 73,000 (104,000), Guliston (Gulistan) 71,000.

GEOGRAPHY: AREA: 172,741 sq.mi.-447,515 sq.km. LOCATION: Uzbekistan is located in Central Asia, bordering Kazakhstan* on the northwest, north, and northeast, Kyrgyzstan on the east, Tajikistan on the southeast, Afghanistan on the south, and Turkmenistan on the south and west. PHYSICAL GEOGRAPHY: The country is divided into four topographical regions: the Ustyurt Plateau and the delta and plains of the lower Amu Darya River in the northwest;

the Kyzyl Kum Desert, which lies between the Amu Darya and Sty Darya Rivers and cuts across the northern provinces east of the Aral Sea; the foothills of the Pamir and Altai mountains in the southeast, and the Tien Shan Range east of Tashkent; and the fertile oases of the Fergana Valley between the Alai and Tien Shan Ranges. The principal rivers are the Amu Darya, Sry Darya, and Zeravshan. ADMINISTRATIVE DIVISIONS: Twelve provinces or wiloyatlar (singular—wiloyat) and one autonomous republic, Karakalpakstan. POLITICAL STATUS: Uzbekistan was recognized as an independent state in 1991.

INDEPENDENCE DECLARATIONS: TURKESTAN: 16 December 1917 (from Russia); UZBEKISTAN: 31 August 1991 (from the Soviet Union).

FLAG: The Uzbek national flag, the official flag of the republic, is a horizontal tricolor of blue, white, and pale green, the stripes separated by narrow red stripes and bearing, on the upper hoist, a small white crescent moon and twelve white five-pointed stars in three rows of stars, three stars in the top row, four stars in the middle, and five stars in the bottom row, all on the blue stripe.

PEOPLE: Ethnically, Uzbekistan occupies a kind of bridge between the Turkic and Persian worlds. While various ethnic groups historically occupied different economic niches, they were united by their common history and their Islamic religion. Bilingualism was seen as normal for many centuries, not only among the educated elite but among the common people as well. Command of three or four languages was not exceptional. The Uzbek-dominated society and culture were formed on a multiethnic and multilingual basis.

Uzbek—an estimated 71.5% of the population, numbering about 16,655,000. The Uzbeks are a Central Asian people of mixed Turkic, Caucasian, and Mongol background. The most numerous nation in Central Asia, the Uzbeks are divided into ninety-two distinct tribes collectively called Uzbek after a fourteenth-century chief of the Golden Horde, Uzbeg Khan.

The language of the Uzbeks, called Northern Uzbek, is an East Turkic language of the Turkic group of languages. The language, which is used throughout Central Asia, is spoken in three major dialects and is written in the Cyrillic script. Many Uzbeks are bilingual in Russian. There is much Persian influence in the Uzbek language and culture.

The Uzbeks are mostly Hanafi Sunni Muslims, as are most of the republic's non-Uzbek national groups. The Uzbeks tend to be more secular than the other Central Asians. Physically the Uzbeks more closely resemble the Turks or Iranians than the Mongols.

Russian—an estimated 7.1% of the population, numbering about 1,650,000. The large Slav population is mostly concentrated in the major cities, particularly Tashkent and Samarkand, with overall Slav numbers dropping dramatically since Uzbek independence in 1991. Seeking better economic opportunities or security, many ethnic Russians have returned to Russia, taking their badly needed technical and administrative skills with them.

Settled in the region during the Soviet era, the Russians mostly came as workers or administrators. Until recent decades the Slavs predominated in Tashkent and the other large cities of the region. The Russians are the largest Christian population in the country, mostly belonging to the Russian Orthodox Church.

Tajik—an estimated 5.2% of the population, numbering about 1,210,000.

The Tajiks are an Iranian people, more numerous in neighboring Tajikistan. Their language is a West Iranian language related to the Farsi language of Iran. The majority are Sunni Muslim, with a minority adhering to the Shi'a branch of Islam.

Tajik sources estimate the number of ethnic Tajiks in Uzbekistan at over 2 million. More militant Tajik nationalists have laid claim to the Samarkand and Bukhara regions of Uzbekistan on the grounds that the two regions were predominantly Tajik before 1917.

Kazakh—an estimated 3.6% of the population, numbering about 841,000.

The Kazakhs, of mixed Turkic and Mongol background, are former nomads living mostly in the northern districts of the country and in the area south of the Aral Sea. The majority of the Kazakhs more closely resemble their Mongol ancestors than the other Central Asian peoples, but their culture and language belong to the Turkic world.

Their language, a West Turkic language, is related to Uzbek, which has influenced the dialect spoken by the Kazakhs in Uzbekistan. Their language, like Uzbek, is written in the Cyrillic alphabet. The majority of the Kazakhs are Sunni Muslims.

Karakalpak—an estimated 2.1% of the population, numbering about 465,000.

The Karakalpak, also called Tudzit or Kara-Kalpak, meaning Black Caps, are the least numerous of the major Central Asian peoples. Of mixed origins, the Karakalpak include in their ancestry Orguz and Kipchak Turks, Mongols, and Iranians. They developed as a separate people in the fifteenth century. Although more Turkic in appearance than the neighboring Kazakhs, the Karakalpaks are more closely related to them than to the Uzbeks. The status of women, more advanced than in the rest of Uzbekistan, is considered one of the few positive legacies of the Communist era.

The Karakalpak are concentrated along the lower Amu Darya River and around the southern coast of the Aral Sea, where many are fishermen. The Karakalpak territory came under Soviet authority in 1920. In 1925 the area became an autonomous region of Kazakh Autonomous Republic. In 1932 the Soviet authorities transferred the region to the Russian Federation and upgraded its status to that of an autonomous republic. Four years later the Soviets again transferred the small republic to the authority of the Uzbek Soviet Socialist Republic. Following Uzbekistan independence in 1991, the republic, called Qoraqalpoghiston or Karakalpakstan, was granted autonomous status, with Nukus as its capital.

The Karakalpaks speak an Aralo-Caspian language of the West Turkic languages. The language is sometimes classed by scholars as a dialect of Kazakh, although it developed as a separate literary language after the Russian Revolution. Even though the Karakalpaks' sense of separate identity is well developed, their status as a Kazakh subgroup or a separate national group is still debated.

Tatar—an estimated 1.3% of the population, numbering about 302,000.

The Tatars, more numerous in the Tatarstan republic of the Russian Federation, are a Turkic people speaking a West Turkic language. The majority came to Uzbekistan as administrators soon after the Russian conquest of the region in the nineteenth century, as the authorities believed that the Sunni Muslim Tatars would have more in common with the newly conquered peoples of Central Asia than would Christian Russians.

Most of the Tatars are concentrated in the larger Uzbek cities, and many speak Russian and Uzbek as well as the Tatar language. The most widely dispersed of the nations of the former Soviet Union, many Tatars have returned to Tatarstan in the Russian Federation since the collapse of the Soviet Union in 1991.

Turkmen—estimated at less than 1% of the population, numbering about 229,000.

The Turkmen, also called Turcomen, are a Central Asian people related to the Uzbeks. They form part of the larger Turkmen population of the Republic of Turkmenistan. Divided along tribal lines, the Turkmen live mostly in the southern provinces along the international border with Turkmenistan.

Former nomads, the Sunni Muslim Turkmen speak an Orguz Turkic language of the West Altaic language group. The Turkmen language is spoken in at least eleven separate dialects and is written in the Cyrillic alphabet.

Korean—estimated at less than 1% of the population, numbering about 186,000.

The Korean population lives mostly in the eastern districts around Tashkent. Most of the Korean population was deported from the sensitive border areas of the Russian Far East during the Stalin years. Some Korean groups claim an ethnic population of up to 250,000 in Uzbekistan.

The majority of the Koreans are Buddhists, with a substantial minority professing atheism. Most of the Koreans live in urban areas. The government of South Korea has established contact with the scattered Korean populations since Uzbek independence in 1991 and is giving the new state substantial aid to be used partly for the welfare of the ethnic Koreans.

Kyrgyz—estimated at less than 1% of the population, numbering about 183,000.

The only Central Asian people with predominantly Mongol physical features, they are Turkic in language and culture. Their language, a West Turkic language related to Uzbek, became a viable language only after the Russian Revolution and the infusion of Russian words.

A Sunni Muslim people, the Kyrgyz tend to be more devout than the more sophisticated, urbanized Uzbeks. Conflicts between the two peoples over water and land rights led to violent ethnic confrontations in 1990.

Crimean Tatar—estimated at less than 1% of the population, numbering about 167,000.

The Crimean Tatar population of Kyrgyzstan is part of a larger nation deported from the Crimean Peninsula by the Stalinist government in 1944. The language of the Crimean Tatars is a West Turkic language related to Turkish. In Soviet censuses, up to 1989, they were counted as ethnic Tatars, but the languages and cultures are quite different.

Dumped at rail sidings across Central Asia following the terrifying trip in closed cattle cars from Europe in 1944, thousands died of hunger and exposure. The Crimean Tatars were not rehabilitated along with the other deported nations in the 1950s, but remained in exile, mostly in Uzbekistan. The Muslim Crimean Tatars have prospered in exile, but a movement to return to their homeland, now in independent Ukraine,* has led to the departure of some 50,000 for the Crimea since 1991.

The charge of treason against the Crimean Tatar nation was not formally lifted until 1967, and even then they were not permitted to return to the Crimea. A long and concerted campaign for the right to return ended with the dissolution of the Soviet Union in 1991. In 1988 a few managed to reenter the Crimea and take possession of unoccupied pieces of land. In 1990 they began to leave their long exile in Uzbekistan in large numbers.

Ukrainian—estimated at less than 1% of the population, numbering about 152,000.

The Ukrainians, mostly settled in the region during the 1950s and 1960s, are concentrated around Tashkent and in the cities of the subtropical Fergana Valley. Like the Russians, the Ukrainians came to the region as administrators and industrial workers in Soviet government–sponsored migrations.

Since Ukrainian independence in 1991, and the increasingly difficult economic problems in Uzbekistan, over 50,000 ethnic Ukrainians have left the republic, mostly for Ukraine, but also for areas of European Russia and the United States.

Meskhtekian—estimated at less than 1% of the population, numbering about 110,000.

The Meskhtekians, also called Meskhtekian Turks, are the descendants of Muslim Georgians called Meskhi, Armenian Muslims called Khemsils, Shi'a Muslim Ajars, Kurds, and Karapapakh Turks deported from Soviet Georgia* in 1944. Even though the German army never reached their homeland in southwestern Georgia, over 130,000 were driven from their homes and shipped east in closed cattle cars. Thousands died of hunger, thirst, and exposure on the long trip east. Dumped at rail sidings across Central Asia, they were often left without food or water. The Meskhtekians claim that over 50,000 of their people died as a direct result of the deportations and the deprivations suffered in their Central Asian exile.

The Meskhtekian peoples formed a nation in exile, including the development of a separate Meskhtekian language that combines the Laz dialect of Georgian and admixtures from several Turkish dialects. In 1968 they were the last group to be cleared of the treason charge. Released from KGB supervision, many moved to the Fergana Valley.

Forbidden to return to their Georgian homeland, the Shi'a Muslim Meskhtekians prospered in exile until June 1989, when fighting broke out between Meskhtekians and Uzbeks in the Fergana Valley. An Uzbek nationalist demonstration turned into a pogrom as the Sunni Muslim Uzbeks turned on the entire Meskhtekian population of the region. Enraged Uzbeks hunted the terrified Meskhtekians through a week of violence, rape, and murder. Over a hundred Meskhtekians died in the violence before the Red Army evacuated 74,000 Meskhtekians to camps outside the urban areas.

Jew—estimated at less than 1% of the population, numbering about 100,000.

The Jewish population of Uzbekistan is divided between the European Jews who settled in or were deported to the region during the Soviet era, and the native Jewish people, the Bukharan Jews.

The European Jews, numbering about 70,000, are mostly Russian-speaking, although Yiddish is still spoken. The majority live in Tashkent and Samarkand. Immigration to the United States and Israel has increased since the dissolution of the Soviet Union in 1991.

The Bukharan Jews, numbering about 30,000, have lived in the region since ancient times. Their cultural center is the city of Bukhara. Their language, called Bukharic or Bukharian, is a Southwestern Iranian dialect related to Tajiki and is written in the Hebrew script.

Fergana Turk (counted as ethnic Uzbek)—estimated at less than 1% of the population, numbering about 60,000.

The Fergana Turks, the descendants of Turkish migrants, live in the Fergana Valley in eastern Uzbekistan. Formerly Turkish-speaking, they now speak a dialect of Uzbek, and are counted as ethnic Uzbeks. Culturally, the Turks have maintained many of their ancient traditions and customs. The Fergana Turks are Sunni Muslims.

Armenian—estimated at less than 1% of the population, numbering about 47,000.

The Armenian population of Uzbekistan, concentrated in the capital, Tashkent, was settled in the region or deported during the Stalin era. They mostly speak Russian as their first language, while speaking Armenian at home or among themselves.

The overwhelming majority of Armenians are Gregorian Christians with their religious center at Echmiadzin, near the Armenian capital city of Yerevan. A small number of the Armenian population belong to the Roman Catholic Church. The small Muslim Armenian minority, called Khemsils or Khemshins, is also represented.

An unknown number of the Uzbek Armenians have emigrated since the last Soviet census in 1989. However, the majority have shunned Armenia,* with its political and economic chaos, in favor of southern Russia.

Azeri—estimated at less than 1% of the population, numbering about 43,000.

The Azeris, more of whom live in Azerbaijan* across the Caspian Sea, are a Turkic people of mixed Turkic and Caucasian ancestry. Their language is a Turkic language of the West Turkic group of Altaic languages. They speak the Northern Azeri dialect of the language.

The main concentrations of the Azeri population are in the southeastern districts. The Azeri population in Uzbekistan is mostly rural. The majority of the Northern Azeris are Sunni Muslims, while the majority of the population of the Republic of Azerbaijan is Shi'a Muslim.

German—estimated at less than 1% of the population, numbering about 38,000.

The Germans of Uzbekistan are mostly the descendants of the German populations of European Russia deported to Central Asia in 1941, when Stalin's ally, Hitler, launched his invasion of the Soviet Union.

Many of the Germans speak Russian as their first language while retaining archaic South German dialects brought to Russia by their ancestors in the eighteenth century. Many have taken advantage of the German government's aid to return to Germany. However, in Germany many face discrimination, as few speak standard German and culturally they have absorbed many Slavic traits. Employment problems and discrimination in Germany have slowed the pace of emigration.

Bashkort (Bashkir)—estimated at less than 1% of the population, numbering about 36,000.

The Bashkort, of mixed Finnic, Turkic, and Mongol ancestry, mostly live in the Fergana Valley of eastern Uzbekistan. Their language, a Turko-Tatar language related to Tatar, is spoken as the mother language, but the majority use Russian or Uzbek to communicate with other national groups.

Uighur—estimated at less than 1% of the population, numbering about 36,000.

The Uighurs of Uzbekistan are mostly refugees who fled Chinese repression in the so-called Eastern Turkestan region of China. The descendants of the Dzungars, the Left Hand, the left wing of the hordes of the medieval Mongol empire, the Uighurs speak an East Turkic language related to Uzbek. The majority are Sunni Muslims.

Persian (Iranian)—estimated at less than 1% of the population, numbering about 32,000.

The Iranian inhabitants of Uzbekistan, called Persians, are mostly rural and work as collective farm workers, mostly in the southeastern districts. The descendants of the ancient inhabitants of the region, the Iranians are related to the Tajiks and the Iranians of Iran.

Their language, Western Farsi, is spoken by only about 30% as the first language, as most are bilingual in Uzbek or Tajiki. The Persians are Shi'a Muslims, but are less religious than their kin in the Islamic Republic of Iran.

Belarussian—estimated at less than 1% of the population, numbering about 28,000.

The Belarussians in the country, the majority the descendants of colonists who settled in the northern provinces, are mostly Russian speakers and belong to the Russian Orthodox Church. A minority, mostly Roman Catholic, were deported to the region during and after World War II when the Soviets took control of the eastern provinces of Poland.

The Belarussian population, like that of the other Slav groups, is being reduced by immigration to Europe. More than 20,000 Belarussians are believed to have left Uzbekistan since the census of 1989.

Mordvin—estimated at less than 1% of the population, numbering about 14,000.

The Mordvins, more numerous in the Mordvin Republic of the Russian Federation, are a Finnic people, the descendants of the pre-Slavic populations of the Volga River region of European Russia.

Many are the descendants of anti-Communist or anti-Stalin deportees deported to Central Asia during the Stalin era. The majority are Orthodox and speak Russian as their first language. The language of the national group is Ezrya, one of the two major dialects of Mordvin, a Finnic language that constitutes a separate branch of the Volga-Baltic language group.

Chavash (Chuvash)—estimated at less than 1% of the population, numbering about 9,000.

The Chavash, called Chuvash by the Slavs, are the descendants of the medieval Bulgar people of the valley of the Volga River in European Russia, with later admixtures of Turkic and Finnic peoples. The majority of the Chavash in Uzbekistan were settled in the region after World War II. Their homeland now forms a member state of the Russian Federation.

Their language, though of basic Turkic structure, forms the separate Bulgaric branch of the West Altaic group of languages and is only distantly related to the Turkic languages. The Uzbek Chavash mostly speak Russian as their first language.

Ossetian—estimated at less than 1% of the population, numbering about 6,000.

The Ossetians of Uzbekistan, calling themselves Iristi, are an Iranian people whose homeland, which forms a member state of the Russian Federation, is located in the Caucasus region of southern European Russia.

The Ossetian language, an East Iranian language, remains the mother language of the national group, but the majority use Russian in Uzbekistan. Most of the Ossetians are Russian Orthodox, but with a substantial Sunni Muslim minority.

Georgian—estimated at less than 1% of the population, numbering about 4,000.

The Georgian population, mostly deported to the region during World War II, is concentrated in Tashkent and the eastern provinces. In Uzbekistan the Georgians mostly use Russian, the lingua franca of the region, while retaining their own national language within the group. Since 1991 many have left the region to return to the newly independent Republic of Georgia.

Moldovan—estimated at less than 1% of the population, numbering about 3,000.

The Moldovans of Uzbekistan, mostly the descendants of deportees of the World War II era, are ethnically Romanian, but use the Cyrillic alphabet instead of the Latin. The majority are Orthodox Christians and are concentrated in Tashkent.

THE NATION: An ancient region, inhabited as early as 3000 B.C., Central

Asia developed sophisticated civilizations along the Silk Road, the legendary trade route that connected China and the East to the Mediterranean and the West. Converted to Islam by Arab invaders in the seventh and eighth centuries, Central Asia became a center of Islamic learning and Muslim Persian civilization with flourishing cities and an extensive trade and agriculture based on vast irrigation systems.

Seljuk Turkic tribes conquered the area in the eleventh and twelfth centuries, maintaining the tradition of open trade and irrigated agriculture. The Turkic conquerors mixed with the Persian oasis dwellers to form the Uzbek nation. The Seljuk Turks founded the Khorezm state, later called Khiva. The Seljuks' Turkic language and culture dominated the area.

Devastated by invading Mongols in the thirteenth century, the region later came under the rule of several successor states as the Mongols' Golden Horde broke up. The destruction of the irrigation system had a profound influence on the decline of the region.

The area again flourished under the rule of Tamerlane, who established his capital at Samarkand, in the late fourteenth century. The Uzbeks, a remnant of the Golden Horde, conquered Central Asia from the east between 1490 and 1505, eventually expanding their empire into present Afghanistan, Iran, and China. In 1555 the Uzbeks moved the capital of the region from Samarkand to Bukhara.

Internal conflicts split the Uzbek empire in the seventeenth century, with the Uzbek states of Bukhara and Khorezm (Khiva) emerging as regional powers. In 1619–21 the Russians established diplomatic contact between Moscow and Bukhara. The first military expedition to Khiva, in 1717, ended in a massacre of the Russian troops, bringing an end to Russian contacts with the region for several decades.

The Uzbeks, the most powerful people in Central Asia, ruled the other ethnic groups in the region, but remained divided along regional and clan lines. Although dominated by the Uzbeks, the states in the region were multiethnic and multilingual. The population of the Bukhara state in the eighteenth century was estimated at about a third Uzbek, with the rest being Tajik, Turkmen, Kyrgyz, Arab, Persian, and Bukharan Jews. The inhabitants of Khiva were about half Uzbek, with large Turkmen and Karakalpak populations in the northern and southern provinces.

The Uzbek Mangit dynasty began to rise to power in the Khanate of Bukhara in 1747. In 1759 the Chinese conquered the Tarim Basin to the east, sending a flood of Muslim refugees fleeing to Bukhara and Kokand. The Uzbek Kungrat dynasty began to take power in the state of Khiva in 1763. In 1784–85 the Uzbek Mangit dynasty succeeded the Astrakanids as the rulers of the Khanate of Bukhara and adopted the title emir, changing the name of the state to the Emirate of Bukhara.

In 1798 a third Uzbek state, the Khanate of Kokand, emerged in the area known as Turkestan. Soon after, in 1804, the Kungrat dynasty of Khiva adopted the title of khan. Their state, the Khanate of Khiva, which controlled the left bank of the Amu Darya River south of the Aral Sea, became a powerful rival to neighboring Bukhara.

Russian troops invaded the region in 1865, and in June of that year they took control of the Uzbek stronghold at Tashkent. In 1867 the conquerors established a colonial government, the Governorate-General of Turkestan, with Tashkent as its capital. The next year they took control of the ancient city of Samarkand.

The Uzbek states in the region, under growing Russian influence, were forced to accept the status of Russian protectorates—the Emirate of Bukhara in 1868, and the Khanate of Khiva in 1873. The Russians annexed the Khanate of Kokand outright in 1876, bringing most of Central Asia under their colonial rule. Slavic colonists were settled in the annexed region, enjoying special privileges as the overseers of the harsh Russian colonial administration. In 1884 the Russians introduced American cotton into Turkestan.

The Central Asians, led by the Uzbeks with calls to Muslim solidarity, rose in revolt in the Fergana Valley in 1885. The rebellion, put down with great brutality, was quickly ended. However, uprisings among the volatile population continued sporadically, including a serious threat to Russian rule at Andijan in 1898.

In 1906 the Russians completed laying the tracks of the Orenburg-Tashkent Railroad, linking Turkestan to European Russia. The rail link, bringing settlers, goods, and revolutionary ideals, also brought Russian soldiers quickly to quell each serious threat to the colonial rule of the region.

Revolutionary ideas, spreading from European Russia, greatly affected the Muslim intellectual elite. Dissatisfied with Russian interference in the affairs of the Uzbek states, they began to form revolutionary groups. In 1909, an anti-Russian group known as the Young Bukharans was formed in Bukhara.

The Uzbeks, as a Muslim people, were exempted from military duty in the empire, and therefore remained relatively untouched by World War I until 1916. Desperate for manpower, the Russian authorities attempted to conscript 250,000 Central Asian Muslims for labor battalions at the front. The conscription, resisted by the Muslim peoples of the region, sparked a widespread rebellion that was eventually overtaken by the Russian Revolution, which spread outward from Petrograd in February 1917.

The revolution in Russia resulted in the establishment of the Tashkent Committee of the Provisional Government and the rival Tashkent Soviet of Workers' and Peasants' Deputies. In April 1917 the first Muslim congress in Tashkent demanded the end of Russian colonization and the return of confiscated lands. In September a second congress proposed the creation of an autonomous federal republic in Turkestan.

The October Revolution, the Bolshevik coup in Russia, galvanized the local Bolsheviks, who seized power from the Tashkent Committee. On 15 November a congress of Soviets decided to exclude Muslims from local government. The Muslims, meeting in Kokand, created a rival Muslim Provisional Government of Autonomous Turkestan.

Outraged by the Bolsheviks' antireligious stance and threatened by the Bolshevik forces at Tashkent, the Muslim government declared Turkestan independent on 16 December 1917, the declaration closely followed by those of the former protectorates. On 17 December the authorities in Bukhara declared the emirate independent, and on 23 December the Khanate of Khiva followed suit.

The rival Bolshevik government rejected the declarations, and in January 1918 fighting broke out in the region. The ill-equipped Muslims were easily defeated, and in February the Bolshevik forces overran the Muslim capital at Kokand. Given leave to loot the city, the Bolshevik troops wantonly destroyed ancient monuments, and the city's population of 120,000 was killed or dispersed.

In Khiva and Bukhara turmoil increased as competing ethnic groups fought over water and land and conservative Muslim elements increasingly opposed the liberal intelligentsia, the Young Khivans and the Young Bukharans. In February 1918 the Young Bukharans presented the emir with a list of conditions, which he refused. Bolshevik troops invaded the state, but were defeated and retreated to Tashkent. In March 1918 the Russian Civil War began, lessening pressure on the two independent states.

The Bolshevik government in Tashkent, in April 1918, established the Turkestan Autonomous Soviet Socialist Republic. In July 1919 a congress of the Communist Party of Turkestan voted to exclude Muslims from government posts in Turkestan, alienating their Muslim Communist allies. Many Muslims join the Basmachi Muslim rebel groups operating in the region.

In February 1920 Bolshevik troops invaded the Khanate of Khiva in support of the Young Khivans. The khan was deposed, and the Tashkent government recognized the Young Khivans as the legitimate government of the People's Republic of Khorezm.

The overthrow of the Khivan khanate, in 1920, opened the way to Bukhara. The Young Bukharans staged a revolt in August 1920 and requested Soviet assistance. As previously planned, Soviet troops quickly moved in, and heavy fighting ensued. It appeared that the Bukharan forces would repeat their victory of 1918, but on 2 September 1920 the city of Bukhara fell and the Bukharan People's Republic was proclaimed. The emir and many followers escaped to the mountains, and in 1921 moved on into Afghanistan.

Throughout 1922–23 the Communists extended their authority in the Khivan and Bukharan states, undermining the liberalizing government of the Young Khivans and Young Bukharans. In 1924, ignoring strong Uzbek protests, the Communists took complete control of Khiva and Bukhara, and Central Asia was divided along ethnic lines, the new states admitted to the Soviet Union as constituent republics.

The Basmachis, Muslim rebel groups, continued to harass the Soviet authorities from mountain strongholds. Thousands of Muslims fled Communist rule, joining the Basmachis or crossing the frontiers into Afghanistan and China. Under Stalin's rule after 1924, the Soviet administration became even more oppressive. In 1928 an anti-Islamic campaign was launched, with Islamic courts and schools disbanded and mosques turned into museums, factories, and schools.

The forced collectivization of the Uzbeks, between 1928 and 1933, was carried out with great brutality. In 1937–38 Stalin accused the party leadership in Uzbekistan of activities counter to the revolution and carried out a purge, which eliminated some three-quarters of the party hierarchy.

With the beginning of World War II, the Stalinist terror was somewhat relaxed as troops were sent to the front in European Russia. In a bid to win Muslim support, the Soviet government granted Islam official status in the USSR in 1942. To administer the Muslim religion, four spiritual directorates were established, one in the Uzbek capital, Tashkent.

After the war, as part of the Communist economic integration, the rich agricultural lands around the Aral Sea were turned over to cotton production, to the exclusion of the traditional crops. The republican government of Uzbekistan, staffed by party loyalists, needed only to deliver the Soviet cotton quotas in order to maintain their positions and their near feudal powers. A clannish, authoritarian Communist hierarchy developed under Stalin's rule based on a notoriously corrupt system dubbed "Feudal Socialism" by dissidents.

The hold of the Communist appointees held firm until the late 1980s. The reforms instituted by Mikhail Gorbachev in 1987 hastened the growth of opposition groups. The disclosure of massive government fraud and corruption as well as the extent of previously undisclosed environmental disasters, aroused the dormant Uzbek national movement in 1988–89. The virtual destruction of the Aral Sea, drying up and heavily polluted by chemicals used in cotton production, became an explosive nationalist issue.

Ethnic and economic disputes led to serious violence between Uzbeks and other national groups in the republic, covertly provoked by the Communist regime as a means of deflecting the growing nationalist opposition. The division of water resources in the dry region became a cause for violence.

In the aftermath of the failed Soviet coup in August 1991, the Uzbek republican government, under nationalist pressure, reluctantly declared Uzbekistan independent on 31 August 1991. The new state, beset by massive economic, environmental, and ethnic problems, quickly moved to outlaw the Communist Party, while the former Communist loyalists adopted Uzbek nationalism as the new ideology.

The state, in the Communist Central Asian tradition, continued to be dominated by Uzbekistan's Tashkent and Samarkand clans, to the exclusion of clans in other parts of the country, particularly the powerful Fergana Valley clans. In December 1991, Islom Karimov, the former Communist Party head, was elected president. A March 1995 referendum, approved by a reported 99.6% of the voters, extended Karimov's term until 2000.

The country, which shares borders with all the Central Asian states, has begun to compete with Russia for regional influence in Central Asia. The Uzbeks, the traditionally dominant national group in the vast region, consider theirs the most important of the former Soviet republics in the region. Uzbek power, along with the presence of large Uzbek minorities in the neighboring states, has intimidated the other regional states, which fear Uzbek irredentism and political pressure.

In 1994, led by Uzbekistan, a political and economic union, the Central Asian

Union, was formed among Uzbekistan, Kazakhstan, and Kyrgyzstan. In spite of efforts to cooperate, one issue, access to water, is increasingly dividing the Central Asian states.

The slow implementation of political and economic reforms and the oppression of Uzbek opposition and nationalist groups has sparked an increasing number of protests against President Karimov and rule by the former Communists. The modern Uzbek republic is little different from the former Soviet republic, with the system of near-feudal autocracy continuing to dominate.

In 1995 the Uzbek government signed an agreement with the South Koreans to provide books, training, and aid for the large ethnic Korean population in the republic. The national groups with ties to the industrialized countries, particularly the Koreans and Germans, have become a source of much-needed financial aid.

The Uzbek government, in spite of growing ties to other Islamic countries, has sought a wide range of diplomatic ties. In September 1997, the Uzbeks upgraded their consulate in Tel Aviv, established in 1992, to the position of their official embassy in Israel. Responding to criticism from some militant Muslim groups, government officials recalled that Jews have been living in Uzbekistan for centuries and that many European Jews found refuge in the region during World War II.

The exodus of thousands of Slavs to Russia has hampered efforts to modernize the economy, but despite efforts to reassure the Slavs that they have a place in Uzbekistan, the government proclaimed Uzbek the official state language. Emphasis in all levels of Uzbek society is on the Uzbek population, to the detriment of the other national groups in the republic, while protests and dissident views are quickly handled in the traditional ways.

SELECTED BIBLIOGRAPHY:

Allworth, Edward A. *The Modern Uzbeks: From the Fourteenth Century to the Present. A Cultural History.* 1990.

Critchlow, James. *Nationalism in Uzbekistan: Soviet Republic's Road to Sovereignty.* 1991.

Kalter, Johannes, ed. *Uzbekistan: Heirs to the Silk Road.* 1997.

Kangas, Roger D. *Uzbekistan in the Twentieth Century: Political Development and the Evolution of Power.* 1998.

McLeod, Calum, and Bradley Mayhew. *Uzbekistan: The Golden Road to Samarkand.* 1997.

YUGOSLAVIA

Serbia and Montenegro; Srbija-Crna Gora; Federal Republic of Yugoslavia; Federativna Republika Jugoslavija; Savezna Republika

CAPITAL: Beograd (Belgrade)

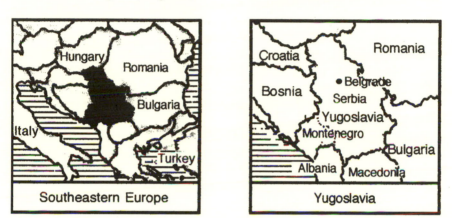

Southeastern Europe

Yugoslavia

POPULATION: (98e) 10,683,000 : 6,698,000 Serbs and 630,000 Montene-grins in Yugoslavia. MAJOR NATIONAL GROUPS: (98e) Serbian 62.7%, Al-banian (Kosovar) 17.1%, Montenegrin 5.9%, Magyar (Hungarian) 3.7%, Muslim 3.2%, Rom (Gypsy) 2.4%, Romanian 1.5%, Croat, Slovak, Bulgarian, Ruthene, Ukrainian, Turk, Pole, German, Czech, Russian, Jew. MAJOR LANGUAGES: Serbian, Albanian, Hungarian, Rom languages, Romanian, Slovak, Russian. MAJOR RELIGIONS: Serbian Orthodox 65%, Muslim 20%, Roman Catholic 5%, Protestant, Jewish, Russian Orthodox. MAJOR CITIES: (98e) SERBIA: Beograd (Belgrade) 1,121,000 (2,108,000), Novi Sad 196,000 (265,000), Nish 184,000 (326,000), Pristina 118,000, Kragujevac 105,000 (180,000), Subotica 97,000, Zrenjanin 88,000, Leskovac 71,000, Sabac 68,000, Sombor 66,000, Smedrovo 65,000, Prizen 57,000, Kosovska Mitovica 55,000, Cacak 54,000, Pec 54,000, Pozarevac 53,000, Kikinda 53,000, Titovo Uzice 50,000. MON-TENEGRO: Podgorica 90,000, Cetinje 17,000.

GEOGRAPHY: AREA: 39,449 sq.mi.-102,173 sq.km. SERBIA: 34,117 sq.mi.-88,361 sq.km. MONTENEGRO: 5,332 sq.mi.-13,812 sq.km. LOCA-TION: Yugoslavia now consists of the republics Montenegro and Serbia with its semiautonomous provinces of Kosovo and Vojvodina (also Voivodina or Voyvodina). The country is located on the Balkan Peninsula of southeastern Europe and is bounded by the Adriatic Sea and Albania on the southwest, Bosnia and Herzegovina* to the west, Croatia* to the northwest, Hungary on the north, Romania and Bulgaria on the east, and Macedonia* to the southeast. PHYSICAL

GEOGRAPHY: The northern region of Serbia lies on the southern extremity of the Central Danubian Plain. In the south is the valley of the Sava River, and to the east and west of the Danube River basin lie the Serbian Highlands and the East Serbian Mountains. In the southwest, in Kosovo, are the basins of the Kosovo Polje and Metonija Rivers. Montenegro, lying between Serbia and the Adriatic Sea, is divided into three distinct regions, the lowlands of the Adriatic, the mountainous region in the west, and the highlands in the north and east. Montenegro's small coastline is Yugoslavia's only outlet to the Mediterranean Sea. ADMINISTRATIVE DIVISIONS: Two republics (pokajine, singular—pokajina); and two nominally autonomous provinces. POLITICAL STATUS: Serbia and Montenegro have asserted the formation of a joint independent state, but the federation of the two states has not been formally recognized by the United States. The U.S. view is that the Socialist Federal Republic of Yugoslavia (SFRY) has disappeared and that none of the successor republics represents its continuation. The United Nations seat held by the SFRY has been inherited by the Federal Republic of Yugoslavia.

FLAG: The flag of the Federal Republic of Yugoslavia is a horizontal tricolor of blue, white, and red. OTHER FLAGS: The flags of both Serbia and Montenegro are horizontal tricolors of red, blue, and white.

INDEPENDENCE: 11 April 1992 (from Socialist Federal Republic of Yugoslavia—SFRY).

PEOPLE: An estimated thirty-seven different ethnic groups inhabit the Federal Republic of Yugoslavia. However, only two, the Serbs and Montenegrins, are represented in the federal government. Except for a brief period during postwar reconstruction in the 1950s, birth rates in Serbia and Montenegro as a whole have been falling. However, two different demographic patterns have emerged: a very high birthrate among the Albanian, Rom, and Muslim populations, and the very low birthrate of the Serb, Hungarian, Slovak, Romanian, Bulgarian, and other nationalities. The two distinct patterns have further divided the federation into territorial, ethnic, religious, and linguistic rivals.

Serb (Serbian)—an estimated 62.7% of the population, numbering about 6,698,000.

The Serbs are a South Slav people, the most numerous of the nations that made up the former Yugoslav state. Although the Serbs are ethnically related to the other South Slav peoples—the Croats, Slovenes, Slavic Muslims, and Macedonians—Serbian culture and history have shaped the nation and separated the Serbs from their South Slav kin.

The Serbian language, now claimed as a separate language, is a dialect of Serbo-Croatian, although written in the Cyrillic alphabet, while Croatian is written in the Latin alphabet. Serbo-Croatian is spoken in four major dialects, with the literary language based on the Stokavian dialect. The majority of the Serbs belong to the independent Serbian Orthodox Church, which forms an integral part of Serbian culture.

Albanian (Kosovar)—an estimated 17.1% of the population, numbering about 1,825,000.

The Albanian population of Yugoslavia is concentrated in the southwestern region, the nominally autonomous province of Kosovo. The Albanians call themselves Shiptars; in Yugoslavia they are normally called Kosovars. The Kosovars speak the Gheg or northern dialect of Albanian, and are mostly Sunni Muslims, with Orthodox and Roman Catholic minorities.

The Kosovars are mostly peasant farmers, although a very high birthrate, possibly Europe's highest, has accelerated urbanization in recent decades. Kosovar nationalists claim an ethnic Albanian population in excess of 2.3 million in Yugoslavia.

Montenegrin—an estimated 5.9% of the population, numbering about 630,000.

The Montenegrins are a South Slav people originally of Serb origin. Separated by the Turkish conquest of much of the Balkan Peninsula in the fourteenth and fifteenth centuries, the Serbs in the region called Crna Gora, Black Mountain, developed a distinct culture and dialect in their mountain homeland.

The dialect of the Montenegrins, free of the five centuries of Turkish influence that have shaped the Serbian dialects, is inherently intelligible with Serbian, which most Montenegrins speak as a second language. The majority of the Montenegrins are Orthodox Christians. In 1993 their church, the Montenegrin Orthodox Church, officially separated from the Serbian Orthodox hierarchy.

Hungarian (Magyar)—an estimated 3.7% of the population, numbering about 395,000.

The Hungarian population is concentrated in the northern region, the nominally autonomous region of Vojvodina, which formed part of Hungary (which lies just to the north) until 1918. Most of the Hungarians live in the flat plains of the Danube and Tisza River regions, Yugoslavia's most fertile and productive.

The Magyar language, the first language of the Hungarians in Yugoslavia, is an Ugrian language of the Finno-Ugrian languages. Most of the Hungarians speak Serbian as their second language. The majority are Roman Catholic, with an important Protestant minority.

Muslim (Sanjaki Muslim)—an estimated 3.2% of the population, numbering about 340,000.

The Muslim population of Yugoslavia is concentrated in the mountainous southern Sanjak region of Serbia, which straddles the Serbia-Montenegrin border. Sanjaki Muslim sources claim a national population of over half a million in Yugoslavia.

The Sanjaki Muslims speak a dialect of Serbo-Croatian that, like Serbian, is written in the Cyrillic alphabet. The dialect shows a marked Turkish influence. The culture of the Muslims is closely tied to their Sunni Muslim religion. The Sanjaki Muslims are often called Turks by the Orthodox Serbs; the term is considered derogatory in Yugoslavia.

The Muslim population of the Sanjak region is descended from Slavs who converted to Islam and the Turkish military aristocracy that settled in the region under Ottoman rule, giving the Sanjakis the right to claim that they are the original inhabitants of the region. Radical Serb nationalists claim that the Muslims settled in the region only in the seventeenth and eighteenth centuries.

Rom (Gypsy)—an estimated 2.4% of the population, numbering about 256,000.

The majority of the Rom in Yugoslavia are ethnic Jerlídes, who live in southern Serbia and Kosovo. A small minority, around 40,000, are ethnic Sasítka Romá, and mostly live in the northern region of Vojvodina. As in many other countries, the Rom of Yugoslavia have suffered discrimination for centuries. Rom political groups claim an ethnic Rom population three or four times the official estimates.

The languages of the Rom include the majority Balkan Romani, which is spoken in three major dialects. Most of the Jerlídes speak the Arlija dialect, with smaller numbers speaking Dzambazi and Tinners Romani. The small northern Rom population, who call themselves Rommanes, speak Sinte Romani dialects that have been influenced by Austrian German. Many of the Rom groups also speak a Slav dialect called Romano-Serbian, also known as Tent Gypsy. The southern Rom groups are mostly Sunni Muslims, and the small northern group is mostly Orthodox Christian.

Romanian—an estimated 1.5% of the population, numbering about 160,000.

The Romanian population of Yugoslavia forms part of the Vlach branch of the Romanian nation. The Romanians live mostly in the Vojvodina region, concentrated in the Timok Valley along the border with Romania. Some Romanian sources claim an ethnic Romanian population of between 200,000 and 300,000, while others claim numbers of up to 500,000 in Yugoslavia. Most of the Romanians in Yugoslavia are Roman or Uniate Catholics, with a substantial number belonging to the separate Romanian Orthodox Church.

The Romanians speak an Eastern Romance language, which in Yugoslavia is spoken in a dialect, often called Daco-Romanian or Vlach. The dialect, which developed while the region formed part of the Austrian, later Austrian-Hungarian, Empire, is free of the Turkic and Slav influences of standard Romanian.

Croat—estimated at less than 1% of the population, numbering about 105,000.

The Croat population, mostly living in the Eastern Slavonia region of northwestern Serbia, forms part of the larger Croatian nation in neighboring Croatia. The Croat population, estimated at 215,000 in 1991, has fallen to about 105,000 since the dissolution of Yugoslavia and the war between Croatia and Serbia in 1991–92.

The language spoken by the Croats is closely related to Serbian, but is written in the Latin alphabet. Religion is also a dividing issue, as most Croats are fervently Roman Catholic.

Slovak—estimated at less than 1% of the population, numbering about 95,000.

The Slovak population of Yugoslavia, concentrated in the northern Vojvodina region, is estimated by some Slovak sources to number over 120,000. Most of the Slovaks are farmers in the fertile plains of the northern river valleys.

The Slovaks speak a West Slav language, but most also speak the Serbo-Croatian language, which, like the Croats, they write in the Latin alphabet. The Slovak language has official status as a regional language in Vojvodina. Most of the Yugoslav Slovaks are Roman Catholic.

Bulgarian—estimated at less than 1% of the population, numbering about 67,000.

The Yugoslav Bulgarians live mostly in the Dmitrovgrad and Bosiljgrad districts of eastern Serbia, along the international border with Bulgaria. A smaller number, mostly Roman Catholic, live in the northern Banat region of Vojvodina.

The Bulgarians, who speak a related South Slav language, but which is not inherently intelligible to Serbian, are mostly Orthodox Christians. During both world wars Bulgarian military forces have occupied the border region, which they claimed historically belonged to Bulgaria.

Ruthene (Ruthenian)—estimated at less than 1% of the population, numbering about 34,000.

The Ruthenes are ethnic Ukrainians separated from the other Ukrainian peoples by nearly a thousand years of Hungarian rule. The Ruthenes of Yugoslavia settled in the northern Banat area of Vojvodina during the rule of the Hungarian kingdom. Although a Ukrainian people, the Ruthenes, also called Rusyn or Carpatho-Rusyn, consider themselves a distinct nation.

The Ruthenes of Ukraine* and Slovakia* speak Rusyn, a dialect of Ukrainian. However, the Ruthenes of Yugoslavia speak an eastern Slovak dialect called Sarish. The majority of the Ruthenes in Yugoslavia are Roman Catholic or belong to the separate Ruthene Uniate Church.

Ukrainian—estimated at less than 1% of the population, numbering about 23,000.

The Ukrainians, concentrated in the northern region of Vojvodina, are part of the larger Ukrainian people of Ukrainian Galicia or Western Ukraine. Settled in the region during the period of Austrian rule, the Ukrainians are mostly farmers and herdsmen.

The language spoken by the Yugoslav Ukrainians is a dialect of Ukrainian, but the majority also speak Serbian as their second language. Most of the Ukrainians are Uniate Catholics, with an Orthodox minority.

Turk—estimated at less than 1% of the population, numbering about 21,000.

The Turkish population of Yugoslavia, mostly living in the southern districts near the Macedonian border, is the remnant of a formerly large Turkish population that lived in the region until World War I. The Turks, like the other Muslim peoples of Yugoslavia, have suffered discrimination in education and employment.

Pole—estimated at less than 1% of the population, numbering about 12,000.

The Poles live in the northern Vojvodina, where they settled during the centuries of rule by the Hapsburg empire. The Poles speak a West Slav language along with Serb, and the majority are Roman Catholic.

German—estimated at less than 1% of the population, numbering about 10,000.

Settled in the region in the early nineteenth century, the German population is part of a formerly much larger Austrian population that lived in the northern Banat and Slavonia regions. Most of the Austrian population left the region after World War I, with another exodus during World War II.

Czech—estimated at less than 1% of the population, numbering about 8,000.

The Czechs of Yugoslavia were also settled in the region during the Habsburg era and live in the northern districts of the Vojvodina. Although the Czechs speak a West Slav language, the first language of the Yugoslav Czechs is usually Serbian. The majority are Roman Catholic with an important Protestant minority.

Russian—estimated at less than 1% of the population, numbering about 5,000.

The Russians, mostly living in central Serbia, are the descendants of Russian settlers who colonized the region following the withdrawal of the Turks in the nineteenth century. Most of the Russians speak Serbian as their first language and, like the Serbs, are Orthodox Christians.

Jew—estimated at less than 1% of the population, numbering about 3,000.

The Jews of Yugoslavia are the remnant of a much larger population most of which was massacred during World War II, mainly at the hands of the Fascist German and Croatian forces, but also by anti-Semitic Serbs. The majority of the remaining Jewish population lives in the Serbian capital, Belgrade.

NATION: Celts are thought to have settled the northern plains in the third century B.C. They lived in agricultural villages in the river valleys, but never united in a state system. Celtic remains are numerous in the northern Vojvodina region. In the first century A.D. the Romans controlled the western region, which formed part of Roman Illyricum. In A.D. 274 the founder of the Byzantine Empire, Constantine the Great, was born at present Nis.

Overrun by Huns and Goths in the fifth century as Roman power weakened, the region was again under the rule of the Eastern Roman Empire, the Byzantine Empire, in the early sixth century. The Byzantines rebuilt much of the former Roman region, founding towns and cities that were colonized by Orthodox Christian peoples from other parts of the empire.

In the seventh century Slavic tribes, pushed across the Danube into Byzantine Moesia by the Avars, settled the region. In the east the tribes settled the fertile lands around the rivers Zeta, Tara, Piva, Drina, Ibar, and Morava. The eastern tribes, called Serbs, came under the hegemony of the Byzantine Empire and were converted to Orthodox Christianity. In the ninth century the Bulgarians held the area before the Byzantines again extended their rule to the region.

Unity among the fractious Serbian clans was not achieved until the end of the eleventh century and the Serbian expansion into Montenegro, where the independent state of Zeta was established in 1081. In 1170 Stefan Nemanja established the Nemanjic dynasty in the Serb state of Raska, and in 1217 Serbia became a kingdom, with Stefan I crowned as the first king of the Serbs.

The kingdom, beset by dynastic struggles, lost territory to Hungary and Bulgaria. The Serb state, overshadowed by the Bulgarian kingdom, was a minor kingdom until the rule of Stephen Dushan, who became king in 1331 and had himself crowned tsar in 1346. Under his rule Serbia became the most powerful state of the Balkan Peninsula, most of which it absorbed. The multiethnic kingdom included Serbs, Greeks, Bulgars, and Albanians. The fourteenth century also marked the zenith of the Serbian Orthodox Church, which was central to the formation of the Serb culture and identity.

Soon after Stephen's death, in 1355, the Serbian empire collapsed, and the Serbs came under pressure from the expanding Ottoman Empire of the Turks. The Serbs were defeated by the Turks in 1371, but the decisive Battle of Kosovo sealed the fate of the Serbian nation in 1389.

The Serbs rallied the Christian peoples of the region against the advancing Turks, putting together an alliance of Christian states determined to stop the Ottoman advance into the Balkan Peninsula. On 20 June 1389 a large force comprised mostly of Serbs, but also including Bosnians, Montenegrins, and Albanians, met the Ottoman army on the elevated plain called Kosovo Polje, the Field of Blackbirds, and was defeated. Serb legend tells of blackbirds feasting on the thousands of dead for weeks after the battle.

The Turks allowed the Serbs to remain semi-independent in a diminished and divided Serbia while paying tribute to the Ottoman rulers. In the west, the Montenegrins retained a precarious independence in their mountain strongholds, their fierce warriors defeating Turkish attempts to conquer their small state. In 1459 the Turks, taking advantage of quarrels over the Serb succession, annexed the vassal state of Serbia. In 1521 Belgrade and the other northern districts held by Hungary also came under Ottoman rule.

Turkish rule in Serbia was among the most oppressive in the vast Ottoman Empire. Most of the Serbian nobility was annihilated and their lands distributed to the Turkish military aristocracy. The Christian peasants, the *rayas*, were treated little better than slaves. Although the Serbs were forbidden to possess weapons, uprisings were frequent.

Many Christian Serbs fled to Hungary and Austria to escape Turkish rule or to fight the Turkish occupiers of their homeland. In 1683, while Vienna was surrounded by a huge Turkish army, the Serbs rose in rebellion, drawing off much-needed Turkish troops and supplies. Although Christian armies relieved Vienna and advanced into Turkish territory, the Serbs were again defeated.

In what is known in Serbian history as the Great Serbian Exodus, a religious leader, Patriarch Arsenija, led some 200,000 Serbs, protected by the Austrian army, north out of Turkish-held territory. The refugees were settled in the Austrian frontier regions in Slavonia and Vojvodina in 1690. Organized along military lines, the Serbian settlements were charged with guarding the frontier between the Austrian and Ottoman empires. The Turkish reverses in wars with

Austria and Russia in the seventeenth and eighteenth centuries revived Serbian hopes for independence.

In 1804 a Serbian patriot called Karageorge led a successful uprising against the Turks. In 1806 his forces captured Belgrade, where the entire Turkish population was massacred, and in 1808 he was proclaimed the hereditary chief of the Serbs. Karageorge joined the Russians in war on the Turks, but was abandoned when the Russians made peace in 1812. By 1813 the Turks had recovered all the Serbian territories. In 1817 Milosh Obrenovich had Karageorge assassinated and was named prince of Serbia by the Serbian leaders.

The Serbs' traditional ally, Russia, forced the weakened Ottoman government to grant Serbia autonomy in 1829 and in 1830 to recognize Milosh Obrenovich as Serbia's hereditary prince. Under the agreement the Turks maintained nominal control over Serbia, which was convulsed by bloody feuds between the Karageorgevich and Obrenovich families.

The European powers, at the 1856 Congress of Paris, recognized Ottoman rule, but placed Serbia under the collective guarantee of the leading powers. In 1867 the last Turkish troops were finally withdrawn from the Serbian state. Serbia then signed a series of secret alliances with Montenegro, Romania, and Greece aimed at dividing up the remaining European territories of the decadent Ottoman empire. Serbian independence was settled by the Treaty of Berlin, which ended the Russo-Turkish War in 1878 but disappointed the Serbs' territorial ambitions by placing the former Turkish territories of Bosnia and Herzegovina under Austrian rule. The treaty also recognized Montenegro as an independent state.

The Austrian presence in the region prevented a return of the Turks, but in the early twentieth century relations between the Austrians and the Serbs soured. By 1905 Serbian policy had become nationalistic and anti-Austrian, as the Habsburgs, whose empire included all the territory north of Belgrade, were seen as frustrating Serbian aspirations to unite the South Slavs in an expanded Serbian-dominated state. Up to World War I the region was in constant flux as shifting alliances among Serbia, Turkey, Bulgaria, and Greece led to two Balkan wars in 1912 and 1913. The wars allowed Serbia to take control of the Turkish regions of Sanjak and Macedonia and made Serbia the strongest state in the Balkans.

The conflict between Serbia and the Habsburgs was suddenly heightened by the assassination of the Habsburg heir, Archduke Francis Ferdinand, by a Serb nationalist, Gavrilo Princip, in the Bosnian capital, Sarajevo, on 28 June 1914. On 23 July Austria sent a harsh ultimatum to the Serbian government. Supported by the Russians, the Serbs accepted some of the Austrian demands, but refused or hedged on others. On 28 July Austria-Hungary and its ally, Germany, declared war on Serbia. Russian mobilization quickly extended the war to the east, and by early August most of Europe was at war.

The Serbian army held out for over a year, until the autumn of 1915, when the army and the Serbian government were forced to withdraw to the Greek island of Corfu. On Corfu the representatives of the various South Slav nations proclaimed, in July 1917, their eventual unification under the rule of the Serbian king. At the end of the war, in November 1918, Montenegro joined the new state, and the Kingdom of the Serbs, Croats, and Slovenes was formally proclaimed.

The country, beset by bitter ethnic feuds and oppressive domination by the Serbs, lurched from crisis to crisis during the 1920s. In 1929 King Alexander proclaimed a dictatorship and changed the name of the country to Yugoslavia. He dissolved the parliament, and the internal borders were redrawn to erase the historic ethnic borders. The newly formed provinces were placed under iron-fisted military governors sent from Belgrade.

The dictatorship ended in 1931, but the domination of the Serbs continued. In 1934 the government's conflict with Croatian and Macedonian nationalists culminated in King Alexander's assassination. Unresolved social issues, combined with the effects of the global depression of the 1930s, aided the growth of extremist groups on both the right and left.

In 1941 German, Italian, Bulgarian, and Hungarian forces invaded Yugoslavia, which was divided into several distinct regions. Hundreds of thousands of Serbs died, many in massacres carried out by the forces of the Fascist Croatian state allied to Germany. Although several partisan groups fought the Fascists, the Communist group led by Josip Broz, known as Tito, gradually gained control of Yugoslavia as Axis defeat neared.

Tito, having gained wide support, took power in 1945. In 1946 a Soviet-style constitution was adopted, which gave each of the member states of the federation cultural and some political autonomy, although power remained centered in the Communist Party. Internal ethnic divisions were suppressed during the Tito era, although not extinguished.

Tito's death in 1980 ended Communist Yugoslavia's strong leadership. He was replaced by a rotating presidency concerned with holding the country together and dealing with the chronic economic crisis. The disparity between the richer northern republics of Slovenia* and Croatia and the poorer republics, particularly Serbia, led to renewed regional and ethnic friction as the country experienced a severe economic crisis.

In May 1981 the Albanian minority in Kosovo revolted against Serbian oppression, setting off a Serbian nationalist backlash. While the other republics distanced themselves from the central government, Serbs were allowed to dominate the Yugoslav army (JNA) as well as key positions in the federal government and state enterprises. Serbian nationalism, which called for the solution of the national question in Yugoslavia by the creation of a Greater Serbia, uniting all ethnic Serbs in a single state, was endorsed by the Serbian Academy of Arts and Sciences in 1986.

In 1987 hard-liner Slobodan Miloshevich was elected president of Serbia, and in 1988 he began moves to restrict the autonomy of Kosovo and Vojvodina, setting off a serious crisis between Serbia and the western republics, Croatia and Slovenia, which supported the Albanians of Kosovo and the Hungarians of Vojvodina. Miloshevich's embrace of extreme Serb nationalism deepened the crisis hanging over the federation.

The collapse of communism in most of eastern Europe in 1989 loosened the ties between the constituent republics even further. In 1990 all of the republics elected nationalist governments, except Serbia and Montenegro, where the re-named Communists, led by Miloshevich, retained power. As friction between the republics heightened and the Serbian government became increasingly bel-ligerent, Croatia, Slovenia, and then Macedonia pushed for independence. Mon-tenegro backed Serbia, and in Bosnia-Herzegovina a three-way ethnic split threatened violence.

Miloshevich's Serbian government, dreaming of a Greater Serbia, encouraged the ethnic Serb minorities in Croatia and Bosnia to rebel. In October 1990 the Serb minority in the Croatian region of Krajina declared autonomy. Croatian forces sought to quell the uprising, while the Serb-led federal army intervened on the side of the Serbs. The Serbian Communist government, taking on an increasingly nationalist rhetoric, backed the creation of a Greater Serbia that would unite all the Serbian-populated regions of the peninsula.

In June 1991 Croatia and Slovenia declared independence, ending hopes of holding the Yugoslav state together. Bosnia and Macedonia soon followed. The federal army, the JNA, took control of a quarter of Croatia before a cease-fire could be arranged, and moved into Bosnia to support ethnic Serbs there. The deliberate targeting of civilian populations by Serb irregulars and the JNA out-raged the international community, but feeble attempts to intervene failed to halt the spreading Balkan war.

The European Community (EC) put forward a plan, in October 1991, for a looser federation of Yugoslavia that would give the republics economic, polit-ical, and cultural autonomy. Of the six former Yugoslav republics that attended the EC conference, only the government of Serbia rejected the proposals. The Serb military, following victories in Croatia, firmly rejected any compromise with the other republics, while President Miloshevich claimed to speak for all the ethnic Serbs living anywhere in the former Yugoslavia.

The international community branded Serbia and its ally Montenegro as the aggressors in the vicious Balkan wars and imposed economic sanctions that crippled their economies but did little to end the fighting in Bosnia. As the Bosnian war dragged on, stories of Serb atrocities and the policy of expelling civilian populations from Serb-claimed territory, called ethnic cleansing, further hardened the attitude of the world community toward the rump Yugoslav state.

Within Serbia, Miloshevich catered to the nationalist sentiment by further tightening restrictions on the non-Serb national groups, including a reign of terror directed against the large Albanian population. Extremist Serb national groups called for the cleansing of all non-Serbs from Serbian lands. The Al-banians responded with nonviolent resistance. In early 1992, they voted in an underground referendum for independence.

The EC foreign ministers imposed economic sanctions on Serbia and Montenegro in November 1991. In December, the government of tiny Montenegro announced that, unlike the other Yugoslav republics, it would not be asking for EC recognition, but would stick by its traditional ally, Serbia. However, the ethnic Albanians of Kosovo asked for EC recognition of an independent Kosovar state, which they had declared after a secret referendum. The European Community, fearful of being drawn into the widening Balkan conflict, finally recognized the independence of Croatia and Slovenia, but refused to recognize any other state in the region.

On 11 April 1992 the largest and smallest of the former Yugoslav republics, Serbia and Montenegro, controlled by renamed Communist parties, formally established the Federal Republic of Yugoslavia. On 27 April the federal assembly adopted a constitution of the new Yugoslav state, which claimed to be the direct heir of the former Communist Yugoslav federation. The United States and the EC countries refused recognition. In December 1993, despite growing opposition to the Miloshevich regime, the majority of the Serbian population voted to return his administration in parliamentary elections.

The Montenegrins, in spite of their participation in the war, particularly their assault on the medieval city of Dubrovnik on Croatia's Adriatic coast, had begun to distance themselves from Miloshevich's Serbia by 1992. Although ignoring calls by Montenegrin nationalist groups for declarations of neutrality and independence, the government of the small state became increasingly less pliant. The Montenegrin Orthodox Church, in 1993, officially separated from the Serbian Orthodox Church. In an attempt to quell rising separatist sentiment, the government transferred the capital of Montenegro from the Tito-era city of Podgorica to the historic capital, Cetinje, in 1994.

The United States, frustrated at feeble EC efforts to end the fighting in Bosnia, applied diplomacy and threats to force the Serbian government, as representative of the Serbian population of Bosnia, to agree to the 1995 Dayton Accords. President Miloshevich represented the Bosnian Serbs, and although many of their leaders were dissatisfied with the accords, the situation on the battlefield, where they were losing much of their conquered territory, left them little choice. The accords split the Bosnian state into a Bosnian Serb statelet and a Muslim-Croat federation, but specifically forbid the unification of the Bosnian Serb region with Serbia.

The end of the war in Bosnia opened the way for Yugoslav recognition by European Union states. Although the United States has refused to recognize Yugoslavia as the successor to the former Socialist Yugoslavia, most European Union countries have recognized the new federal republic in spite of continuing repression of the Albanian minority in Kosovo and the lack of freedom within the country.

The Serbian people, weary of war and their status as international pariahs, and frustrated by economic chaos, began a series of mass protests against President Miloshevich in November 1996. Hundreds of thousands marched through

Belgrade and other urban centers. The protests, led by Serbia's opposition leaders, failed to unseat Miloshevich, but forced the Serbian government to abandon some of its hard-line rhetoric.

A major stumbling block to better relations between Yugoslavia and the other former Yugoslav states is the lack of an agreement on the division of the properties and assets of the former Socialist Federal Republic of Yugoslavia (SFYR). The Yugoslav government wants to keep the bulk of the wealth and argues that the other states should get less because they voluntarily left Yugoslavia. The other governments want the assets divided on the basis of the republics' pre-1991 payments to the federal budget, to which Slovenia and Croatia were the principal contributors.

In July 1997 Miloshevich was elected president of the federal Yugoslav state, as the constitution of Serbia had prevented him from seeking a third term as president of the constituent republic of Serbia. Until his election the presidency of Yugoslavia had been largely a ceremonial post, but he immediately set about gathering power to his new title. The dream of a "Greater Serbia" seems set to haunt the Balkan Peninsula well into the twenty-first century.

A young reformer, Milo Djukanovic, a pro-Western foe of Yugoslav President Slobodan Milosevich, won a close election in Montenegro in October 1997 and took office, over Serbian protests of fraud, on 15 January 1998. The inauguration of the new president of the tiny republic set off violent confrontations between his supporters and hard-line supporters of Milosevich in which forty people were injured.

A brutal police attack on villages suspected of supporting separatists in the tense province of Kosovo in March 1998 left over fifty people dead and many more injured. Hundreds fled into the mountains to escape the attacks. The attacks set off a series of mass demonstrations in the province in support of an autonomous Kosovo free of oppressive Serbian domination. Many Kosovar Albanians now see no alternative to violent resistance, possibly setting the stage for yet another Balkan war.

SELECTED BIBLIOGRAPHY:

Branka, Margas. *The Destruction of Yugoslavia.* 1993.

Judah, Tim. *The Serbs: History, Myth and the Destruction of Yugoslavia.* 1997.

Petrovich, Michael B. *A History of Modern Serbia, 1904–1918.* 1976.

Silber, Laura, and Allan Little. *Yugoslavia: Death of a Nation.* 1997.

Thompson, Mark. *A Paper House: The Ending of Yugoslavia.* 1993.

Largest National Groups with 1998 Population Estimates Listed by State

ARMENIA

Armenian	3,300,000
Assyrian	6,000
Azerbaijani	10,000
Belarussian	3,000
Greek	5,000
Kurd	64,000
Rom (Gypsy)	8,000
Russian	52,000
Ukrainian	8,000

AZERBAIJAN

Armenian	175,000
Avar	53,000
Azeri (Azerbaijani)	6,663,000
Belarussian	5,000
Georgian	92,000
Jew	6,000
Kurd	108,000
Lezgi (Lezgin)	173,000
Russian	185,000

Talysh (Talish)	141,000
Tatar	32,000
Tsakhur	16,000
Turk	19,000
Ukrainian	32,000

BELARUS

Belarussian	8,170,000
Jew	112,000
Latvian	5,000
Lithuanian	11,000
Pole	427,000
Rom (Gypsy)	115,000
Russian	1,135,000
Tatar	72,000
Ukrainian	302,000

BOSNIA AND HERZEGOVINA

Albanian	25,000
Arab	30,000
Bosniak (Muslim)	1,122,000
Croat (Bosnian Croat)	655,000
Jew	17,000
Montenegrin	32,000
Rom (Gypsy)	65,000
Serb (Bosnian Serb)	1,060,000
Turk (Rumelian Turk)	50,000

CROATIA

Albanian	12,000
Bosnian	45,000
Croat	3,678,000
Istrian	(245,000)
Czech	14,000
Italian	120,000

Magyar (Hungarian)	170,000
Montenegrin	10,000
Muslim	50,000
Serb	480,000
Slovene	25,000

CZECH REPUBLIC

Czech	8,498,000
Moravian	(1,388,000)
Silesian	(45,000)
German	52,000
Magyar (Hungarian)	21,000
Pole	63,000
Rom (Gypsy)	32,000
Russian	6,000
Slovak	377,000
Ukrainian and Ruthenian	11,000

ERITREA

Adeni Arab	18,000
Afar	265,000
Bedawi (Beja)	120,000
Bilen	70,000
Hadenoa	20,000
Kunama	145,000
Nara	65,000
Raishada	37,000
Saho	145,000
Tigré	1,130,000
Tigrinya (Tigrigna)	1,584,000

ESTONIA

Belarussian	23,000
Chavash (Chuvash)	1,000
Estonian	940,000

Finn	18,000
Ingrian	15,000
Latvian	2,000
Lithuanian	2,000
Rom (Gypsy)	3,000
Russian	420,000
Tatar	5,000
Ukrainian	39,000

ETHIOPIA

Aari (Shankilla)	1,000,000
Afar	500,000
Agaw (Agau)	1,000,000
Alaba	90,000
Amhara	14,000,000
Bambala (Burji)	80,000
Basketto	100,000
Bedawie (Beja)	300,000
Bench (Gimira)	85,000
Dawro	175,000
Gamo	450,000
Gawwada (Kawwada)	75,000
Gedeo (Darassa)	600,000
Gofa	160,000
Gumuz (Shanquilla)	70,000
Gurage	1,700,000
Hadiyya	1,000,000
Harari (Adare)	50,000
Hausa	55,000
Kaffa	500,000
Kambaata	1,000,000
Komso	200,000
Libido	120,000
Me'en	60,000
Melo	80,000
Nuer (Naath)	50,000

Oromo	16,000,000
Shakacho (Mocha)	80,000
Sidamo (Sidama)	5,000,000
Somali	3,500,000
Tigrean (Tigrinya)	6,000,000
Wolaytta	3,000,000
Xamir	75,000
Yemma	500,000

GEORGIA

Abkhaz (Abkhazian)	110,000
Armenian	398,000
Assyrian	7,000
Azeri (Azerbaijani)	355,000
Belarussian	4,000
Georgian	3,990,000
Ajar (Ajarian)	(275,000)
Greek	112,000
Jew	18,000
Kurd	40,000
Meskhtekian	15,000
Ossetian	170,000
Russian	270,000
Tatar	5,000
Ukrainian	45,000

KAZAKHSTAN

Azeri (Azerbaijani)	105,000
Bashkort (Bashkir)	24,000
Belarussian	180,000
Chavash (Chuvash)	22,000
Chechen	55,000
Dungan (Hui)	35,000
Georgian	7,000
German	805,000
Greek	50,000

Ingush	22,000
Jew	20,000
Kazakh	7,721,000
Korean	110,000
Kurd	28,000
Kyrgyz	15,000
Lezgi (Lezgian)	17,000
Lithuanian	10,000
Mari	9,000
Moldovan and Romanian	33,000
Mordvin	38,000
Ossetian	4,000
Pole	65,000
Russian	5,375,000
Tajik	30,000
Tatar	395,000
Turk	53,000
Turkmen	3,000
Udmurt	17,000
Uighur (Uyghur)	300,000
Ukrainian	875,000
Uzbek and Karakalpak	360,000

KYRGYZSTAN

Armenian	3,000
Azeri	18,000
Bashkort (Bashkir)	3,000
Belarussian	7,000
Chavash (Chuvash)	2,000
Crimean Tatar	42,000
Dungan (Hui)	75,000
German	95,000
Kazakh	40,000
Korean	20,000
Kurd	15,000
Kyrgyz (Kirgiz)	2,410,000

Mordvin	5,000
Russian	850,000
Tajik	39,000
Tatar	80,000
Turk	23,000
Uighur	45,000
Ukrainian	100,000
Uzbek	560,000

LATVIA

Armenian	3,000
Belarussian	105,000
Estonian	3,000
Jew	13,000
Latvian	1,420,000
Latgalian	(500,000)
Lithuanian	30,000
Liv (Livonian)	1,500
Pole	60,000
Rom (Gypsy)	8,000
Russian	765,000
Tatar	6,000
Ukrainian	67,000

LITHUANIA

Belarussian	45,000
Jew	6,000
Karaim (Karaite)	3,000
Latvian	4,000
Lithuanian	3,005,000
Pole	250,000
Russian	300,000
Tatar	5,000
Ukrainian	35,000

MACEDONIA

Albanian	475,000
Bulgarian	11,000
Croat	3,000
Greek	21,000
Jew	2,000
Macedonian	1,400,000
Muslim	31,000
Rom (Gypsy)	47,000
Serb and Montenegrin	45,000
Turk	85,000
Vlach	10,000

MOLDOVA

Belarussian	20,000
Bulgarian	85,000
Gagauz	179,000
German	7,000
Jew	35,000
Moldovan	2,832,000
Rom (Gypsy)	138,000
Russian	538,000
Tatar	2,000
Ukrainian	552,000

NAMIBIA

Baster	38,000
Caprivian	75,000
Colored	90,000
Damara	120,000
Diriku	5,000
Herero (Herrero)	140,000
Kavango	152,000
Kwambi	6,000

Kwangali	5,000
Mbukushu	6,000
Nama	85,000
Ovambo	840,000
San (Bushmen)	48,000
Tswana	8,000
White	117,000

RUSSIA

Abaza (Abazin)	40,000
Adygei	129,000
Agul	24,000
Ajai	76,000
Akhvakh	6,000
Altai	73,000
Andi	11,000
Armenian	528,000
Assyrian	30,000
Avar	572,000
Azeri (Azerbaijani)	342,000
Balkar	91,000
Bashkort (Bashkir)	2,310,000
Belarussian	1,185,000
Bezhta	3,000
Botlikh	12,000
Buryat	455,000
Chamalal	13,000
Chavash (Chuvash)	2,255,000
Chechen	924,000
Chukot (Chukchi)	36,000
Chulym	12,000
Circassian (Cherkess)	76,000
Crimean Tatar	22,000
Dargin	373,000
Dido	9,000
Dolgan	8,000

Estonian	55,000
Even	16,000
Evenki	34,000
Finn	106,000
Georgian	130,000
German	894,000
Ghodoberi	3,000
Greek	105,000
Hunzib	2,000
Ingrian	85,000
Ingush	287,000
Itel'men	3,000
Jew	833,000
Kabardin	443,000
Kalmyk (Kalmuck)	210,000
Karachai	159,000
Karata	13,000
Karel (Karelian)	250,000
Kazakh	649,000
Khakas	87,000
Khanty	29,000
Komi	432,000
Komi-Permyak	175,000
Korean	312,000
Koryak (Nymylany)	12,000
Kumyk	267,000
Lak	107,000
Latvian	27,000
Lezgin	258,000
Lithuanian	64,000
Mansi	13,000
Mari	765,000
Moldovan and Romanian	182,000
Mordvin	1,842,000
Nanai (Nanay)	13,000
Nenets	38,000
Nivkhi	6,000
Nogai	81,000

Ossetian	503,000
Pole	97,000
Rom (Gypsy)	345,000
Russian	115,502,000
Rutul	23,000
Sakha (Yakut)	520,000
Sami (Lapp)	2,000
Selkup	5,000
Serb (Serbian)	11,000
Shor	21,000
Tabasaran	110,000
Tajik	42,000
Tat	12,000
Tatar	6,621,000
Tindi	8,000
Tsakhur	11,000
Tuvan	245,000
Udmurt	1,120,000
Ukrainian	4,297,000
Ulchi	3,000
Uzbek	63,000
Vep (Veps)	17,000

SLOVAKIA

Czech	60,000
German	5,000
Jew	6,000
Magyar (Hungarian)	570,000
Pole	6,000
Rom (Gypsy)	80,000
Russian	2,000
Ruthene (Carpatho-Rusyn)	75,000
Serb (Serbian)	2,000
Slovak	4,556,000
Ukrainian	22,000

SLOVENIA

Croat	48,000
Czech	2,000
Friuli	7,000
German	20,000
Italian	20,000
Magyar (Hungarian)	20,000
Muslim	28,000
Serb (Serbian)	40,000
Slovak	5,000
Slovene	1,795,000
Istrian	(37,000)

TAJIKISTAN

Arab	2,000
Armenian	6,000
Baluch (Baluchi)	5,000
Bashkort (Bashkir)	7,000
Jew	11,000
Kazakh	11,000
Korean	23,000
Kyrgyz	98,000
Ossetian	10,000
Pakhtu	13,000
Persian	31,000
Russian	190,000
Tajik	4,045,000
Yagnobi	(805,000)
Pamiri	(175,000)
Tatar	105,000
Turkmen	18,000
Uighur	4,000
Ukrainian	61,000
Uzbek	1,515,000

TURKMENISTAN

Armenian	31,000
Azeri (Azerbaijani)	37,000
Baluch (Baluchi)	28,000
Bashkort (Bashkir)	2,000
Belarussian	5,000
Jew	2,000
Karakalpak	3,000
Kazakh	137,000
Korean	3,000
Kurd	3,000
Lezgi (Lezgian)	13,000
Mordvin	3,000
Russian	337,000
Tatar	83,000
Turkmen	3,260,000
Ukrainian	48,000
Uzbek	440,000

UKRAINE

Albanian	5,000
Armenian	54,000
Bashkort (Bashkir)	5,000
Belarussian	360,000
Bulgarian	224,000
Crimean Tatar	185,000
Czech	29,000
Gagauz	35,000
Georgian	25,000
German	37,000
Greek	226,000
Hungarian	178,000
Jew	265,000
Kazakh	7,000
Moldovan	310,000

Mordvin	21,000
Ossetian	5,000
Pole	1,237,000
Rom (Gypsy)	258,000
Romanian	152,000
Russian	9,485,000
Slovak	12,000
Tatar	103,000
Ukrainian	38,265,000
Ruthene	(1,550,000)
Uzbek	10,000

UZBEKISTAN

Armenian	47,000
Azeri (Azerbaijani)	43,000
Bashkort (Bashkir)	36,000
Belarussian	28,000
Chavash (Chuvash)	9,000
Crimean Tatar	167,000
Fergana Turk	60,000
Georgian	4,000
German	38,000
Jew	100,000
Karakalpak	465,000
Kazakh	841,000
Korean	186,000
Kyrgyz	183,000
Meskhtekian	110,000
Moldovan	3,000
Mordvin	14,000
Ossetian	6,000
Persian	32,000
Russian	1,650,000
Tajik	1,210,000
Tatar	302,000
Turkmen	229,000

Uighur	36,000
Ukrainian	152,000
Uzbek	16,655,000

YUGOSLAVIA

Albanian (Kosovar)	1,825,000
Bulgarian	67,000
Croat	105,000
Czech	8,000
German	10,000
Jew	3,000
Magyar (Hungarian)	395,000
Montenegrin	630,000
Muslim (Sanjaki Muslim)	340,000
Pole	12,000
Rom (Gypsy)	256,000
Romanian	160,000
Russian	5,000
Ruthene (Carpatho-Rusyn)	34,000
Serb (Serbian)	6,698,000
Slovak	95,000
Turk	21,000
Ukrainian	23,000

Appendix B

Declarations of Independence

States and Regions	Date Independence Declared	From
Armenia	28 May 1918	Russian and Ottoman Empires
	23 September 1991	USSR
Artsakh (Nagorno-Karabakh)	31 December 1991	Republic of Azerbaijan
Azerbaijan	28 May 1918	Russian Empire
	30 August 1991	USSR
Iranian Azerbaijan	8 September 1945	Iran
Belarus	25 March 1918	Russian Empire
	25 August 1991	USSR
Bosnia and Herzegovina	3 March 1992	SFRY
Croatia	10 April 1941	Kingdom of Yugoslavia
	25 June 1991	SFRY
Czech Republic	28 October 1918	Austria (Austro-Hungarian Empire)
	1 January 1993	Czechoslovakia
Eritrea	24 May 1993	PDRE
Estonia	24 February 1918	Russian Empire
	20 August 1991	USSR
Ethiopia (Federal Republic of)	24 May 1993	PDRE
Georgia	26 May 1918	Russian Empire
	9 April 1991	USSR

Kazakhstan	16 December 1917	Russia
	16 December 1991	USSR
Kyrgyzstan	31 August 1991	USSR
Latvia	18 November 1918	Russian Empire
	21 August 1991	USSR
Lithuania	16 February 1918	Russian Empire
	11 March 1990	USSR
Macedonia	2 August 1903	Ottoman Empire
	8 September 1944	Kingdom of Yugoslavia
	17 September 1991	SFRY
Moldova	23 December 1917	Russian Empire
	27 August 1991	USSR
Namibia	21 March 1990	South Africa
Russian Federation	24 August 1991	USSR
Slovakia	30 October 1918	Hungary (Austro-Hungarian Empire)
	14 March 1939	Czechoslovakia
	1 January 1993	Czech and Slovak
Slovenia	25 June 1991	Yugoslavia
Tajikistan	9 September 1991	USSR
Turkmenistan	27 October 1991	USSR
Ukraine	22 January 1918	Russian Empire
	24 August 1991	USSR
Western Ukraine	14 November 1918	Austria (Austro-Hungarian Empire)
	6 October 1941	USSR
Carpatho-Ukraine	2 March 1939	Czechoslovakia
Uzbekistan	31 August 1991	USSR
Yugoslavia	11 April 1992	SFRY

PDRE = People's Democratic Republic of Ethiopia
SFRY = Socialist Federal Republic of Yugoslavia
USSR =Union of Soviet Socialist Republics

Index

The page numbers set in **boldface** indicate the location of the main entry.

About the Author

JAMES MINAHAN is an independent researcher living in Barcelona, Spain. He is the author of *Nations Without States: A Historical Dictionary of Contemporary National Movements* (Greenwood, 1996), which was named an ALA/RASD 1996 Outstanding Reference Source.